Bad English

Manchester University Press

Bad English

Literature, multilingualism, and the politics of language in contemporary Britain

Rachael Gilmour

Manchester University Press

Copyright © Rachael Gilmour 2020

The right of Rachael Gilmour to be identified as the author of this work has been asserted by her in accordance with the Copyright, Designs and Patents Act 1988.

Published by Manchester University Press
Oxford Road, Manchester M13 9PL
www.manchesteruniversitypress.co.uk

British Library Cataloguing-in-Publication Data is available

ISBN 978 1 5261 0884 5 hardback
ISBN 978 1 5261 6382 0 paperback

First published by Manchester University Press in hardback 2020

This edition published 2022

The publisher has no responsibility for the persistence or accuracy of URLs for any external or third-party internet websites referred to in this book, and does not guarantee that any content on such websites is, or will remain, accurate or appropriate.

Typeset by Servis Filmsetting Ltd, Stockport, Cheshire

Contents

List of figures   *page* vi
Acknowledgements   vii
The New Union Flag Project   xi

Introduction: Bad English   1
1. Thi langwij a thi guhtr   38
2. Dictionary trawling   78
3. Prosthetic language   101
4. 'Passing my voice into theirs'   138
5. Living in translation   168
6. 'The language is the border'   205
Conclusions: 'Say Parsley'   236

Bibliography   248
Index   273

List of figures

1. Image from Xiaolu Guo, *I Am China* (London: Chatto & Windus, 2014), p. 70.   *page* 191
2. Image by Chris Walker (@doodlebank) https://twitter.com/ doodlebank/status/1067765392876154882.   244
3. Image by Chris Walker (@doodlebank) https://twitter.com/ doodlebank/status/1067765392876154882.   245

Every effort has been made to obtain permission to reproduce copyright material, and the publisher will be pleased to be informed of any errors and omissions for correction in future editions.

Acknowledgements

This book began its life in a chance conversation with Anamik Saha a few years ago, and it has been enriched and sustained by many other friends along the way. I'm delighted to thank my wonderful colleagues in the School of English and Drama, Queen Mary University of London, including Tamara Atkin, Shahidha Bari, Andrea Brady, Chris Campbell, the much-missed Mary Condé, Nadia Davids, Zara Dinnen, Patrick Flanery, Matt Ingleby, Catherine Maxwell, Sam McBean, Susheila Nasta, Lucinda Newns, kitt price, and Nadia Valman. Many conversations with friends – about language, translation, the institutions of literature, and literary form – have helped these ideas to take shape: my particular thanks to Rehana Ahmed, Nadia Atia, Asha Panesar Bourne, Omar Garcia, Sam Halliday, Suzanne Hobson, David James, Javed Majeed, Nisha Ramayya, Bill Schwarz, and Andrew van der Vlies. I've also been lucky to be part of the Queen Mary Postcolonial Seminar collective, which includes (as well as some of those named above) Pragya Dhital, Lesley James, Adhira Mangalagiri, Chris Moffat, Shital Pravinchandra, and Rob Waters. My thanks to the brilliant postgraduate researchers from whom I've learned over the years: Lara Atkin, Roger Blanton, Xiaoran Hu, Cathie Jayakumar-Hazra, Ellen Jones, Karina Lickorish Quinn, Y-Lynn Ong, Rob Waters – now a colleague – and James Williams. Conversations with my committed and curious undergraduate and postgraduate students at Queen Mary have often shown me how to see things in new ways; something that's also true of students from two local Tower Hamlets secondary schools with whom I worked on a three-year creative project called 'Reading/Writing Multilingualism'.

It is thanks to a one-year British Academy Mid-Career Fellowship that much additional research for this book was completed, making it a richer and better project. Thanks too to Gladstone's Library, where I did a significant amount of the writing. I've been lucky to be able to talk about these ideas as they've developed at conferences and in invited lectures at Stellenbosch University and Rhodes University in South Africa, Utrecht in the Netherlands, Berne in Switzerland, and Bremen in Germany, as well as Queen Mary University of London, Sheffield University, the School of Oriental and African Studies, the School of Advanced Studies, University of Oxford, and King's College London. Timely ideas have come out of conversations with Fiona Doloughan, James Procter, and Wendy McMahon, as well as all those involved with two brilliant conferences organised by Wen-Chin Ouyang, Jane Hiddleston, and Nora Parr as part of the Creative Multilingualism project (SOAS/Oxford), in particular Karyn Nykvist and Brigitte Rath. I owe a lasting debt to Tony Crowley and his work on the politics of language, without which I'd probably be doing something else entirely. Daljit Nagra and Raman Mundair have been generous friends to the project, as well as two of its subjects.

For reading and commenting on work-in-progress on various of these chapters, I'd like to thank my friend and co-editor at the *Journal of Commonwealth Literature*, Claire Chambers, as well as Rehana Ahmed, Sheela Banerjee, Nisha Ramayya, and particularly Nadia Atia, who tackled the whole manuscript and to whom I owe favours in perpetuity. My thanks too to the whole team at Manchester University Press, as well as to the anonymous readers they solicited, whose thoughts and care for this project also helped to shape it. Any remaining errors are of course mine.

In a minor failure of planning, I allowed final completion of this manuscript to collide with becoming Head of English at Queen Mary. It's been a strenuous pleasure doing both at the same time, but it wouldn't have been possible without the support, understanding, and graciousness of the whole School of English and Drama team, and in particular Warren Boutcher, Lara Fothergill, Caiomhe McAvinchey, and the inestimable Bev Stewart. Outside academia, good friends have heard these ideas rehearsed, and put up with me while it was all happening, in particular Sarah Arnott, Sarah Durham, Francesca Favia, Vanessa Ganguin, Sharon Glasgow, Claire Lanyon, Rose Macdonald, and Sarah Shanson. I wish Fiona Struthers were here to see it in print (particularly the bits about music in chapter three).

Thanks, as ever, to my wonderful mum and stepdad, Ray and Derrick. I'm grateful for the love and support of my extended family of Dales, Gilmours, Raznicks, Libovitches, Poles, Sandlers, Smiths, and Fursts; and for the memory of Jo Wright and Judy Libovitch. My father, Philip Sandler, is the difficult polyglot whose pleasure in languages was his best gift to me, even if he would perhaps have argued with me about some of the things I say in this book.

And finally: my endless thanks to Jonathan, with whom it's been a delight – as always – to share the journey, and whose care, patience, and ability to make me see the funny side deserve an acknowledgements page of their own; and to Ella and Ava, whose own adventures in language accompanied this book as it grew. This book is for these, my very special three, with love.

* * *

Earlier versions of parts of chapters three, four, and five have appeared as:
' "Ah'm the man ae a thoosand tongues": multilingual Scottishness and its limits', in Rachael Gilmour and Tamar Steinitz (eds) *Multilingual Currents in Literature, Language and Culture* (London and New York: Routledge, 2018).
'Punning in Punglish, sounding "poreign": Daljit Nagra and the politics of language', *Interventions: International Journal of Postcolonial Studies* 17:5 (2015), 686–705.
'Living between languages: the politics of translation in Leila Aboulela's *Minaret* and Xiaolu Guo's *A Concise Chinese-English Dictionary for Lovers'*, *Journal of Commonwealth Literature* 47:2 (June 2012), 207–227.

My thanks for permission to reproduce extracts from the following:
Tom Leonard, *Intimate Voices: Selected Work 1965-1983* (Buckfastleigh: etruscan books, 2003). Reproduced by kind permission of Sonia Leonard.
Robert Crawford and W. N. Herbert, *Sharawaggi: Poems in Scots* (Edinburgh: Polygon, 1990). Reproduced by permission of the licensor through PLSclear.

David Kinloch, 'Mamapoules', in Robert Crawford, W. N. Herbert, David Kinloch, Peter McCarey, Richard Price, and Alan Riach, *Contraflow on the Super Highway* (London: Southfields Press and Gairfish, 1994). Reproduced by kind permission of David Kinloch.

David Kinloch, *Paris-Forfar* (Edinburgh: Polygon, 1994). Reproduced by permission of the licensor through PLSclear.

Daniel O'Rourke (ed.) *Dream State: The New Scottish Poets* (Edinburgh: Polygon, 1994). Reproduced by permission of the licensor through PLSclear.

Raman Mundair, *Lovers, Liars, Conjurers and Thieves* (Leeds: Peepal Tree Press, 2003). Reproduced by kind permission of Raman Mundair and Peepal Tree Press.

Raman Mundair, *A Choreographer's Cartography* (Leeds: Peepal Tree Press, 2007). Reproduced by kind permission of Raman Mundair and Peepal Tree Press.

Daljit Nagra, *Look We Have Coming to Dover!* (London: Faber, 2007). Reproduced by kind permission of Daljit Nagra and Faber & Faber Ltd.

Daljit Nagra, *Tippoo Sultan's Incredible White-Man-Eating Tiger-Toy Machine!!!* (London: Faber, 2011). Reproduced by kind permission of Daljit Nagra and Faber & Faber Ltd.

David Herd and Anna Pincus (eds), *Refugee Tales* ([Manchester]: Comma Press, 2016). Reproduced by kind permission of Comma Press.

The New Union Flag Project

The New Union Flag project, by the artist Gil Mualem-Doron, reimagines the Union Flag in a way that reflects the changing society in which we live, acknowledging and celebrating the communities that have contributed to the UK's cultural legacy. Re-created with fabric designs from all over the world, the New Union Flag transforms the traditional Union Jack from an archetype of uniformity into a dynamic and celebratory on-going performance of diversity. While it appears on this book's cover as a static image, it is in fact a constantly evolving entity.

From 2015, when it was first exhibited at Peckham Platform, the New Union Flag has evolved every few months with the contributions of participants from various national and ethnic backgrounds. For five years now, it has engaged tens of thousands of people through gallery exhibitions (Turner Contemporary, Tate Modern, the Southbank Centre, People's History Museum – Manchester, Liverpool Museum), numerous cultural events, school visits, festivals, rallies, and workshops.

The New Union Flag project also includes portraits of people who would like to see it adopted as the national flag, as well as others who don't, and recordings of conversations with them. The New Union Flag project is an ongoing project, and, pending funding, another national tour is planned for 2021.

More information about the project, short films, and photography can be found at: www.http://gildoron.co.uk

Introduction: Bad English

Language is my home, I say; not one particular language.
Vahni Capildeo, 'Five Measures of Expatriation'[1]

At an event at the School of Oriental and African Studies in London in early 2018, the Trinidadian British poet Vahni Capildeo was asked about their multilingual poetics. What was it, the questioner asked, that made them mix up so many different kinds of language in their poetry? Well, they were usually thinking in more than one language, Capildeo replied – and they had simply 'stopped translating'.[2] A commonplace assumption was neatly illuminated by that well-meant question: that literature usually *is* in one particular language, and that writing which uses different kinds of language is anomalous and therefore remarkable. Just as illuminating was Capildeo's response: that their poetry is what happens when one stops translating a multilingual consciousness and experience of the world into monolingual English.

The exchange took place in the basement of a bookshop in Bloomsbury; and indeed, what could be more resonantly appropriate, recalling Euro-American modernism's plurilingual language experiments and linguistic estrangements, its portrayal of 'languages that were neither fully English nor fully foreign'?[3] Yet, while accounting for experimental poetry that is sometimes a wild assemblage of fragments of different kinds of language – words spliced, diced, wilfully misheard – Capildeo's comments nevertheless located it in relation to the resolute *everydayness* of multilingual subjectivity. Thinking in, being surrounded by, and using an ever-changing repertoire of linguistic resources is just how someone like them – who grew up in Trinidad, lives in Britain, has travelled around Europe, as well as having had the admittedly less commonplace experience of studying Old Norse and translation theory at Oxford – experiences the world. In the contemporary moment in Britain, partly thanks to processes that include migration, globalisation, new technology, and urbanisation, it is fairly unexceptional to have access to a wide range of languages, bits of language, codes, and registers from which to make meanings.[4] Though in fact, of course, Britain has never been monolingual, and its languages, most especially English, have been shaped by ceaseless traffic within and beyond its national borders.

In the prose poetry sequence 'Five Measures of Expatriation', Capildeo describes the conjuring of multiple words from different registers and languages as 'a kind of bee dance' – syncopated, back-and-forth, cross-pollinating. On the one hand they locate this practice in 'the fluidity and zigzagging of Trinidadian speech': language that wears its histories on its sleeve in the meshing of 'flowery translations of Sanskrit' and Catholic liturgy with 'the tricksy shrug and bread-and-curses everydayness of Spanish-French-Portuguese-Syrian-Chinese-Scottish-Irish-(English)'. On the other, it is an outcome of their 'expatriation': of the move to Britain, of linguistic displacement, and of the consequent and unnerving sense of their own language as experienced by others – language perceived as different, anomalous, foreign, *accented*.[5] In a party game in which each participant says the first word that comes to mind, prompted by the word the person before has said, producing 'outrages and banalities and brilliance', Capildeo's poetic speaker describes being paralysed by 'hesitation and a stammer' – by the summoning up of wrong words, too many words, or no words at all. Capildeo asks: 'Was everyone else pretending to have one-word events in their brains, while secretly choosing from a *retentissante* horde?'[6] Language, they reiterate, is their home, but 'not one particular language'.

Capildeo's self-conscious self-positioning in the gap between *languages* as supposedly distinct, orderly, complete, self-contained systems and *language* as a dynamic assemblage of resources, registers, and styles is representative of some of the core questions with which this book is concerned. As many of the authors it examines are keenly aware, the idea of 'a language' or 'the language' is an invention (a colonial one, at that), and one that carries weighty ideological power.[7]

So what happens to literary language, and the idea of language in literature, when the ideological force of English monolingualism comes under pressure from an actually occurring diversity of languages, registers, codes, and styles, in literature that is concerned at its centre, as Capildeo's poetry is, with ideas about language and their implications? In Capildeo's case it is hard to miss the postcolonial dynamics at work in an articulation of language that operates in relation to Trinidad, whose linguistic landscape is shaped by residues of slavery, indenture, and colonialism, and by an English that once dominated in the name of imperial rule and now does so in the name of global communication and economic opportunity. There is also the particular effect of experiencing your own language as something exterior and alien that comes with arriving as a racialised (post)colonial speaker in the metropole. Like Frantz Fanon's 'r-eating man from Martinique', Capildeo dramatises the experience of suddenly hearing one's own recalcitrant, racially marked speech as a kind of unwilled sound effect: ' "Hello!" My voice reverted to a kind of Trinidadian that it had never used in Trinidad: a birdlike screech'.[8] Here a speaker experiences their own 'tone' in the double sense in which Rey Chow uses the term, visual and audial, of being 'racialized by language'.[9]

There is a studied ambiguity to Capildeo's putting English in parentheses: 'Spanish-French-Portuguese-Syrian-Chinese-Scottish-Irish-(English)'. Set apart from its others, English appears to maintain its ideological claim to be imagined separate and distinct. Its parentheses are exclusionary, an assertion of dominance, and a refusal to mingle. But they cannot altogether hold English apart from its hyphenated relationship to all these other forms of language, in a Trinidadian linguistic landscape shaped by slavery, empire, and migration. So perhaps those parentheses mark subordination, as well as exclusion: an English no longer able to assert its unitary nature, become open to its others. In the poem 'Two Foreign', Capildeo writes:

> if this language is the sole
> to carry over
> how we were war-thrown,
> tens, dizzens, thon thorn
> honour a tension,
> learnt our statues: lesteners,

let's lessen to poems:
but these words have class issues;
is it she'd rase or e-race
unnatural disasters? swap
swamp?[10]

This compressed sequence of words points to a monologic English
that is both the only ('sole') language in which to claim sanctuary for
the 'war-thrown', and the essence (soul) of the nation, yet which is
freighted with 'tension', 'class issues' (not only issues of class, but the
matter of how the language classifies), and race.[11] It is a language which
'lessons' and 'lessens' its learner, who responds with creative homophonic mishearings and the double meanings they create – as when 'on
our attention' becomes 'honour a tension' – that bring into plain sight
the ambivalent experience of being an outsider, 'two foreign', to the
language and the histories with which it comes: 'lesson | to the museum
pornograph. | Phono-, okay'.[12] As the poem progresses, it seeks to
overcome this monologic 'lesson[ing]' both by intralingual associative
wordplay and by borrowing promiscuously across English's supposedly
shored-up borders: from the Glasgow Scots of poet Tom Leonard ('it
izny | that'), Old English ('thorn'), dialectal English ('pote'), Icelandic
('the stjörnu I stjeer by'). Turning mispronunciation into multilingual
aspiration, the poem concludes by transforming linguistic faultlines
into 'vaultlines'.[13]

Capildeo's poetry addresses itself to an English in Britain that has,
since 2001, been shored up as a language of national belonging; and
this intensified antipathy to multilingualism is one important context
for this book. Over the past almost two decades, English language com-
petence (measured by language testing) has increasingly come to be
legislated for in Britain as a requirement of entry and citizenship, while
public and political discourse has ever more intensively focused on
other languages and their speakers as threats to the national order. In
the words of Boris Johnson, at a Conservative Party leadership hustings in July 2019 prior to his inauguration as Prime Minister: 'Too
often there are parts of our country … where English is not spoken by
some people as their first language and that needs to be changed'.[14] As
Deborah Cameron puts it in an article from 2013,

Today, discourse on the status of English and the presence of other languages in Britain is ubiquitous, and the anxiety is being voiced most insistently not by racist fringe parties or the popular tabloid press, but by the UK government itself.[15]

As each new iteration of immigration law has intensified language testing requirements, learning and speaking English is cast in public and political discourse as the means to become a successful, integrated citizen. It is this pedagogic and disciplinary object, a valorised and mandated English, which appears, and is partially dismantled, in 'Two Foreign'. Capildeo's poetic tools are multilingualism, etymology, and the disjuncture between what Garrett Stewart calls the 'graphotext' and 'phonotext'[16] – or, put another way, the hearing (and the wilful mishearing) of the written word – by which to ruffle English's surface, to coax it to show its ideological underpinnings and at the same time revealing its capacity to be transfigured.

Published more than fifty years earlier, in a different historical moment – of postwar immigration, and the era of decolonisation – the 'vernacular landscape' of fellow Trinidadian Sam Selvon's *The Lonely Londoners* also resonates with these dual aspects of English: ideological conveyor of national and imperial power, nonetheless susceptible to critical reshaping.[17] Selvon's polyphonic modernist metropolis, fabricated out of the linguistic resources of London on the one hand and Trinidad and the wider Caribbean on the other, is a city caught in the uneven throes of being creolised.[18] In his confected literary vernacular, Selvon casts the provisional and fragile making of a society of West Indians in postwar London, mapped through a language-world shared between narrator, characters, and reader that offers a sense of commonality outside 'the received, "standard" London'.[19] For Selvon's characters, arriving as colonially educated West Indians steeped in British culture and with the anticipation of the English language as a shared linguistic commons, comes the shock of racial overdetermination, and English does not prove to be a shared communicative medium that can pass through their newly discovered 'blackness'. Selvon's is a language-world in which acts of speaking across London's racial divides are perpetually being suspended, circuits of communication broken off or foreclosed, from Moses' earnest attempt to express the predicament of West Indians in London to an unheeding news reporter, to

Galahad's unheard efforts to talk publicly about 'the colour problem' at Speaker's Corner, or when Daisy says to Galahad:

> 'What did you say? You know it will take me some time to understand everything you say. The way you West Indians speak!'
> 'What wrong with it?' Galahad ask. 'Is English we speaking.'[20]

As Mervyn Morris puts it, 'Daisy's problem is the unfamiliar sound of the Trinidadian' – but, once again, the outcome is the evaporation of Galahad's meaning on the way to its intended recipient.[21] In 'Calypso in London', a short story in Selvon's *Ways of Sunlight*, Hotboy and Mangohead write a calypso about the 1956 Suez Crisis, fantasising that they will hear it 'playing all about in London, and people going wild when they hear it', and Mangohead suggests they 'might even get it play by the BBC'. Yet, by the end of the story, their calypso has disappeared without trace:

> But up to now I can't hear it playing or singing anywhere, though I sure the number was really hearts, and would make some money for the boys if it catch on and sell.[22]

But even if Selvon's London is a city in which the utterances of his West Indian characters are all too easily lost, Hotboy and Mangohead's calypso is also a symbol of language always being generated, always on the move. The linguistic medium shared by Selvon's characters doesn't emanate from some pure point of origin in the West Indies, but is an outcome of their living in London – in *The Lonely Londoners* even Cap, who is Nigerian, spends enough time with 'the boys' to 'forget proper English', so that 'many times you would mistake him for a West Indian, he get so hep'.[23] New words and phrases appear constantly, most famously in the redefining and remapping of London in language – Marble Arch ('the Arch') becomes a place to 'coast a lime', Bayswater is renamed 'the Water', Piccadilly Circus 'the Circus', and Big City, with his perpetual mishearings, develops a whole alternative toponymy for London: 'From Pentonvilla right up to Musket Hill, all about by Claphand Common. I bet you can't call a name in London that I don't know where it is.'[24] In Selvon's short story 'Working the Transport', the bus depot resonates to the improvised sounds of what its protagonist Change, in a moment of inspiration, dubs 'hip and hit', which fleetingly becomes a music and dance craze among the teddy boys and girls 'south of the river'.[25] Selvon's polyphonic city is a world of signs: the words people speak, advertising, print media, voices amplified and recorded. Indeed, in the short story 'My Girl and the City', London is little more than an exhilarating, overwhelming experience of linguistic acceleration – '[h]urtling in the underground from station to station, mind the doors, missed it!, there is no substitute for wool' – amid which the West Indian writer-narrator fires off his own 'precious words' obsessively, across buses and under the din of trains:

> My words bumped against people's faces, on the glass window of the bus; they found passage between 'fares please' and once I got to writing things on a piece of paper and pushing my hand over two seats.[26]

Selvon's nascently postcolonial city, being linguistically transformed by postwar migration, social change, global connectedness, and new technology – even while the ideological and racial power of the standard language persists – lays the groundwork for some of the questions which are central to this book. In it I argue that living in and between multiple forms of language, being surrounded by diverse symbolic resources of all kinds, is one kind of contemporary everyday experience – in Britain's cities, and increasingly beyond them. In the context of accelerated patterns of migration, global communication, electronic media, and rapid social change, we live in 'distinctly and intensely polyglot' times.[27] Friction between such experiences of languaging and the idea that there is a singularity called 'English' is a generative force for writers like Capildeo, and others I explore in *Bad English*. In this way, their work also renders inescapable some of the myths by which monolingualism operates. These include seemingly commonplace ideas like 'mother tongue' and 'native speaker', as well as the operations of what Deborah Cameron calls 'verbal hygiene': the 'motley collection of discourses and practices through which people attempt to "clean up" language and make its structure or its use conform more closely to their ideals of beauty, truth, efficiency, logic, correctness and civility'.[28] English, as an official, institutionalised form of language, thus appears exposed as an ideological far more than a linguistic object.

Ideologies of English

Another abiding myth, as Dennis Ager observes, is that the English language in Britain is in fact somehow apolitical – simply existing, in the
background, like the weather. Ager gives the example of John Simpson,
chief editor of the *OED*, writing in the *Guardian* in 1995:

> The English language has never had a state-registered guardian.
> English is already such a patchwork language that the Word Police
> would hardly know where to start. Instead of an academy, we've
> ruled ourselves and allowed the natural forces of change to be curbed
> only loosely by general dogma and prejudice.[29]

Unlike France, so an argument like Simpson's goes, with the controlling
oversight of the Academy, or the US with its English-Only campaign,
English in Britain is 'a simple reflection of a mysterious social consensus'.[30] Certainly, as Deborah Cameron argues, it is only since 2001 that
there has been a decisive shift towards state legislation of language in
Britain mandating the learning and use of English.[31] Yet debates were
already raging at the turn of the twentieth century about declining language standards, and the need for language standardisation and spelling
reform – concerns of the Society for Pure English, which was founded
in 1913.[32] From the 1960s to the present, the period I examine in this
book, as Britain has been transformed by forces including immigration,
rapid social change, devolution, technology, and globalisation, language
in various guises has been a recurrent concern of political discourse and
public policy-making, and a preoccupation of journalists, educationalists, community activists, and academics, as well as the writers who are
my central concern. The 'standard English' debates and the Secretary of
State for Education's Better English Campaign of the 1980s and 1990s,
and discussions of the relationship between language testing and immigration law, are just two signal examples of the ways in which arguments
about language appear in public and political discourse, and become
part of government policy or state legislation.[33] Instances could be
multiplied – the question of minority languages within the UK National
Curriculum, for example, in which Welsh and Gaelic can be used as
media of instruction whereas 'non-native' community languages like
Punjabi, Hindi, and Urdu are studied through the medium of English
under the aegis of 'modern foreign languages'. As these few examples

suggest, debates about language are rarely, if ever, 'just' about language: they are about what counts as native and what counts as foreign, about definitions of purity and impurity, about race, class, or national belonging. The point, then, is how many other things we are *really* talking about when we are talking about language. The prescription of particular kinds of language as desirable or otherwise recurrently casts them as carrying particular kinds of values – as emblems of modernity, progressiveness, rationality, national cohesion, or as harbingers of social ills that range from school underachievement and declining literacy rates to civic disorder and social breakdown.[34] As this book will argue, and as the writers it discusses are often keenly aware, Britain has been and remains dominated by a powerful monolingualist ideology – all the more forceful for being diffused and so often couched in the idiom of 'common sense' – that sees English as identical with the national order.

Two kinds of argument about language, never entirely distinct from each other, have recurred in Britain with great regularity. The first focuses on threats to standards of English propriety as harbingers of social disintegration. In a BBC radio interview in 1988, for example, the Conservative politician Norman Tebbit associated a decline in grammar teaching in schools with a rise in football hooliganism.[35] Three years later, the writer and newspaper columnist Keith Waterhouse observed that 'Bad English … is part of the general corrosion of the quality of life, like vandalism, litter, and graffiti'.[36] The second focuses on anxieties about the encroachment of other kinds of language as dangerous to a state of (monolingual) linguistic order, resting on a logic of either/or which dictates that the growth of other languages must mean a decline of English, or that to speak another language implies a kind of inevitable disloyalty. The *Express* newspaper, reporting on the 2011 Office for National Statistics Census results, which included questions about language for the first time and which revealed that in some inner-city areas 40 per cent of people speak a language other than English, ran with the cover headline 'Migrants shun the English language'.[37] The *Sun* followed the same non sequitur that speaking another language must mean not being able to speak English and concluded that 'many migrants have no interest in learning English because they simply don't want to integrate'.[38]

What these examples also demonstrate with some clarity is the way in which arguments about language focalise or make speakable other kinds of ideas – about immigration, race, class, social change, national identity – and the kinds of fears which may be conjured through invocations of linguistic difference. In his infamous 1968 'rivers of blood' speech, Enoch Powell proffered apocalyptic visions of a British nation transformed not just by racial but by linguistic alterity so as to be made literally unintelligible. He recounted the story of an elderly white woman terrorised by the immigrants who had taken over her street and her neighbourhood:

> When she goes to the shops, she is followed by children, charming, wide-grinning picaninnies. They cannot speak English, but one word they know. 'Racialist', they chant.[39]

The fearful image of children in Britain who 'cannot speak English' is one which recurs, for example in shrill news reporting on inner-city schools in which the majority of pupils speak a language other than English at home.[40] Into the figure of the child is invested a particular kind of fear: of a future Britain that has become linguistically disordered, even incomprehensible.

In the 1970s and 1980s, a number of prominent British sociolinguists were arguing that the main problem for children in Britain was in fact the ways in which ideologies of race and class were conflated with language, and the monolingualist ideology of linguistic correctness, and made the case for integrating different kinds of language in the school classroom, including all non-standard varieties of English, and for the value of bilingual education. Viv Edwards, for example, conducted research which demonstrated the prejudice and lack of comprehension directed towards Caribbean creole language forms on the part of many British teachers – who regarded them as 'sloppy', or 'jungle talk' – and connected this, as black educational campaigners did, with the disproportionate number of black children being sent to ESN ('educationally subnormal') schools.[41] As Peter Trudgill argued in *Accent, Dialect and the School*,

> The fact that no one language is 'better' than any other is important for the role of language in education. This is because the same thing is equally true of different varieties of the same language. ... All English dialects are equally complex, structured and valid linguistic systems. There is no linguistic evidence whatsoever for suggesting

that one dialect is more 'expressive' or 'logical' than any other, or for postulating that there are any 'primitive', 'inadequate' or 'debased' English dialects.[42]

Educationalists of the 'new right', meanwhile, were appalled at what they interpreted as attacks on standard English and notions of linguistic propriety. John Honey, in his pamphlet 'The Language Trap: Race, Class, and the "Standard English" Issue in British Schools', attacked what he described as a 'pseudo-scientific' 'new orthodoxy' as the source of declining educational standards and cultural crisis.[43] Taking Jamaican Creole as an example of a variety of language 'being actively promoted by some educationists', with support from 'specialists in linguistics', he diagnosed the danger not just of linguistic but social and racial disorder:

> the use of these forms of 'Black English' is cultivated for the most part among the disaffected young and, at least in present-day Britain, this variety is actually learned as a second language by adolescent blacks (who already speak standard English or one of its regional variants) in order to assert their subgroup's differences from mainstream culture and their scorn for those who identify or collaborate with that culture. Its use is often accompanied by other anti-authority behaviour, including gang membership which is sometimes crime-oriented and involved in drug use; and the creole may be used on occasions specifically in order to irritate and confuse police or other representatives of authority such as teachers or youth club workers who happen to be white. ... In these, as in many other groups, the conscious choice of non-standard forms in preference to standard English also serve 'sexist' purposes, emphasizing the more dubious forms of machismo and male exclusiveness.[44]

Associating Jamaican Creole with a raft of social ills – anti-authoritarianism, violence, crime, drug use, misogyny – Honey accused its defenders of 'promoting social divisiveness, aggression and even criminality'.[45] Threats to standard English were threats of descent into racial chaos and societal collapse. Even Lord Scarman, in his report on the causes of the 1981 Brixton riots, associated issues of language with civil disorder. Though focusing largely on social, political, and economic factors, on issues in housing and employment as well as discriminatory policing tactics, the Scarman Report also insisted that language – specifically, young black people's supposed lack of proficiency in English – had played a role in the disturbances. Going forward, steps needed to be taken to ensure that

> children should leave school able to speak, read and write effectively in the language of British society, i.e. English. This is of the first importance if young black people are to have a chance to make their way, and to contribute to the extent they have it in them to do, to British society.[46]

These specific associations between black speech and criminality are the ones John Agard satirises in his 1985 poem 'Listen Mr Oxford Don'. Subverting a word that had come to unambiguously signify black criminal violence – 'mugging' – Agard's speaker sardonically observes:

> I ent have no gun
> I ent have no knife
> But mugging de Queen's English
> Is the story of my life[47]

Armed with nothing more than 'mih human breath' – in his hands, itself a 'dangerous weapon' – Agard's speaker combats the whole conjoined linguistic and juridical system that would condemn him:

> So mek dem send one big word after me
> I ent serving no jail sentence
> I slashing suffix in self-defence
> I bashing future wit present tense
> And if necessary
>
> I making de Queen's English accessory/to my offence[48]

Deft and funny, Agard's poem celebrates the dexterity with which it moves between linguistic codes, syncopating the capabilities of vernacular speech, poetic form, 'de Queen's English' and 'de Oxford dictionary', while it uses all of them to expose the repressive power of discourses of black criminality, and their relationship to representations of creole language forms as expressively insufficient or a threat – a violent threat – to the standard language.

Nevertheless, such associations are remarkably persistent. In August 2011, on the BBC's *Newsnight* programme, discussing the civil disorder which had just taken place in several British cities, the historian David Starkey explicitly invoked Enoch Powell but also seemed to be channelling John Honey. The riots had taken place following the deadly police shooting of an unarmed black man, Mark Duggan, in Tottenham, London; but Starkey laid the *real* blame for them on a Britain become alien, racially and linguistically disordered, under the influence of black culture:

> The whites have become black. A particular sort of violent, destructive, nihilistic, gangster culture has become the fashion.
>
> And black and white, boy and girl, operate in this language together, this language which is wholly false, which is this Jamaican patois that's been intruded in England, and this is why so many of us have this sense of literally a foreign country.[49]

Starkey's target was the language and culture of young black people – even worse, that of 'the whites' who 'have become black' – but in general the locus of such linguistic anxieties in Britain has shifted since 2001 towards South Asian languages and their speakers. As Adrian Blackledge observes, these languages have come to be routinely associated in public and political discourse with a variety of social ills ranging from marital and intergenerational disharmony, social segregation, educational underachievement, poverty, and mental illness, through to violent extremism, civil disorder, and threats to the integrity of the nation.[50] These discourses about language have a political function – they imply particular communities' culpability for their own exclusion, which would melt away if they would simply speak proper English like everyone else. They demonstrate, too, the way in which language becomes a screen onto which to project what are in fact other kinds of anxieties – anxieties about race, about class. But they also speak to a *fear* of other languages: of being in 'a foreign country' at home, of not understanding, of languages imagined as a threat. In our recent times, we have seen this kind of linguaphobia and the fearful logic of either/ or manifest in violent physical attacks on people for speaking languages other than English in public spaces like buses, trains, and city streets: 'speak English in England!'[51]

Bad English

Perhaps because of the supposedly commonsensical idea that England is fundamentally monolingual – in Wales or in Scotland, where chapter one begins, the situation is somewhat different – or because of the pervasive assumption that language diversity is only of marginal concern, questions about language and multilingualism have for the most part been seen as little more than incidental to the field of literature in Britain. This is in marked contrast to the situation in the US, where literary multilingualism has been a field of critical inquiry for more than twenty years, often explicitly in the context of 'English-Only' language politics and concomitant struggles to assert the value (and inescapability) of US language diversity: from Werner Sollors's edited *Multilingual America: Transnationalism, Ethnicity, and the Languages of American Literature* (1998) and Michael North's *The Dialect of Modernism: Race, Language, and Twentieth-Century Literature* (1994), through Doris Sommer's *Bilingual Aesthetics: A New Sentimental Education* (2004), Martha J. Cutter's *Lost and Found in Translation: Contemporary Ethnic American Writing and the Politics of Language Diversity* (2005), Hana Wirth-Nesher's *Call It English: The Languages of Jewish American Literature* (2006), Maria Lauret's *Wanderwords: Language Migration in American Literature* (2014), with an increasingly transnational gyre in Azade Seyhan's *Writing Outside the Nation* (2001), Brian Lennon's *In Babel's Shadow: Multilingual Literatures, Monolingual States* (2010), and Yasemin Yildiz's *Beyond the Mother Tongue: The Postmonolingual Condition* (2012), as well as Emily Apter's *The Translation Zone: A New Comparative Literature* (2006) and *Against World Literature: On the Politics of Untranslatability* (2013).[52] Perhaps the most significant in the context of my discussion is Joshua L. Miller's *Accented America: The Cultural Politics of Multilingual Modernism* (2011), for the way Miller moves between literature and wider discourses about language, from politics and popular culture to linguistics and philology, to make an argument for understanding the literature of the first third of the twentieth century in the US as indivisible from its shifting language politics.[53]

   As Miller points out for the US and as is true for Britain too, the literary field is also multilingual in the sense that there is a wealth of literature being written and published in other languages – Somali poetry,

Arabic novels – that lies beyond the scope of this book. What the writers I examine here have in common is a shared focus on English, as a matrix language for their writing and as an object of scrutiny. This book draws together writers living and working in England and Scotland, unified neither by race nor class, and a survey of the diverse critical fields that encompass them is instructive. Scholarship on the work of black and Asian writers in Britain has been, as a rule, more attentive to thematic concerns of race and identity than to questions of language and form, with some notable exceptions, like James Procter's *Dwelling Places: Postwar Black British Writing* (2003). Lars Ole Sauerberg's *Intercultural Voices in Contemporary British Literature* (2001) is a rare and innovative foray into this field, whereas Jeremy Scott's *The Demotic Voice in Contemporary British Fiction* (2009) is carefully attentive to style but takes a somewhat restricted view of what constitutes a 'demotic voice', as a property of white British, mostly male writers. In Scotland, by contrast, the relationship of literature to language politics appears inescapably visible in the agonistic relations between English, Scots, and Gaelic. In Robert Crawford's ground-breaking *Devolving English Literature* (1992), for example, parsing the history and politics of language in Scotland provides the ground to argue for a radical assault on the propriety of English from all of its peripheries, from Scotland to the north of England, Ireland, the Caribbean, and Australia.[54] As I'll argue in chapters one and two, the idea of a shared experience of language with writers from the Caribbean and elsewhere provides a fertile – though sometimes risky – strategy for white Scottish writers, Crawford among them, in imagining the lineaments of a shared anti-colonial internationalism.

In fact, many of the writers under examination in this book are prone to associating themselves with diverse kinds of literary language experiments and insurrectionary language politics. Vahni Capildeo gives nods not just to Tom Leonard's vernacular Scots poetics but to the Nigerian novelist Amos Tutuola and his hallucinatory non-standard English. The Glasgow writer James Kelman cites influences that include the anticolonial vernacular politics of the London-based Caribbean Artists Movement and Nigerian Ken Saro-Wiwa's 'rotten English' novel *Sozaboy*. French-Norwegian poet Caroline Bergvall points towards the radical multilingualism of American/Japanese/German writer Yoko Tawada and the Caribbean poet and theorist

Édouard Glissant's 'relational poetics'.[55] These transnational connections offer, among other things, means to think about language in
expansive ways that bypass the confines of the nation, even as each of
the writers I've mentioned remains often antagonistically conscious of
the mutual imbrication of the English language and the British state. It
is also worth noting in passing here the range of these writers' various
involvements with the theory and *techne* of translation, language, and
linguistics: James Kelman's relationship with Noam Chomsky, David
Kinloch's practice as a translator of French, Daljit Nagra's programme
for BBC radio about the colonial Anglo-Indian glossary *Hobson-Jobson*,
Vahni Capildeo's Oxford MPhil in Old Norse and translation studies
and work as an OED lexicographer.

As all of this goes to suggest, a central contention of this book is
that this is a field of writing – growing, diverse, complex – which is
highly metalinguistic: it is *about* language, not as a transparent medium
for our experiences and their expression but as an object in itself. It
reflects self-consciously on the experiences of using, mixing, translating, speaking, listening to, losing, and acquiring different kinds of
language. Writers here produce synthesised written vernaculars and
probe the attendant paradoxes of writing as a technology to reproduce
voice. They use visual-textual means to represent languages encountering each other: images, orthographies, visual experiments, facing-page
translations, paratexts like glossaries, literary code-switching, and
weird new forms of English.[56] They employ metaphors for how language travels and mixes, from music to digital technology to oceanic
currents, and they narrativise scenes of ordinary and extraordinary
linguistic encounter taking place in streets, homes, classrooms, shops,
mosques, and asylum centres. They probe the stakes of using different
kinds of language that operate at scales smaller and bigger than the
nation, in relation to the powerful unitary language that continues
to ideologically shore up the nation state and its borders. For reasons
which are probably quite clear by now, although the central focus of
this book is literature, it is also interested (as many of these writers are)
in all the other ways in which ideas about language circulate: in arguments about citizenship or education, in political discourse and legislation, in Home Office policy, in streets and playgrounds, in newspapers,
television, or on Twitter.

In exploring all of this, this book rebuffs the view that language difference and language politics are somehow irrelevant or marginal to contemporary Britain and makes an argument for their constitutive centrality to a literature produced by a growing range of novelists and poets whose inside/outside relationship to English in its institution-alised forms is the generative force of their writing. Thus, while the central imperative of this book is the work of literary analysis, it (I hope respectfully) draws on a range of fields which are concerned with ideas about language. Postcolonial studies has for obvious reasons never been able to overlook the politics of language and linguistic inequality and I'm indebted in particular to Rey Chow's parsing of 'languaging as a postcolonial experience' and Mary Louise Pratt's theorisation of the colonial dynamics of language contact. Mikhail Bakhtin, Pierre Bourdieu, Michel Foucault, and Jacques Derrida each in their different and irreplaceable ways help us to understand the history, dynamics, and variegated, often covert operations of the ideological object called 'a language'. In applied linguistics, concepts of multilingualism some-times glibly invoked in literary studies come under sustained critical scrutiny, while the linguistic regimes and ideologies of contemporary Britain are made plain, as in the scholarship of Deborah Cameron, Jan Blommaert, Alastair Pennycook, Sinfree Makoni, and Adrian Blackledge among others.

With the work of applied linguists particularly in mind, a couple of linguistic issues are worth discussing a little further. The first is that, as will probably already be obvious, a monolithic language called 'English' (as opposed to many different kinds of 'Englishes') is largely an inven-tion, albeit a hugely powerful one. I'll be using the term 'English' as a catch-all, and sometimes 'standard English' to denote the language in its overtly codified and prescribed forms, while attending to how both of these ideologically constructed objects are parsed, historicised, dramatised, contested, recalibrated, translated, or otherwise bent out of shape in the literary and other texts I examine. Equally, as I've sug-gested above, it's important to underline that 'multilingualism' itself is also not one thing, or way of thinking about language, but several. In its most conventional received sense, meaning something like 'more than one language', multilingualism still rests on the assumption that there is such a thing as 'a language', of which there can be more than one: that languages are singular, bounded, discrete, countable, stable entities.[57] Yet – as Vahni Capildeo's poetry suggests – this is to ignore the lived reality of how language is actually used, particularly in linguistically complex, 'super-diverse' (to use Steven Vertovec's phrase) urban environments, in which speakers are surrounded by symbolic resources of all kinds and often have correspondingly highly diverse language repertoires, drawing adaptively from the range of linguistic resources at their disposal.[58] In an increasingly digitally connected, mediatised world, these include different forms of communication that broach the supposed divide between the linguistic and the visual, or 'multimodality'.[59]

The interplay which this book uncovers between language politics and literary form is both antagonistic and productive, as it traces literature's articulation of experiences of linguistic alienation and ambivalence, of struggle, of worrying exposure and visibility through language, as well as the productivity and making-new of radical language practices. It is all too easy, in literary scholarship, to romanticise linguistic 'hybridity' or 'multilingualism' or what John McLeod calls 'enabling cosmopolitanism' as necessarily positive or progressive.[60] As Sebastian Groes writes of *The Satanic Verses* (and as is undoubtedly true), Rushdie's dazzlingly polyphonic novel 'approaches London as a text … to linguistically unstitch the metropolis and to open up spaces into which the immigrants can inscribe themselves'.[61] But that 'opening up' has always come at a cost, as we see in Selvon's London-set novels and short stories, or the work of black British poets of the 1970s and 1980s like Linton Kwesi Johnson, in whose writing the city is a system which can be acted upon resistantly – albeit with great individual and collective effort – through the acts of occupying, moving through, and speaking in it. The London of the present day is both one of the most linguistically diverse cities on earth and often, on those grounds, celebrated as a site of particular postcolonial conviviality. It is also the central node in the UK's national system of exclusion, dispersal, surveillance, and control of refugees – in David Farrier's words, 'an outpost of the border located deep within the national territory'.[62] Any liberatory, mobile view of language and culture has to reckon with the fact that not all people are equally mobile, nor under circumstances of their own choosing; that not all multilingualisms are the same, nor are their resources evenly distributed. Some confer privilege, and others danger.[63] Bakhtinian heteroglossia, hybridity, and improvisatory linguistic creativity on the one hand meet linguistic normativity, surveillance, and securitisation on the other. Even if we all carry the power of Google Translate in our pockets, as Rebecca Walkowitz reminds us at the start of *Born Translated*, you still have to pass an English language proficiency test to qualify for a UK visa.[64] As Emily Apter cautions in 'Translation at the checkpoint', there is a (neoliberal) politics to imagining translation as a frictionless trade in meanings.[65] This is an imagining that has real-life, even life-or-death consequences within the UK asylum system, which provides perhaps the starkest example of 'dangerous multilingualism', as I discuss in chapter six.

Underpinning the arguments of this book is not only the conviction that the issue of language diversity in Britain, and its relationship to literature, remains underemphasised and underexamined, but also the attendant question: what different configurations of literary field and discipline might we need if we were to understand language diversity as a constituent of, rather than anomalous to, Britain and Britishness? One of the claims in this book is that decolonisation, patterns of migration, and a digitally networked globe all make this more intensively so now than ever – and that language needs to be a constituent part of any account of Britain's becoming-postcolonial. But in actual fact, the commonplaceness of language diversity in Britain is no new thing, and the idea of a monolingual 'English' literary culture was a relatively late invention, as Leonard Foster's ground-breaking *The Poet's Tongues* made clear as long ago as 1970.[66] Monolingualism as a way of thinking, as David Gramling underlines in *The Invention of Monolingualism,* came to real fruition in Europe in the eighteenth century.[67] It was a fantastically powerful invention, the mesh making possible new national, institutional, civic, and imperial modes of governance, though always in tension with actually occurring language diversity. And literature, above all, was a key site for the production and promulgation of monolingualism as an ideology. Linda Mugglestone and Robert Crawford both chart the ways in which English 'correct usage' was extrapolated from literature; Gauri Viswanathan, and most recently Aamir Mufti, how those models were exported via the British Empire and persist into the present.[68] The 'standard' language appeared in the field of literature as the language of authorial and narrative voice, of the material and social world, and of psychic interiority. Other kinds of language – literary representations of raced and classed voices, or foreign speech – appeared in the form of dialogue, set off in inverted commas and

marked with distinctions of vocabulary, orthography, grammar, and
syntax, often with sentimental or comic overtones. Examples abound,
from Henry Fielding to Elizabeth Gaskell, Charles Dickens to Rudyard
Kipling; to reread the 'classics' of English children's literature like
Frances Hodgson Burnett's *The Secret Garden*, as I ended up doing not
too long ago with my own children, is to be brought up short by the
politics of literary language and voice.[69] The Scottish novelist James
Kelman, whose work I discuss in chapters one and six, has written at
length of the distinction in the English novel between the language of
narration and that of its marginalised 'colonial servants and underlings' as encapsulating whole structures of classed and racial power:[70]

> In prose fiction I saw the distinction between dialogue and narrative
> as a summation of the political system; it was simply another method
> of exclusion, of marginalising and disenfranchising different peoples,
> cultures and communities.[71]

These are literary conventions still going strong in the late twentieth
century and beyond, of course, and not only in egregious examples
like Martin Amis's *London Fields* (1989). But they also represent language politics that have never been uncontested, and certainly from the
first half of the twentieth century onward these were conventions of
literary language and linguistic propriety undergoing seismic and irre-
versible challenge under a complex of influences: literary modernism's
polyphonic linguistic experimentalism; the 'new' linguistics and new
approaches to language; anticolonial internationalism and decolonisation; migration; urbanisation and rapid social change; globalisation;
innovations in communication technology; devolution. It is the literary
impact of all of these that, in varying proportions, I chart in this book.

My focus here is on writers whose work is highly, self-consciously
metalinguistic: who write poetry and prose that is *about* language, which
dramatises different kinds of language encountering one another and
asks, very centrally, what this means for us individually, collectively,
politically, aesthetically. Moving back and forth across the Scotland/
England border, my aim is partly to defuse what is a somewhat conventional focus on London, certainly in thinking about Britain's postcoloniality (though I am no pioneer in this regard, given important recent
projects like *Postcolonial Manchester* and James Procter and Jackie

Kay's *Out of Bounds*),[72] and equally, perhaps, a somewhat conventional focus on Scotland when thinking about multilingualism. Scotland, certainly, with its linguistic landscape of English, Scots, and Gaelic, makes it impossible to forget that Britain is not and never has been 'monolingual'. It also raises the question of how one thinks about 'native' and 'foreign', or 'endogamous' and 'exogamous' multilingualisms. I was drawn by white Scottish writers like James Kelman who see their work, on the ground of language, as part of an anticolonial or internationalist project, and by Scottish Asian writers like Raman Mundair and Suhayl Saadi who in their language experiments confound the 'native'/ 'foreign' dichotomy altogether. Nevertheless, the patterns I've tried to trace and the connections I've sought to make, taken together with the constraints of this being only one book-length study, have meant that there are no Welsh writers here, nor Irish writers mentioned more than incidentally.

Indeed, a more comprehensive study of literary multilingualism and vernacular experimentalism in Britain, inflected by a complex of the factors I've been discussing, could draw in writers in Britain as different as Alison Flett, Janice Galloway, Tony Harrison, Linton Kwesi Johnson, Anthony Joseph, Eimear McBride, Paul Muldoon, Grace Nichols, Salman Rushdie, Warsan Shire, Irvine Welsh, and Tony White (to give an idiosyncratic and nothing-like-exhaustive list).[73] Working to develop new strategies of literary mimesis to represent the social realities of an increasingly language-diverse Britain, in the 1970s and 1980s writers like Farrukh Dhondy and Ravinder Randhawa were using code-switching, glossaries, and scenes of incomprehension and language attrition between generations to represent life in multilingual British Asian communities.[74] Zadie Smith's famously polyphonic *White Teeth* opens onto a radically heteroglot London in which, as her character Samad observes, 'only the immigrants can speak Queen's English these days'.[75] Smith's novel is one critically and commercially successful example of writing which exploits the novel's heteroglossia in a dazzling polyphony of voices; another, well known for different reasons, is Salman Rushdie's *The Satanic Verses*. Yet in the terms of a fundamentally monolingualist publishing industry, only certain kinds of language diversity are likely to sell – as Brian Lennon argues, there is little space in mainstream markets for 'a radically, anarchically plurilingual literature' – and these are constraints within which writers work often highly self-consciously.[76] What Yaseen Noorani calls 'soft multilingualism', which emphasises 'translatability and inter-linguistic transparence', is very different to a 'hard multilingualism' that insists on linguistic difference and incommensurability.[77] Certain kinds of linguistic difference may be construed as attractively exotic, or they may fulfil demands that writers be 'representative' or 'authentic' – writing that, as the poet Daljit Nagra (the subject of chapter four) puts it, fills 'the gap in the market'.[78] The marketable frisson of urban 'authenticity' may well have had something to do with the six-figure advance given for Gautam Malkani's hugely hyped 2006 novel *Londonstani*, which in the end was both celebrated and condemned for its linguistic mix of English, Punjabi and Urdu, rap lyrics and mobile phone text-speak. In a review for the *Independent* the Scottish Asian writer Suhayl Saadi, whose work I discuss in chapter two, ascribed to the novel a tendency to linguistic caricature redolent of 'shabby, 21st-century Orientalism'.[79]

My concern in this book is with a range of literary texts which I see as representing something of the cutting edge of this field of literature: writing which is metalinguistically *about* as much as *in* language, which is prone to reflecting on some of the questions I sketch above, often conscious of extraliterary discourses about language even as it reflects on new ways of shaping 'English' in the presence of other kinds of language. This is not to say that it traces patterns of consensus – often quite the opposite. As Saadi's comments on Malkani's novel above make clear, there is no positive agreement on what a responsible literary multilingualism should look like; nor indeed on what a language is, what the place of an individual speaker is within it, how we conceive of linguistic community, how translation should proceed, how we represent different kinds of language and to what purpose, or any of the other questions which are inevitably attendant on the question of multilingualism in literature. As I hope this book will show, this is a field of literature that uncovers and probes the politics of language, so often so well concealed. Yet it is as schismatic and ambivalent as any other about the conclusions it draws.

In chapter one, the Scottish writers James Kelman and Tom Leonard probe the evident distance between the written norms of standard English and the Scots language world of white working-class Glasgow, finding in the dynamics between writing and speech a synecdoche of the class system. Drawing on postcolonial literature and

Chomskyan linguistic thought, and seeking solidarity in particular with Caribbean and black British writers, both seek on the grounds of language to reconcile a committed literary localism with an expansive anticolonial internationalism. Yet whereas Kelman and Leonard both invest in a literary language politics drawn from the Scots vernacular, for the poets I discuss in chapter two, working as academics and translators as well as poets, Scots exists not as the lived language of everyday experience but as a highly synthetic, neologistic medium, obviously indebted to Hugh MacDiarmid's 'synthetic Scots', salvaged and reinvented from sources as diverse as antiquarian dictionaries, contemporary media culture, and digital technology. Robert Crawford's early, ambitious techno-Scots poetry casts itself, in its unsystematicity and unboundedness, as capable of internationalising English – part of a wider movement of 'barbarian' linguistic-literary insurrection across the formerly colonised world. Yet as David Kinloch's intimate poetry suggests, often written in a queer, dictionary-trawled Scots always on the verge of vanishing, there are also wagers and risks to claims of solidarity on the grounds of language.

In chapter three, I take up the polyglot poetry and prose of Suhayl Saadi and Raman Mundair, writers who choose a Scottish identification that brings with it a semi-peripheral internationalism of minor languages, in tune with Scottish literature's inclination to, in Cairns Craig's words, provide 'resistance [to] a world system which sees small and marginal cultures as irrelevant to its logic'.[80] Saadi, a Glasgow novelist and poet born in the north of England, whose parents are from Pakistan, and Mundair, a poet and multimedia artist born in India, who grew up in Manchester and who has lived in Scotland, and mostly in Shetland, since 2002, stage scenes of linguistic prosthesis and performance throughout their writing, treating languages not as fully interior systems of meaning but as samples, sounds and fragments. Both reflect Rey Chow's insistence that, for the postcolonial subject, the encounter with 'language as a foreign object', with which one must 'wrestle in order to survive', is to be able to recognise more fully its reality as 'prosthetic': 'Whereupon even what feels like an inalienable interiority, such as the way one speaks, is – dare I say it? – impermanent, detachable, and (ex)changeable'.[81] As both Saadi's work and Mundair's are at pains to point out – for example in Mundair's poetry in Shetland Scots – no particular form of language has an essential, autochthonous relationship to the inner self, despite nativist fantasies to the contrary. The question that remains, then, is where this leaves questions of the linguistically authentic or inauthentic, experimental or commodified, radical or self-exoticised, and where a politics of language that accepts no such fixed distinctions can be located.

The marketability of the racialised poetic voice, as I mention above, is the subject of Daljit Nagra's poem 'Booking Khan Singh Kumar':

> Did *you* make me for the gap in the market
> Did *I* make me for the gap in the market[82]

In chapter four, I examine how Nagra's poetry, too, plays fast and loose – often riskily so – with notions of linguistic authenticity and performance. His highly stylised British Punjabi poetic voices play out self-consciously against a backdrop of British linguistic racism, from the 'racist television programming' of the 1970s and 1980s to contemporary stigmatisation of South Asian languages in political and popular discourse.[83] Nagra casts his work as that of 'reclamation', reinstituting complexity, depth, and ambivalence to performed voices that are nevertheless stylised works of mimicry, haunted by the legacies of British racism. The constant question in Nagra's poetry, I argue, is that of linguistic provenance: where words come from, what histories they carry with them, the potentiality and peril of using language which is in Bakhtin's terms always 'half someone else's'.[84] Nagra's poems unsettle English in dizzying intertextual, etymological, and translingual patterns of infinite regression, with a particular emphasis on how the English language, and the contemporary multilingualism against which it is often antagonistically pitted, are equal products of a shared colonial and imperial history.

Whereas Nagra's poetry is largely oriented toward English, Leila Aboulela and Xiaolu Guo, whose writing I discuss in chapter five, consider the dynamics of language and linguistic exchange in novels for whose women protagonists translation is the lived experience of communication and consciousness, a permanent and inevitable state of existence, and English a linguistic medium to be travelled into and out of. Aboulela writes in the conscious recognition of a global Islam in which the majority do not speak the language of the Qur'an, Arabic, and about Muslim communities in Britain in which multilingualism and transnational connectivity are everyday facts. For Guo, the back-and-forth transit between English and Chinese is at the centre of a 'multimodal' way of seeing in which all kinds of systems of meaning – linguistic, visual, filmic – are in dynamic, mutually energising relation and tension with one another.[85] Comparing these two very different writers as examples of what Waïl Hassan calls 'translational literature' reveals two very different conceptualisations of the relationship of the individual to language and the nature of translation.[86] Aboulela, regarding translation as fidelity, finds earthbound acts of translation inevitably falling short, and imagines spaces beyond the constraints of human signification and exegesis. Guo, seeing translation as icon-oclastic and transformative, invests in it as a form of self-dissolution and self-remaking with individually and collectively radical creative potential.

Guo's *I Am China*, a novel full of analogues and echoes, proffers two alternative visions of translation: Iona, a London-based Scottish translator whose work teaches her about human connectivity and who learns how to live fully and ethically through translation, is doubled by Jian, a Chinese political dissident whose lived experience, like Iona's, has been structured through translation but who, as an asylum seeker and illegal worker in Europe, experiences it in its far less liberating, cosmopolitan articulations. The relationship of language to regimes of border security is my concern in chapter six, which begins by considering the asylum seeker as perhaps the pre-eminent multilingual figure of our times, whose position is one of grave danger when faced with the monolingualist ideology of the nation state and its enactment in asylum law. In this final chapter I consider how a range of literary texts – the *Refugee Tales* project, James Kelman's *Translated Accounts: A Novel*, and Brian Chikwava's *Harare North* – conjure asylum as a regime of 'hostile language'.[87] Both Kelman's and Chikwava's linguistic experimentalism operates to make a self-enclosed language-world of paranoia, confusion, fear, and grief, constantly threatened with its own violent appropriation, which satirises and upends the asylum system's demands for transparent testimony in an English supposedly infinitely capable of transmitting meaning without loss. Considering the risks posed to speakers by coercive institutional regimes of language, Caroline Bergvall, with whose poetry and performance art I conclude, reflects: 'The pronunciation of a given word exposes the identity of the speaker. To speak becomes a give-away. Are you one of us, not one of us?'[88]

Though concerned with transnationalism, and in dialogue with scholarship that takes transnationalism as its overarching premise, this book is very much concerned with language and the nation, and the particular status of the English language in Britain. The way in which lingering postimperial nostalgia works through language can be seen in visionary articulations of a post-Brexit 'Global Britain' imagined as being about to reclaim its status as the centre of the English-speaking world.[89] Arguments about 'correct' language, meanwhile, continue to mediate classed and regional power. Although it is by now a given in the field of literary studies that literature is governed by transnational and global flows, seeming to travel faster and further – between spaces, media, languages – than ever before, languages and national borders continue to be largely synonymous with one another, and the power of the nation and the state have not gone anywhere. English as a global language continues to feed Britain's ambitions as a key cultural, economic, and geopolitical power in the world, while the same language is used to define the parameters and perimeters of the nation. This is true quite literally, in regimes of border security and immigration law that depend on the use of English and require evidence of English proficiency as a condition of entry or residency. It's also true symbolically, in discourses about citizenship, community cohesion, public services, religious extremism, education, parenting, and family life that use 'English' to mark endogamous from exogamous, belonging from not-belonging, desirable from undesirable.

This approach aims to keep the operations of the nation and the state in view – as these authors do, to greater or lesser extents – over ideas of transnationalism that buy into the idea that borders, certainly of the national kind, are transcended and overridden by global cultural flows. There is a politics to this, of course, in common with a turn away from the idea of the mobile and exilic towards a better recognition of the constraints on movement.[90] World literature scholarship, concerned as it is with how texts travel, taking multilingualism – rightly – as a global phenomenon and literature as a world field, focuses on the transnational coordinates of literature that declares itself multilingual. These are approaches, then, which focus on literature that readies itself for translation, and think about how it travels. Such approaches inevitably focus on the novel as a form, by and large, for the good reason that it is novels that most readily travel in this way, and on particular kinds of literary multilingualism that critique the monolingualist demands of world literary markets while still bearing them in mind. This is, for example, the concern of Rebecca Walkowitz's recent *Born Translated*. Some of what follows could be thought about in these ways – Leila Aboulela's stylistically level English prose, shot through with scepticism about the processes of translation which it nevertheless appears ready for, could perhaps be said to be 'born translated' in Walkowitz's terms.[91] Daljit Nagra's work has been included in the *Norton Anthology of English Literature*.[92] In another kind of linguistic travelling, that of self-translation, Caroline Bergvall performs her work in multiple languages across Europe and the US.[93] A number of these writers also think in their work about the political implications of monolingualist linguistic globalisation and the demand for translatability. As David Gramling observes of James Kelman's *Translated Accounts: A Novel*, it is concerned with 'a twenty-first century where "human rights" are tantamount to "the right to have one's human rights translated, and translatable, globally"'.[94] But this critique of Kelman's, which in *Translated Accounts* and elsewhere claims the right of minor languages and marginalised voices to be heard, is important to the coordinates of this project, which is not interested in literature primarily for its world-travelling capabilities (indeed, some of this writing doesn't travel well at all)[95] but for how, why, and in what ways it reflects on English in relation to other kinds of language.

Finally, a note on the 'bad English' in *Bad English*. According to the peerless arbiter of English usage, the *OED*, 'bad' has numerous meanings. These include 'not good', 'of little worth', 'debased, counterfeit, false', 'containing or characterised by errors, faulty … erroneous, wrong', 'troublesome, vexing, trying, difficult'. And they also include: 'slang (orig. U.S.). Formidable, good. (Sometimes with repeated vowel, for emphasis.)', 'as a general term of approbation: good, excellent, impressive; esp. stylish or attractive', 'originally in African-American usage. Of a person: (originally) dangerous or menacing to a degree which inspires awe or admiration; impressively tough, uncompromising, or combative; (in later use also) possessing other desirable attributes to an impressive degree; esp. formidably skilled'. That 'bad' has extended its meanings through the influence of African American

Vernacular English to imply 'good' and 'skilled' seems resonantly appropriate to the arguments that are foundational to this book: that English in Britain carries an immense and often troublesome institutional and ideological freight, and that it can also be made to reflect critically upon itself, even to contradict itself, by being opened up to its various others. Correspondingly, the linguistically self-reflexive literature which *Bad English* explores thinks about 'bad English' in a number of connected ways. First, it examines the psychic, social, political, and historical operations and effects of English in its institutionalised and official forms, and thinks about how these may be 'vexing'. It interrogates English monolingualism and linguaphobia, and parses out their relationship to ideologies of class and race, and also gender and sexuality. It finds the histories of empire that lie half-submerged in English, and their inescapable relationship to its current status as a global and literary language – to what Aamir Mufti calls 'the *cultural system* of English'.[96] And, in doing so, it considers the damage ideas about English inflict on its linguistic others, and the people who use them. Second, and relatedly, it thinks about what is going on when people use, or are accused of using, 'bad English', and what that means: English that is inflected by other forms of language; English that is non-standard lexically, grammatically, syntactically; English that *sounds foreign*. And third, it puts English into articulation with other kinds of language and makes 'bad English' – incorrect, impure, weird, surprising, 'uncompromising', and often 'formidably skilled' – the medium for literary experiment and expression. Of course, 'bad English' is also an accusation sometimes levelled at these writers: at James Kelman, when he won the Booker Prize for *How Late It Was, How Late,* being accused of writing from 'transcripts' of 'a maundering old drunk', or at Xiaolu Guo being urged to write her second novel in 'grown up English'.[97] It will be obvious, I hope, that this book is a riposte to such unimaginative, monolingualist critical positions. Its approach to 'bad English' is to see it as a way of asking questions about and doing new things with language. In pursuing it, *Bad English* traces literature's reflections on language and subjectivity, language and history, language and nation, language and world. And it discovers a constellation of ways in which English is being remade and reshaped in Britain, in critical relation to its ongoing status as an emblem of state and nation, as well as of global power.

Notes

1 Vahni Capildeo, 'Five Measures of Expatriation', in *Measures of Expatriation* (Manchester: Carcanet, 2016), p. 101.

2 Vahni Capildeo, 'Mother tongues: multilingual identities' panel discussion, *Multilingualisms in World Literature*, School of Oriental and African Studies, 18 January 2018.

3 John Marx, *The Modernist Novel and the Decline of Empire* (Cambridge: Cambridge University Press, 2005), p. 2. For further discussion of multilingualism in modernist literature, see also Juliet Taylor-Batty, *Multilingualism in Modernist Fiction* (Basingstoke: Palgrave, 2013); Steven G. Yao, *Translation and the Languages of Modernism: Gender, Politics, Language* (Basingstoke: Palgrave, 2002); James Williams, *Multilingualism and the Twentieth Century Novel: Polyglot Passages* (Basingstoke: Palgrave, 2019).

4 See, for example, Sinfree Makoni and Alastair Pennycook (eds) *Disinventing and Reconstituting Languages* (Clevedon: Multilingual Matters, 2006); Alastair Pennycook and Emi Otsuji, *Metrolingualism: Language in the City* (London and New York: Routledge, 2015).

5 Capildeo, 'Five Measures of Expatriation', p. 100.

6 Capildeo, 'Five Measures of Expatriation', p. 101.

7 On the inventedness of 'languages' as discrete, countable entities, see Makoni and Pennycook (eds) *Disinventing and Reconstituting Languages*. On the colonial history of '*languages, conceptions of languageness* and the *metalanguages* used to describe them' (p. 1), see pp. 4–15 and passim.

8 Capildeo, 'Five Measures of Expatriation', p. 94.

9 Rey Chow, *Not Like a Native Speaker: On Languaging as a Postcolonial Experience* (New York: Columbia University Press, 2014), pp. 8–9.

10 Vahni Capildeo, 'Two Foreign', in *Venus as a Bear* (Manchester: Carcanet, 2018), p. 46.

11 The word 'swamp' occupies a particularly toxic position within the lexicon of racism in Britain. In a 1978 *World in Action* interview, Margaret Thatcher stole a march on the far right on the question of immigration: 'people are really rather afraid that this country might be rather swamped by people with a different culture and, you know, the British character has done so much for democracy, for law and done so much throughout the world that if there is any fear that it might be swamped people are going to react and be rather hostile to those coming in'. The Metropolitan Police's notorious 'Swamp 81' campaign of harrassment against black people in Brixton, London led to the 1981 Brixton riots. See Scarman Report, *The Brixton Disorders 10–12 April 1981* (London: Penguin, 1982).

12 Capildeo, 'Two Foreign', p. 46.

13 Capildeo, 'Two Foreign', p. 46.

14 Boris Johnson, quoted in Josh Halliday and Libby Brooks, 'Johnson pledges to make all immigrants learn English', *Guardian*, 5 July 2019. www.theguar dian.com/politics/2019/jul/05/johnson-pledges-to-make-all-immigrants-learn-english.

15 Deborah Cameron, 'The one, the many and the Other: representing multi- and monolingualism in post-9/11 verbal hygiene', *Critical Multilingualism Studies* 1:2 (2013), 65. See also David Gramling, *The Invention of Monolingualism* (London and New York: Bloomsbury, 2016), p. 25.

16 Garrett Stewart, *Reading Voices: Literature and the Phonotext* (Berkeley, Los Angeles, and Oxford: University of California Press, 1990).

17 James Procter, *Dwelling Places: Postwar Black British Writing* (Manchester: Manchester University Press, 2003), p. 55. Capildeo has written about their relationship with fellow Trinidadian Selvon's work in '*A Brighter Sun*: "I still want to see how the story unfolds" – Conversations with a novel', in Malachi McIntosh (ed.) *Beyond Calypso: Rereading Sam Selvon* (Kingston, Jamaica: Randle, 2016) [ebook], n.pag.

18 On Selvon's creolised city, see Bill Schwarz, 'Creolization, West One. Sam Selvon in London', *Anthurium: A Caribbean Studies Journal* 11:2 (2014), 1–22.

19 Procter, *Dwelling Places*, p. 55.

20 Sam Selvon, *The Lonely Londoners* [1956] (London: Penguin, 2006), p. 82.

21 Mervyn Morris, *Is English We Speaking and Other Essays* (Kingston, Jamaica: Randle, 1999), p. 1.

22 Sam Selvon, 'Calypso in London', in *Ways of Sunlight* [1957] (London: Longman, 1979), p. 131.

23 Selvon cited in Procter, *Dwelling Places*, p. 48; Selvon, *The Lonely Londoners*, p. 35.

24 Selvon, *The Lonely Londoners*, p. 91.

25 Sam Selvon, 'Working the Transport', in *Ways of Sunlight*, pp. 132–138.

26 Sam Selvon, 'My Girl and the City', in *Ways of Sunlight*, pp. 180–183.

27 Jan Blommaert, Sirpa Leppänen, and Massimiliano Spotti, 'Endangering multilingualism', in Jan Blommaert, Sirpa Leppänen, Päivi Pahta and Tiina Räisänen (eds) *Dangerous Multilingualism: Northern Perspectives on Order, Purity and Normality* (Basingstoke: Palgrave, 2012), p. 9. See also Pennycook and Otsuji, *Metrolingualism*, p. 46; Steven Vertovec, 'Super-diversity and its implications', *Ethnic and Racial Studies* 30:6 (2007), 1024–1054; Susanne Wessendorf, *Commonplace Diversity: Social Relations in a Super-Diverse Context* (Basingstoke: Palgrave, 2014).

28 Deborah Cameron, *Verbal Hygiene*, 2nd edition (London and New York: Routledge, 2012), p. vii. On 'mother tongue' and 'native speaker', see Rajendra Singh (ed.) *The Native Speaker: Multilingual Perspectives* (New Delhi: Sage, 1998); Thomas Paul Bonfiglio, *Mother Tongues and Nations: The Invention of the Native Speaker* (Berlin and New York: Mouton De Gruyter, 2010); Gramling, *The Invention of Monolingualism.*

29 John Simpson, *Guardian*, 27 December 1995. Quoted in Dennis Ager, *Ideology and Image: Britain and Language* (Clevedon: Multilingual Matters, 2003), p. 1.

30 Ager, *Ideology and Image*, p. 1.

31 Cameron, 'The one, the many and the Other', 63–64.

32 Michael North, *The Dialect of Modernism: Race, Language, and Twentieth-Century Literature* (Oxford and New York: Oxford University Press, 1994), pp. 12–16.

33 Ager, *Ideology and Image*; Tony Bex and Richard Watts, *Standard English: The Widening Debate* (London and New York: Routledge, 1999); Tony Crowley, *Standard English and the Politics of Language* (Basingstoke: Palgrave, 2003); Adrian Blackledge, *Discourse and Power in a Multilingual World* (Amsterdam and Philadelphia: John Benjamins, 2005).

34 See Jan Blommaert, 'The debate is open', in Jan Blommaert (ed.) *Language Ideological Debates* (Berlin and New York: Mouton de Gruyter, 1999), pp. 1–38.

35 Crowley, *Standard English and the Politics of Language*, p. 249.

36 Keith Waterhouse, quoted in Ager, *Ideology and Image*, p. 83.

37 Sarah O'Grady, 'Migrants shun the English language', *Daily Express*, 31 January 2013. www.express.co.uk/news/uk/374550/Migrants-shun-the-English-language.

38 Graeme Wilson, 'English is a second language for 40% in parts of Britain', *Sun*, 5 March 2013. On UK press reporting of the 2011 census results, see Cameron, 'The one, the many and the Other', 66–67.

39 Enoch Powell, speech to the Conservative Association, Birmingham, 20 April 1968. Reprinted in *Daily Telegraph*, 6 November 2007.

40 For instance, Susannah Hills, 'Children who speak English as their main language at home are now in the MINORITY in 1,600 schools across Britain', *Daily Mail*, 22 March 2012, www.dailymail.co.uk/news/article-2118846/Children-English-home-language-MINORITY-1-600-school-Britain.html; Vickiie Oliphant, 'More than one MILLION schoolchildren do not speak English as first language', *Daily Express*, 2 September 2017, www.express.co.uk/news/uk/849283/immigration-news-children-speak-english-first-second-language-school; Max Evans, 'School becomes first in Britain to teach English as a FOREIGN language', *Daily Express*, 24 March

2014, www.express.co.uk/news/uk/466589/British-school-to-teach-English
-as-a-FOREIGN-language. See also, for example, David Wright and Gavin
Brookes, '"This is England, speak English!": a corpus-assisted critical study
of language ideologies in the right-leaning British press', *Critical Discourse
Studies* 16:1 (2019), 56–83.

41 Viv Edwards, *The West Indian Language Issue in British Schools: Challenges
and Responses* (London: Routledge and Kegan Paul, 1979); see also Viv
Edwards, *West Indian Language: Attitudes and the School* (Derby: National
Association for Multi-Racial Education, 1976) and Bernard Coard's influential *How the West Indian Child is Made Educationally Subnormal in the
British School System* (London: New Beacon, 1971). Evidence of negative
attitudes to creole languages in British schools, as well as arguments for
their potential role in mainstream education and emphasis on their expressive potential, can also be found in Peter Trudgill, *Language, Dialect and
the School* (London: Edward Arnold, 1975); David Sutcliffe, *British Black
English* (London: Blackwell, 1983); David Sutcliffe and Ansel Wong (eds)
*The Language of the Black Experience: Cultural Expression Through Word
and Sound in the Caribbean and Black Britain* (London: Blackwell, 1986).

42 Trudgill, *Language, Dialect and the School*, p. 26.

43 For discussion of Honey's arguments, their contexts and effects, see
Crowley, *Standard English and the Politics of Language*, chapters 7 and 8.

44 John Honey, 'The Language Trap: Race, Class and the "Standard English"
Issue in British Schools' (Middlesex: National Council for Educational
Standards, 1983), p. 26.

45 Honey, 'The Language Trap', p. 27.

46 Scarman Report, pp. 165–166. My thanks to James Procter for pointing out
the significance of language in Lord Scarman's findings.

47 John Agard, 'Listen Mr Oxford Don', in *Mangoes and Bullets: Selected and
New Poems 1972–1984* (London and Sydney: Pluto Press, 1985), p. 44. I've
discussed this poem in detail in 'Doing voices: reading language as craft
in black British poetry', *Journal of Commonwealth Literature* 49:3 (2014),
343–357. As Hall et al. argued in *Policing the Crisis*, analysing the discourses
around the British 'mugging' scare of 1972–3, 'Few would deny that, for all
practical purposes, the terms "mugging" and "black crime" are now virtually synonymous. … The two are indissolubly linked: each term references
the other in both the official and public consciousness'. Stuart Hall, Chas
Critcher, Tony Jefferson, John Clarke, and Brian Roberts, *Policing the Crisis:
Mugging, the State, and Law and Order* (London: Macmillan, 1978), p. 327.

48 Agard, 'Listen Mr Oxford Don', p. 44.

49 'England riots: David Starkey defends Newsnight remarks', *BBC News*, 20
August 2011. www.bbc.co.uk/news/uk-14601813.

50 Blackledge, *Discourse and Power in a Multilingual World*, p. vii.

51 'Woman told to speak English in London tube attack', *Guardian*, 13 April 2018. www.theguardian.com/uk-news/2018/apr/13/woman-attacked-on-tube-and-told-to-speak-english-in-england. '"Put up with your f****** bla bla bla": passenger launches into shocking racist rant because he cannot understand couple talking on a train', *Daily Mail*, 20 March 2018. www.dailymail.co.uk/news/article-5523391/Racist-London-train-attacks-pair-dont-speak-English.htm. This isn't solely a UK phenomenon, of course. In May 2018, a video went viral of a lawyer named Aaron Schlossberg berating workers in a New York restaurant for speaking Spanish to one another, saying to another employee: 'your staff is speaking Spanish to customers when they should be speaking English ... this is America'. Demonstrating the imbrication of race, language, and regimes of border security, Schlossberg threatened to call US Immigration and Customs Enforcement (as well as, perversely, alleging that their welfare payments were coming out of his taxes). Activists responded by holding a Mexican-themed street party outside his Manhattan apartment, complete with a GoFundMe-sponsored mariachi band. Sam Wolfson, 'New Yorkers respond to lawyer's racist rant with "Latin party" outside his house', *Guardian*, 18 May 2018. www.theguardian.com/us-news/2018/may/18/aaron-schlossberg-racist-lawyer-new-york-latin-party.

52 North, *The Dialect of Modernism*; Werner Sollors (ed.) *Multilingual America: Transnationalism, Ethnicity, and the Languages of American Literature* (New York: New York University Press, 1998); Doris Sommer, *Bilingual Aesthetics: A New Sentimental Education* (Durham, NC and London: Duke University Press, 2004); Martha J. Cutter, *Lost and Found in Translation: Contemporary Ethnic American Writing and the Politics of Language Diversity* (Chapel Hill: University of North Carolina Press, 2005); Hana Wirth-Nesher, *Call It English: The Languages of Jewish American Literature* (Princeton: Princeton University Press, 2006); Maria Lauret, *Wanderwords: Language Migration in American Literature* (New York: Bloomsbury, 2014); Azade Seyhan, *Writing Outside the Nation* (Princeton and New York: Princeton University Press, 2001); Brian Lennon, *In Babel's Shadow: Multilingual Literatures, Monolingual States* (Minneapolis: University of Minnesota Press, 2010); Yasemin Yildiz, *Beyond the Mother Tongue: The Postmonolingual Condition* (New York: Fordham University Press, 2012); Emily Apter, *The Translation Zone: A New Comparative Literature* (Princeton and Oxford: Princeton University Press, 2006); Emily Apter, *Against World Literature: On the Politics of Untranslatability* (London: Verso, 2013). Other significant works of US scholarship concerned with literary multilingualism and language

experiment include Steven G. Kellman (ed.) *The Translingual Imagination* (Lincoln and London: University of Nebraska Press, 2000) and Evelyn Nien-Ming Ch'ien, *Weird English* (Cambridge, MA: Harvard University Press, 2004).

53 Joshua L. Miller, *Accented America: The Cultural Politics of Multilingual Modernism* (Oxford and New York: Oxford University Press, 2011).

54 Robert Crawford, *Devolving English Literature* (Oxford: Clarendon, 1992). See chapter 6: 'Barbarians'.

55 See Édouard Glissant, *Poetics of Relation*, trans. Betsy Wing (Ann Arbor: University of Michigan Press, 1997).

56 The authority on 'weird' English is Ch'ien, *Weird English*.

57 Makoni and Pennycook argue that the idea of countable, discrete 'languages' is an idea with a history rooted in European colonialism and the rise of the nation state, and that ideas of 'multilingualism' too often proceed from this starting point, 'start[ing] with the enumerative strategy of counting languages and romanticizing a plurality based on these putative language counts'; Makoni and Pennycook (eds) *Disinventing and Reconstituting Languages*, p. 16.

58 Vertovec, 'Super-diversity and its implications'. See also Jens Normann Jørgensen, M. S. Karrebæk, L. M. Madsen, and J. S. Møller, 'Polylanguaging in superdiversity', *Diversities* 13:2 (2011). Available at: www.unesco.org/shs/diversities/vol13/issue2/art2.

59 On multimodality, see, for example, Gunther Kress, *Multimodality: A Social Semiotic Approach to Contemporary Communication* (London and New York: Routledge, 2010).

60 John McLeod, 'European tribes: transcultural diasporic encounters', in Michelle Keown, David Murphy, and James Procter (eds) *Comparing Postcolonial Diasporas* (Basingstoke: Palgrave, 2009), pp. 19–36.

61 Sebastian Groes, *The Making of London: London in Contemporary Literature* (Basingstoke: Palgrave, 2011), p. 15.

62 David Farrier, *Postcolonial Asylum: Seeking Sanctuary Before the Law* (Liverpool: Liverpool University Press, 2011), p. 4.

63 On 'dangerous multilingualism', see Blommaert, Leppänen, and Spotti, 'Endangering multilingualism'. On the need to distinguish between different kinds of language diversity with different political stakes, see Ben Rampton, Jan Blommaert, Karel Arnaut, and Massimiliano Spotti, 'Introduction: superdiversity and sociolinguistics', *Tilburg Papers in Culture Studies* (2015), 14.

64 Rebecca Walkowitz, *Born Translated: The Contemporary Novel in an Age of World Literature* (New York: Columbia University Press, 2015), p. 1.

65 Emily Apter, 'Translation at the checkpoint', *Journal of Postcolonial Writing* 50:1 (2014), p. 59.

66 Leonard Foster, *The Poet's Tongues: Multilingualism in Literature* (Cambridge: Cambridge University Press, 1970).

67 Gramling, *The Invention of Monolingualism*.

68 Linda Mugglestone, *Talking Proper: The Rise and Fall of the English Accent as a Social Symbol* (Oxford: Oxford University Press, 2003); Crawford, *Devolving English Literature*; Gauri Viswanathan, *Masks of Conquest: Literary Study and British Rule in India*, revised edition (New York: Columbia University Press, 2014); Aamir R. Mufti, *Forget English! Orientalisms and World Literatures* (Cambridge, MA: Harvard University Press, 2016).

69 See Norman Page, *Speech in the English Novel*, 2nd edition (New Jersey: Humanities Press International, 1988).

70 James Kelman, 'Elitism and English literature, speaking as a writer', in *'And the Judges Said …': Essays* (Edinburgh: Polygon, 2008), p. 61.

71 Kelman, '"And the judges said …"', in *'And the Judges Said …': Essays*, p. 41.

72 Lynne Pearce, Corinne Fowler, and Robert Crawshaw, *Postcolonial Manchester: Diaspora Space and the Evolution of Literary Culture* (Manchester: Manchester University Press, 2015); Jackie Kay, James Procter, and Gemma Robinson, *Out of Bounds: British Black and Asian Poets* (Tarset: Bloodaxe, 2012).

73 See Linton Kwesi Johnson, *Mi Revalueshanary Fren: Selected Poems* (London: Penguin, 2002); Salman Rushdie, *The Satanic Verses* (London: Viking, 1988); Grace Nichols, *The Fat Black Woman's Poems* (London: Virago, 1984); Tony Harrison, *Collected Poems* (London: Viking, 2007); Alison Flett, *Whit Lassyz Ur Inty* (Edinburgh: Thirsty Books, 2004); Tony White, *Foxy-T* (London: Faber, 2004); Anthony Joseph, *Teragaton* (London: Poison Engine Press, 1997); Eimear McBride, *A Girl is a Half-Formed Thing* (Norwich: Galley Beggar Press, 2013); Janice Galloway, *The Trick is to Keep Breathing* (Edinburgh: Polygon, 1989).

74 Farrukh Dhondy, *East End at Your Feet* (London: Topliners, 1976), *Come to Mecca and Other Stories* (London: Collins, 1978), *Bombay Duck* (London: Jonathan Cape, 1990); Ravinder Randhawa, *A Wicked Old Woman* (London: The Women's Press, 1987).

75 Zadie Smith, *White Teeth* (London: Penguin Books, 2001), p. 181.

76 Lennon, *In Babel's Shadow*, p. 165.

77 Yaseen Noorani, 'Hard and soft multilingualism', *Critical Multilingualism Studies* 1:2 (2013), 9.

78 Daljit Nagra, 'Booking Khan Singh Kumar', in *Look We Have Coming to Dover!* (London: Faber, 2007), p. 6.

79 Suhayl Saadi, 'Londonstani, by Gautam Malkani: a tale of gangsta Sikh', Independent, 21 April 2006. www.independent.co.uk/arts-entertainment/ books/reviews/londonstani-by-gautam-malkani-6103175.html. Gautam Malkani, Londonstani (London: Harper Collins, 2006). Less scepticism has been directed at what one critic called the 'miraculous' London-Ghanaian first-person narration of Stephen Kelman's 2011 Booker-shortlisted debut Pigeon English, loosely based on the story of the murdered London school-boy Damilola Taylor. Lewis Jones, 'Pigeon English by Stephen Kelman', Daily Telegraph, 7 March 2011. www.telegraph.co.uk/culture/books/ bookreviews/8362385/Pigeon-English-by-Stephen-Kelman-review.html. Stephen Kelman, Pigeon English (London: Bloomsbury, 2011). Kelman's title is a play on the homophonic relationship between the 'pidgin' of its young Ghanaian protagonist, living on a London estate, and the feral pigeon he secretly adopts.

80 Cairns Craig, 'Beyond reason: Hume, Seth, Macmurray and Scotland's postmodernity', in Eleanor Bell and Gavin Miller (eds) Scotland in Theory: Reflections on Culture and Literature (Amsterdam and New York: Rodopi, 2004), p. 259.

81 Chow, Not Like a Native Speaker, pp. 14–15.

82 Nagra, 'Booking Khan Singh Kumar', p. 6.

83 Claire Chambers, '"Meddl[ing] with my type": an interview with Daljit Nagra', Crossings: Journal of Migration and Culture 1 (2010), 92.

84 Mikhail Bakhtin, 'Discourse in the novel', in The Dialogic Imagination: Four Essays, trans. Caryl Emerson and Michael Holquist (Austin: University of Texas Press, 1981), pp. 293–294.

85 Fiona Doloughan, Contemporary Narrative: Textual Production, Multimodality and Multiliteracies (London and New York: Continuum, 2011), p. 2.

86 Waïl Hassan, 'Agency and translational literature: Ahdaf Soueif's The Map of Love', PMLA 121:3 (2006), 754.

87 Rachel Holmes, 'The Barrister's Tale', in David Herd and Anna Pincus (eds) Refugee Tales II ([Manchester]: Comma Press, 2017), p. 55.

88 Caroline Bergvall and Ciarán Maher, 'Say: "Parsley"', Arnolfini, Bristol, UK, May–July 2010. www.arnolfini.org.uk/whatson/caroline-bergvall-cir an-maher-say-parsley.

89 Theresa May, speech at Lancaster House, Daily Telegraph, 17 January 2017 www.telegraph.co.uk/politics/2017/01/17/theresa-mays-brexit-speech-fu ll/; James Blitz, 'Post-Brexit delusions about Empire 2.0', Financial Times, 7 March 2017. www.ft.com/content/bc29987e-034e-11e7-ace0-1ce02ef0 def9.

90 Simon Gikandi, for example, asks what it would mean to consider the

refugee, rather than the exile or émigré, as the quintessential outsider for our times. Simon Gikandi, 'Between roots and routes: cosmopolitanism and the claims of locality', in Janet Wilson, Cristina Sandru, and Sarah Lawson Welsh (eds) *Rerouting the Postcolonial: New Directions for the New Millennium* (London and New York: Routledge, 2009), pp. 22–35.

91 Walkowitz, *Born Translated*.

92 Jahan Ramazani (ed.) *Norton Anthology of English Literature: The Twentieth and Twenty-First Centuries* (London and New York: Norton, 2018).

93 Karin Nyqvist, for example, has reflected on the multidirectional multilingualism of Bergvall's performance of *Drift* in Italian. Karin Nyqvist, 'Multilingual political activism in the work of Caroline Bergvall', *Performing Multilingualism in World Literatures: Aesthetics and Activism*, 20–22 September 2018, Exeter College, University of Oxford.

94 Gramling, *The Invention of Monolingualism*, p. 163.

95 For example Suhayl Saadi's novel *Psychoraag*, feted in the Scottish press but largely ignored south of the border in England, and certainly not 'translation ready' (which is not to say that it is not translatable), or Raman Mundair's passage from Punjabi into English into Shetland Scots – a decisive political step away from 'global' language.

96 Mufti, *Forget English!*, p. 12.

97 Alan Clark, 'A prize insult to the courage of Scotland's finest', *Mail on Sunday*, 23 October 1994; Jonathan Mirsky, 'Cute pidgin pie', *Spectator*, 15 February 2007, n.pag. http://archive.spectator.co.uk/article/17th-febru ary-2007/25/cute-pidgin-pie.

1

Thi langwij a thi guhtr

Owing to the influx of Irish and foreign languages in the industrial areas near Glasgow the dialect has become hopelessly corrupt.

'Introduction' to the *Scottish National Dictionary* (1931)[1]

would you swear tay swerr
and not abjure
the extra-semantic kinetics
uv thi fuckin poor

Tom Leonard, 'ah knew a linguist wance'[2]

It was in a 1990 essay about John La Rose, the Trinidad-born, London-based poet, trade unionist, language activist, Caribbean Artists Movement founder, educational campaigner, and founder of Caribbean and black British publishing house New Beacon, that the Glasgow writer James Kelman recalled something of the genesis of his own literary language politics. He recounted how, sitting in Paisley Central Library a decade earlier, he had stumbled across the library's small 'Ethnic' section – stocked from the 1979 New Beacon catalogue, as well as the Heinemann African Writers Series – and discovered the English language in the throes of being decolonised.[3] Encountering the experimental, irreverent 'Anglophone' writing of Caribbean and African writers like Sam Selvon, Amos Tutuola, and Ayi Kwei Armah, as a white, working-class Glaswegian aspiring novelist, he recalled his response as one of recognition and identification. It was in the work of these 'other English-language writers from other marginalised cultures' – their common ground their peripherality to the operations of English – that he had found the means to interpret the situation of urban working-class Scotland:

> Although using the English language, these writers were NOT working to assimilate their own cultural experience within standard prose form which is possible only through ultimate surrender. Surrender was the last thing on their mind. They were attacking and the attack was formal and methodical; like Sam Selvon they were laying claim to the language, allowing their culture to breathe in it.[4]

Kelman paints a scene of linguistic decolonisation opening out before him from a bookshelf in Paisley Central Library. As a speaker of contemporary, urban Glasgow Scots – a working-class vernacular commonly stigmatised as 'bad English' – his struggle as a writer was to parse out the relationship between his own language-world and that of the English novel.[5] Encountering postcolonial literature offered him the means to interpret working-class Glasgow's situation in relation to the operations of English as a globally dominant language, wielding power derived from histories of empire. It also, in the work of writers like Selvon or Tutuola, provided examples of localised, vernacularised, non-standard, *new* literary Englishes.[6] Thus he presents an understanding of his own local contexts as stemming from an internationalist perspective, which provides, in turn, responses to related problems of literary language and form. Because, for Kelman, the central conundrum is a set of dominant linguistic ideologies that he sees as rooted in English literature, and specifically in the formal conventions of the novel.

The issue, then, is of a shared relationship not only to the English language, but also to 'standard prose form': how the relationship of English to its others is reified within the history of the English novel. As Kelman has often argued, standard English constitutes the language-world of novelistic narration, its often-omniscient voice. It also extends into the voice of the novel's protagonists and, through free indirect style, into their inner worlds. It is a form of language that flows unmarked, in fact, through all novelistic dimensions of exterior reality and inner depth. Dialogue, meanwhile, provides a container for what is other than standard English: the voices of a minor cast of 'colonial servants and underlings'.[7] These, by contrast, are all surface

effect without depth or interiority – 'stumb[ling] along in a series of
behaviourist activity; automatons, cardboard cut-outs'.[8] Their language
is given with a range of simulated, exaggerated 'peculiar speech man-
nerisms or patterns', not so much attempts at linguistic realism as
visual markers of their distance from the fully realised language-world
of the narration (Conrad's 'Mistah Kurtz, he dead').[9] A Glaswegian
character in English literature, Kelman argues in his essay 'The importance of Glasgow in my work', can be recognised as a 'cut-out figure':
drunk, violent, without 'a solitary "thought" in his entire life', whose
language appears as 'a stream of gobbledegook … a cross between
semaphore and morse code; apostrophes here and apostrophes there;
a strange hotchpotch of bad phonetics and horrendous spelling'.[10] At
the margins of the English novel, among the 'colonial servants and
underlings' and 'cut-out' Glaswegians, race and class intersect and are
fixed in place by a division between narration and dialogue that is 'a
summation of the political system'.[11] The English novel at its most
centred, argues Kelman, is not just a vehicle for standard English and
the systems of power it represents, but its primary ideological cheerleader. The achievement of Sam Selvon or Amos Tutuola – or Ken
Saro-Wiwa, whose influence on Kelman is perhaps the greatest – is to
upend these conventions, to displace standard English as the language
of narration.[12] This, then, is the lesson Kelman presents himself as
having started to learn in the 'Ethnic' section of Paisley Central Library.

 In this chapter, I probe the connection proposed here by Kelman:
between a Scottish experience of language oriented by the never-
entirely-distinct relationship between English and Scots, and a political internationalism grounded in what Kelman's friend and fellow
Glasgow writer Tom Leonard calls an 'international pattern' of literary insurgency against standard English.[13] Approaches to Scots and
English by Kelman and Leonard, working from the starting point of the
spoken vernacular, as well as the radically denaturalised versions of literary Scots that I will go on to explore in chapter two, take aim via Scots
at the monolingualist myths of English: of its boundedness, orderliness,
rationality, expressiveness, fairness, capacious sufficiency. In a range
of inventively visible vernaculars, marked in lexis, orthography, and
syntax, they puncture the fiction that writing and speech are identical;
and they point to the systems of power which English, or the myths
of English, hold in place. In all of this, the direction of travel is not

only inwards, towards the local and the specific, but outwards towards different kinds of internationalism that might displace English's dis-ingenuous claims as a neutral global lingua franca with other ways of imagining connection in language.

Reclaiming the local

In their essays, both Kelman and Leonard have often discussed issues of 'standard English', 'prescriptive grammar', and 'received pronunciation' – linguistic and literary norms which, as they analyse them, are problem-atic not only because they are class-bound, dictated by and associated with an English elite, but also because they assume a direct correspond-ence between the written and spoken word. In *Talking Proper*, Linda Mugglestone historicises many of the founding myths of the standard language, including the supposed identity between written standard English and 'correct' English speech, which originates with the drive to establish agreed linguistic standards in the ever-expanding Anglosphere of the eighteenth and nineteenth centuries. Developed and promoted in the work of grammarians, rhetoricians, and elocution masters, coincid-ing with and naturalised in the form of the novel, the 'ideal of the literate speaker', as Mugglestone puts it, crystallised the idea that there was one correct way to write English and one correct way to speak it. Thus, in place of the assumption that one written sign might have any number of spoken realisations – and 'in spite of the manifest incompatibility of grapheme and phoneme in English' – was asserted the position that there was one 'correct' phonological realisation for each written word.[14] Kelman satirises the embeddedness of these conventions in the English novel, in which protagonists speak an English which is 'absolutely splen-didly proper and pure and pristinely accurate', uttered in 'Colons and semicolons! Straight out of their mouths!'[15]

As Leonard points out in 'On reclaiming the local', divergence from these norms is associated with lack and absence in English poetry as well. In poetry, attention to the properties of voice lies perhaps closer to the surface than in the novel, the directness of lyric unmediated by third-person narration; but the propensity of poetry to 'speak' in the first person still leaves intact the assumption that it is in standard English that poetic self-consciousness, just as much as narrative authority, is made manifest. Working-class speakers, meanwhile, remain 'trapped in the expression of their own personal language', which is rendered by orthographic conventions that stand not so much for the actual sounds of spoken language as visual markers of deficit and absence:[16]

> Those apostrophes that indicate the 'and of the writer 'elping out the reader, indicating by sign the prescriptive norm from which a 'character' is 'deviating'. The character can't talk proper words, so the writer-narrator indicates where there's bits missed out, so you can better understand. The apostrophes indicate a supposed deficiency which the reader, over the head of the persona as it were, must supply. The personae are trapped within the closed value-system that denigrates their use of language, while the writer-narrator communicates with the reader over their heads.[17]

Orthographic absences, 'bits missed out', stand in for other kinds of deficit: a lack of self-consciousness, of intellectual sophistication, or of the capacity to understand the laughs and nods shared between writer and reader 'over their heads'. Leonard's pointed use of the word 'deficiency' seems to signal a relationship not just to literature but to linguistic theory: specifically, to Basil Bernstein's hugely influential linguistic deficit model. In 1971, Bernstein had published *Class, Codes and Social Control*, in which he argued, broadly, that whereas middle-class speakers had access to an 'elaborated code' characterised by range, expressivity, and the capacity for abstraction, working-class speakers were more likely to use a 'restricted code' that is localised, concrete, and referential.[18] Leonard's 'deficiency' gestures to a continuity between sociolinguistic and literary approaches to language as a 'closed value-system'.

In fact, Bernstein's 'deficit model' belongs to a broad field of struggle over language in the 1970s and 1980s (to which it was frequently co-opted, whether favourably or unfavourably, accurately or inaccurately). In applied linguistics in the UK, the US, and across the decolonising world, questions were being asked about the relationship between language and class, gender, race, and power; about the relationship between language and imperialism; about the normative force of standard languages; and about how new understandings of language could be built in the name of social justice.[19] These forces can be seen at work in feminist linguistics, in the development of creole linguistics as language activism in the Caribbean, in work on African American

Vernacular English and Ebonics in the US. In literature too, the norms
of English as they had historically been dictated by the former imperial
metropole, Britain, were coming to be challenged, and it is precisely in
this sense that what Leonard called 'reclaiming the local' laid claim to
be part of an 'international pattern' of insurgency, hastening the 'breakdown in prescriptive grammar' across the Anglophone world.[20] In
concrete and sound poetry, L=A=N=G=U=A=G=E poetry, Caribbean
poetry, and the work of American modernists like William Carlos
Williams as well as 'new – and multiple – voices in British poetry,
from a variety of class/cultural backgrounds', language was becoming
'an object in itself', interrogated in 'its components of lexis, syntax,
and phonology'.[21] Leonard's own highly localised vernacular aesthetics
form part of this 'international pattern', insofar as they are committed
to overturning ideas about linguistic propriety or Bernsteinian 'deficiency' as well as showing how language is 'an object in the world – the
world is not an object in it'.[22] In this way Leonard, as does Kelman, tries
to show how a genuinely radical, egalitarian, internationalist politics is
indivisible from a politics of language that values, respects, and makes
central the language practices of ordinary speakers, not as objects of
knowledge but as its creators.

   In a 1988 essay on Noam Chomsky, Kelman gathered together
the two sides of Chomsky's work to argue that his theory of universal
grammar is a crystallisation in the sphere of linguistic theory of his
emphasis as a political theorist on the experiences of the disenfranchised. Kelman underlined how Chomskyan linguistic theory, rooted
not in language as an idealised object but 'as it is actually used', made
its proper object of study the language practice of ordinary people. In
this interpretation of Chomsky what is at stake is the contention that
any study of language must take account of its limitless capacity for
innovation, in the hands of all speakers; powers of creativity, abstract
reasoning, and critical judgement are functions of 'innate forms of
knowledge' and thus the property of all.[23] As Kelman quoted from
Chomsky's *Language and Problems of Knowledge*:

> In normal speech one does not merely repeat what one has heard
> but produces new linguistic forms – often new in one's experience
> or even in the history of language – and there are no limits to such
> innovation.[24]

For Kelman, Chomsky's is a pronouncement on the infinite expressive capabilities of ordinary language, and thus a fundamental call to a democratic politics founded on the judgements of ordinary people.

In 1990, at Kelman's invitation, Chomsky visited Glasgow as keynote speaker at a two-day conference entitled 'Self-Determination and Power'. Among the three hundred participants, from local activists to poets from South Africa and the former Soviet Union, were John La Rose and fellow black activists and educationalists Gus John and and Roxy Harris, who spoke on the subject of Caribbean language and literature.[25] Interviewing La Rose after the event, Kelman wanted to reflect on the politics of 'commitment' in black British activism of the 1970s and 1980s, which he saw as rooted in a lived, shared, 'working language' which connects 'politics, culture', and 'social life' as one indivisible experience. Thinking about the language activism of the Caribbean Artists Movement and the Black Education Movement in validating creole language forms as central to an anticolonial politics and aesthetics and as media for the production of knowledge, and about the work of poets like Linton Kwesi Johnson to forge a radical vernacular poetics,[26] Kelman tried to apply those lessons to white working-class Scotland:

> [T]here's all these different things: here's a writer, here's a poet and here also is a working language. All these things that say this is our culture, this is our language. We can discuss it, here are artworks, all of that. These things are central to a person becoming valid as a person. ... Whereas part of the colonial experience – as it is also in Scotland – is you're taught to be ashamed of your culture, you know, inferiorisation. If you're down here in London and a guy starts talking in a strong Scottish accent you wind up blushing with embarrassment. Thinking about that effect in the 1970s where that is part and parcel of the self-confidence of going into the street, of challenging authority and not being put down by authority: the right to self-defence. All these things become part of valuing yourself and your community.[27]

Scotland, empire, language

The 1980s and 1990s saw a growing internationalising of Scottish writing: through translation, through engagement with Europe and the European project, as well as in relation to the kind of insurgent, critical global Anglophony with which Leonard and Kelman aligned themselves.[28] In the field of Scottish studies, arguments were made for the applicability of postcolonial theory to Scottish contexts,[29] even if, as Kelman pointed out, 'the old myth that "there is no racism in Scotland"' was little more than a convenient fiction, at a time when the racist far right was surging in Scotland, just as in England and across wider Europe.[30] If what Berthold Schoene has called Scotland's 'British postcolonial condition' is undeniable, then so is its ambivalent and complex relationship to that condition, given the extensive implication of Scots and Scotland in the British Empire, and the consequently 'duplicitous, conflicting status of Scotland as both (internal and external) colonising *and* colonised nation'.[31] As Carla Sassi puts it, Scotland is a 'stateless nation' that has constructed its identity 'in opposition to unjust cultural and political marginalisation within the United Kingdom', but this construction has been vouchsafed by a sometimes oppressive silence around Scotland's role in the British Empire:

> testimonies of how enthusiastically modern Scots identified with the imperial enterprise are omnipresent in the cities that were the hub of the Empire, from street names in Glasgow's Merchant City and Edinburgh's New Town, from collections of imperial memorabilia on display in museums and stately houses, to small kitschy objects on sale in second-hand shops or car-boot sales.[32]

Sassi marks the material traces of a history by which Scotland's industrialisation and urbanisation were built on imperial trade, and much of its philosophical and political energies devoted to underpinning the Empire. The Empire, including the slave trade, brought wealth to Scotland's institutions and to those members of its upper and middle classes who profited as investors, bankers, traders, plantation owners, colonial officials; but this is not to say that a proportion of its lower classes did not benefit, too. This is so even though, for swathes of the working-class Scots population – and notably an urban proletariat who Tom Leonard describes as 'a colony within a colony' – its consequences 'were *and remain* economic and social deprivation on a scale disproportionate in British experience'.[33]

To think about the 1707 Act of Union – ground zero, in many ways, for the dominance of the English language in Scotland – is also to face some of the difficulties of thinking about Scotland postcolonially. The Act incorporated a no longer self-governing Scotland as a subordinate part of a newly minted Britain and instituted English as its language of power and administration, at the expense of both Scots and Gaelic, while it also set the stage for Scotland's enthusiastic participation in the expansion of Empire.[34] In the realm of language, the effects of the Act brought the purposeful stigmatisation and suppression of 'Scotticisms' in literature and public discourse in the name of 'purifying' Scottish English. As Robert Crawford points out, these processes were to a large extent self-administered by members of the Scottish intelligentsia, who were keen to secure for Scotland an expanding role in the growing economic and intellectual markets of the newly defined Union and the British Empire:

> To play a full part, Scottish people would have to move from using Scots to using English, an English which was fully acceptable to the dominant partner in the political union. This English, it was argued, both had to replace Scots and had to be purged of what we would now call 'markers of Scottish cultural difference'.[35]

Following this logic, Scottish writers were urged to expunge 'Scotticisms' from their work. Scottish rhetoricians and elocution masters, armed with models of language use for the purposes of 'improvement' drawn from English literary works, sought to influence the spoken language of Scottish polite society – Thomas Sheridan's *Course of Lectures on Elocution*, for example, were delivered to Edinburgh audiences anxious 'to cure themselves of a provincial or vicious pronunciation'.[36] There is an unmissable irony, given the extent to which working-class varieties of the Scots language and its speakers have been marginalised through the comparative labelling of their speech as 'bad', 'wrong', or 'incorrect', that it has been in Scotland and in Scottish writing that some of the most influential arguments for the 'purification' of English, including the convergence of the written standard with notions of 'correct' spoken English, have been staged.[37] It is not too much of an exaggeration to say, as Crawford does, that both 'standard English' and the institutions of English literature – elevated, in the first instance, as models of linguistic propriety – have been in many ways 'a Scottish invention'.[38] This was a relationship replicated across the Empire using

Scottish expertise: the classic imperialist assertion of English as vehicle of modernity and Empire, Thomas Macaulay's 'Minute on Indian Education', was written by the son of a Scottish Highlander.

It was also a relationship which saw the elevation of Scotland's idealised linguistic past at the expense of its actually occurring contemporary language forms. With English invested as the language of modernity, the languages of the Scottish poetic tradition, Lowland Scots and Gaelic – increasingly marginalised as languages of everyday speech – were reinvented as objects of antiquarian curiosity or nostalgia, temporally relocated as the Scottish past to English's modern present. Heritage societies celebrated an elevated, idealised poetic tradition, while publishers did a booming trade in antiquarian treatises on rural Scots and Gaelic. The contemporary languages of a rapidly changing Scotland, meanwhile, and notably the urban, working-class varieties of Scots which thrived in Scotland's newly industrialised belt, fed by immigration from the Highlands, Ireland, and northern England, were overwhelmingly condemned. Duncan McNaught, president of the Burns Club, wrote in 1901 of the 'degraded', 'mongrel' character of modern Scots: 'nine-tenths of so-called modern Scots is a concrete of vulgarised, imperfect English in which are sparsely embedded more or less corrupted forms of the lovely words with which Burns wove his verbal magic'.[39] Such attacks associated the allegedly debased, unsystematic, jumbled nature of modern urban Scots with its susceptibility to undesirable mixing: a 'mongrel patois' or a 'wonderful gibberish' best described as 'Glasgow-Irish' – an unmistakeable dig at its suspect Catholic, as well as working-class, tendencies.[40] As the introduction to *The Scottish National Dictionary* (1931) most famously put it: 'owing to the influx of Irish and foreign languages in the industrial areas near Glasgow the dialect has become hopelessly corrupt'.[41]

Tom Leonard's linguistic kinetics

The first poem of Tom Leonard's 'Unrelated Incidents' sequence reflects on prevailing attitudes to working-class urban Scots. In an unmissable dig at the poet Hugh MacDiarmid's well-known dismissal of Ian Hamilton Finlay's early literary attempts at Glasgow demotic as 'the language of the gutter',[42] its narrator recounts a conversation with

an unnamed other, a fellow Glaswegian who condemns 'thi langwij a |
thi guhtr' as

> awright fur
> funny stuff
> ur
> Stanley Bax-
> ter ur but
> luv n science
> n thaht naw
>
> thi langwij
> a thi
> intillect hi
> said thi lang-
> wij a thi intill-
> ects Inglish[43]

In an act of comic comeuppance, the poem's punchline comes when
this interlocutor strides confidently through lift doors and falls 'eight |
storeys | doon thi | empty | lift shaft'.[44] Internalised linguicism may make
you want to step away from your language, to turn and condemn it as
though it isn't yours, the poem warns, but be careful where you're step-
ping just in case there's no ground there. Meanwhile, though, Leonard's
defamiliarising orthography is busy making visually strange what are
in fact alphabetic representations of commonly realised English pro-
nunciations that are not particular to Glasgow at all: 'intillect', 'Inglish',
'langwij'. In other words, while at first glance the poem appears to be
dramatising the distinction between Scots and English, it is also underlining how the latter functions as an ideological fantasy of the identity
between speech and writing – a 'langwij | a thi | intillect' that is, in actual
fact, a chimera. As the next poem in the sequence tells us, it is about time
that we started to think of 'lang- | wij izza | sound-system', about 'thi dif-
| frince tween | sound | n object n | symbol'.

> iz
> god said ti
> adam:
>
> a doant kerr
> fyi caw it

an apple
ur
an aippl –
jist leeit
alane![45]

Leonard challenges the supposition that one set of sounds, or one symbol, has a more direct relationship to the object it symbolises, or a greater capacity to represent an external reality – knowledge is knowledge, whether you call it an 'apple' or an 'aippl'. A Bernsteinian idea of linguistic deficit ('awright fur | funny stuff') is countered by a putatively Chomskyan perspective whereby the joke is on those who cannot square working-class speech with metalinguistic self-reflexivity: 'ma language is disgraceful', insists 'sum wee smout thit thoat ah hudny read chomsky'.[46] '[A] knew a linguist wance', writes Leonard in 'Ghostie Men', who has made an object of study of the language she once spoke: 'shi used tay git oanty mi | ah wish I could talk like you | ahv lost my accent'.

thi crux iz sayz ah
shiftin ma register
tay speak tay a linguist

would you swear tay swerr
and not abjure
the extra-semantic kinetics
uv thi fuckin poor[47]

With great disingenuousness, the linguist claims to have 'lost [her] accent' – she of all people should know that there is no speech without 'accent' – while the speaker's dextrous movement between 'register[s]' gives the lie to her claim that to gain one code is to lose another. His injunction to 'swear tay swerr', meanwhile, underlines what would be at stake for her to return to a working-class Scots vernacular not as an object of study, but as a living form of speech. 'Swear' and 'swerr' stand, not only as different orthographic markings of the 'same' sign, but also as tokens of two different systems of meaning and value. Both 'swear' and 'abjure' are English words with enunciatory power in law: to utter them meaningfully is to act on the world, to commit or renounce. The speaker uses them to call on the 'linguist' to fully recognise and take on – rather than fetishise and condescend to – Scottish working-class speech, in which 'swerr' words also possess power ('kinetics' refers to the effect of force on the motion of objects) that, like that of 'swear' or 'abjure', far exceeds their strictly 'semantic' meaning. Both 'swearing' and 'swerring', the poem suggests, are speech acts that tell us about how language acts on the world.

Language conceived 'izza | sound-system' begins with voice, just as voice is what gives both 'swearing' and 'swerring' their power. Thinking about William Carlos Williams, Leonard writes: 'What I like about Williams is his voice. What I like about Williams is his presentation of voice as a fact, as a fact in itself and as a factor in his relationship with the world as he heard it, listened to it, spoke it.'[48] In 'Jist Ti Let Yi Know (from the American of Carlos Williams)' it is Williams's voice, and its relation to everyday lived experience, which Leonard reflexively activates in all its audibility as he turns the sensual pleasure of Williams's cold, sweet plums, pilfered from 'the icebox' in 'This is Just To Say', into the equal satisfaction of cold cans of strong lager:

Ahv drank
thi speshlz
that wurrin
thi frij

n thit
yiwurr probbli
hodn back
furthi pahrti

Aright
they wur great
thaht stroang
thaht cawld[49]

Leonard's versioning brings Williams's colloquial New Jersey into counterpoint with his working-class Glasgow vernacular – as, for example, when in the third stanza Leonard's unapologetic 'Aright' underscores the disingenuousness we hear in Williams's 'Forgive me', from a speaker enraptured by the memory of eating plums 'so sweet | and so cold'. Generating its own meanings through acoustic echoes of a translated original underscored in all its voiced vernacularity, Leonard's poem also subverts the assumption that the visibly differentiated classed or raced 'voice' in poetry – even one which so ostentatiously courts stereotype – can be reduced to the unreconstructed idiolectal orality of 'an individual speaker speaking'.[50]

In fact, attention to voice helps to expose the fictions of the standard language, including the artificiality of alphabetic writing as a technology for the reproduction of speech. 'Unrelated Incidents 8' begins with the opening line of the Gospel of John in the King James Bible: 'in the beginning was the word'. Starting with this injunction to see the word as stable origin and self-identical anchor of meaning, originating from the urtext of national, religious, and linguistic Englishness, the poem dissolves it progressively over the lines which follow into its constituent sounds. Letters become phonemes, segmental boundaries break down, from 'in thi beginning was thi wurd' to 'nthibiginninwuzthiwurd', before concluding: 'in the beginning was the sound'. Replacing 'word' with 'sound' as language's point of origin also reveals, though, the unsettled relationship between them. As Leonard reflects in an essay titled 'Honest':

> Yi write doon a wurd, nyi sayti yirsell, that's no thi way a say it. Nif yi tryti write it doon thi way yi say it, yi end up wi thi page covered in letters stuck thigithir, nwee dots above hof thi letters, in fact, yi end up wi wanna they thingz yid needti huv took a course in phonetics ti be able ti read. ... But ifyi write down 'doon' wan minute, nwrite doon 'down' thi nixt, people say yir beein inconsistent. But ifyi sayti sumdy, 'Whaira yi afti?' nthey say 'Whut?' nyou say, 'Where are you off to?' they don't say 'That's no whutyi said thi furst time.' They'll probably say sumhm like, 'Doon thi road!' anif you say, 'What?' they usually say, 'Down the road!' the second time – though no always. Course, they never really say, 'Doon thi road!' or 'Down the road!' at all. Least, they never say it the way it's spelt. Coz it *izny* spelt, when they say it, is it?[51]

Leonard here, again, denaturalises the convention whereby one written sign stands for all its different realisations in speech. Prioritising the acoustic particularity of one kind of spoken language – Glasgow Scots – he draws attention both to the workings of alphabetic writing as a technology to evoke the sounds of a human voice, and to the inescapable distance between writing and the voice it is supposed to represent. Not just standard English orthography (the spelling of individual words), but also segmental boundaries (the spaces between words) start to break down 'if yi tryti write it doon thi way yi say it': 'yi end up wi thi page covered in letters stuck thigithir'.

In the sequence 'Six Glasgow Poems', first published in 1968, Leonard puts this language into poetic practice – for example in the rapid articulation born of the collective excitement of a group of truanting children dodging fares on the bus: 'we aw skiptwirr ferz njumptaffit thi lights | YIR AW PINE THEY FERZ THIMORRA'.[52] The concluding poem of the sequence, 'Good Style', acknowledges that it is 'helluva hard tay read theez init':

> stull
> if yi canny unnirston thim jiss clear aff then
> gawn
> get tay fuck ootma road[53]

It is not, of course, that being 'hard tay read' is necessarily considered by literary gatekeepers as anathema to 'good style' – as the poem slyly reminds us, difficulty can, as in modernism, be considered precisely as a benchmark of literary value – but that the written representation of such working-class speech is conventionally associated with simplicity and unselfconsciousness, and thus has no right to be difficult. The poem assails its would-be critics with what could be said to be, from such an elite perspective, the anticipated litany of macho clichés, empty threats, and impotent aggression: 'ahmaz goodiz thi lota yiz so ah um | ah no whit ahm dayn', he writes, 'stick thi bootnyi good style | so ah wull'.[54] In the midst of all this, 'no' is double-voiced, hovering between two linguistic 'value-systems'.[55] As the lingering trace of standard English, it is the negative judgement of the 'professional' reader: a 'no' to the poem's claim to 'good style'. This 'no' is an assertion of the speaker's unliterariness – a sign that he does not, in fact, 'know what he's doing', since he can only ever be a character in someone else's narrative, object to another's subject. Contextualised by both voice and syntax, though, 'no' is not the standard English negative determiner but the Glasgow Scots active verb, making a claim to vernacular 'knowing' – 'ah no whit ahm dayn' – and to the right to be difficult, from the baseline of the demotic, as a statement of purpose to rewrite the definition of 'good style'.

Leonard's claim of 'good style' for vernacularity can be read in emphatically localist terms, and as part of the 'international pattern' to which he claims allegiance. As he has observed:

> The same linguistic politics of colonisation and counter-colonisation occurs in different and many parts of the world, throwing up the same stratagems that the locally mainstream will put into some little locally marginalised classification-box. My phonetic dialect work is sometimes bracketed – outside Scotland that is – with counter-colonial Black writers like John Agard, Jean Binta Breeze, Linton Kwesi Johnson. I'm happy enough with that.[56]

Though the most common connection made by critics is between Leonard and Linton Kwesi Johnson,[57] it is Agard's 'Listen Mr Oxford Don' (1985) which the double-voicedness of 'Good Style' most readily calls to mind. Agard's poem addresses the eponymous gatekeeper of linguistic authority in a creolised literary voice that slides artfully between speech and writing, playing with assumptions about black vernacular speech, including its association with black criminality, before laying claim to *all* forms of language as the poet's to use: 'I making de Queen's English accessory | to my offence'.[58]

In 1990, Leonard wrote a review for the *Glasgow Herald* of black British sociolinguist and education campaigner Roxy Harris's *Language and Power* (1990), a collection of teaching materials compiled by Harris as part of the Inner London Education Authority's Afro-Caribbean Language and Literacy Project. In it, Leonard argues for the utility of Harris's project for Scottish readers, connecting Scottish with Caribbean/black British language contexts both by analogy, in terms of a shared experience of linguistic domination, and by the shared, material history which that commonality unearths. He suggests that Caribbean creole forms of language and working-class urban Scots have in common the 'contempt' heaped upon them. An account of Jamaican Creole from 1858 – 'their pronunciation is abominable, and the rising generation, not withstanding the pains taken to educate them, retain the villainous "patois" of their parents' – should remind readers of 'parallels for Scotland … The last such anti-Glasgow speech letter I saw a couple of months back got the Evening Times star letter

award'.[59] Scottish readers have something to learn from the activist
uses of poetry in London's black community in contesting the value of
vernacular language.[60] But they also have something to learn about the
historical connections which the parallel reveals. The names of some
of Glasgow's oldest streets, Leonard points out, like Jamaica Street,
opened in 1763, recall the city's foundational relationship to slavery in
the Caribbean. Confirming the connectedness of submerged histories
of oppression occluded in the naming of Glasgow's newly minted aspi-
rational 'Merchants Quarter', Leonard writes:

> The abominable conditions endured by children and adults
> working in such as the tobacco processing factories, according to
> Parliamentary Reports, links these bygone factory workers with their
> slave counterparts overseas. The link lives on in the contempt heaped
> on the language varieties spoken by the descendants of both.[61]

In the introduction to *Radical Renfrew*, published the same year,
Leonard restates the material connection between histories of slavery
in the Caribbean and urban proletarianisation in Scotland – 'one group
laboured long hours to extract raw materials which the other laboured
long hours to finish into manufactured goods' – that is affirmed in a
shared experience of language.[62] The 'highly political questions' about
language posed to writers in both contexts are therefore analogous:
whether accepting the use of standard English is 'an acceptance of colonial status'; how to develop a poetic lexis out of a language marked by
marginalisation and attrition; whether synthesising a written literary
language out of 'the language as spoken' is to risk being reduced to a
straightforward 'model of an individual speaker speaking'.[63]

As Leonard goes on to argue, for the reader and writer in Scotland,
the analogy with histories of slavery pulls the politics of language into
sharp focus: 'when one sees the historic connection between slave and
proletariat embodied in the language, one sees more clearly the actual
nature of derisive laughter at working-class speech and accent today;
one sees what forces are behind the vehemence with which a child
will be told to alter his or her language when addressing a superior'.[64]
Undeniably, the history of slavery here is being used as an instrument
by which to heighten white Scottish working-class language-political
consciousness. But, at the same time, what Leonard identifies in lan-

guage is a means to excavate a connected history by more than analogy: the history of what Carla Sassi calls 'an invisible transatlantic region, stretching from Scotland to the Caribbean archipelago',

> both a geo-political space across conventional borders and conventional historical categories and representations, which was the site of violent colonial encounters as well as of similar or parallel fates, micro-histories shaped by the same imperialist ideology, and an imagined space, created through the centuries by all those who moved across and settled within it – travellers, merchants, African slaves, exiles or tourists.[65]

As Sassi goes on to point out, recovering this sense of transatlantic connection in the past is a way to reclaim it for the present; as Leonard does, insisting that the experience of linguistic marginalisation implies not only a necessarily internationalist solidarity, but also recognition of the shared material histories that have forged the relationship of linguistic centre to periphery. Leonard's position calls on Scots to interpret their local conditions in internationalist terms.

Yet this is a risky move insofar as Leonard's call to solidarity rests on making histories of Scottish proletarianisation and Caribbean slavery analogous. Its vernacular politics erase race as an explanatory category in favour of class. And (in a move by no means unique to him, of course) Leonard implicitly lays Scotland's complicit role in the Caribbean, in the atrocity of slavery, at the door of *other* Scots – a comprador middle class. The reality is of course far more complex. As Jackie Kay's poem *The Lamplighter* recalls, Scotland and the Caribbean have been mutually constituted through the history of the slave trade:

> In 1770 on the slave island of Jamaica
> There were one hundred Black people
> Called MacDonald;
> A quarter of the island's people
> Were Scottish.[66]

The slave woman Black Harriot goes on to comment on the brutality and rape which underpins this shared history: 'My daughters have Scottish blood. | Scotland has my blood'.[67] This gendered dimension to what Leonard sees fit to erase from Scotland's Caribbean history is telling, insofar as it reveals the highly masculine orientation of his work. His assaults on the conventions of English often parody working-class Glasgow machismo, but they also risk reproducing it as they 'put thi boot in'.[68]

Nevertheless, these are blind spots in a language politics that strives to assert an internationalist solidarity on the grounds of the local, understanding linguistic marginalisation as the means by which people worldwide are denied agency. As a poem in *Reports from the Present* puts it:

> And their judges spoke with one dialect
> but the condemned spoke with many voices.
>
> And the prisons were full of many voices,
> but never the dialect of the judges.
>
> And the judges said:
>   'No-one is above the law'.[69]

Abstracted from any specific context, the poem speaks a particular kind of truth about the power of English, and its relationship to all those other forms of language, the 'many voices' subordinated or unheard in a discursive logic that operates only within the confines of 'one dialect'. This matters at the scale of the Glasgow local, to a language 'awrite fur | funny stuff', and it matters at an international scale, standing for all the ways in which the meanings made by subordinate groups – those being marginalised, oppressed, enslaved, or bombed – are discounted or erased.

Leonard's essay 'On reclaiming the local', which starts with the specificity of vernacular voice, concludes with the 1991 US-led bombing of Iraq and Kuwait:

> It's in the reification of linguistic codes and their possession by dom-
> inant and powerful classes wherein lies real danger, now literally
> for the whole world. That reification will always contain as part of
> its mechanics the device to maintain the illusion that social conflict
> does not exist, or that such conflict as exists can be meaningfully
> recreated, and resolved, within its own perimeter. Self-expression
> outside that code becomes simply a mechanism of self-elimination.
> The dominant refuse to recognise that all language is an instrument

of consciousness: instead, it is held as a symptom. Others don't 'have' a language – they 'are' it. In dismissing the language, one dismisses the existence of its users – or rather, one chooses to believe that they have dismissed themselves. The 'local' becomes that which can be bombed from 30,000 feet.[70]

'Operation Desert Storm' was war waged from the air: some estimates give the destructive power of the high explosives used in the first month of the conflict alone as greater than that of the combined Allied forces in World War Two. New technological advances in mapping and 'smart bombs' gave the sense that this was war as simulation – a seeming Baudrillardian simulacrum (and Baudrillard himself wrote *The Gulf War Did Not Take Place* along precisely such lines). With unprecedented levels of media coverage, carefully controlled by military planners, viewers around the world saw round-the-clock images of the bombardment, filmed from US planes and the noses of 'smart bombs' and presented as a 'clean' war. Systematically downplaying the actual violence that was taking place, news images rarely showed the human destruction wrought by all this technology, and victims were rarely seen and more rarely heard. For Leonard, the aerial bombardment of people in Iraq and Kuwait – death delivered technologically from 30,000 feet – stands as the apotheosis, the logical endgame, of geopolitical power that is fundamentally antidiscursive, and that can see the 'local' as nothing more than collateral damage.[71]

A voice in the distance: James Kelman

James Kelman's essay '"And the judges said …"', addressing problems of literary language, takes its title from Tom Leonard's poem, in which the 'one dialect' of juridical power and law pronounces over the 'many voices' of the condemned. Sharing with Leonard's poem an understanding of the relationship of monolingualist ideology with state power and violence, Kelman turns to find this captured in English literature, where standard English is forever normalised as the language of narrative authority, rationality, and interiority, while the voices of English's others pop up in dialogue only to insist on their own often-comical insufficiency. This is, he writes, nothing more than a 'summation of the political system': 'simply another method of exclusion, of marginalising and disenfranchising different peoples, cultures and communities'.[72] Regimes of language, whether of the law, the state, or the English novel, possess real-world force.

For his example of resistance to this system Kelman turns to Ken Saro-Wiwa, the Nigerian poet, novelist, and activist for whose release from prison he had campaigned, and who had then only recently been executed by the Nigerian government. In particular, Kelman recommends Saro-Wiwa's novel *Sozaboy*, and 'what he says about his use of English in the author's note'.[73] Here Saro-Wiwa famously writes:

> Sozaboy's language is what I call 'rotten English', a mixture of Nigerian pidgin English, broken English and occasional flashes of good, even idiomatic English. This language is disordered and disorderly. Born of a mediocre education and severely limited opportunities, it borrows words, patterns and images freely from the mother-tongue and finds expression in a very limited English vocabulary.[74]

Sozaboy, or Mene, is the novel's narrator, whose language is an improvisational, heteroglot projection of both his external circumstances and his inner life. Meanwhile, the language of power that looms over him is an anti-dialogic, colonising, 'big big grammar' or 'fine fine English', to which he aspires but which he can never master, that exists only to express authority and command obedience. Saro-Wiwa serves as Kelman's model for innovation with language that begins with synthesis of an individual voice, and there are repeated echoes of *Sozaboy*'s 'rotten English' throughout his work; he also stands for the connection between a localised perspective and a struggle for international solidarity that equally contest the exclusionary ideologies of nation states. Recalling contemporary Britain's stringent regime of border security, Kelman speculates on what would have happened if Saro-Wiwa had come seeking sanctuary. He asks: would he have been 'kept here pending a decision' or 'been found dead in a British cell, suffocated in mysterious circumstances, cause unknown?' Perhaps the Home Secretary would have made a special case because he was a well-known writer, supported by Amnesty International.[75] Thought about this way, the 'standard third party narrative voice' is a synecdoche for regimes of language which ascribe agency and rationality to some individuals and not others; which treat only some human lives as worth protecting or mourning.[76] Saro-Wiwa's 'rotten English', meanwhile, speaks the 'disordered and disorderly' experience of those from whom national and international systems of law withhold protection.

Kelman's first published novel, *The Busconductor Hines* (1984), is a study in the relationship between vernacular voice and narrative perspective. There is no clear stylistic distinction between the novel's third-person narration, dialogue, and the interior voice of the novel's protagonist, Hines. An at times performatively exaggerated pastiche of external, objective narrative authority – 'Although predisposed toward speculative musings the Busconductor Hines cannot be described as a dreamer' – blends into free indirect discourse that seems to directly channel Hines's inner world: 'sorry. Sorry sorry sorry. Really and truly. How could anybody even think such a thing. He definitely doesnt mean it. Not at all, honest to christ he doesnt, he just has a bad tongue, things come out, they do sir sorry sir please sir'.[77] If anything, it is Hines who appears to be narrating himself in the third person, even as that narration is constructed around a pervasive and mistrustful uncertainty about the relationship between language, narration, and interior consciousness:

> Silence is a remarkable how-d'ye-do. Hines would wish to maintain it. His mouth gets him into difficulties. His language contains his brains and his brains are a singular kettle of fish. He often feels like slitting his head open to have a look at the mess in a mirror. It is a peculiar notion. Hines is, however, peculiar. And genuinely regards himself as such.[78]

As Kelman has observed, 'it is very possible … that Hines could be writing the novel' – like Moses in Sam Selvon's *The Lonely Londoners*, imagining, at the novel's end, writing 'a book like that, what everybody would buy', a book which might closely resemble the one we hold in our hands.[79] Yet throughout the novel, as Hines wavers uncertainly between being the subject and object of narration, the mechanisms of narrative authority are sprung open. What is the relationship between the voices we are hearing, who is it who is telling us Hines's thoughts and actions?

> Here auld yin my wife's fucked off and left me I mean what's the fucking game at all, your fucking daft patter, eh, leave us alone ya

cunt for fuck sake. This isnt Hines who's talking. It's a voice. This is a
voice doing talking which he listens to. He doesnt think like it at all.
What does he think like. Fuck off. He thinks like anybody else under
the circumstances, the circumstances which are oddly normal.[80]

Hines's words are interrupted by a question as to their provenance –
'this isnt Hines who's talking'. The voice, which is the voice of his speech
being narrated, appears to Hines too: 'this is a voice doing talking
which he listens to'. But though it is supposed to sound like him, it is
one which he doesn't recognise: 'he doesnt think like it at all'. On the
one hand, perhaps his spoken words do not match his thoughts – what
does he think like, he asks. On the other, perhaps third-person narration is also part of the problem, the intrusive and estranging experience
of someone else recounting your thoughts, utterances, and actions. As
thought, speech, and narration start to come apart, he pushes the question away altogether, telling his own doubts – perhaps the narrator and
reader as well – to 'fuck off'.

The point of Kelman's vernacular language, in other words, is not
to represent some kind of working-class verisimilitude, but to point
to Hines's complex interior life, and also the difficulty with which this
can be given up to the narrative conventions of the novel.[81] *How Late
It Was, How Late* (1994), again, pivots on the indistinct boundary
between protagonist Sammy's internal and external worlds. The novel
begins with Sammy blinded after a beating from police – or in the language of the narrative, 'sodjers', an echo of the 'sozas' (soldiers) of Saro-
Wiwa's *Sozaboy* – and, like Saro-Wiwa's protagonist-narrator Mene,
Sammy is caught out by the gaps between his own language-world and
an authoritative and oppressive language of authority. Throughout the
novel, Sammy finds himself lost, disbelieved, and persecuted within
a system of benefits assessors, police, and doctors who – blurring the
distinction between real-world and narrative authority – appear like
disinterested or antagonistic narrators, co-opting his voice as a weapon
against him. As he tries to give an honest account to the 'Sightloss'
assessor at 'Central Medical', for example,

> Ach my own stupidity son a wee altercation with the sodjers; they
> gave me a doing. Sammy shrugged. One of these things; I was silly
> and so were they.

They gave ye a doing?
Aye.
And ye're saying ye were silly?
…
The boy had started hitting the keyboard again.
What're ye writing that down? said Sammy.
Yeh.
Well I'd prefer ye not to.
I've got to but Mr Samuels.
How?
Cause it's material.
…
We're required to do it.
Sammy sniffed. Ye no got a delete button?
Yeh but no for this operation. If the customer doesnt want something
in they're supposed to not say it. Once it's in it cannay come out. I
dont have the authority.[82]

In a literal rendering of linguistic appropriation, the 'operation' of
authority takes Sammy's words and he is powerless to claim them back
again: 'once it's in it cannay come out'. Power, meanwhile, is enacted
in the novel in language that is obscurantist, manipulative, often perverse – Sammy is a 'customer', for example, even when he is being disbelieved, denied benefits, or in handcuffs. Conversations proceed like
a communicative hall of mirrors, as, for example, in discussion with
the medical assessor Dr Logan, who is supposedly assessing Sammy's
blindness:

Eh how do ye go about it?
Go about it?
Eh, if ye wanted a guide-dog, or a white stick; how d'ye go about
getting them?
I'm afraid I dont follow.
Right eh just if'v ye no got the money I mean to buy them, I mean,
what do ye approach a charity?
Well I dare say that if a claim in respect of a found dysfunction is
allowed then an application in respect of a customer's wants that may
be consistent with the found dysfunction becomes open to discharge
by the appropriate charitable agency.
So I should approach a charity?

...
Eh?
I beg your pardon?
Have I to approach a charity? I mean ... should I approach a charity?
That's entirely up to yourself.
Yeh but
You may approach a charity at any time.
Yeh but I'm just saying
The doctor sighed.[83]

Sammy considers that perhaps it is his expression that is unclear (as
he has been told before, his 'colloquialisms' can be hard for those with
authority to understand), syntactically correcting himself: 'should
I approach a charity?' But in fact he has misunderstood the whole
purpose of the interview, which is to probe his case for falsehoods, not
to treat him as a person in need of help:

See I was just wondering there eh about eh the future and that, my
eyes ...
I've stated that it would be wise to proceed on the assumption that
should the alleged dysfunction be found
Aye sorry for interrupting doctor but see when you say 'alleged'?
Yes?
Are ye saying that you dont really think I'm blind?
Pardon?
Ye saying ye dont think I'm blind?
Of course not.
Well what are ye saying?
I told you a minute ago.
Could ye repeat it please?
In respect of the visual stimuli presented you appeared unable to
respond.
So ye're no saying I'm blind?
It's not for me to say.
Aye but you're a doctor.
Yes.
So ye can give me an opinion?
Anyone can give an opinion.
Aye but to do with medical things.
Mister Samuels, I have people waiting to see me.

Christ sake!
I find your language offensive.[84]

Sammy finds himself unable to understand, never mind conform to, the obscure communicative rules of those who have power over him, while his own language is used to make judgements about him. 'Dont use the word "cunts" again, it doesnay fit in the computer', says the police officer interrogating him at one point.[85] Later, he is advised:

Look eh pardon me; just one thing, ye're gony have to watch yer language; sorry; but every second word's fuck. If ye listen to me ye'll see I try to keep an eye on the auld words.[86]

In *How Late It Was, How Late*, the language of working-class speakers provides the means to dismiss them, even when they try to appropriate the tools of standard English. The advice above comes from Ally who, like Sammy, has spent time in prison and recalls sending a 'press-release to the letter pages of all the qualities' while campaigning against his wrongful conviction:

Dear sir, I says, or madam, I says, to the editor: I says, if you ask me the authorities are making a major error victimising all these innocent people. With respect, I says, it just serves to educate them in the protocols and procedures of the due processes of state and this cannot be good for society as a whole, I says, bla bla bla. I was a sarcastic bugger even then.

…

Naw, but what they done, just to show me who was boss, one of the qualities DID publish my letter. But see I had made a bloomer, I spelt 'victimising' wrong, I spelt it with an 'o' for 'victom' instead of with an 'i' for 'victim'. So they just left it in. and then they done an insert, the buggers, they stuck a wee SIC beside it. That was all they done. So easy! Hh![87]

All it takes, Ally tells Sammy, is one 'wee SIC' to discredit an uppity working-class attempt to turn the language of power against itself. This is a lesson not lost on Sammy, who has also been victimised by the police, in fact, precisely because he presses his case in the language of authority – 'I need to speak to a third party', he tells them, 'I want to report this dysfunction man I'm suffering a sightloss'. 'Another yin said: Give the guy his due, he knows his rights and regulations.'[88]

Thus on one level the novel narrates an external language-world in which every variety open to Sammy seems only to marginalise him further. Yet, at the same time, the effect of Kelman's narrative is to focus on the linguistic construction of Sammy's interior consciousness, as he feels his way – literally – through a world which he can no longer see. As Simon Kövesi puts it, 'He assesses his physical situation: his pains, his damage; then through simile, and then memory, he tries to express, ostensibly to himself, a conception of what he is experiencing.'[89] Sammy's sense-making works through interior narrative, at a remove from the narratives which are simultaneously being made about him: 'That was for him but no for the sodjers. It was him that needed it, the story':[90]

> Ah fuck it man stories, stories, life's full of stories, they're there to help ye out, when ye're in trouble, deep shit, they come to the rescue, and one thing ye learn in life is stories. Sammy's head was fucking full of them.[91]

The obstacles around which Sammy must navigate in *How Late It Was, How Late*, just as much as those of the physical world in which he must newly orient himself without the benefit of sight, are the linguistic conventions of a dominant culture in which his only real options are either to remain silent or, by speaking, to indict himself. But his own inner world represents a different kind of linguistic order incipiently trying to assert itself: a responsive means to interpret and understand what is happening to him through word, image, and analogy. As Sammy himself observes, his hearing newly sharpened, straining to attend to the prosody of an individual voice, each person has in their possession their own, fundamentally unique language:

> A voice in the distance. He listened hard but couldnay make sense of it. It seemed to be going in circles, up the scale and down the scale. It was funny how people had their own voices, everybody in the world, everybody that had ever been.[92]

It is both an obvious and a necessary point to make that this kind of attentiveness, with its attendant recognition of the limits of one's own vantage point of interpretation, was lost on some of the novel's critics. As others have observed, the novel's dramatisation of language politics – the gulf of dislocation between Sammy's language world and those who are to decide his case, the assumptions they make about his inability or unwillingness to conform to their communicative rules – to an extent anticipated its own reception by the English literary establishment. When *How Late It Was, How Late* won the Booker Prize in 1994, one of the judging panel, Rabbi Julia Neuberger, nevertheless spoke out to condemn the award as 'a disgrace'. For the *Mail on Sunday*, Alan Clark questioned whether Kelman's novel could be described as a '"book"' at all – 'Compiled? Scripted? I am trying to avoid the word "written"':

> The work consists of a series of transcripts taken from a running tape (there can be no other explanation) of a maundering old drunk who has been at the window table in the public bar since opening time.[93]

Not a book – not even writing – Kelman's novel was nothing more than transcripts from the public bar, where the proles sit. In *The Times*, Simon Jenkins accused Kelman of 'literary vandalism':

> My reeking companion demanded attention like a two-year-old. He told me his so-called life story, requested money with menaces, swore and eventually relieved himself into the seat.[94]

It is not hard to spot the elitist language politics at work in these responses to *How Late It Was, How Late* as a barbarian attack on the very concept of literary value. Placed outside of considerations of literary style or form, for these reviewers Kelman's novel resembles nothing so much as an assault on the unsuspecting middle-class English reader by one of the bit-part Scottish drunks he finds at the margins of English literature: violent, infantile, without 'a solitary "thought" in his entire life', his language 'a stream of gobbledygook'.[95] Kelman's uncompromising Booker Prize acceptance speech, published under the title 'Elitist slurs are racism by another name', responded by restating his allegiance both to Glasgow working-class culture and to a 'much wider process – or movement – toward decolonisation and self-determination … premised on a rejection of the cultural values of imperial or colonial authority'.[96]

Thus, rather than resorting to reified ideas of Scottishness, or Glaswegianness, Kelman stakes a claim instead on the structural relationship between a specifically local experience of language in working-class Glasgow and an international pattern of struggle for self-determination. As he has observed of his own spoken language:

> There is nothing about the language used by folk in and around Glasgow ... that makes it generally distinct from any other city in the sense that it is a language composed of all sorts of particular influences, the usual industrial or post industrial situation where different cultures have intermingled for a great number of years. In the case of my own family we fit neatly into the pattern, one grandparent was a Gaelic speaker from Lewis, another was from a non-Gaelic speaking family in Dalmally, up near Oban, another grandparent came from the east coast, the Macduff region; a great grandparent came from Northumberland ... All of these are at play in my work, as filtered through my own perspective that, okay, is Glaswegian, but in these terms 'Glaswegian' is a late twentieth century construct.[97]

This language – the version of language 'at play in my work', Kelman says – is unbounded ('the language used by folk in and around Glasgow') and the only name he is prepared to give it is in shudder quotes: '"Glaswegian"'. It is language defined by flux, not a pure container of identity but a 'late twentieth century construct', bound to the socioeconomic realities of the place where it is spoken but also idiosyncratic, 'composed of all sorts of particular influences' – constituted, to borrow Sinfree Makoni and Alastair Pennycook's terms, not as a discrete and stable entity but in terms of 'stylistic inventories, stylistic commons'.[98] This is, Kelman points out, a globally commonplace, late-modern experience of language, just like that to be found in 'any other city'. And, as a living riposte to fantasies about linguistic purity, it is a model for an anti-purist language politics and literary aesthetics. Thus, Kelman faces down the blood-and-soil nationalist version of Scottishness while at the same time trying to resist the homogenising force of English. Both are enacted at the difficult interface between English and Scots. But at the same time Kelman's internationalism insists on the recognition of other, yet more profound kinds of marginalisation and disenfranchisement that are made possible through what he sees as English's capacity for violence.

In *You Have to Be Careful in the Land of the Free* (2004), politics, race, and language are all invoked to determine who is excluded from and who is admitted to the paranoid, isolationist, dystopian US in which the novel is set – implicitly, in the context of 9/11 and the so-called 'War on Terror'. The novel's Glasgow-born protagonist-narrator, Jeremiah, is not only a 'furnir' but a political undesirable who, under a regime of intense US border securitisation, must carry and produce on demand his ID, a 'Class III Red Card' marking him as an 'unintegratit' social-ist.[99] His voice makes it hard to hide – 'as soon as I open my mouth I am an unassimilatit alien fucker', a fact about which he is constantly, paranoiacally aware.[100] Fantasising about the association between lin-guistic and political dissidence, he imagines being deported 'under Section 2 of the Extremist Outporings [sic] legislation, my use of Alien English deemed to produce terror among true-born true-breeds'.[101] Indeed, Jeremiah's narration could perhaps provoke nativist terror, constructed as it is as a synthetic melee of Glasgow Scots, exaggerated phonetic representations of American, Mexican, French, and other accents, among other miscellaneous linguistic material such as adver-tising jingles and song lyrics. But while his voice makes his difference audible and his safety sometimes precarious, nevertheless he has race, language, and nationality on his side, as 'an Inkliz-spaking pink-faced caucasian frae a blood-and-soil motherland'.[102] Indeed, though he claims persecuted solidarity with other 'immigrants', he is just as often advantaged by his whiteness and the fact that he speaks English, as when he gets work as an airport security operative, right by the 'Patriot Holding Centers' which house 'asylum-seeking furnir suspects'.[103] In other words, his claims to linguistic marginalisation are heard against a constant background hum of other, more profound forms of alterity. He is an aspiring (though so far failing) writer in English who imagines earning a fortune through global publishing: for example by selling 'high erotica' online across 'the inkliz-language-speaking world'. In a satire on English's global dominance as a source for translation, he imagines reaching a host of other languages via automated 'translation programs':

> eg. inkliz-pampangan, inkliz-senga, inkliz-kirghitz, inkliz-ewe, inkliz-livonian, inkliz-kurdish, inkliz-gandi, inkliz-adamanese, inkliz-grabar, inkliz-khalkha, inkliz-zapotec, inkliz-n to the power-n.[104]

This roll call – of minority languages, declining languages, moribund languages, languages whose speakers have been marginalised and persecuted – represents English steamrollering its others while it multiplies itself by translation: 'inkliz-n to the power-n'. Meanwhile there is no sight, no sound, no roll call at all of the languages spoken by the unnamed, unseen 'furin folks' who populate the 'Patriot Holding Centers' at every airport and along the US–Mexico border.

In *You Have to Be Careful in the Land of the Free*, Kelman presents us with the paradoxical spectacle of 'Inkliz' travelling globally in its least transparent form, while reflecting on the expanding reach of English as a synecdoche for global power. For Kelman, as for Tom Leonard, the specificity of the individual voice is the starting point for a political internationalism that insists on the right of all people over their own language, and over the language which is used about them. At one point, Jeremiah watches a TV show in which a panel of experts debate the so-called 'persian bet', in which an epidemic of plane crashes has resulted in America's starving and suicidal underclass taking out bets on their chances of dying on flights. With so many people living 'so far below what official government experts reckoned it took to stay alive', the term 'income' has simply been abolished. Still, the experts ask,

> What do we mean by 'stay alive'? What do poverty-stricken folks mean by 'stay alive'? Do 'we' have the right to assume that 'the wish to stay alive' even exists let alone as a universal?[105]

To claim the right to represent other people in language they have no control over lays the groundwork for other kinds of violence. As Kelman argues in his essay on Chomsky, in the realm of international politics and law, the words which are used to describe atrocity are subjected to a 'slow trudge through semantics', the purpose of which is to abstract them from the experiences they denote and to sidestep the responsibility to act in solidarity with those who suffer them. In phrasing which closely echoes that above, he writes:

> What do we mean by pain? What do we mean by suffering?
>   Around this point the terms get surrounded, captured by inverted commas – e.g. what do we mean by 'torture' – thus throwing into

doubt the very existence of the experience. A distinction is created
between the actual experience and the 'concept of the experience'. In
creating this distinction a closed system is put into operation: only
those who specialise in discussing concepts will be admitted. The
actual experience of atrocity becomes redundant.[106]

What starts in Kelman's writing from the original ground of
Glasgow and the specificities of the individual voice moves outwards
towards these figures of displacement, atrocity, and suffering. This is
a movement I will return to in chapter six, when I consider Kelman's
Translated Accounts (2001) as a fully deterritorialised response to
the brutality in which English is implicated, as it is manifest both in
international law and in the British asylum system. Kelman, at the
same time, is carefully cognisant of the risks of claiming solidarity,
questioning what claims of connection it's possible or legitimate to
make. As he frankly admits at the start of his essay celebrating John La
Rose, even though in the 1980s he knew and admired the work of the
Caribbean Artists Movement, and the black political, social, and cultural activism and self-determination represented by New Beacon and
the George Padmore Institute, and even though mutual friends were
encouraging him to meet La Rose, he had prevaricated about making
an initial approach. Uncomfortable, equivocal, and anxious, he had
been conscious of his own whiteness, and about 'crossing certain social
barriers, in this instance, colour and racial'.[107] Even so, the connection
with La Rose, and with the networks of black intellectuals, activists,
and artists around him, made possible new ways of thinking about
self-determination, mutuality, and collective action. Kelman became,
for example, an active participant in the International Fair of Radical
Black and Third World Books, including twice helping to bring it to
Scotland. As Mitch Miller and Johnny Rodger recount, when *How
Late It Was, How Late* won the Booker Prize in 1994, a full-length BBC
Arts programme was devoted to Kelman. The sociolinguist and black
educational campaigner Roxy Harris was interviewed, and discussed at
length the relationship between Scotland and the Caribbean, between
class and race, and 'shared ground in struggles over language' that connected Kelman to a writer like Sam Selvon.[108] But when the programme
was aired, Harris was shocked to discover that his contribution had
been left on the cutting room floor, along with '[a]ny portrayal ... of the

network of international and radical connections' or Kelman's 'shared ground across the globe'.[109]

These 'international and radical connections' – occluded in the BBC's account in favour of a particularist, 'angry primitive' (in Harris's words) version of Kelman – are precisely what this chapter has sought to unearth.[110] For both Kelman and Leonard, writing from a vantage point of working-class vernacularity, and forced confrontation with the conventions of the standard language and the linguicism that accompanies them, is the starting point for a politics that articulates the local into an internationalist solidarity. At the centre of their writing, and dramatising these struggles at work, both insist on the creativity of marginalised, ordinary speech forms, of language as it is used in everyday life as the starting point for literary expression, even as it always operates in the shadow of standard English. In the next chapter, I'll turn to Scottish poets whose internationalism is grounded in *un*vernacularity: in a critical turn away from the idea of belonging in language in any unproblematic way. Working through translation, but also through an approach to language – Scots specifically – in which synthesis and artifice are the point, their work asks: what does it mean to write in language which you *don't* speak, what risks does that entail, and what kinds of connections does it make possible?

Notes

1 William Grant, 'Introduction', in William Grant (ed.) *The Scottish National Dictionary*, Vol. 1 (Edinburgh: Scottish National Dictionary Association, 1931), p. xxvii.

2 Tom Leonard, 'Ghostie Men', in *Intimate Voices: Selected Work 1965–1983* (Buckfastleigh: etruscan books, 2003), p. 127.

3 James Kelman, 'Say hello to John La Rose', in James Kelman, *'And the Judges Said …': Essays* (Edinburgh: Polygon, 2008), pp. 226–227.

4 Kelman, 'Say hello to John La Rose', p. 227.

5 Roderick Watson, 'The double tongue', *Translation and Literature* 9:2 (2000), 175. On pejorative attitudes to Scots in political, cultural, and educational discourse, but also among its speakers, see J. Derrick McClure, 'Lowland Scots: an ambivalent national tongue', in McClure (ed.) *Scots and its Literature* (Amsterdam: Benjamins, 1995), pp. 5–19; Johann Wolfgang Unger, *The Discursive Construction of the Scots Language:*

Education, Politics and Everyday Life (Amsterdam and Philadelphia: John Benjamins, 2013).

6 On postcolonial literary 'englishes', the classic account is Bill Ashcroft, Gareth Griffiths, and Helen Tiffin, *The Empire Writes Back: Theory and Practice in Postcolonial Literatures*, 2nd edition (London and New York: Routledge, 2002).

7 James Kelman, 'Elitism and English Literature, speaking as a writer', in Kelman, *'And the Judges Said...'*, p. 60.

8 James Kelman, 'The importance of Glasgow in my work', in James Kelman, *Some Recent Attacks: Essays Cultural and Political* (Stirling: AK Press, 1992), p. 82.

9 Kelman, 'Elitism and English literature, speaking as a writer', p. 60. See also, for example, Duncan McLean, 'James Kelman interviewed', *Edinburgh Review* 71 (1985), 64–80.

10 Kelman, 'The importance of Glasgow in my work', p. 82.

11 James Kelman, '"And the judges said …"', in Kelman, *'And the Judges Said …'*, p. 41.

12 I'll discuss Ken Saro-Wiwa's influence on Kelman's writing and thinking on language more in due course, in this chapter and again in chapter six. On Kelman's relationship to Saro-Wiwa and Tutuola, see also Iain Lambert, 'This is not sarcasm believe me yours sincerely: James Kelman, Ken Saro-Wiwa and Amos Tutuola', in Michael Gardiner and Graeme Macdonald (eds) *Scottish Literature and Postcolonial Literature* (Edinburgh: Edinburgh University Press, 2011), pp. 198–209.

13 Tom Leonard, 'Introduction', in Tom Leonard (ed.) *Radical Renfrew: Poetry from the French Revolution to the First World War by Poets Born, or Sometime Resident in, the County of Renfrewshire* (Edinburgh: Polygon, 1990), p. xxvi.

14 Linda Mugglestone, *Talking Proper: The Rise and Fall of the English Accent as a Social Symbol* (Oxford: Oxford University Press, 2003), p. 173.

15 Kelman, 'The importance of Glasgow in my work', p. 82.

16 For an overview of English literary conventions for the representation of 'dialect', see, for example, Norman Page, *Speech in the English Novel*, 2nd edition (New Jersey: Humanities Press International, 1988), pp. 55–96; but in particular Jane Hodson, *Dialect in Film and Literature* (Basingstoke and New York: Palgrave Macmillan, 2014).

17 Tom Leonard, 'On reclaiming the local', in Tom Leonard, *Reports from the Present: Selected Work 1982-1994* (London: Jonathan Cape, 1995), p. 40.

18 Basil Bernstein, *Class, Codes and Control: Theoretical Studies Towards a Sociology of Language* (London: Routledge, 1971).

19 See Monica Heller and Bonnie McElhinny, *Language, Capitalism, Colonialism: Toward a Critical History* (Toronto: University of Toronto Press, 2017).

20 Leonard, 'Introduction', in *Radical Renfrew*, pp. xxv-xxvi; Tom Leonard, 'The Locust Tree in Flower, and why it had difficulty flowering in Britain', in Tom Leonard, *Definite Articles: Selected Prose 1973–2012* (Okehampton: etruscan books / Edinburgh: WP Books, 2013), p. 78.

21 Leonard, 'The Locust Tree in Flower', pp. 76, 78.

22 Leonard, 'The Locust Tree in Flower', p. 82. Robert Crawford terms this field of literature 'barbarian' writing, including such poets as Tony Harrison, whose speaker in 'Them & [uz]' proclaims 'RIP RP', determining to use 'my name and my own voice: [uz] [uz] [uz]'. Robert Crawford, *Devolving English Literature* (Oxford: Clarendon Press, 1992), p. 283.

23 James Kelman, 'A reading from the work of Noam Chomsky and the Scottish tradition in the philosophy of common sense', in Kelman, *'And the Judges Said ...'*, pp. 140–186.

24 Noam Chomsky quoted in Kelman, 'A reading from the work of Noam Chomsky', p. 156.

25 For a detailed account of the 'Self Determination and Power' event, see 'Two days in Govan' in Mitch Miller and Johnny Rodger, *The Red Cockatoo: James Kelman and the Art of Commitment* (Dingwall: Sandstone, 2011), pp. 157–212.

26 I discuss CAM, the Black Education Movement, poetry, and radical language politics in Rachael Gilmour, '"Sight, sound and meaning": voice/print transitions in black British poetry', in Kate McLoughlin (ed.) *Flower/Power: British Literature in Transition Volume 2, 1960–1980* (Cambridge: Cambridge University Press, 2019), pp. 86–101.

27 James Kelman, 'An interview with John La Rose', in Kelman, *'And the Judges Said ...'*, p. 242.

28 See, for example, Crawford, *Devolving English Literature*; Alan Riach, 'Tradition and the new alliance: Scotland and the Caribbean', *Gairfish: The McAvantgarde* (1992), 135–144.

29 See, for example, Berthold Schoene, 'A passage to Scotland: Scottish literature and the British postcolonial condition', *Scotlands* 2:1 (1995), 107–122; Michael Gardiner, 'Democracy and Scottish postcoloniality', *Scotlands* 3:2 (1996), 24–41; Liam Connell, 'Modes of marginality: Scottish literature and the uses of postcolonial theory', *Comparative Studies of South Asia, Africa and the Middle East* 23:1–2 (2003), 41–53; Graeme Macdonald, 'Postcolonialism and Scottish Studies', *New Formations* 59 (2006), 115–131.

30 James Kelman, 'Introduction', in Kelman, *'And the Judges Said ...'*, p. 10;

'Racism and the Maastricht Treaty', in Kelman, *'And the Judges Said …'*, p. 350.

31 Schoene, 'A passage to Scotland'; Macdonald, 'Postcolonialism and Scottish Studies', 118. On Scotland's relationship to the British Empire, see also T. M. Devine, *Scotland's Empire 1600–1815* (London: Allen Lane, 2003); John M. MacKenzie and T. M. Devine (eds) *Scotland and the British Empire* (Oxford: Oxford University Press, 2011).

32 Carla Sassi, 'Acts of (un)willed amnesia: dis-appearing figurations of the Caribbean in post-Union Scottish literature', in Giovanna Covi, Joan Annim-Addo, Velma Pollard, and Carla Sassi (eds) *Caribbean-Scottish Relations: Colonial and Contemporary Inscriptions in History, Language and Literature* (London: Mango Publishing, 2007), p. 133.

33 Macdonald, 'Postcolonialism and Scottish Studies', 118.

34 See Carla Sassi, 'Issues of memory, issues of identity: interrogating Scotland's mnemonic fictions of the Caribbean', in J. Derrick McClure, Karoline Szatek-Tudor, and Rosa E. Penna (eds) *'What Countrey's This? And Whither are we Gone?': Papers presented at the Twelfth Conference on the Literature of Region and Nation* (Newcastle: Cambridge Scholars Publishing, 2010), p. 104.

35 Crawford, *Devolving English Literature*, p. 18.

36 Crawford, *Devolving English Literature*, p. 23. On the significance of Scottish elocution masters to the standardisation of English, see also Tony Crowley, *Standard English and the Politics of Language,* 2nd edition (Basingstoke: Palgrave, 2003).

37 A. J. Aitken, 'Bad Scots: some superstitions about Scots speech', *Scottish Language* 1 (1982), 42.

38 Crawford, *Devolving English Literature*, p. 15.

39 Duncan McNaught quoted in Aitken, 'Bad Scots', 32.

40 T. D. Robb quoted in Leonard, 'Introduction', in *Radical Renfrew*, p. xxiii; R. de B. Trotter quoted in Aitken, 'Bad Scots', 32.

41 William Grant, 'Introduction', in William Grant (ed.) *The Scottish National Dictionary, Vol. 1* (Edinburgh: Scottish National Dictionary Association, 1931), p. xxvii.

42 Kirsten Matthews, 'A democracy of voices', in Matt McGuire and Colin Nicholson (eds) *The Edinburgh Companion to Contemporary Scottish Poetry* (Edinburgh: Edinburgh University Press, 2009), p. 88.

43 Tom Leonard, 'Unrelated Incidents 1', in Tom Leonard, *Intimate Voices: Selected Work 1965–1983* (Buckfastleigh: etruscan books, 2003), p. 92.

44 Leonard, 'Unrelated Incidents 1', p. 93.

45 Leonard, 'Unrelated Incidents 2', in *Intimate Voices*, p. 94.

46 Leonard, 'Ghostie Men', in *Intimate Voices*, p. 134.

47 Leonard, 'Ghostie Men', p. 127.
48 Leonard, 'The Locust Tree in Flower', p. 74.
49 Leonard, 'Jist Ti Let Yi Know', in *Intimate Voices*, p. 37.
50 Leonard, 'Introduction', in *Radical Renfrew*, p. xxv.
51 Leonard, 'Honest', in *Intimate Voices*, p. 78.
52 Leonard, 'A Scream', in *Intimate Voices*, p. 8.
53 Leonard, 'Good Style', in *Intimate Voices*, p. 10.
54 Leonard, 'Good Style', in *Intimate Voices*, p. 10.
55 Leonard, 'On reclaiming the local', p. 40.
56 Tom Leonard, 'The sound of poetry', in Attila Dósa, *Beyond Identity: New Horizons in Modern Scottish Poetry* (Amsterdam: Rodopi, 2009), p. 186.
57 For discussion of Leonard's work in relation to black British poetry, see David Nowell Smith, 'Langwij a thi guhtr', in Abigail Lang and David Nowell Smith (eds) *Modernist Legacies: Trends and Faultlines in British Poetry Today* (Basingstoke: Palgrave, 2015), pp. 177–191. For readings of his poetry specifically in relation to that of the British Jamaican poet Linton Kwesi Johnson, see Liam Connell and Victoria Sheppard, 'Race, nation, class and language use in Tom Leonard's *Intimate Voices* and Linton Kwesi Johnson's *Mi Revalueshanery Fren*', in Michael Gardiner, Graeme Macdonald, and Niall O'Gallagher (eds) *Scottish Literature and Postcolonial Literature: Comparative Texts and Critical Perspectives* (Edinburgh: Edinburgh University Press, 2011), pp. 173–184; Donald Wesling, 'Bakhtin and the social poetics of dialect', in Donald Wesling, *Bakhtin and the Social Moorings of Poetry* (Cranbury, NJ, London, and Mississauga, Canada: Associated University Presses, 2003), pp. 61–76. Somewhat ironically (for my purposes) Wesling concludes his chapter by dismissing the idea of a book about 'poetries in dialects of English' because 'there is no sufficient audience either for dialect poetry or for its defence' (p. 76).
58 John Agard, 'Listen Mr Oxford Don', in *Mangoes and Bullets: Selected and New Poems 1972–1984* (London and Sydney: Pluto Press, 1985), p. 44. On Agard's poem, see Tony Crowley, *Language in History: Theories and Texts* (London: Routledge, 1996), pp. 51–52; Mervyn Morris, 'Is English we speaking', in Mervyn Morris, *Is English We Speaking and Other Essays* (Kingston: Randle, 1999), pp. 11–12; Lars Ole Sauerberg, *Intercultural Voices in Contemporary British Literature: The Implosion of Empire* (Basingstoke: Palgrave, 2001), p. 69; Jahan Ramazani, *The Hybrid Muse: Postcolonial Poetry in English* (Chicago: University of Chicago Press, 2001), p. 15; Jahan Ramazani, 'Black British poetry and the translocal', in Neil Corcoran (ed.) *The Cambridge Companion to Twentieth-Century English Poetry* (Cambridge: Cambridge University Press, 2007), p. 208; Rachael Gilmour, 'Doing voices: reading language as craft in Black British

poetry', *Journal of Commonwealth Literature* 49:3 (2014), 343–357. I discuss the discursively produced connection between black British language and criminality in the Introduction.

59 Tom Leonard, 'Language and power', in Tom Leonard, *Definite Articles: Selected Prose 1973–2012* (Okehampton: etruscan books / Edinburgh: WP Books, 2013), p. 13.

60 Leonard, 'Language and power', p. 13.

61 Leonard, 'Language and power', p. 13.

62 Leonard, 'Introduction', in *Radical Renfrew*, p. xxv.

63 Leonard, 'Introduction', in *Radical Renfrew*, p. xxv.

64 Leonard, 'Introduction', in *Radical Renfrew*, pp. xxv-xxvi.

65 Sassi, 'Issues of memory', pp. 101–102.

66 Jackie Kay, *The Lamplighter* (Tarset: Bloodaxe Books, 2008), p. 81. Quoted in Sassi, 'Issues of memory'.

67 Kay, *The Lamplighter*, p. 81. Quoted in Sassi, 'Issues of memory'.

68 This is an argument made by David Kinloch in 'A queer Glaswegian voice', in Dimitris Asimakoulas and Margaret Rogers (eds) *Translation and Opposition* (Bristol: Multilingual Matters, 2011). I'll discuss this essay of Kinloch's further in chapter two. For a critique of the masculinist perspective of James Kelman's writing as well, see Neil McMillan, 'Wilting, or the "poor wee boy" syndrome: Kelman and masculinity', *Edinburgh Review* 108 (2001), 41–55.

69 Tom Leonard, 'Situations theoretical and contemporary', in Tom Leonard, *Reports from the Present: Selected Work 1982–1994* (London: Jonathan Cape, 1995), p. 17.

70 Leonard, 'On reclaiming the local', p. 41.

71 Important work on language, translation, and the technologies of war since 9/11 includes Emily Apter, *The Translation Zone: A New Comparative Literature* (Princeton and Oxford: Princeton University Press, 2006), chapter 1: 'Translation after 9/11: mistranslating the art of war'; Emily Apter, 'Translation at the checkpoint', *Journal of Postcolonial Writing* 50:1 (2013), 56–74; Mary Louise Pratt, 'Harm's way: language and the contemporary arts of war', *PMLA* 124:5 (2009), 1515–1531. Pratt discusses the Phraselator, a handheld translation device devised by the US military in the 1990s for conflict settings. The Phraselator's user can choose the English sentence they want to say and the machine will play a recorded version of the corresponding sentence in the target language; however, the machine has no capacity to understand what is said back to it. As Pratt observes, '[i]t embodies to a fault the one-way mission of psychological operations: to convey, influence, induce, reinforce. You can use it to ask a question, but when it comes to deciphering a reply, you are

on your own. It can give a command, but if someone wants to explain why the order is a bad idea, the machine is no help. The Phraselator, in other words, is an instrument of pure interpellation.' Pratt, 'Harm's way', 1519.

72 Kelman, ' "And the judges said …" ', p. 41.

73 Kelman, ' "And the judges said …" ', p. 41.

74 Ken Saro-Wiwa, 'Author's Note', in Ken Saro-Wiwa, *Sozaboy: A Novel in Rotten English* (New York: Longman, 1994).

75 Kelman, ' "And the judges said …" ', p. 43.

76 James Kelman quoted in Terence Patrick Murphy, ' "Getting rid of that standard third party narrative voice": the development of James Kelman's early authorial style', *Language and Literature* 15:2 (2006), 187.

77 James Kelman, *The Busconductor Hines* (London: Orion, 1992), p. 93.

78 Kelman, *Busconductor Hines,* p. 213.

79 Fabio L. Vericat, 'Letting the writing do the talking: denationalising English and James Kelman's *Translated Accounts*', *Scottish Literary Review* 3:1 (2011), 131, citing Kelman in McLean, 'James Kelman interviewed', 65. Samuel Selvon, *The Lonely Londoners* (Harlow: Longman, 1986), p. 142. Echoes of *The Lonely Londoners* can also be heard in Hines's renaming of the city, as 'High Amenity Zone K', 'the district of D', reminiscent of Selvon's protagonists' renaming of London as 'the Water', 'the Circus' – overwriting the networks of power and authority which have historically named and defined Glasgow's urban space, including for empire and slavery.

80 Kelman, *Busconductor Hines*, p. 167.

81 See Fiona Doloughan, *English as a Literature in Translation* (London and New York: Bloomsbury, 2016), p. 92.

82 James Kelman, *How Late It Was, How Late* (London: Vintage, 1998), p. 98.

83 Kelman, *How Late It Was, How Late*, pp. 223–224.

84 Kelman, *How Late It Was, How Late*, p. 225.

85 Kelman, *How Late It Was, How Late*, p. 160.

86 Kelman, *How Late It Was, How Late*, p. 238.

87 Kelman, *How Late It Was, How Late*, p. 300.

88 Kelman, *How Late It Was, How Late*, p. 20.

89 Simon Kövesi, *James Kelman* (Manchester: Manchester University Press, 2007), p. 140.

90 Kelman, *How Late It Was, How Late*, p. 25.

91 Kelman, *How Late It Was, How Late*, p. 52.

92 Kelman, *How Late It Was, How Late*, p. 207.

93 Alan Clark, 'A prize insult to the courage of Scotland's finest', *Mail on Sunday*, 23 October 1994.

94   Simon Jenkins, 'An expletive of a winner', *The Times*, 15 October 1994, 20.
95   Kelman, 'The importance of Glasgow in my work', p. 82.
96   James Kelman, 'Elitist slurs are racism by another name', *Scotland on Sunday*, 16 October 1994, Spectrum supplement, 2.
97   Kelman, 'The importance of Glasgow in my work', p. 84.
98   Sinfree Makoni and Alastair Pennycook, 'Disinventing and reconstituting languages', in Sinfree Makoni and Alastair Pennycook (eds) *Disinventing and Reconstituting Languages* (Clevedon: Multilingual Matters, 2007), p. 14.
99   James Kelman, *You Have to be Careful in the Land of the Free* (London: Penguin, 2004), p. 151.
100 Kelman, *You Have to be Careful*, p. 37.
101 Kelman, *You Have to be Careful*, p. 267.
102 Kelman, *You Have to be Careful*, p. 132.
103 Kelman, *You Have to be Careful*, p. 136.
104 Kelman, *You Have to be Careful*, p. 214.
105 Kelman, *You Have to be Careful*, p. 127.
106 Kelman, 'A reading from the work of Noam Chomsky', p. 166.
107 Kelman, 'Say hello to John La Rose', p. 217.
108 Miller and Rodger, *The Red Cockatoo*, p. 153.
109 Miller and Rodger, *The Red Cockatoo*, pp. 153–154. Just one signal example of the kinds of connections and solidarities occluded in the BBC's, along with many other accounts of Kelman, is the book launch of *How Late It Was, How Late*, held at a benefit night in Southall, south London, to raise money for the Stephen Lawrence Family Campaign. Stephen Lawrence was a black teenager murdered by racists in London in 1993 – the mishandled police investigation of which would lead, eventually, to the Macpherson Report, branding the Metropolitan Police 'institutionally racist' – and the family's campaign aimed to push Stephen's murder into the media spotlight and push for the arrest of his killers. Driving down in a hired bus from Glasgow to the Dominion Centre, Southall, Kelman and his fellow Scottish writers, including Margaret Cook and the Gaelic poet aonghas macneacail, shared the stage with the South African poet Mandla Langa, poets Kamal Kaddourah from Lebanon and Randhir Sandhu from India, John La Rose and Linton Kwesi Johnson, Scottish blues band The Blues Poets, as well as Stephen's mother Doreen, who spoke 'in the most powerful and moving terms' about her son's murder and the family's campaign. Kelman, 'Introduction', in *'And the Judges Said …'*, p. 24.
110 Miller and Rodger, *The Red Cockatoo*, p. 154, quoting Roxy Harris in interview.

2

Dictionary trawling

There is no passport to this country,
It exists only as a quality of the language.

W. N. Herbert, 'Dingle Dell'[1]

In the writing of Tom Leonard and James Kelman, discussed in the previous chapter, social and political life proceeds through the inevitable
and constant friction of linguistic difference – trying to make ourselves
understood, negotiating others' linguistic demands, being judged by
the language we speak – and it is made possible through common-
alities and solidarities based on linguistic self-recognition. Thinking
and writing from the starting point of working-class Glaswegian Scots,
invested in the politics of the vernacular, and using it to jibe at the
naturalised conventions of English literary form and the standard language, they see theirs as an internationalist insurgency shared with
other speakers marginalised by class and by race from English's vested
cultural power. Pivotal to all of this is their regard for language as the
individual and collective property of its speakers, and an expression of
their identity, even as it is also recognised as highly mediated through
the technology and conventions of print and always ghosted by the
figure of standard English.

In this chapter, I turn to Scottish poets whose work also responds
to language as an inescapable and fraught social fact. Yet, whereas for
Kelman and Leonard a language community is a class community, and
class serves as a primary explanatory category – for Leonard in particular, it was Scotland's middle classes as much as an English elite who

were responsible for the linguistic, cultural, material, and political marginalisation of the Scottish urban poor – these writers set their sights on
Scotland and Scottishness, and a linguistic terrain defined by its diversity. Instead of a commitment to vernacular language as a site of possible solidarities, Scotland's complicated histories of multilingualism and
language loss and reinvention lead them to question the possibility of
belonging in language in any uncontested way. Considering the movement between languages – and the concomitant experience of being an
outsider to language – as distinctively Scottish experiences leads them
to consider language as something provisional, that can be lost, gained,
or claimed. Translation becomes central, as both a figure and a practice, to foreground Scotland's always already multilingual social reality
between English, Scots, and Gaelic, and as a means to travel beyond
Scotland to claim European and international belonging. And, for some
writers, language itself comes to appear as a kind of assemblage: something that can be shattered or lost, and by that logic also constructed or
built. The practice of 'dictionary trawling', drawn in part from the 'synthetic Scots' of Scottish modernist poet Hugh MacDiarmid – salvaging
and recombining linguistic material from Scots antiquarian sources
into a highly and self-consciously artificial, ultra-modern poetic language – provides a provisional means of drawing fractured linguistic
pasts into the present, and of trying to anticipate new ways of being in
language.[2] Both strategies – translation, and a synthetic approach to
Scots – allow for the imagining of an internationalist, outward-looking
Scottishness untethered by nationalist myths. But at the same time,
they also mean having to think about what it means to claim different
kinds of language as yours to use.

The period addressed in this chapter, roughly the mid-1980s to the
mid-1990s, is bookended by two referendums on a devolved Scottish
assembly, the latter of which in 1997 led to the inauguration of the
Scottish parliament at Holyrood. 1979, by contrast, saw a failed bid at
devolution – in a referendum in which a majority voted yes, but turnout
failed to reach a high enough bar (40 per cent of the eligible electorate
casting a 'yes' vote) to compel its enactment. The British parliamen-
tary election which followed saw Margaret Thatcher's Conservative
government ushered into power, immediately voting down the as-yet-
unimplemented Scotland Act which would have granted Scotland its
own assembly. The subsequent decade, with the deindustrialisation and

free market economics that defined the 1980s under Thatcherism, was by many measures a disaster for Scotland, bringing the hollowing-out of Scotland's industries and industrial communities, soaring unemployment, and economic decline. At the same time – and partly in response, in a nation that continued to be not-(yet)-a-nation – Scottish artists and writers continued to reflect on the odd nature of 'Scottishness'. And many tried to imagine this in expansive, outward-looking forms that used the grounds of language as a means to turn towards Europe and the wider world.

For some, this outward turn was enacted in literal terms, making use of a capacity to travel facilitated often, at least in part, by class and education. Writers went south to study at English universities, moved to other parts of Europe, travelled, and returned to Scotland. It is in this period, the 1980s and early 1990s, that Eleanor Bell identifies a related, pervasive interest in Scottish poetry in the Scots figure of the stravaiger, or wanderer[3] – one who travels across all Scotland's borders, internal and external, between languages as well as across spaces. Some, echoing Tom Leonard and James Kelman, asserted a fundamental relationality between Scotland and Britain's postcolonial peripheries on the grounds of a shared experience of language. In an interview with the Guyanese novelist, essayist, and poet Wilson Harris published in 1992, Alan Riach claimed a largely 'unrecognised and undiscussed' link between Scottish and Caribbean writing. In particular, he suggested to Harris, Scottish writers had much to learn from the Caribbean about how to understand their own necessarily 'heterogeneous' language resources as 'potentially creative and liberating rather than debilitating'.[4] In *Devolving English Literature*, published in the same year, Robert Crawford argued for the relationship of Scottish writing to an insurgency against the dominating power of standard English from all its 'provincial' and 'barbarian' peripheries, from Ireland and the north of England to Australia and the Caribbean.[5] Meanwhile, Scottish writers were also engaging with translation in newly intensified ways, translating between all the languages of Scotland and into them from others, as a means to engage with poetry beyond English, and also to stake a claim on the connection between Scotland's own internal multilingualism and Scottish poetry's internationalist aspirations. For example, Tom Hubbard gives copious examples of translation of poetry into Scots from across Europe and Latin America from the later 1980s to the 2000s, and of Scots poetry's correspondingly evident 'international concerns'.[6] The journal *Verse*, established by Robert Crawford and David Kinloch in 1985 while both were students at Oxford, published up-and-coming Scottish poets alongside international poetry in English translation (from Pier Paolo Pasolini and Jorge Luis Borges to new poets emerging from Eastern Europe) and an international roster of radical Anglophone poetry from such figures as Seamus Heaney, Tony Harrison, Les Murray, and John Ashbery. As W. N. Herbert argued in 1990 in the first issue of the poetry journal *Gairfish*, Scottish literature's outward-looking, translational orientation – exemplified, for Herbert, by a James Kelman Europeanised as 'the Robbe-Grillet of Glesceranto', as well as Robin Fulton, the Norway-based Scottish translator of Tranströmer and Lagerkvist into English – stood in stark contrast to the 'unEuropean shallowness' of English writing.[7] Accustomed by virtue of Scottishness to living with the perpetual fact of linguistic difference, Herbert and his fellow poets were – he argued – European by definition.

Herbert pitched *Gairfish*'s project – dedicated to 'all the languages of Scotland', to 'the radical reappraisal of Scottish culture', and to 'the greatest possible plurality stemming from a Scottish base'[8] – as partly emerging from his own Oxford-born experience of straddling the linguistic fault-line between England and Scotland. 'I don't know how many times I've been criticized by Scots for picking up an English accent', he wrote, nor 'mocked by the English for not pronouncing something just so, the way "we" do'.[9] Herbert suggests that for him there is something particularly *enabling* about this experience: being between forms of language, unable to make any claim to straightforward linguistic belonging, becomes a way of evading both English linguistic chauvinism ('the subliminal crusade for Received Pronunciation') and Scottish parochialism ('balanc[ing] dictionaries on their shoulders in lieu of chips (despite having written them)').[10] The sensation of being an outsider to language, which Herbert describes as both unsettling and liberating, has specific resonances in a Scottish context, where distinctions between varieties of English, Scots, Gaelic, and other languages also mark other kinds of distinctions: between urban and rural, working- and middle-class, Highland and Lowland, between generations, between 'indigenous' Scots and incomers, as well as the demarcation of the England/Scotland border. As John Corbett puts it of language in Scotland: '[o]ur others are everywhere, within and outwith our political boundaries'.[11] The arguable inevitability, in Scotland, of linguistic insider/outsiderness, is also tied to its histories of language loss: of rural Scots, and even more so of Gaelic. As Iain Galbraith observes, the convention that the facing-page English translation of poetry in Scots or Gaelic is provided for readers outside Scotland is a fiction, given that most Scottish readers will not be able to read the 'original'. Indeed, the two versions of the poem – both often written by the poet, and regularly confounding the conventional relationship between 'original' and 'translation' or 'source' and 'target' – may be said to make their meanings out of the fact of their translational relationship to one another.[12] Reflecting this complex and aporic linguistic field, central to the work of many Scottish poets writing in the 1980s and 1990s are motifs of encounter between different forms of language, evocations of linguistic insider/outsiderness, or of language made distant and strange. On the one hand, these say something about the history of Scotland and the nature of Scottishness. On the other, they make a particular kind of claim to internationalism – to a Scottishness always already ready to travel linguistically, to be in the presence of linguistic others, to translate.

The anthology *Dream State: The New Scottish Poets*, published in 1994, aimed to showcase the diversity of the 'new' Scottish poetry and laid claim to a revitalised, outward-looking Scottishness. As editor Daniel O'Rourke observed in his introduction, *Dream State* represented a generation of Scottish poets, all under 40 at the time, who had come of age politically in the 1970s. Many had been first old enough to vote in 1979: in the Scottish devolution referendum, which saw hopes for a devolved Scottish assembly dashed for a generation, and in the UK general election that installed Margaret Thatcher's Conservative government, widely viewed as a catastrophe for Scotland.[13] Against the blows of 1979 – standing for Scotland's ongoing political, economic, and cultural marginalisation by an establishment located in London and the decimation of Scottish industries and communities under Thatcherism, but also for the disappointments of an inward-looking, anachronistic Scots nationalism – O'Rourke pitched the *Dream State* poets' bid to be 'newly Scottish and yet unbounded', laying claim to a Scottishness that was capacious and plural from the outset, framed by Alasdair Gray's dictum that 'the first people in Scotland to call themselves Scots, were

immigrants'.[14] O'Rourke's introduction focused confidently and opti-
mistically on language diversity as a defining feature of contemporary
Scottishness. The 'distinct and thriving poetic tongues' of Scots and
Gaelic served as a source of enrichment for 'Scotland's newest poetry'.
Central to his vision is a definitively Scottish multilingualism, located
within European and international circuits of translation and cultural
circulation and in relation to the 'languages' of global consumer capitalism, information technology, and digital communication.[15]

Simultaneously, though, many of the *Dream State* poets described a
linguistic landscape marked by absences and aporias, by the attrition of
Scots and Gaelic, and by Scotland's complex histories as both centre and
periphery, nation and not-nation. Over and over, language becomes
the ground on which to express both a polyglot, outward-looking
internationalism and the fissiparous, paradoxical nature of contemporary Scottishness: language is something which has been lost, even
if that also means it's something which can be found or reinvented.
Iain Bamforth, discussing his own use of Scots words and 'occasional
dictionary-trawling', describes his language as evidencing 'those dis-
continuities, time-lapses and demons' which have 'made us modern'.[16]
W. N. Herbert remarks similarly about his own poetry:

> In Scots I pretend that my basic speech – Dundonian – hasn't been
> atrophied by cultural neglect, and still has access to the broad vocab-
> ulary of the Scots dictionary. This creates the language of a quasi-
> fictional country, one which offers a critique of the present status of
> 'Scotland'.[17]

This half-'pretend' Scots, suggests Herbert, a fabricated 'language
which is not really a language', is a wholly apt medium to express 'a
country which is not quite a country', the discrepant realities of which
can only be reached through linguistic distance and estrangement. The
task of language is to express 'the truth about Scotland': a state of being
which needs an in-between, doubled (or 'forked') fictitious language to
express it, trawled from its own pasts and possible futures. 'The truth
about Scotland, perhaps, can only be situated between the dominant
and suppressed parts of language, in the region of the forked tongue'.[18]

In the poetry collection *Contraflow on the Super Highway* (1994),
Richard Price gave the name of 'Informationists' to the loose circle of

(young, male) poets whose work was contained therein – Price, Herbert, Crawford, Kinloch, Peter McCarey, and Alan Riach – and he argued that what united their poetry was the distinctively Scottish yet internationalist experience of living across 'linguistic faultline[s]', of which those between English, Scots, and Gaelic were only the most obvious.[19] Influenced by Hugh MacDiarmid's modernist synthetic Scots and by the translational internationalism of Edwin Morgan, Informationist poetry was written predominantly in English, but was often marked by a self-reflexive concern with English's relationship to other kinds of language, and in particular by varying degrees of engagement with Scots. Yet, as Price emphasised, the *Contraflow* poets' concern was neither with 'everyday' language nor indeed with 'Scots *as such*' – which was 'not quite the point for Informationists'.[20] He referred instead to a shudder-quoted ' "Scots" ', archly and knowingly fabricated, somewhat distant from language anyone might speak, the name not so much for a kind of language as a practice of language-making. Informationist ' "Scots" ' stood for an untotalisable linguistic amalgam, synthesised through archaeology, reinvention, or fantasy, blurring urban and rural, 'prosaic' and 'academic', atrophied, dominant, and emerging forms, and drawn from sources as various as antiquarian dictionaries and 'the international vocabulary of multinational companies and transglobal information networks'.[21] This was 'a Scots which may draw from the forgotten past in the same breath as it creates words imagined from the distant future'.[22]

This 'super-saturated mix'n'match approach to Scots' may speak to Scotland and Scottish experience, but it also, argues Price, models a way of understanding language that is appropriate to the whole 'postmodern world'.[23] Relational, situational, fabricated, globalised, this ' "Scots" ' confounds the idea of a singular language and a singular national culture, challenging monolingualist ideologies of linguistic purity, hygiene, order, and good governance. The 'paradox of the foreignness' of Informationist ' "Scots" ' makes it, in fact, an intentional analogue for English made productively foreign to itself:[24]

> The extraordinary possibilities of Scots, much more those of Scotland itself, teach the Informationist user of English that English itself can be used to define nuances of experience 'standard' English poets and other poets in English have shied away from.[25]

Holding a postmodern mirror up to English, this version of Scots
– what Price calls 'the most fictitious language in Scotland' – represents a de-essentialised, decentred vision of language beyond the
nation. Jettisoning conventional ideas of language community almost
altogether, 'Informationism' instead suggests that what defines
Scottishness, *and* beyond it the whole of the 'postmodern world', is the
schism between monologic, nation-based ideologies of linguistic good
order and language's actually occurring productive unruliness.[26]

English 'ungutenberged'

W. N. Herbert and Robert Crawford's co-authored *Sharawaggi: Poems
in Scots* (1990), incorporating both poets' Scots poetry as well as Scots
translations from Vietnamese (Crawford) and Spanish and Italian
(Herbert), would seem to exemplify this project particularly well.[27]
Crawford's poems, given in facing-page Scots–English 'translation',
offer something of a pastiche of the conventions of English translation
in both Scots and Gaelic poetry, and a play on the assumed relationship
between a hard-to-read 'original' and an accessible translated 'copy'.
His Scots is neither a conventional literary Scots nor a version of everyday spoken Scots – which he, in any case, does not speak.[28] Rather, it is
a postmodern, flamboyantly artificial techno-Scots: a MacDiarmidian
synthetic, salvaged, and invented language combining neologisms,
found and obscure words trawled from old dictionaries, Scots literature, and antiquarian sources with an Anglobal lexis of consumer capitalism and computer technology. Owning up fully to this state of affairs,
Crawford's Scots and English versions are also mutually constituting
and, as Kathleen McPhilemy has observed, insistent on a back-and-
forth movement of reading by which this becomes evident. Given the
difficult density of the Scots, she suggests, the reader may be tempted
to abandon it for the 'apparently more accessible' English. However,
'after being dragged headlong' through the poetry's 'minimally punctuated rush of imagery', he or she will be forced back towards the
Scots to find the line breaks and movement of verse which 'serve to
steady the poem'.[29] This oscillating movement between both versions,
jumping back and forth across the page division, points precisely to
how meaning is being made at the interface between them, and thus
to 'translation' not as a linear direction of travel from source to target

but as a feedback loop or continuous circuit. As an extension of arguments made in the poetry itself, this movement tries to short-circuit both the sometime nostalgia and parochialism that may be associated with Scots and the prescriptive presumptions of English.

The English in Crawford's poetry is often made to seem pointedly laboured in comparison to a dextrous Scots. 'Burns Beyond Edinburgh' celebrates the poetry of an earthily radical Robert Burns, before he was co-opted by a twee Burnsiana that sees him commodified and 'prettified | fur printed towels'.[30] Burns's Scots in the poem is a language of transatlantic modernity – 'Ma wurds sky oot wih Coancoard's soanic bangs' – taking flight while its English 'translation' lumbers ponderously behind. '[A]h bide hamshakelled', for example, is given as 'I endure defiantly like a cow whose head is fastened to its forelegs': a hamshackled English, inescapably earthbound while the neologistic Scots skies oot over the Atlantic.[31] Yet the division between the two versions is also a fictitious line of demarcation, in that the poem's 'Scots' and 'English' are more markers standing for visions of language than they are distinct languages in any stricter sense. The poems' Scots lexis, from 'Coancoard' to 'hamshakelled', is borrowed from English into Scots only to be 'translated' back into English again. Throughout Crawford's poetry, language operates as one continuous field of meaning-making that jibes at the artificial 'border' that lies between its pages. 'Fur Thi Muse of Synthesis', for example, enacts through the interplay of facing-page Scots and English versions the celebration of proliferating meaning through 'synthesis' which it also thematises:

Interkat intercommuner, intercommunin	Intricate negotiator between facts
At aw leid's interfaces, skeich	at variance, having intercourse
Tae interpone a hooch that intermells	at all language's interfaces, apt
An interverts auld jorrams tae reconduct	to startlingly interpose a cry
Aureat thru lingua franca, intercommoun	of joy that intermingles and
Thru joie-de-vivre-wurds, guttir thru	appropriates to a new, unfamiliar
dictionar	use old slow, melancholy
	boatsongs to reconduct high
	diction through common speech,
	the language of conversation
	through exclamations of delight,
	gutter through dictionary[32]

In the push-and-pull between versions, it appears on one level to be the task of English translation to impose order. The neologism 'intercommuner' | 'intercommunin' | 'intercommoun' polysemously signifies all kinds of communing, communicating, coupling, while the English breaks it down into deadeningly stable, variant meanings: 'negotiator between factions at variance', 'having intercourse', 'the language of conversation'. Yet the translational loop between the two, resisting closure, serves to remind the English of its own irrepressible openness to difference; this is what the loan words 'aureat', 'lingua franca', 'joie-de-vivre' also continue to insist on from the left-hand side of the page, making their own joyful claim about how English has never respected its own ethnonational borders. Crawford's poetry is strewn with images of synthesis, network, interface – computer semiconductors, erotic couplings, chemical reactions, and crystallographic growth – that are figures for imagining both Scottishness and the languages that express it expansively, translingually, synthetically, beyond the nation.

Unlike that of Hugh MacDiarmid, Crawford's Scots aims to open its arms to the 'gutter', as he puts it in 'Fur Thi Muse of Synthesis' – perhaps the gutter at the edge of page, beyond the printed word, but certainly the gutter out of which MacDiarmid dismissively accused Ian Hamilton Finlay of getting his Glasgow vernacular. But though referencing 'common speech', in fact Scots as everyday language is no more a concern of Crawford's work than it is of MacDiarmid's. It is collateral to the work of modernist defamiliarisation, the target of which, in Crawford's case, is really English: an English which, disencumbered from myths of its own purity, might be freed to polyamorously 'intercommune' with other kinds of language. In 'Thi Unbiggars', MacDiarmid's poetry lines up alongside Alexander Graham Bell's telephone and John Logie Baird's television as globe-travelling Scottish technologies of synthesised vernacularity:

Thru transatlantic raips	Through transatlantic cables the
Purall-leid gairfushed wi licht, ram-stam	language of the common people
an ungutenberged –	porpoised with light, headlong
Thi wey yi speik ut. Loo's ramfeezlement	and freed from the regimentation
fizzed.	of print – the way you speak it.
Aa yon toapiaries o RP English	Love's confused discourse fizzed.
Wer buzz-saa'd, thi wurld keekit thru	All those topiaries of Received
Wan wee lit windae	Pronunciation English were buzz-
	sawed, the world peeked through
	one small lit window[33]

Crawford's combinatorial language repurposes Scots out of antiquarian sources for new technologies ('raips' for 'cables'), plays alliteratively
between Scots and English ('ramfeezlement fizzed'), and neologises
English nouns into Scots adjectives or verbs ('ungutenberged', 'buzz-
saaed'). In doing so, the language remains recognisably Scottish while
at once appearing as insistently outward-moving as the technologies
it celebrates. Scots' history of linguistic marginalisation, and its consequent unstandardised or 'ungutenberged' nature, is celebrated here
as a sort of liberation, out of which a dizzyingly plastic poetic language
might be built, synthesising the debris of the past with a lexicon of the
present and the future without concern for boundaries of language or
propriety. Yet Scots itself, never mind the 'language of the common
people' or 'thi wey yi speik ut', are hardly the targets here. Instead the
aim is, ultimately, to 'ungutenberg' English as a poetic medium, to
'buzz-saa' its neat 'toapiaries'.

Sharawaggi proved critically divisive. For some, it was a vital and
liberating linguistic experiment with an unmistakeable and radical
antinationalist and internationalist politics – what Jeffrey Skoblow
calls 'an affirmation of linguistic renaissance (in the general context
of penury, inanition, and catastrophe) that subverts the very premise
of identity as a national phenomenon'.[34] Yet for others, the project
dealt flippantly with Scots, overlooking its material, cultural, social,
historical, and political realities and actually occurring diversity and
rich literary capabilities in order to perform a flamboyant exhibition
of intellectualised, postmodern linguistic knowingness. Tom Hubbard
called the collection 'sophomoric smart-assery', archly observing that
'Robert Crawford ... and the Scots language did not detain each other
for long'.[35] Certainly, Crawford's Scots in Sharawaggi is synthetic, even
fictitious: an assertion of the right to *make language up*. Reading at
the interface with this artificial Scots, he seems to suggest, a reader
may finally be able to recognise how English has never been the stable,
self-identical, bounded entity it claims to be. In this sense, Sharawaggi
aims at what Crawford calls, in his ground-breaking critical work
Devolving English Literature, published two years later, the 'barbarian
broadside' on English's authority taking place from all of its peripheries: from Scotland, Ireland, the Caribbean, Australia, the north of
England.[36] Yet both the project itself and some of the criticism it has
drawn point to the implications of linguistic performativity which, as

we will see in this and subsequent chapters, shadow other writers as well. Exposing the fiction of English's neutrality, by the adoption of other, wilfully artificial kinds of language, suggests all language is synthetic: there is no 'natural' language, no one-to-one correspondence between language and the interior self. Yet it also provides a simultaneous reminder that all language comes from *somewhere*: it all has a history, a context, a politics. In particular, at English's insurrectionary margins, the idea of all language as artifice comes up against the assumed relationship of certain kinds of language to particularities of experience – including to the expression of individual and collective, marginalised or submerged subjectivities or histories. What, then, does it mean to claim, or use, a particular kind of language – one that isn't strictly 'yours'?

Queering language

In an essay titled 'The apology of a dictionary trawler', David Kinloch recounts how his own 'interest in Scots' derived from the discovery that his grandfather, a contemporary of Hugh MacDiarmid, had written Scots poetry.[37] Yet though Kinloch studied French at Oxford and became both a practising translator and translation theorist, nevertheless he represents Scots as a language that refuses to yield an easy fluency to him. While contemporaries could write 'screeds of synthetic Scots poetry',[38] he struggled with 'connectives, personal pronouns, all the little words that get you from phrase to phrase':[39]

> [I]t seemed to me as I laboured with my dictionary, as I tried to link its words up to make poems, that there was far more poetry in them when I left them in their squat paragraphs than when they swarmed forlornly about my white page looking for some connective to hold onto.[40]

Kinloch describes Scots words as unamenable to being integrated to new structures of grammar and syntax. Their 'poetry' remains tethered to the contexts in which he finds them: to the materiality of the dictionary, to its 'squat paragraphs' and the definitions and etymologies they record.

This tethering is evident when Kinloch uses Scots words in his poetry. They exist in relation to the pages of the dictionary from which they are drawn, erupting out of them unpredictably, springing into the present while still tied to the past, dissident words resisting any efforts at assimilation. In the prose-poem 'Dustie-Fute', the Scottish narrator is surprised by the sudden appearance of the old Scots word *dustie-fute* ('acrobat') from Jamieson's *Etymological Dictionary of the Scottish Language*, arriving alone and 'bewildered' on his Paris windowsill. For this speaker, longing to belong to a new city, the word is as out of place as he is in the 'living metropolis', and no help in 'tam[ing]' its 'strangeness'.[41] What, he asks, can an old Scots word have to say to contemporary Paris? 'What can *dustie-fute* have to say to a night like this? How can it dangle on its hyphen down into the rue Geoffrey L'Ansier'? Yet this is merely until 'dustie-fute', mining its own etymology from Jamieson's *Dictionary,* reveals its history of travel into Scots via a literal translation of French 'pieds poudreux', in turn derived from the Latin 'pede-pulverosi':[42]

> He reaches deep into his base latinity, into his *pede-pulverosi* and French descendants pull out their own *pieds poudreux.* Dustie-fute remembers previous lives amid the plate glass of Les Halles … and for a second Beaubourg words graze Scottish glass then glance apart.[43]

Disruptively and acrobatically performing its 'motley' etymology, 'dustie-fute' tells a story of Scots as a European language, not necessarily routed via English; and, thereby, also of how all language is haunted by the ghosts of other language.[44]

In his 2011 essay 'A queer Glaswegian voice', Kinloch writes of his attraction to translation, as both a figure and a practice, for developing his own poetic language. He recounts his experience of growing up 'as a gay, middle-class teenager' in Glasgow in the 1970s, and limns his ambivalent orientation to the working-class voices he heard around him, alienated on grounds of both class and sexuality from 'some of the macho characteristics of Glasgow culture'.[45] Tom Leonard's poetry both attracted and provoked him – pitched against the kind of middle-class, university-educated privilege he himself possessed, and nonetheless compelling as a model of linguistic dexterity and language politics 'ghosted by the figure of translation' and dedicated to 'the accents and contestation of the inferiorities of our own local place'.[46] Despite this, Kinloch concludes, Leonard's commitment to those who 'live outside the narrative' cannot extend as far as a queer solidarity, undercut as it is by the extent to which it 'seemed to me to remain in thrall – to some extent drew inevitable sustenance from' the macho, heteronormative conventions it often satirises but cannot entirely disavow.[47] Though Leonard remained as 'a constant goad, an insulting incitement to dig beneath my own middle-class complacencies', wrote Kinloch, it was Edwin Morgan, and above all Hugh MacDiarmid – whose work he engaged with properly for the first time when living in Paris, being 'involved on a daily basis in translation activity of one kind or another', and therefore able to access the translational energies of MacDiarmid's synthetic Scots for the first time – who provided the models for the 'confected vernacular' of his 'queer Glaswegian voice'.[48] A self-consciously synthesised language, Kinloch's Scots stands for dissident sexualities and disjunct temporalities, for a travelling, translational experience of being both in and out of place in language, as the titles of some of his collections – *Paris-Forfar* (1994), *Un Tour d'Écosse* (2001) – suggest.[49]

In 'The apology of a dictionary trawler', written two decades earlier, Kinloch contrasts his own literary Scots, gleaned in fragments of lexis from dictionaries and antiquarian sources, with that of his grandfather, 'rooted' in the 'living framework' of the language. Time, language loss, urbanisation stand as barriers between him and his grandfather's language, just as class and sexuality stand between him and the Glasgow Scots of Leonard. But the point of his hoard of dictionary fragments – of his 'dictionary trawled' Scots – is, quite precisely, its elusiveness and fragility. It is a code that stands not just for the language dislocated between generations, between grandfather and grandson, or 'the difficulty of many writers of my generation who would like to write in Scots more fluently than they are able'. Even more importantly, at the height of the UK AIDS crisis and in the context of institutionalised homophobia and prejudice (of which Section 28 of the Local Government Act 1988, prohibiting the promotion of 'the acceptability of homosexuality as a pretended family relationship', is the most notorious example), the language operates as 'a kind of metaphor for the queer and wonderful tongue that is dying prematurely in the mouths of young men killed off by AIDS'.[50] A slender skein of connection between the living and the dead, Scots disrupts the English surface of Kinloch's poetry, as a figure for translation, for the restitution of loss, and as a queer lexis. As he writes of 'Dustie-Fute':

> In this poem, the old Scots word for a troubadour or jongleur, juggler or merchant, jumps out of Jamieson's Dictionary and, rather like Orpheus, sails off on the Renfrew Ferry into an Underworld of secret or suppressed languages.[51]

Travelling in the realms of 'secret or suppressed languages', like a Scottish Polari, the dustie-fute is language brought to 'boisterous', peripatetic life while always remaining – like Orpheus in the Underworld – in the presence of death. In one version of Kinloch's poem 'Gurliewhirkie', the title's gloss from Jamieson's *Scottish Dictionary* is an epigraph which looms menacingly over the poem: '*Unforeseen evil, dark, dismal, premeditated revenge. It is scarcely possible to know the origin of terms of such uncouth combination and indefinite meaning.*'[52] The poem's speaker and his lover, aboard the Renfrew Ferry, hear old Scots words come to sudden life as 'people', 'invisible brothers': '*greengown, dustie-fute, rinker, rintherout, set, abstraklous, alamonti, afftak, baghash, amplefeyst, let-abee for let-abee*'. As they 'horde' [sic] the words on the deck, 'warmed between our hands', the threat of the poem's title takes effect: 'It's then the gurliewhirkie gets to work: just as we're about to understand their throats are cut.' Cutting their throats, killing and silencing in one gesture, the gurliewhirkie overwrites its own Scots sounds with English in the consonantal echo of 'gets to work'; and the Scots words break down, dissolving, fading again, and disappearing beneath the surface of the water.

In 'The Love That Dare Not', as in 'Gurliewhirkie', dictionary trawling is an intimate act to be shared between lovers. Against the language-destroying power of the AIDS virus ('the illness … forming the syntax of your end'), the poem's speaker flings out old Scots words like spells to hold back the moment when 'the last page of this dictionary has been turned', recalling a love played out in those pages. 'I trace you back, nudging you, as I used to, from word to word':

> The days you called me *rinker*, a tall, thin, long-legged horse, a bloody harridan, I called you *rintherout*, a gadabout, a needy, homeless

vagrant, like the tongue we spoke between the sheets. Our life as
mobile and happy as the half a dozen Scottish verbs I'd push across a
page on Sunday afternoons, trying to select a single meaning.[53]

Scots in Kinloch's poems is a language lived 'between the sheets', taken
from the pages of dictionaries into the mouths of lovers, as 'vagrant'
words to be used for speaking intimacies. With unbearable hope, the
speaker of 'The Love That Dare Not' tries to hold off death's leaden
objecthood with the energy of a 'Scottish verb' and its resistance to 'a
single meaning':

> Or you might find us under *set* which seats, places hens on eggs in
> order to hatch them, assigns work, settles, gets in order; puts milk
> into a pan for the cream to rise, sets fishing-lines or nets, works
> according to a pattern, plants potatoes, makes, impels, includes,
> besets, brings to a halt and puzzles, nauseates, disgusts, marks
> game, lets, leases, sends, dispatches, becomes, suits, beseems, sits,
> ceases to grow, becomes mature, stiffens, congeals, starts, begins,
> sets off.[54]

'Set' in Scots is about the quotidian, all the ordinary textures of a shared
life; it may be an end, or a beginning. It also tells us something about
etymology itself as the means to hold open the possibility of other
meanings, or other futures.

    In Kinloch's poetry the possibilities of connection in language are
always tentative, alive to the possibility or imminence of their own
destruction. There is an elegiac aspect to this, in the context of his
consistent concern with the ravages of AIDS on gay men's bodies and
bonds of love. But there is also another kind of politics at work, in his
attention to and caution about the possibilities of solidarity in language. As he points out in his arguments about Tom Leonard's Scots,
there is no Glaswegian voice, never mind a Scottish voice, which can
stand for all, regardless of gender, sexuality, or class. Kinloch's is a
translational politics, insofar as to move between languages is the point:
to reflect on one's language from the outside is to see its limits – just
as Leonard's poetry serves as a 'goad' to probe his own 'middle-class
complacencies'. But it is also signally cautious about the colonising
capabilities of translation, or of the assumption that another's language
can readily become ours.

In 'Mamapoules', one of Kinloch's poems from *Dream State*, an imagined mutuality between Scotland and the Caribbean gives way to a reflection on the limits of postcolonial solidarity imagined through language. The poem's title is glossed as 'gays' in Barbadian Creole: the speaker and his lover, who is evidently ill with AIDS, are holidaying in Barbados, enduring the hostile stares of their fellow holidaymakers. It is only their Bajan guide, Adolphus Job, who 'laughs *with* us', his laughter a 'jab ... | against the prejudice that shipped | his forbears here' even as its simultaneous target is the homophobic prejudice directed at them.[55] In apparent recognition of both this shared experience and this shared history, it is Adolphus who finds 'in our red hair' a 'wisp' of the 'Perjonnies': Scots convicts shipped to the Caribbean

> whose Scottish
> Misdemeanour earned Atlantic
> Breakers. Not for them the Caribbean
>
> Side of sugar clubs, green
> Pitches of fast-bowling snorklers,
> Simply 'Windward parishes' of shifting
> Sand they christened 'Scotland'.[56]

The ambiguity of the 'misdemeanour' – committed somehow by virtue of Scottishness – draws this history still closer to that of Adolphus Job, and away from that of the Scottish plantocracy to which their entitled, oblivious fellow holidaymakers appear to be heirs. The speaker and his lover, 'seek[ing] a tongue | To mark this difference', find it in Adolphus Job's Creole speech:

> a dialect
> Whose English grammar's strung
> With the surf of unfamiliar
> words: some, forgotten Scots,
>
> Some African, most a bevelled
> English slurred by sun
> And contempt for tyranny.[57]

Adolphus's speech memorialises connected histories of language scattered through loss and devastation – like that of the speaker's lover, too, for whom the return journey, too rapid, like coming up from deep water too fast, 'will jinx his tongue | His English shattered'.[58] Yet the poem both offers and withholds this hope of recognition. The speaker and his lover hear Adolphus's language filtered through racist stereotypes of the Caribbean – it is 'laid-back', 'out of step with "progress"', 'aborted, exiled, | Enslaved'.[59] His language mediated through theirs, his voice reaches the reader only via scare-quoted mimicry embedded within the speaker's narrating English:

> He 'visits us de Plantation House',
>
> Points out 'de doctor-booby hummin
> At de cotton-tree', 'chats
> Down' the ticket girls.

Though the speaker and his partner 'seek a tongue | to mark this difference', reaching out towards a language that 'tugs at our | Ears', and words that are 'tiny | Genes of sound encoding | Colours, difference', their mimicry of Adolphus Job's voice nevertheless looks suspiciously like an act of colonial appropriation.[60] There is a studied ambiguity as to whether they are, or are not, included as part of 'the master race on holiday' which, in the end,

> Can't understand its own tongue
> Talking back to it:
> Black vowels, convicted consonants
>
> Queer as the politeness of their hosts'.[61]

Even Adolphus Job's solicitous politeness appears open to multiple interpretations. To holidaymakers it may be nothing more than funny (the conventional signification of Scots 'queer'[62]); to the speaker and his partner it may feel like 'queer' affirmation; but the poem can give no final answer to the reasons behind (or the authenticity of) the welcome he offers. Nor indeed as to whose word 'mamapoules' is, the title that doesn't appear in the poem – this is a pejorative term, in Bajan Creole.

'Mamapoules' does seem to long for a sense of identification and commonality, a 'laughing *with*' and together; it is suggestive of all kinds of possible contiguity across divides of language, geography, history, race, and sexuality. But there is a sense in which each seemingly simple act of communication – laughter, politeness, everyday conversation – is pregnant with ambivalence, ready to break down in the poem's final act of 'shatter[ing]'. The aspiration to solidarity is important, particularly one born from recognition of both shared experiences of marginalisation and shared histories between Scotland and the Caribbean. But experiences of linguistic peripherality are striated and differentiated by race, class, gender, sexuality, economics, history. In the end, the lovers in 'Mamapoules' are privileged consumers in the global tourism market that employs Adolphus Job, even if they are marginalised in other ways. While the practice of 'dictionary-trawling' seems to reject notions of linguistic authenticity or belonging altogether – if all language is assemblage, all language can be ours – 'Mamapoules' quietly cautions about the risks of staking a claim on another's language.

Both Robert Crawford and David Kinloch perform self-conscious acts of 'dictionary-trawling', working with unintegrated, salvaged language with no pretence to linguistic naturalism; but despite this commonality, and though friends and occasional collaborators, they nevertheless take very different approaches to the writing of Scots. In Crawford's Scots poetry, it is a language of the future, built from spare parts: travelling insistently outwards from its ostensibly Scottish origins into an international sphere. For Kinloch, by contrast, Scots is a fragile, precarious, provisional language of connection across divides that are hard to bridge. In the following chapter, I'm going to pursue another idea shared to an extent by both and by the wider project of Informationist poetry: that of language as something fundamentally provisional, detachable, composite, and performative. This is a sense of language shared by postcolonial Scottish writers who, as I'll argue through the work of Suhayl Saadi and Raman Mundair, have particular reason to see language as fully prosthetic. In their writing, not only the expressive possibilities but also the individual, social, and political implications of a 'mix'n'match' experience of language come inescapably to the fore.

Notes

1 W. N. Herbert, 'Dingle Dell', in *Forked Tongue* (Newcastle: Bloodaxe, 1994), p. 40.

2 Matthew Hart describes MacDiarmid's modernist internationalist project of synthetic Scots thus: 'to modernize Scots and Scotland from a position within the vernacular, reattaching the nation to the international sphere by synthesizing the language of the future from the debris of the past'. Matthew Hart, *Nations of Nothing but Poetry: Modernism, Transnationalism, and Synthetic Vernacular Writing* (Oxford: Oxford University Press, 2010), p. 59.

3 Eleanor Bell, 'Old country, new dreams: Scottish poetry since the 1970s', in Ian Brown (ed.) *Edinburgh History of Scottish Literature. Vol. 3. Modern Transformations: New Identities* (Edinburgh: Edinburgh University Press, 2007), pp. 190–191.

4 Alan Riach, 'Wilson Harris interviewed by Alan Riach', in Alan Riach and Mark Williams (eds) *The Radical Imagination: Lectures and Talks by Wilson Harris* (Liège: Université de Liège, 1992), pp. 37, 46. See also Alan Riach, 'Tradition and the new alliance: Scotland and the Caribbean', *Gairfish: The McAvantgarde* (1992), 135–144.

5 Robert Crawford, 'Chapter 6: Barbarians', in *Devolving English Literature* (Oxford: Clarendon Press, 1992), pp. 271–305.

6 Tom Hubbard gives copious examples of translation of poetry from across Europe and Latin America into Scots from the late 1980s to the 2000s, and of Scots poetry's correspondingly evident 'international concerns'. Tom Hubbard, 'Contemporary poetry in Scots', in Matt McGuire and Colin Nicholson (eds) *The Edinburgh Companion to Contemporary Scottish Poetry* (Edinburgh: Edinburgh University Press, 2009), p. 38. On translation into Scots, see also, for example, John Corbett, *Written in the Language of the Scottish Nation: A History of Literary Translation into Scots* (Clevedon: Multilingual Matters, 1998). For a contemporary example – Palestinian poetry translated into English, Scots, and Gaelic by leading Scottish writers – see Henry Bell and Sarah Irving (eds) *A Bird Is Not a Stone: An Anthology of Contemporary Palestinian Poetry* (Glasgow: Freight Books, 2014).

7 W. N. Herbert, 'A sense of porpoise', *Gairfish* 1 (1990), i.

8 Front matter, *Gairfish*, 1991 onwards.

9 Herbert, 'A sense of porpoise', ii.

10 Herbert, 'A sense of porpoise', ii.

11 John Corbett, 'A double realm: Scottish literary translation in the twenty-first century', in Berthold Schoene (ed.) *The Edinburgh Companion to Contemporary Scottish Literature* (Edinburgh: Edinburgh University Press, 2007), p. 337.

12 Iain Galbraith, 'To hear ourselves as others hear us: towards an anthology of twentieth-century Scottish poetry in German', *Translation and Literature* 9:2 (2000), 153–170.

13 Scottish antipathy to the Conservatives under Margaret Thatcher is a matter of record. As well as introducing the hated poll tax to Scotland a year before it was rolled out in England, the Conservative government was responsible for the decimation of Scottish industries in the 1980s, leading to soaring unemployment and the gutting of working-class industrial communities.

14 Alasdair Gray, *Why Scots Should Rule Scotland*, quoted in Daniel O'Rourke, 'Introduction', in Daniel O'Rourke (ed.) *Dream State: The New Scottish Poets* (Edinburgh: Polygon, 1994), pp. xvii-xviii. The vaunted internationalism of the *Dream State* poets took varied forms: Alison Kermack, for example, connected her experiments with working-class Edinburgh Scots to explore the complex textures and interiorities of women's lives to the influence of African American poet and playwright Ntozake Shange (p. 192). Robert Alan Jamieson's Shetland Scots poetry looked out across the north Atlantic to Scandinavian writers like Knut Hamsun and William Heinesen (p. 54).

15 O'Rourke, 'Introduction', in *Dream State*, p. xxiii.

16 Iain Bamforth in O'Rourke (ed.) *Dream State*, p. 95.

17 W. N. Herbert, in O'Rourke (ed.) *Dream State*, p. 144.

18 W. N. Herbert, in O'Rourke (ed.) *Dream State:*, p. 144.

19 Richard Price, 'Approaching the Informationists', in Robert Crawford, W. N. Herbert, David Kinloch, Peter McCarey, Richard Price, and Alan Riach, *Contraflow on the Super Highway* (London: Southfields Press and Gairfish, 1994), p. viii.

20 Price, 'Approaching the Informationists', pp. viii-ix.

21 Price, 'Approaching the Informationists', p. viii.

22 Price, 'Approaching the Informationists', p. viii.

23 Price, 'Approaching the Informationists', p. ix.

24 Richard Price, 'Atlantis', *Verse* 15:1–2 (1998), 25. Herbert, elsewhere, describes synthetic Scots as having the capacity to to 'criticize', 'include', or 'extend' English. W. N. Herbert, 'Carrying MacDiarmid on', *Chapman* 69–70 (1992), 20.

25 Price, 'Approaching the Informationists', p. ix.

26 On language and postmodernity, see, for example, Jan Blommaert, 'Language, asylum and the national order', *Current Anthropology* 50:4 (2009), 415–441.

27 Robert Crawford and W. N. Herbert, *Sharawaggi: Poems in Scots* (Edinburgh: Polygon, 1990). Crawford includes Scots poems 'fae the Vietnamese' of Chê Lan Viên, with the translator Mai Lan; Herbert includes Scots translations/adaptations of poems by Pablo Neruda and Mario Luzi.

28 As he discusses in an interview with Attila Dósa, Crawford did not grow

up in a Scots-speaking family. 'Robert Crawford: the emphatic soul', in Attila Dósa, *Beyond Identity: New Horizons in Modern Scottish Poetry* (Amsterdam: Rodopi: 2009), p. 84.

29 Kathleen McPhilemy, 'Poetry in Scots: a view from the outside', *Gairfish: The McAvantgarde* (1992), 127.

30 Robert Crawford, 'Burns Beyond Edinburgh', in Crawford and Herbert, *Sharawaggi*, p. 48.

31 Crawford, 'Burns Beyond Edinburgh', pp. 48–49.

32 Robert Crawford, 'Fur Thi Muse O Synthesis', in Crawford and Herbert, *Sharawaggi*, pp. 70–71.

33 Robert Crawford, 'Thi Unbiggars', in Crawford and Herbert, *Sharawaggi*, pp. 72–73.

34 Jeffrey Skoblow, *Dooble Tongue: Scots, Burns, Contradiction* (Newark: University of Delaware Press, 2001), p. 38.

35 Tom Hubbard, 'Contemporary poetry in Scots', in Matt McGuire and Colin Nicholson (eds) *The Edinburgh Companion to Contemporary Scottish Poetry* (Edinburgh: Edinburgh University Press, 2009), p. 37. Hubbard also (p. 37) quotes George Gunn's attack on Informationist poetry as 'just another kind of English Department imperialism'.

36 Crawford, 'Chapter 6: Barbarians', in *Devolving English Literature*.

37 David Kinloch, 'The apology of a dictionary trawler', in Crawford et al., *Contraflow on the Super Highway*, p. 5.

38 Kinloch, 'The apology of a dictionary trawler', p. 4.

39 Kinloch, 'The apology of a dictionary trawler', p. 5.

40 Kinloch, 'The apology of a dictionary trawler', p. 5.

41 David Kinloch, 'Dustie-fute', in *Paris-Forfar* (Edinburgh: Polygon, 1994), p. 30.

42 John Jamieson, *An Etymological Dictionary of the Scottish Language, Vol. 1* (Edinburgh: Edinburgh University Press, 1808), n.pag.

43 Kinloch, 'Dustie-fute', pp. 30–31.

44 Kinloch, 'Dustie-fute', p. 30.

45 David Kinloch, 'A queer Glaswegian voice', in Dimitris Asimakoulas and Margaret Rogers (eds) *Translation and Opposition* (Bristol: Multilingual Matters, 2011), pp. 129–130.

46 Kinloch, 'A queer Glaswegian voice', pp. 130, 143.

47 Kinloch, 'A queer Glaswegian voice', p. 133.

48 Kinloch, 'A queer Glaswegian voice', pp. 136, 144.

49 David Kinloch, *Paris-Forfar* (Edinburgh: Polygon, 1994); *Un Tour d'Écosse* (Manchester: Carcanet, 2001).

50 David Kinloch, in O'Rourke (ed.) *Dream State*, p. 72.

51 Kinloch, in O'Rourke (ed.) *Dream State*, p. 72.

52 David Kinloch, 'Gurliewhirkie', in *Paris-Forfar*, p. 35.
53 David Kinloch, 'The Love That Dare Not', in O'Rourke (ed.) *Dream State*, p. 74.
54 Kinloch, 'The Love That Dare Not', p. 75.
55 David Kinloch, 'Mamapoules', in Crawford et al., *Contraflow on the Super Highway*, p. 49.
56 Kinloch, 'Mamapoules', p. 49. 'Scotland' is a district in the Barbados parish of St Andrew (named equally of course for its Scottish namesake).
57 Kinloch, 'Mamapoules', p. 49.
58 Kinloch, 'Mamapoules', p. 51.
59 Kinloch, 'Mamapoules', p. 50.
60 Kinloch, 'Mamapoules', p. 50.
61 Kinloch, 'Mamapoules', p. 50.
62 The *Scots Word Book* gives 'queer, adj.' as 'amusing'. William Graham, *The Scots Word Book* (Edinburgh: Ramsay Head Press, 1978), p. 166.

3

Prosthetic language

Some of the most powerful myths underlying the idea of monolingualism have to do with ideas of the 'native speaker' and the 'mother tongue'. For the 'native speaker', language – *the* language – is assumed to be something organic, interior, possessed as by right, and used without impediment. The 'mother tongue', meanwhile, holds the idea of being born into a language, 'the site of nativity and pure origin' from which we come and to which we belong.[1] Operating far below the level of consciously held belief, these ideas about language work so effectively by appearing commonsensical.[2] As the previous chapters have already suggested, they run counter to other ways in which language is experienced: as something fragmentary, diverse, diffuse, untotalisable; as codes to be adopted, imposed, practised, lost, acquired, or invented.[3] Yet their power lies in their ubiquity, and in the pronouncements which they make – without ever seeming to – about what a language is, about who authentically belongs in language and who has authority as a speaker, as well as about language's intrinsic, self-evident, and given interiority.

As Rey Chow, for one, points out, 'postcolonial scenes of languaging' in particular serve to trouble this kind of perception. For postcolonial subjects having to move between different forms of language, whether chosen or imposed, the straightforward possession of 'a language' is not necessarily obvious at all. Moreover, questions of linguistic authority and ownership are also by definition exclusionary, and often highly racialised – such as the prevailing association of 'native speaker' English with whiteness.[4] What, under these circumstances, could any kind of straightforward idea of belonging in language possibly look like? Yet, considering the 'shock, humiliation, rage, and melancholy' that may define the postcolonial subject's enforced encounter with a colonising language, and the alienating experience of being racialised in and through language, Chow nevertheless argues (as she admits, 'counterintuitive[ly]') that this experience also confers a privileged vantage point.[5] To encounter 'language as a foreign object', with which one must 'wrestle in order to survive', she suggests, is to be able to recognise more fully the reality of language as 'prosthetic': 'Whereupon even what feels like an inalienable interiority, such as the way one speaks, is – dare I say it? – impermanent, detachable, and (ex)changeable'.[6] Just as Derrida puts it for French in *Monolingualism of the Other*, language is not something singular, which it is possible to possess – and this becomes apparent with particular force in 'the postcolonial scene of languaging'.[7]

In this chapter I examine the work of two Scottish Asian authors, the novelist and poet Suhayl Saadi and the poet, playwright, and multimedia artist Raman Mundair, both of whom explore what it means to be a postcolonial subject moving between different, chosen or imposed, linguistic forms. Each to a greater or lesser extent chooses a Scottish identification, and with it a semi-peripheral internationalism of minor languages, in allegiance with Scottish literature's inclination to, in Cairns Craig's words, provide 'resistance [to] a world system which sees small and marginal cultures as irrelevant to its logic'.[8] Nevertheless, both express a deep scepticism towards superficial celebrations of a multilingual, post-ethnic Scottishness, finding inescapable the ways in which identifications of race and class, insider and outsider, are enforced in and through language.[9] Out of this recognition, inculcated by multilingual, postcolonial subjecthood, of language as something imposed from the outside and fundamentally exterior to ourselves, comes a linguistic-philosophical view – a conviction in Saadi's case, whereas Mundair also maintains a complicated, ambivalent attachment to the idea of the 'mother tongue' – of language as prosthetic: where fully inhabiting it, owning it, or maybe even understanding it are no longer entirely the point.

In an essay called 'Being Scottish', Saadi poses his title as a provisional assemblage, its profusion gesturing towards an irrepressibly polyglot way of 'being Scottish':

> I celluloid my forehead and hastily scribble: SCOTTISH. But that
> is inadequate, so I add: English, British, Pakistani, Indian, Afghan,
> Sadozai, Asian, European, Black (-ish), Minority Ethnic, Male,
> Non-resident, 21st Century person, 15th Century being, Glaswegian,
> middle-class, Writer, Seeker, Lover, Physician, Agha Jaan, Son,
> English-speaking, Music-loving, Left-leaning. ... until I run out of
> space and time and ink.[10]

This litany of descriptors poses both challenges to conventions
about Scottishness (this Scottishness is a black(-ish) Scottishness, a
middle-class Scottishness, a non-resident Scottishness) and a riposte
to ideas of national belonging at all. Scottishness, as a roomy container
for perversity and paradox, is celebrated by Saadi for encompassing
'all things polyglot, musical and oceanic' rather than 'walls, stridency
and final definitions'. Indeed, also thinking in aquatic imagery, Raman
Mundair uses the Shetland Scots *shoormal*, the shifting space where
the sea meets the shore, to think about how language flows and connects. As both Saadi's and Mundair's writing is at pains to point out
– for instance, in Mundair's poetry in Shetland Scots – despite nativist
fantasies to the contrary, no particular form of language has an essential, autochthonous relationship to the inner self. Saadi is 'Agha Jaan'
(father) to his Scotland-born child and 'son' to his immigrant parents.
He is not an 'English speaker', with the definitional solidity of a noun,
but 'English-speaking', with the present progressive verb suggesting
something more contingent and combinatory. In Saadi's 'oceanic',
'polyglot' vision, Scottishness is made synonymous with the experience
of language as multiplicity: not of the inhabitation of whole and entire,
fixed linguistic systems, but as fragments and snatches that may be
brought into a constellation of relations, a rewritable 'celluloid' surface
onto which new meanings can be imprinted 'until I run out of space
and time and ink'.[11] At the same time, the same image can't help but
hint at tensions – between 'all things polyglot' and the affixing of labels,
between the idea of a unified identity and something more unruly and
complex, between the idea that languages and identities are there to be
claimed and the raciolinguistic ideologies that get in the way – which it
will be the concern of this chapter to consider.

'Ah'm the man ae a thoosand tongues': multilingual Scottishness and its limits

When Saadi's hallucinatory, flamboyantly multilingual novel *Psychoraag* was published in 2006, he was keen to distance himself from comparisons drawn by critics – on grounds, perhaps, of a South Asian, postmodern linguistic experimentalism – with Salman Rushdie. He had little in common, he insisted, with Rushdie's elite metropolitan, 'Oxford educated upper class English' perspective nor, for that matter, with what he termed 'the Hyper-Hip Multicoloured Multicultural Metropolitan London-Oxbridge "Liberal" Literary Mafia'.[12] His nearer affinity and allegiance, he claimed, was to Scottish writers, and particularly James Kelman, in their concern with class and capital, and the material, historical, and social dynamics of linguistic marginalisation.[13]

'Diversity', Saadi has argued, is a defining characteristic of Scottish literature, both because of Scotland's own internal heterogeneity and because of Scottish writers' propensity for 'gazing out' transnationally, which is at least as old as the British Empire.[14] At the same time, though, there are conditions which are necessary for the entry of certain *kinds* of 'diversity' into literature and, in a scene dominated by the 'London-Oxbridge "Liberal" Literary Mafia', that entry is not made any easier by being in Scotland.[15] Discussing the mechanisms by which writing gets written and published – the role of arts funding, arts councils, publishers, university curricula, and critics in shaping the field of literature – Saadi argues that too much of the literary market, for writers like him, is dominated by the demands of 'safe multiculturalism'. There is a seemingly boundless appetite for novels with 'Orientalist covers – a sari-clad henna-daubed Indian woman pirouetting on a pyramid of spices', a scattering of foreign words, literature that offers an exotic but ultimately safe sense of 'difference' that does not trouble the stability of 'normative absolutes'.[16] The commodified, obedient, and manicured performance of difference that serves to reinforce, rather than trouble, rigid boundaries of race and culture, Saadi defines 'safe multiculturalism' as a new form of imperialism: 'the systems of imperialism have merely adapted – their iron grip, on our consciousness, our labour and our purse, remains as tight as ever'.[17]

Saadi's own poetry, prose, and short stories have been published by independent Scottish publishers or in online forums, and he has

discussed his difficulties in finding publishers for his more linguistically experimental work.[18] *Psychoraag* was critically well received in
the Scottish press, but almost entirely ignored south of the border. As
Ali Smith observed in the one notable exception, a review piece for the
Guardian pointedly titled 'Life beyond the M25': 'the critical silence
that met it down south is an interesting reaction in itself to a book
about race and invisibility, voice and silence, whose central theme is the
question of whether anyone out there is actually listening.'[19] Set among
Glasgow's Pakistani community, the novel is largely written on a continuum between standard Scottish English and Glaswegian Scots while
also performing a visually and stylistically marked multilingualism by
incorporating not only Urdu lexis but also fragments of multiple other
languages, different font sizes and styles, fragments of Arabic script,
capitalisation, upside-down text, right-left reversal of English words,
shattered language fragments, as well as images and shreds of maps.
Saadi recounts how an anonymous reader for a UK publisher reported
of *Psychoraag* that 'the use of unusual words and foreign words is a
difficulty' and 'they seem to be drawn from such a broad range of languages and traditions that their impact and meaning became lost'. Of
this, he remarks sardonically:

> Signalling acute (partly sexual) anxiety at the dissolution of old
> boundaries, this kind of response is no less than fundamental-
> ist monocultural rearguard action disguised as a sensible plea for
> decorum and aptitude.[20]

Psychoraag is set in an Asian community radio station in Glasgow,
Radio Chaandni ('moonlight radio'), on its final night on air. It follows
Zaf, the station's night-shift DJ, through the last ever broadcast of his
Junuune Show (*junuune* meaning 'madness, a trance-like state' according to the novel's glossary,[21] in Urdu, Hindi, Arabic, and Persian), from
midnight to 6.00 a.m. Zaf's on-air persona is flamboyantly multilingual,
mixing Glaswegian Scots and English with a plethora of fragments of
other languages, while the novel's free indirect narration also tacks
between English and Glaswegian Scots, with a scattering of languages
including Urdu, Punjabi, Gaelic, and Arabic. The night's hour-by-hour
progression is followed chapter-by-chapter, and through Zaf's music
playlist; yet both the narrative's linear order and the sequencing of Zaf's

playlist are subject to disruption and doubling throughout the long night of the novel. The narrative travels analeptically to tell the story of Zaf's parents' illicit love affair in Lahore, Pakistan in the late 1950s, and their subsequent journey overland to Glasgow. It is also disrupted by Zaf's memories, of his parents and his childhood, but particularly of his relationships – on the one hand, with his current partner Babs, pale, blonde, Galloway-born, and 'bona fide Scottish, blue and white down to the marrow',[22] and on the other, recalling his Glaswegian-Pakistani ex-girlfriend Zilla and her descent into heroin addiction. The narrative mimics, at times, the psychically disordering effects of absinthe and heroin, both of which Zaf (probably) ingests over the course of the night. Midway through, it splits into two distinct, hallucinatory, parallel narrative realities: one Zaf remaining within the confines of the radio station DJ booth, the other journeying out through the city at night. The novel probes the operations and fissures of race, class, gender, and national and transnational belonging, through a disorientating narrative of linguistic, sensory, and experiential breakdown and recombination.

In the context of the novel's sometime emphasis on polyglot disorientation and undecidability, it is worth noting Saadi's perhaps surprising typographic concession to his eventual publisher, the independent Edinburgh-based Chroma, who insisted on the italicising of 'foreign' words in the text. In an unmistakeable statement on what counts as 'native' and 'foreign', switches between Scottish English, Scots, and Gaelic remain unmarked, while romanised Urdu, Punjabi, Arabic, and other languages are italicised, so that an endogamous 'Scottish' linguistic diversity is typographically marked off from the exogamous or 'foreign'.[23] Nevertheless, the novel's extensive glossary seems bent, at least in part, on undoing the distinction. Incorporating words and phrases from Scots and Gaelic alongside Urdu, Punjabi, Arabic, French, and others, Saadi's glossary emphasises continuities and resonances between them in a heterogeneous vision of global languaging. Reading through its pages, there is an emphasis on minor or obsolete languages (Basque, Occitan), utopian world-languages, or those that operate across (and threaten) national borders (Esperanto, Mexican Spanish). Nevertheless, as Saadi himself has acknowledged, the inclusion of a glossary also risks being read as a 'regressive linguistic-political statement', in terms of what it suggests about the status and the mode of reading of a multilingual text.[24] However, *Psychoraag* includes a series of appendices, not only the glossary but also a playlist and a discography, each of which seemingly offers a different hermeneutic key to make sense of the novel's fragmented narrative, and each of which could be said to raise as many questions as it answers. The playlist reassembles the sequence of music Zaf plays over the course of the night, which becomes increasingly obscure to both the reader and Zaf himself as the novel progresses. Yet its linear chronological sequencing, following the forward temporal motion of the narrative, has no way to account for its analepses and narrative doubling. The alphabetised discography, meanwhile, gives the superficial impression of flicking through Zaf's CD collection, yet shorn of any sense of the complex connections and associations that govern his relationship to the music it contains. Similarly, the glossary, while seeming to offer a sense of 'translatability' to the narrative, in fact insists on being read and interpreted as a commentary in its own right. In it, the pronounced but reasonably superficial multilingualism that consists in words and phrases scattered through the narrative is given in concentrated form that makes a different, though related, set of points about language. As Saadi himself has argued,

> the glossary in *Psychoraag* represents both a hypertextual, etymological exposition and a creative deviance from the psychological intensity of the narrative itself. For example, *hijaab*, the Arabic word for a woman's headscarf (but metaphysically speaking also the term for a protective spiritual 'covering') sits next to *hijerah*, the Urdu word for 'transvestite'. Similarly, *khotay ka lun* (Punjabi for 'you're a donkey's prick') nestles up alongside *Khuda hafez*, which is Persian/Urdu for 'God go with you,' and *khuserah*, the Urdu term for 'effeminate homosexual'. I did not intend to be outrageous; these juxtapositions are alphabetical and I have picked them at random. None the less, the effect is subversive and egalitarian: *Psychoraag* becomes an homage to the work of Diderot's encyclopedists.[25]

Saadi here presents *Psychoraag*'s glossary as a creative endeavour, offering a reading experience that generates its own kind of language politics by partially dissolving ethnolinguistic boundaries in favour of alphabetical contiguity. Both diverting from and reflecting on the narrative itself, it beckons the reader into a backwards-and-forwards movement between main narrative and translational paratext, with new meanings being created through relations both of 'exposition' and 'deviance' between them. Saadi paints the glossary as a heterogeneous and 'egalitarian' space of intimate juxtaposition and homophonic 'nestling', likened to 'the work of Diderot's encyclopedists'.[26] The examples Saadi chooses are obviously significant: giving an etymological account of the Arabic '*hijaab*' – a word which acts as a lightning-rod in mainstream post-9/11 British and European discourses on Islam – while at the same time provocatively underscoring a phonological similarity (and suggesting a ghostly etymological connection) to '*hijerah*'. And yet the glossary also raises discomforting questions. For one thing, how these words 'nestle up alongside' each other and seem to resemble one another, inviting readers to suspect spectral etymological relations between unlikely pairs, is itself a function of the glossary's imposition of the Latin alphabet as an organising principle. The invocation of Diderot also recalls the relationship of European Enlightenment thought to racial thinking (not least in the hands of Scottish Enlightenment philosophers) underpinning slavery and empire, notwithstanding the encyclopedists' celebratory eclecticism. Even the 'subversive and egalitarian' space of *Psychoraag*'s glossary is, therefore, perhaps not quite what it seems. Its resources include '*khuserah*', used as a term of abuse by the novel's violent, hypermasculine Kinnin Park Boys, and translated in the glossary as 'the Urdu term for "effeminate homosexual"'. A multilingual space is not necessarily, as both the novel's narrative and its glossary go to suggest, utopian, or even politically progressive.

Psychoraag's Glasgow, built on the back of the slave trade as Scotland's first city of industry and empire – therefore globally connected by definition, and a city of immigrants – is correspondingly multilingual to its foundations: the contemporary sounds of Glaswegian Scots, English, Urdu, Punjabi, Gujarati, Kashmiri, Swahili, and Pashto are continuous with the polyphony of ghostly voices from its past.[27] Glasgow is 'haunted', not just by the mythic figures of Scottishness ('the Young Pretender and all that', 'Rabbie Burns') but by the Empire that built the city, global from the start: the 'Tobacco Barons', the 'great sailin ships which had been built by the bonnie banks of the Clyde', and 'the sound of marchin boots. The seventy wars of the British Empire which had been fought with Scottish soldiery in the van'.[28] Listening to the city, Zaf can hear the long-ago Irish Gaelic songs of the navvies who built much of

Glasgow, which 'still slunk about the walls – they had been intoned so often in strange, polyphonic choruses that their notes had become inspissated into the grains', and the voices of Jewish immigrants, with their 'fading, twirling mazurkas'.[29] Reversing Herderian romantic nationalist understandings of language as an emanation of a specific place and landscape, Zaf imagines languages becoming 'inspissated' where they are spoken, their words and rhythms embedding in and altering the city's very material fabric. Saadi's Glasgow is multi-voiced, imagined via the polyphonic crackle of radio transmission; as Zaf observes, 'the whole thing wis one big hi-fi system'.[30] Both transmitter and receiver in global flows of language, the city's multilingualism is at the same time highly localised. The language of the Scottish Pakistani 'Kinnin Park Boys', for example – a gang of violent criminals and savvy entrepreneurs, whose fathers took over from the Kinning Park area's Protestant sectarian 'Orange gangs' in the 1980s – bears the traces of unacknowledged, transnational histories of working-class experience:

> They were the sons and grandsons ae the *kisaan* who had powered the buses, the underground trains, the machines of the sweatshop underwear-manufacturers. … [T]hey had clothed the lily-white bodies of whole generations of Scots and then, later, they had filled their stomachs too. You eat what you are. If that was the case, then Glasgae wis Faisalabad a hundred times over. But their sons and daughters had gone in the opposite direction and become Scots. Right down to their gangs and their dancin and their chip-bhatti *sahib* footba tops, they had sipped of the waters of the Clyde and had become cold killers. And they were swearin at him and Ruby in a mixture of Glaswegian and Faisalabadi.
> '*Maa di pudhi!*'
> 'Fuckin *gandu!*'
> 'Oh, *chholae!*'
> '*Teri maa di lun!*'[31]

The history of Glasgow's transformation through Pakistani culture is quite literally submerged – underground, beneath Glaswegians' clothes and in their bellies – while, in an equally unacknowledged set of processes, Pakistani culture has been remade through the filter of Glaswegianness. Along the way, two working-class urban speech forms, Glaswegian Scots and Faisalabad-inflected Urdu, have been transnationally recombined, together with 'stock phrases' from 'East Coast gangsta' culture and American films.[32] The outcome, however, is no kind of liberating hybridity, but a hyper-masculine vernacular in which the oppressive codes of a localised white working-class urban Scots – that of the 'Orange gangs' of Kinning Park – are mixed with Urdu homophobic and misogynistic obscenities and the 'stock phrases' of an implicitly violent, sexist, commodified strand of US culture. Thus for all its transnational, polyglot, apparently improvisatory nature, this is a form of language which splices codes that are equally regressive in compensating for marginalisation through an aggressive masculinity, and which offers a brutal riposte to any easy celebratory account of multilingualism as necessarily progressive.

Zaf himself, Glasgow-born, has 'never learned his own mother tongue', Punjabi: 'not properly so that he would have been able to con-verse in it, to construct meanin from chaos'.[33] His parents, speaking Punjabi between themselves, used English with him 'except when they were angry or upset or when they had forgotten'.[34] In this he resembles other Saadi protagonists, like Sal in 'Ninety-Nine Kissograms', who speaks a Glasgow Scots interspersed with Urdu, which he can't read, and is baffled by the English he encounters in Pakistan which is 'pretty meaningless. A kind ae jumbled-up mix ae auld colonial-speak and Amrikan Gangsta talk'.[35] The living antithesis of the supposedly linguis-tically unified, self-identical speaking subject, fully 'at home' neither in English nor in Punjabi, Zaf articulates his own self-understanding through the motif of musical sampling: 'He liked samples, felt comfort-able with them. He was a sample of Pakistan, thrown at random into Scotland, into its myths. And, in Lahore, he had felt like a sample of Glasgow'.[36] At a willed level, Zaf's is a playful linguistic polymorphism: languages are resources from which he is free to sample at will, and he self-consciously opposes monologisms of all kinds, whether the sup-posedly unassailable purity of 'standard English', the hermeticism of certain strands of Scots nationalism, or the 'people who live in *halaal* universes' as means to stave off the fear of change.[37] In his on-air radio persona, calling himself 'the man ae a thoosand tongues', he greets his listeners in a surfeit of languages:

Hi there, *samaeen. Sat sri akaal, namaste ji, salaam alaikum. Bonjour, Buongiorno, Subax wanaagsan, Nee-haa, Günaydin, Buenos*

*días, Dobro jutro, Làbas rytas, Bom dia, Mirëmëngjes, Guten morgen,
Maidin mhaith dhuit, Molo, Boker tov, Shubh subah, Kalai vanak-
kam, Go Eun A Chim.* Hiya in fifty thousand tongues! Zero wan five
or five meenuts past wan. Bet ye thought Ah wis skimmin doon a
phrase book. But, naw, you'd be wrong. Ah've goat loads ae tongues
in ma heid – thu're aw there, wagglin away, almost singin. A babble.[38]

Zaf's multilingual performance here is characteristically ambivalent.
On the one hand, branching out from Punjabi, Hindi, and Arabic, he
offers greetings in the languages of the city's immigrant communities old and new, from Hebrew to Somali, Irish to Albanian, beaming
out a vision of polyglot Glasgow over the airwaves, which, he tells
his listeners, corresponds to the 'babble' of the 'tongues in ma heid'.
On the other, Zaf's 'fifty thousand tongues' represent a multilingualism of the surface that can progress no further than saying 'hiya': a
market-friendly, unthreatening performance of Glasgow's inclusivity.
It is, in this sense, cut from much the same cloth as the rumoured new
'"Commonwealth Tartan" that anyone could wear, a pretty blue-and-
white woollen skin to wrap around yourself at football matches'.[39] His
on-air persona both ironises and at times flirts with this kind of superficial, self-congratulatory Scottish 'multiculturalism'.

Zaf revels in the flamboyant performativity of his on-air multilingualism, and draws attention to its commodified artificiality: 'Hey,
wu're multilingual oan this station', he tells his listeners: 'Polyethylene
ethnic'.[40] Even his on-air Glaswegian Scots is not strictly 'authentic':
he slips into and out of it, adopting it as part of his radio performance.
He is playfully neologistic: 'Farangoid', he portmanteau-terms his life-
style, which is too much like that of a farangi/white man to please his
mother; with deliberately doubled heresy, he coins the hybrid 'Wahabi
Calvinist' to denote a mindset antithetical to the idea of hybridity.[41]
Yet Zaf's carefully curated multilingualism and language-play does not
always seem fully under his control. When he announces 'Ah'm Zaf-
Zaf-Zaf and Ah'm yer ghost. Host, Ah mean, host', the partial erasure
of 'host' by 'ghost' lends a spectral flimsiness to his exuberant on-air
persona.[42] Later, drunk on absinthe, his English words begin a kind
of disorderly breakdown: 'I just felt a bit faint. Must be that drink.
That buggery blue stuff – green, I mean. Mean I green. Whatever'.[43]
While his omnivorous language practices serve to disrupt apparent

distinctions between authenticity and artifice, they are shot through
with the confusion, anxiety, and contradiction which mark his interior
world. His use of Glaswegian Scots, for example, is worn as a badge of
solidarity with his listeners, but it is also a protectively self-ironising
performance of class that is kept carefully separate from the rest of
his linguistic praxis. Off-air, Glasgow Scots is a source of shame to
him: inadvertently slipping 'intae a broad Glaswegian', he immediately
feels 'like kickin himself in the shins'.[44] Later he admonishes himself,
'Get yourself thegether! Get yourself together, straighten out your words,
down among the lush chords': in Zaf's mind the 'straight' words, the
proper words, are English.[45] He is keenly self-conscious about how race
is 'heard' in language – to borrow Rey Chow's terms, he is acutely tuned
to the 'tones' which signify both the visual and the acoustic dimensions
of racialisation.[46] At one point, on air, he is tempted to use a 'fake Indian
accent'; later, listening to his mother's Punjabi-accented English, he
finds 'he had constantly to resist the temptation to stereotype' her.[47]
This racialised self-consciousness about voice is further complicated by
Zaf's sense of the voicelessness of Pakistanis within Scotland and more
widely in Britain, in which Pakistan is not only seen as 'completely
differently' from the rest of Asia (notably, from India) but 'most of
the time, it wasn't seen at all'. It is 'perceived as bein a repository of
the dirty, the oppressed, the smelly, the cunning and the inscrutable',
its people 'pictured as nameless, liquid hordes that would pour in'.[48]
Above all, 'Pakistanis had remained completely inaudible. They had no
music, no voice, no breath'.[49] Zaf's internalised racism is spliced with
misogyny in his negatively distorted and often highly racialised and
sexualised view of his ex-girlfriend Zilla: 'like a tree charred black by
lightning', she 'could've been an *Asian Babe* if she'd wanted but she'd
had other demons to ride'.[50] Zilla is a silenced presence in the novel: as
Pittin-Hedon notes, she is 'a figure of the suppressed, inaudible voice',
whose final emergence into the narrative, in a violent, hallucinatory
sex scene, 'provokes an explosion of language, which scatters words
on the page as so much shrapnel'.[51] By contrast, Zaf idealises his white
Scottish girlfriend Babs as embodying a full relationship between language and subjectivity: she 'never had to think before she felt, before
she spoke. The words just came out like a river – clear and rushin and
confident. He envied that'.[52] He associates Babs with a romanticised,
putatively authentic Scottishness rooted in language and land, with

'clarsach spaces and bodhrán mountains, unchangin in their unimagi-
nable antiquity'.[53]

Zaf's intermittent fantasies about linguistic and racial purity are
projected, though, against a backdrop of languages endlessly and promiscuously recombining. The novel puts into circulation almost every
conceivable permutation of multilingualism: quotidian language-
mixing, high modernist polyphony, commodified linguistic exoticism,
official celebrations of 'diversity', in a city which has never not been
multilingual to its core. Meanwhile, at the levels of analogy and metaphor, *Psychoraag* explores radical possibilities for linguistic recombination and connectivity, particularly in relation to the practices and
formal properties of music. Sampling – in which recorded sound is
approached as a sequence of disarticulatable components which
may be appropriated, recontextualised, and layered into new sound
sequences – is a governing metaphor in the novel. Insofar as it involves
retaining dim resonances of its source recording, a 'ghostly aurality'
left over from one sequence as it is repurposed into another, sampling
both plays on and self-consciously distorts the idea of 'original' signification.[54] Sampling in Saadi's novel stands for the never-authentic, for
languages and identities fragmenting, travelling, and recombining into
complex new structures in a postcolonial, globalised present. This is
true, too, of the musical technique of counterpoint, which Saadi takes
as a structuring principle for the novel's contrapuntal narrative: counterpoint refers to the polyphonic relationship between voices that differ
from each other rhythmically and melodically, while working together
harmonically, combining into a whole distinct from, and greater than,
the sum of their parts. Both sampling and counterpoint stand as metaphors for how different forms of language, pulled into relation with
one another, become subject to constant, improvisatory recombination
into new forms.[55]

Over the course of one long, hot Glasgow summer's night, Zaf plays
an eclectic mix of vocal tracks on his radio show, with an emphasis
on unexpected fusions and connections, and spanning 'the whole of
recording history'.[56] He begins with the 1990s British Asian political
punk-electronica of Asian Dub Foundation, going on to play everything
from 1960s American psychedelic folk to the Beatles and the Yardbirds,
to Scottish folk and Glaswegian indie rock, to Bollywood playback artists,
to Algerian raï, back to the earliest, turn-of-the-twentieth-century

recordings of Indian tawaif singers. While the novel's playlist and discography give chronological and alphabetical order respectively to its
musical contents, Saadi's narrative itself is concerned with the distort-
ing, disruptive, space-annihilating, time-bending properties of sound
recording, playback, and broadcast technology. Sometimes tracks
blend into one another, overlap, or emerge in multiple versions; at
certain moments, it becomes unclear whether they are playing forwards or backwards. Music and language provide extensions of one
another in the novel's insistently heteroglot exploration of the power of
fragmentation and recombination.

The novel's interest in fragmentation and recombination over
notions of purity and wholeness plays out, too, in typographic and
visual–textual experimentation and bricolage. These strategies disrupt
the apparent linear transparency of the novel's text and, specifically,
they seem to offer a fleeting equivalence in the English text to the
experience of multilingual disruption – for example in right-left reversal which makes English conform momentarily to the directionality
of written Arabic, Urdu, and Hebrew. The association of these typographic techniques to the methods and concerns of Euro-American
modernism is self-consciously evident. At one point, for example, Zaf
plays Stravinsky's *The Rite of Spring*, a piece of music associated more
than any other with high modernism. The music is apt, in a section
of the novel that concerns itself with women's sacrifice, but the reference is oblique: Zaf himself cannot remember what the piece is called
(readers will need to consult the playlist at the back of the book to find
out), never mind what it is about. Instead, he improvises a title, calling
the piece 'Ode to my Father':[57]

> It wis classical – Western classical. Some kind of polytonal thing.
> Modern. Well, not more than a hundred years old, at most. That wis
> modern. ... The swirlin wind produced by the instruments would
> have been strong enough to have blown the iron needle right out of
> its groove, even the strongest of the dancers off the stage, the night
> clean out of its time.[58]

Zaf's response to the power of the music captures its sense of 'newness'
anew, extracted from its long-standing high modernist associations. At
the same time it samples, in the word 'iron', T. S. Eliot's famous review

of the *Rite*, with its commentary on the impact of new technology on perception:

> [I]t did seem to transform the rhythm of the steppes into the scream of the motor horn, the rattle of machinery, the grind of wheels, the beating of iron and steel, the roar of the underground railway, and the other barbaric cries of modern life; and to transform these despairing noises into music.[59]

Euro-American modernism, in other words, is subject to the kind of improvisation and recombination signalled by the raag of the novel's title – a South Asian musical form distinguished, as Saadi's glossary defines it, by the 'interplay of prescribed melodic movement and on-the-spot composition'.[60] Modernism's polyphonic models provide important intertexts for *Psychoraag*'s multilingualism (the novel repeatedly evokes James Joyce, in particular *Ulysses*),[61] but only as elements in a constellation of works of multilingual art to which it responds – for example the early Calcutta sound recordings of Armenian Indian tawaif singer Gauhar Jan:

> The impossibly distant and yet somehow knowing voice of Gauhar Jan, singer-songwriter and polylingual diva, lasered out from Deck A, through the twisted metal of the Radio Chaandni Community Asian Radio Station, out into the cracks of the dawn and beyond. 'Bhairavi'. The vocal cords of Erevan transplanted to Kolkata and the brass horns and thick wax of the Gramophone and Typewriter Company.
>
> …
>
> It seemed as though the words were issuin from several of Gauhar Jan's eleven languages at once. But, more than that, the singin style wis archaic, open throated, somethin from the deep past that lay beyond livin memory. Voices which only the insane could hear, issuin from the trees. Voices strainin with the bonded freedom of words and convention. Wild voices.[62]

Zaf hears in Gauhar Jan's singing voice something which goes beyond sense or signification. The song is incomprehensible to him not because it is not linguistic, but because it represents an excess of language – 'several of Gauhar Jan's eleven languages at once' – in which meaning is transcended by the voice as sound. Polyphonic and plurilingual to the point of incomprehensibility, it is singing which, to use Mladen Dolar's terms,

> [B]rings the voice energetically to the forefront, on purpose, at the expense of meaning. ... Singing takes the distraction of voice seriously, and turns the tables on the signifier; it reverses the hierarchy – let the voice take the upper hand, let the voice be the bearer of what cannot be expressed by words.[63]

In Zaf's interpretation, this voice seems able to go beyond language, to travel in time and space, to cross the boundaries between human and non-human nature – even if this transcendence is ultimately illusory. As he himself acknowledges, voice may 'strain' for freedom but ultimately remains 'bonded' to language.[64]

What is significant is not only the sound of Gauhar Jan's 'wild voices' themselves, but their survival and reproducibility, through the material processes of sound recording and reproduction, from 'brass horns and thick wax' to laser disc, and the capacity of radio broadcasting to transmit them, a century after their recording and thousands of miles away, 'out into the cracks of the dawn and beyond'. Radio transmission is capable, in the novel, of crossing distances of time as well as space: voices of the past cross over with songs yet to be played. Across the airwaves, sounds meld, distort, and recombine while at the same time, it is often implied, none ever truly disappear:

> Well, let me ask ye this: Whit happens tae a particular wavelength aifter a radio station hus stopped usin it? Where dae aw the wurds go? Eh? Does it jis fade away or does it refuse tae disappear? Does it grab the invisible air an take oan a life ae its ane so that, even aifter the radio station's door hus been closed an bolted, the voice goes oan?[65]

In such endless, multidirectional flows, relations of speaker and addressee, transmitter and receiver are not straightforward. Zaf, hearing his own voice 'falling deep into the night', 'over the airwaves, spiralling into the darkness of space', wonders whether anyone is actually listening; at other times, he fantasises about reversing the direction of flow: 'Ah'll put my ear up tae the mike. Don't all answer at wance'.[66]

Voices transmitted via the radio are fragile – they may be lost to static, and tuning to a particular frequency can easily slip. As the narrative travels analeptically to the moment of Zaf's parents' first meeting in 1950s Lahore, a radio emits a sub-audible hum in the background:

> Over in one corner, in the window recess, the Bakelite volume control on a wooden radio had been turned down just after he arrived. But, though it had not been switched off, it seemed to have lost its tuning because he was sure that, underneath everything, he could make out the low, dissonant sound of static.[67]

Right at the end of the novel, the same old valve radio sits in Zaf's father's hospital room:

> [Zaf] tried again and, this time, the set began to emit a low-pitched hum. A faint green light began to glow from behind the glass of the frontage, began to illuminate the tables that ran vertically over its surface and which delineated the frequency wavebands all the way from Thirteen Meters to Long Wave, from the Light Programme to Tangier to Kalundberg, Ankara, Tel Aviv, Tehran and then back again to the Third Programme. And, unmarked, somewhere out over the dark ocean, the remembered voices of Lahore, Karachi, Delhi, Agra. Most of the stations on Jamil Ayaan's radio were long defunct and the wavelengths, which they once had occupied, were now filled with the bark and chatter, the strange burzakh hyper-speak of the disc jockeys with their rhythm-heavy fanfares.[68]

This radio stands both for lost communication and for the possibility of its coming into being. The sound of static is 'dissonant': lacking musicality, made up of multiple, discordant sub-sounds. It is unsettling, unmelodious, and without meaning; yet it also signifies an open channel along which a new signal might be transmitted. On the radio voices are lost, but may also be found. At the novel's end, it is through the radio that Zaf seeks to communicate with his father, who is lost in dementia. Entering his father's linguistic realm, in which past and present merge and in which individuated selves lose their borders, he sings in his father's Punjabi and in the voice of his long-lost brother Qaisar:

> Zaf turned the volume up to full, pushed the fade switch back as far
> as it would go and then some. Leaned forwards into the microphone.
> Whispered. Sang. 'Haa ji, Papa. Qaisar hai.'[69]

These are the final words of Saadi's novel: suspended in the act of
travelling towards their intended recipient. Amid *Psychoraag*'s hyper-
trophic whirl of signs and patterns, of crisscrossing systems of meaning,
it is in fact never clear whether any act of communication is successful.
At one level, undoubtedly, the novel is driven by the urge to interpret,
translate, communicate, and make knowable – for example through
the relationship between main narrative and glossary. In counterpoint,
however, it suspends the circuits of communication: voices circulate
without being sure of reaching their hearers, or of being understood if
they do so. It also thereby, and perhaps more profoundly, dramatises a
surrender to *unknowing*, to the *inability* to understand, as a locus of a
different kind of revelation. Thus, as Zaf plays the Algerian raï of singer
Chaba Fadela, for example, and attempts to continue annotating his
increasingly illegible playlist,

> his writin resembled a hermeneutic form of shorthand, a kind of
> hidden Hebrew or mibbee a revealed Arabic. The syncopated quar-
> ter-tones of Chaba Fadela's voice cut in Kufic across the mornin,
> words transfigured from stone to music to air. It wis a duet with
> Cheb Sahraoui – a call-and-response thing – and, after a few bars, it
> became hard to distinguish between words and instrumentation so
> that the whole was like a flat-woven kilim or a rough woollen prayer
> rug. … And, somehow, this song, this risin, lyrical piece of raï, whose
> words Zaf had no hope of understandin, seemed to penetrate his
> brain, the muscles of his limbs, the lengthenin rubric of his bones,
> so that he felt, liftin inside him, the urge to dance or, at least, to
> move about, to do somethin purely physical. To abrogate his mind,
> his voice, and simply to lose himself in the Rif Berber fractals of the
> Maghrebian night.[70]

The recording Zaf plays is, first of all, a commodity in a global marketplace: Fadela's 1983 'N'sel Fik (You Are Mine)', sung with her then-
husband Cheb Sahraoui, was one of the first raï records to become an
international hit, via the Euro-American music industry's marketing
of so-called 'world music'. In common with the majority of the track's

audience as it travels globally, Zaf is a listener for whom the meaning
of its Arabic lyrics is inaccessible. Excluded from the song at the level
of linguistic signification, his experience – just as with Stravinsky's *Rite*
– dwells instead on its sounds, and the spiralling, ultimately uninter-
pretable connections between systems of meaning which they convey
to him. The textual 'hermeneutic shorthand' of Hebrew and Arabic
blends with the musical 'syncopated quarter-tones' of Fadela's voice,
whose words Zaf imagines as Kufic: an angular, calligraphic Arabic
script, carved in stone, 'transfigured' by her voice from 'stone to music
to air'. Unable to understand the meaning of the words, to Zaf the
human voices and instrumentation become indistinguishable parts of
an acoustic field which, in turn, is likened to 'a flat-woven kilim or a
rough woollen prayer rug' – material objects which, in fact, also possess
their own intricate systems of signification. The excess of meaning in
this passage, from the carving of Kufic to the rubric of bones, beckons
both Zaf and the reader towards an intricately networked decoding.
Yet at the same time, their effect on Zaf is in fact the transcendence
of meaning and a kind of sublime, synaesthetic surrender, abrogating
'his mind, his voice' and calling him 'simply to lose himself in the Rif
Berber fractals of the Maghrebian night'.

This comes close to a fantasy of what Doris Sommer has characterised as the *multilingual sublime*: an experience of linguistic and cultural difference that is truly 'foreign, even fearsome'.[71] Moving beyond
the fear or paralysis of being overwhelmed by difference, Sommer's
sublime constitutes an ethical adjustment not only towards acceptance,
but towards the pleasure of being unsettled by what one does not know
or understand: a 'disturbing sublime' which offers 'more intense effects
than does easily lovable beauty' and 'a thrill of survival close to cathar-
sis'.[72] Such a move, Sommer argues, is an ethical necessity under global
capitalism, dependent on flows of migrant labour, yet haunted by 'the
fear of losing control, given the spectres of violence, scarce resources,
or just clogged institutions'. Facing the challenge, and the perceived
threat, of difference and incomprehension, Sommer argues that by cul-
tivating a disposition of willingness, even of welcome, towards that
which one doesn't understand,

> the enormity that makes any one of us feel small might look inviting,
> if we developed a taste for the sublime. On reflection, society would

exceed any individual imagination; the complexities would excite awe and contemplation and our only partial understanding would safeguard the modesty that democracy depends on.[73]

The jumping-off point for this unsettling, vertiginous experience of the 'multilingual' is, in Zaf's case, a commodified piece of 'world music' which he is still able to experience in all of its strangeness. Multilingualism's radical possibilities are not, therefore, exclusive to an elite and rarefied field of art, nor can they be kept pristine from the operations of capital. *Psychoraag*'s insistence on staging and restaging multilingualism – in music, art, in the sounds of an ordinary street, in conversations and radio transmission, in glib celebrations of multiculturalism, in nationalist or institutionalised forms – is intentionally overwhelming. Linguistic diversity is fundamental, in the novel's imaginary, not only to the formation of individual subjectivity, nor to comprehending contemporary Glasgow, but also to an understanding of the world-system of which they are both products. In Glasgow, as synecdoche for urban late modernity, forms of language mix and combine in a constellation of ways, while opening up new ways of making meaning for the polyglot late-modern urban subject.[74]

Saadi's novel expresses an experience of language as fully prosthetic: 'impermanent, detachable, and (ex)changeable'.[75] On the one hand, Zaf experiences the alienating insight which Derrida presents us with – that not just 'the language', but any language, can never 'be mine'; on the other, he discovers the enabling capability of having access to all language, beyond any nativist claim to ownership. Faced with a whole world of language, endlessly interchangeable, *Psychoraag* suggests there may be (at least) two responses, beyond a withdrawal in nativist fear. The first is Zaf's perpetual longing to interpret, even to be able to say, everything, that manifests as a kind of madness – the paranoia of finding hidden meanings everywhere, the pandictic drive to speak in 'a thousand tongues'. The second is a kind of surrender to alterity without the comfort of a glossary: a surrender to not knowing, Sommer's 'multilingual sublime'. In Saadi's version of the global contemporary, viewed from Glasgow's semi-peripheral vantage point, incomprehension and partial understanding become, increasingly, dimensions of everyday life. Global capitalism may seek to neutralise the radical potential of rapidly recombining and shifting multilingualism but it also makes it inevitable – in ceaseless flows of migration, driven by the demands of capital, and in the global flows that accompany and drive each new technological innovation in cultural reproduction. Overturning Euro-American modernism's sometime elitism, Saadi reclaims popular and commodified cultural forms for his omnivorous multilingualism, while pointing to the marginal vantage points – on grounds of class, race, Scottishness – from which the dynamics of language, denaturalised, become most clearly visible.

Incoming: Raman Mundair's voices

In June 2019, as part of Refugee Festival Scotland, Raman Mundair produced an installation the Centre for Contemporary Arts Glasgow titled 'Sow, Reap and Slowly Savour'. Thinking about how words and foods are borne across borders, 'sown' and 'reaped', Mundair invited women of colour and women with experience of the UK immigration and asylum system to take part by making a table place setting for another woman, to participate in the sharing of a meal, and to contribute to the sound installation by reflecting on language, food, and eating.[76] In a characteristic move, this most recent project of Mundair's thinks about food and language in terms of histories and legacies, as things carried with us and as things to be shared, layered, and combined; neither fully interior nor fully exterior, like the mouth itself, where ingestion and utterance both take place. One of the resulting works of sound art, 'Mu Vich, Ajeeb Jeeb – In my Mouth, Strange and Curious Tongue', sequences and layers women's voices speaking languages including Punjabi, Hindi, Vietnamese, Thai, Malay, and English.[77] Another recording, 'Losing my Tongue', reflects on the 'emotional puzzle' of relating to languages of home which you no longer speak fluently.[78] As Mundair reflects in a Facebook post about the project:

> I lost many things through forced migration, including language – I lost my mother tongue. Schooling in the UK compounded this and in my father's house, for various reasons, I never had the opportunity to learn my languages except by ear. This meant that I often made errors. I still do. My language in/abilities give me away. These in/abilities demonstrate that I am different in every context. They speak to my split tongue, double tongued, strange tongued existence.[79]

In a motif which stretches right across Mundair's work, in repeated scenes of articulation, 'tongues' are both lost and gained. The 'melancholic' rupture and displacement associated with 'losing your mother tongue' recurs, as a loss of 'harmonious relation' to language.[80] But this nostalgic, and even nativist, way of thinking about language is encountered, nevertheless, alongside assertions of language as a 'found object' open to use without claim to pure origins or native belonging.[81]

As will probably already be obvious, 'tongue' is much more than a metaphor in Mundair's work. The body is the site where language is produced, and her poetry often finds mouths or tongues struggling to shape themselves to unfamiliar language, like the child learning English in 'Name Journeys', whose mouth must 'toil … to accommodate the rough musicality of Mancunian vowels'.[82] The child in 'Name Journeys' may resemble Mundair herself, who was born in Ludhiana, India and learned English after moving to Manchester, England at the age of five. A poet, playwright, and multimedia artist, as an adult she has lived and worked in India and Sweden, as well as Scotland, where she has largely been based since 2002 – mostly in Shetland, Scotland's northernmost islands. In the 'about the author' section which concludes Mundair's first poetry collection, *Lovers, Liars, Conjurers and Thieves* (2003), she describes her movement between languages via a characteristically uncanny image:

> My journey started in India, where I left for England in my early years, my tongue flowing with Punjabi and Hindi. Having washed up upon these shores my first generation self grew … immersed in a foreign tongue until memories of my umbilical tongue became diluted.[83]

This passage is in many ways emblematic of how language figures in Mundair's poetry. On one level, it courts a vision that rests on origins and ruptures: an original ease and facility, 'tongue flowing' with language, deposed through migration and entry into 'a foreign tongue'. On another, the 'umbilical tongue' both literalises and makes weird the idea of the 'mother tongue' as being that which connects us to the body of the mother – while Mundair also refrains from declaring which, Punjabi or Hindi, the phrase refers to. As Yasemin Yildiz points out, the idea of the 'mother tongue' grounds a whole complex of ideas which have the deepest purchase on modern concepts of language. The 'mother tongue' is primary articulation, first loyalty, one's *real* language, rooted in a one-to-one relationship between language and self that originates with the mother. As Yildiz puts it, the term 'constitutes a condensed *narrative* about origin and identity', in which '[t]he manufactured proximity between "mother" and "tongue" stages the fantasy … that the mother tongue emanates from the mother's body'.[84]

These are ideas which form a subtext to the opening sequence of *Lovers, Liars, Conjurers and Thieves*, rich as they are in images of mothers, tongues, and scenes of articulation. Poems about a young child's experiences growing up in India – rendering in English an early childhood experienced in Punjabi – proceed to poems about a child's traumatic and dislocating journey from Punjabi into English. Through the course of these poems Mundair seem to both court and disavow the idea of a straightforward relationship to original (linguistic) beginnings. In 'Osmosis', a girl-child's first expressions of sensual pleasure are rendered in an English scattered with Punjabi, just as ingredients 'fall like angels' into her mother's cooking:

> Watching sweet, fragrant
> *methay* fall like angels
> into the *paraat*,
> knowing that soon there will be
> fresh *parathay* with *methay* inside
> and *ghee* melting
> into its crevices,
> and *dhai*, served in small metal bowls
> with indentations that sing
> like steel musical drums[85]

The insertion of individual, romanised Punjabi words for food proffers a quite conventional kind of multilingualism as exotic surface effect, italicised as a flickering visual marker of difference; but these soon give way to something more complex as the pleasure of food, and the pleasure of the sounds of Punjabi, seem to anchor the child's inchoate longings which are directed towards her mother's body. In a poem full of images of things inside other things, she presses her face to the 'special place' between her mother's legs, 'where scent roots me | and leaves me with desires | of burying myself deep inside': a longing to literally return to where she's come from, back to her own original source, but also a sexual awakening in which her mother's body is that of a woman, not her own. Tellingly, the poem concludes with her mother lovingly shooing her from her lap and telling her to 'go and play': there is no judgement here, but nor is there the option of return. The speaker in 'The Folds of my Mother's Sari', meanwhile, recalls how the first milk to pass her lips as an infant was, by 'custom', 'not my mother's own':

> A neighbour took
> my sultana body
> and coaxed my lips
> to clamp aroused
> around my first object of desire.[86]

In place of an initiating moment of plenitude and oneness with the mother, or the mother tongue, the poem subversively stages its primal scene of orality as that of encounter with and desire for what is *different* from the self, and the site of a queer longing. Mundair's poems do not look back towards a lost relationship to anything that might once have been the mother tongue, but they also in any case foreclose any possibility of easy return. The speaker's father's village, revisited in adulthood, has been decimated by industrial decline and outward migration, and stands for a ravaged and disconnected family in which 'remnants of my childhood self' are 'trunked into a musty, shuttered | room' where 'the trunk has been prised | many times in my absence'.[87]

The sequence proceeds to poems that narrate a traumatic and dislocating journey from Punjabi into English. In 'Name Journeys', the act of entering into English takes place inside mouths: in the speaker's mouth, which loses Punjabi like 'milk teeth' and which 'toil[s] to accommodate | the rough musicality of Mancunian vowels', and in 'English mouths', filled by her name with a 'stumble', 'a discordant rhyme'. Both her voice and her name are stripped of 'history and memory' by the move into an alien English, into 'the Anglo echo chamber' in which one's voice comes back distorted. The loss of Punjabi like 'milk teeth' evokes it as a loss of that 'first object of desire' that originally filled her mouth with milk. At the same time, it also possesses a sense of retrospective inevitability: like 'milk teeth', Punjabi is a relic of childhood, but also like milk teeth, it has been acquired only to be lost.[88] This impermanent image recalls Chow's claim that the traumatic experience of enforced linguistic transit is one which reveals all language to be prosthetic. In 'Refractions', even more starkly, the speaker is caught between forms of language, none of which offer any kind of linguistic homeliness, in the communicative labyrinth of trying 'to assimilate'. Her internal language world is 'fused into a calcified | internal loop-de-loop', made up of half-remembered rhymes and phrases of 'broken | Punjabi jammed Bollywood Hindi'. Learning to speak English, meanwhile, is like a stripping and flaying, a 'willing', racialised self-brutalising of mouth and voice:

> I lend myself bleached,
> Willing to the bone-raw,
> Blistered voice
> Unused to dialogue

English – ironised as a set of 'survival essentials' – reduces her to empty, pleading, and stilted repetitions:

> Thank you Thank you
> Very much Very much
> Please Please
> Sorry, so sorry …
> Is this the queue?

This jagged, broken-up syntax moves the speaking 'I' towards her own dissolution: 'How do you say | I think I do not exist?'[89] Later poems retain a lingering sense of language as both embodied and racialised, of the 'bleachedness' of English. In 'The Meeting Point', for example, the speaker travels to Canada to meet her lover, who urges her to ask for a glass of water in a fast food outlet 'in my "nice British accent"'. Wryly, she continues: 'I did, and for the first time ever | my Black Britishness was rewarded'.[90]

As Mundair's poetry insistently emphasises, language is visceral, it happens in bodies: bodies articulate language, and language is experienced in the body. Countering a disembodied ideal of language as neutral medium or unquestionably inner property, she stages scenes of speaking and listening which consider articulation and audition as material, embodied acts. Experimenting with the placing of listeners' bodies in relation to the sounds of a human voice, the 2005 Leicester Art Gallery installation 'A Choreographer's Cartography' played a record-ing of Mundair's eponymous poem read in three different voices, in English and in Punjabi translation, through three different speakers at different points in the room, so that the audience heard it differently depending on where they stood.[91] In 'Apnea', the second of Mundair's 2003 triptych of short films made with the film-maker Lotte Petronella, a Scottish man's voice whispers the lyrics to the Beatles' 'Ticket to Ride'. Shorn of musicality, it becomes the menacing, self-pitying mon-ologue of a controlling lover on his partner's attempts to break free of his grasp, its whispered tones insisting on an unwelcome, closely con-fiding intimacy with the listener.[92]

In 2002, Mundair became Scottish Arts Council Writer in Residence for the Shetland Islands, and she has been based in Scotland, and off and on in Shetland, ever since.[93] Her second collection, *A Choreographer's Cartography* (2007), includes a sequence of poems in Shetland Scots, a form of language she has also used in other work – for example her contribution to *Archipelagos: Writing the North* (2014).[94] The choice of Shetland Scots, a peripheral form of a peripheral form, 'minoritised' with respect to Lowland Scots, which is literarily and culturally domi-nant over Highlands and Islands varieties even as it is marginalised by English, is a pragmatic response to local circumstances – Shetland is where Mundair lives – but also an act of linguistic prosthesis with par-ticular political implications.[95] As Roderick Watson observes of poets who choose to write in an adopted Scots or Gaelic, such acts 'may have local roots', but also embody a wider minoritarian politics, as a wilful gesture of resistance to 'the increasingly global domination of English':

> There may be a more intimate motivation, too, whereby the shift to another language has also led to an untying of the tongue. … It is language, after all, that creates the subject, not vice versa, and to write in Gaelic or Scots (given that the medium is also the message) is to commit to a vision of self and the world that is simultaneously asser-tive and provisional, even perhaps embattled, and always already under threat of neglect, erasure or even extinction. And for some writers this has been like coming home.[96]

For Mundair, the estranging move into Shetland Scots has a prece-dent in the estranging move into English and, before that even, the estranging move into Punjabi – 'coming home' to a kind of language that is as much home as any other. The move enacts a self-translation away from English's global dominance into a linguistically minoritarian identity, while at the same time challenging Shetland Scots' associations with linguistic nativism by an assertive act to embrace the provisional and estranged nature of all language.

In the opening short poem prelude to her sequence concerned with Shetland in *A Choreographer's Cartography*, '60° North', Mundair writes:

> You swallowed my tongue
> left me *fantin*,
> without voice,
>
> Now I look
> for my tongue
> in other people's mouths.

Read against Mundair's earlier work, the poem invites reading in relation to the linguistic dislocation that takes place in the 'Anglo echo chamber' and stakes a postcolonial claim on the right to new tongues. But it is also a reflection on the nature of linguistic commons – as well as a comment on the polymorphous erotics of multilingualism, or the intimacy of using another('s) language, for who but a lover could 'swallow … my tongue'? The speaker is left *'fantin'*, Shetland Scots for hungry or starving: a hunger that craves new languages to break its silence. Playing on orality in all its senses to consider language's intrinsically interactional nature, Mundair coins an uncanny image of linguistic collectivity in which one's tongue has to be found 'in other people's mouths'. Thus the poem is suggestive of what may broadly be said about language – that it is both highly intimate and yet never strictly ours, in the sense that it always comes from somewhere else – as well as asserting the poet's particular right, as one already alienated from her 'own' language, to escape silence by adopting new tongues.

Linguistic nativism, against which the above poem asserts its right to claim a new tongue, is by no means the sole preserve of majoritarian languages and cultures. As Mundair reflects in her 2014 project *Incoming: Some Shetland Voices*, notwithstanding the declining use of Shetland Scots – already a minor form of a minor language, spoken on

islands whose population growth is largely due to in-migration, predominantly from outside Scotland – there is hostility towards 'the idea
of people who were not born in Shetland learning and speaking dialect
themselves'. Writing linguistic nativism right into the body itself, some
even go so far as to suggest that 'folk without Shetland genes are phys-
iologically incapable of producing Shetland words'.[97] Shetland terms
for those who were not born on the islands include not only 'incomers'
but also 'soothmoothers' – a reference to the literal entry point to the
islands, through the south mouth to Lerwick, but also by implication
a southern speaker, a linguistic outsider. *Incoming* sets 'the image that
Shetland projects, and that most Shetlanders convey, of the islands as
a kind, friendly, welcoming place' against pervasive prejudices against
'incomers', including the ingrained assumption that to be a Shetlander
is to be white. Using archaeological, written, and photographic records
to consider the six-thousand-year history of 'incomers' to Shetland,
and recording testimony from contemporary Shetlanders originating
from countries including Bulgaria, China, Burma, Slovenia, and Sri
Lanka, the project asserts theirs *as* 'Shetland voices', a challenge to
Shetland as a linguistically homogeneous and distinct, 'mono-cultural
"white" space'.[98]

The poem sequence 'Stories Fae Da Shoormal' in '60° North', written
in Shetland Scots, was inspired, Mundair has said, by the photographs
of unknown Shetlanders in the Shetland Museum and Archive which
she includes, too, in the *Incoming* project.[99] The *shoormal* of the title is
the island space where the sea meets the shore: that part of the island
which is constantly shape-shifting, open to the sea's flows. The sequence
has five numbered sections, distinct but connected through echoes and
repetitions, each an address by an anonymous speaker (perhaps the
same speaker, perhaps different speakers). Often speaking as aban-
doned lovers, it is unclear whether these are men or women, black
or white, born Shetlander or 'incomer'. In the first section, a speaker
reflects on the dreaming dark of a Shetland night and her sense of
self-presence within it, while the sound of Shetland Scots reflects the
distant cracking ice of the Arctic tundra:

> Unlichted,
> Unshadowed, I canna see
> Mysel, bit I kyen, Ah'm dere. Un-alon,

Awaash o me, awaash o midnicht
Blue. Da skies waash ower me.

Da ice cracks, da Arctic tundra
Shivers, readjusts hits spines,
Sends secret messages idda dialect
Tae hits nerve-endins in Shetlan.
Dir ley lines here
Vibratin, crackin – electric.

On the one hand, this poem appears to endorse the romantic ideal of Shetland's language as an emanation of its landscape, which Mundair plays on, for example, in the onomatopoeic doubled vowel of 'awaash', and a sense of mythic island time. Nevertheless, there is a contradictory sense of flux whereby the island and its 'dialect' are defined by the living, constant 'readjustments' of a world beyond. Correspondingly, the language Mundair uses is not a strictly realised literary Shetland Scots but one which is orthographically and lexically innovative, as in the neologism 'Un-alon'. Through the sequence, Mundair seems at times to teeter on the brink of a mythologised Shetland, but references to the tankers which pass the islands, a reminder of its economic dependence on North Sea oil revenues, or to the camera which has captured the images of the people she gives voice to, recall the present-ness of the islands and their relationship to a material and technological culture. In the final section, the speaker addresses a lover who has abandoned her, the island, and its language – recalling the island's long history, like so many other rural areas, as 'a place of emigration, not immigration'.[100] The town has been 'no big enuff fur dee | ta lose desel', she tells him, and in order to escape he has 'lassoed dy tongue | shapeit him intae a "sooth mooth"', until 'Noo, riggit in black | like a *Reservoir Dug*, du | veils desel in da English | wroucht, wry wit, while | aroond dee shadows | hing fae nooses'. The reference to *Reservoir Dugs* marks the island not as either timeless or remote, but part of a global cultural marketplace, and English as not only the language of London's dominance, but also of US cultural imperialism, even as its phonetic spelling – *Reservoir Dugs* – is a striking visual/acoustic reminder of how all cultural forms are susceptible to remaking through Shetland Scots. Nevertheless, to the speaker, the addressee's adopted, instrumentalised English 'wry wit' – distanced, knowing – is ringed around by 'shadows' which 'hing fae nooses'. English, she insists, is not only the language of a dead love affair, but a deathly language. And in the section of poems which follows, 'Terra Infirma', this deathliness does indeed reveal itself in the brutalities of Britain and the US in the context of the invasion of Iraq and the 'War on Terror'. In these poems, English is the language that provides legitimacy and cover – in phrases like 'shock and awe' – for new forms of imperialism.[101] In 'Piercing Flesh', it is the UK asylum system which is the monologic, exclusionary exemplar of language in the service of state violence. The poem addresses Abas Amini, an Iraqi Kurdish poet and refugee who fled to Britain after escaping prison in Iraq. Amini had been granted asylum, but the UK Home Office decided to appeal the decision and to try to deport him back to Iraq.[102] In response, Amini sewed his eyes, ears, and mouth closed, in protest over his own case and at the UK government's policies on asylum. In his written statement, which Mundair uses as her epigraph, Amini represented his actions as an act of prosthetic signification, in a context where meaningful linguistic communication in the form of testimony has proven useless: 'I sewed my eyes so others could see, I sewed my ears so others could hear, I sewed my mouth to give others a voice.'[103] In Mundair's poem, it is his sewn lips themselves that release a deafening torrent of sound:

> And with your mouth sewn shut
> what a song
> you sang, what a poem
> to pin back deaf ears – what a noise,
> what a cacophony,
> and what a silence
> to greet it.[104]

Amini's 'song', 'poem', 'noise', 'cacophony', untranslatable into the monologic language of authority, are met by 'silence'. The rest of the sequence is scattered with more minor or intimate scenes of difficult and failed communication, where language itself is an unsteady 'terra infirma' on which to rest. 'Detox', for example, reflects the seductive power of digital communication to create illusory intimacy via the addictive thrill of 'words || I read too much into'.[105]

Language is a visceral, embodied experience in Mundair's poetry: mouths long for new tongues, form themselves with pain or delight around the difficult shapes of new sounds. On the one hand, her work claims affinity with the complex and politically charged negotiations of belonging and not-belonging in language that are distinctive of certain strands of black British poetry. On the other hand, she places herself in the company of other contemporary Scottish poets who reflect on language's prosthetic nature and choose to write in adopted languages, such as Jen Hadfield, another 'incomer' who writes using Shetland Scots. Mundair's work is overwhelmingly concerned with the body as the place of articulation, pointing to what happens to bodies using language, and the relationship between how speakers are seen and how they are heard as language emerges from their raced, sexed bodies. What Chow calls 'the lingering work of language in the form of skin tones and sound effects' is evident when it takes travelling as far as Canada to be recognised for your 'nice British accent'.[106] Underlying all of this is no original experience of fully inhabiting language: language is what is other to ourselves, and it is on the basis of this insight that Mundair asserts the freedom to choose her language, as in her Shetland Scots poetry. In choosing, she draws a connection between this highly localised context and other experiences of linguistic marginality, working to uncouple the essentialist association of Shetland Scots with some kind of by-birth Shetlandness, insisting on it as a language as open as any other to the 'incomer'. However, she has recently observed that she still struggles to be recognised as a Shetland poet, or a Shetlander, and that it is a particular property of British rural landscapes to continue to be imagined as white.[107]

Language as something lost and gained is a theme to which Mundair returns in uncanny images of umbilical, divided, strange tongues. Locating language in an undecidable inside/outside position – neither fully internal nor external, like the mouths in which she persistently locates it – she pivots between a conviction in language as prosthesis, and the persistent affective force of a lost and irretrievable 'mother tongue'. In Suhayl Saadi's writing this ideal is inventively and unsettlingly exploded, as in *Psychoraag*, where Zaf, who 'never learned his mother tongue', also has to resist the temptation to mimic his own mother's voice. For Mundair, a complex of desire, loss, and longing is held in the displacement of the fantasy that first language is acquired with the 'mother's milk' by the image of taking that first milk from another.[108] Thinking about language in ways that are attuned to 'skin tones and sound effects', both writers dwell on the visceral, embodied experience of language and of being a speaker, as well as the fully detached and prosthetic disembodiment of the voice through sound recording and transmission. And, through enforced confrontation with language's impermanence, unfixity, and interchangeability, each tries to parse out the enabling potentialities of linguistic unbelonging.

Notes

1 Yasemin Yildiz, *Beyond the Mother Tongue: The Postmonolingual Condition* (New York: Fordham University Press, 2012), p. 67.
2 On the operations of monolingualism as an ideology, and its naturalisation as common sense, see David Gramling, *The Invention of Monolingualism* (London and New York: Bloomsbury, 2016).
3 For key critical accounts of language as a practice see Sinfree Makoni and Alastair Pennycook (eds) *Disinventing and Reconstituting Languages* (Clevedon: Multilingual Matters, 2007); Alastair Pennycook, 'English as a language always in translation', *European Journal of English Studies* 12:1 (2008), 33–47; Alastair Pennycook and Emi Otsuji, *Metrolingualism: Language in the City* (London and New York: Routledge, 2015).
4 As Thomas Bonfiglio argues, both 'mother tongue' and 'native speaker' are concepts underpinned by 'submerged racial, ethnic, and gender ideologies' all the more effective for remaining largely unspoken. Thomas Paul Bonfiglio, *Mother Tongues and Nations: The Invention of the Native Speaker* (Berlin and New York: Mouton De Gruyter, 2010), p. 3. For further critique of the concept of the 'native speaker' see Rey Chow, *Not Like a Native Speaker: On Languaging as a Postcolonial Experience* (New York: Columbia University Press, 2014), pp. 57–60. On raciolinguistics – theorising the mutual imbrication of language and race – see H. Samy Alim, John R. Rickford, and Arnetha F. Ball (eds) *Raciolinguistics: How Language Shapes Our Ideas About Race* (New York: Oxford University Press, 2016); Jonathan Rosa, *Looking Like a Language, Sounding Like a Race: Raciolinguistic Ideologies and the Learning of Latinidad* (New York: Oxford University Press, 2017).
5 Chow, *Not Like a Native Speaker*, p. 14.
6 Chow, *Not Like a Native Speaker*, pp. 14–15.
7 Jacques Derrida, *Monolingualism of the Other; or, The Prosthesis of Origin*, trans. Patrick Mensah (Stanford: Stanford University Press, 1998).
8 Cairns Craig, 'Beyond reason: Hume, Seth, Macmurray and Scotland's postmodernity', in Eleanor Bell and Gavin Miller (eds) *Scotland in*

Theory: Reflections on Culture and Literature (Amsterdam and New York: Rodopi, 2004), p. 259.

9   Berthold Schoene discusses the idea of 'postethnic' Scottishness in 'Going cosmopolitan: reconstructing "Scottishness" in post-devolution criticism', in Berthold Schoene (ed.) *The Edinburgh Companion to Contemporary Scottish Literature* (Edinburgh: Edinburgh University Press, 2007), p. 13.

10 Suhayl Saadi, 'Being Scottish', in Tom Devine and Paddy Logue (eds) *Being Scottish: Personal Reflections on Scottish Identity Today* (Edinburgh: Polygon, 2002), p. 240.

11 Saadi, 'Being Scottish', p. 240.

12 Anna Battista, 'Facts and fictions: interview with writer Suhayl Saadi', *Erasing Clouds* www.erasingclouds.com/0714saadi.html; Suhayl Saadi, '*Psychoraag*: the gods of the door', *Spike Magazine*, n.d., www.spikemagazine.com/0206-suhayl-saadi-censorship-in-the-uk.php.

13 Nick Mitchell, 'Interview – Suhayl Saadi: *Psychoraag*', *Spike Magazine*, 1 April 2006. www.spikemagazine.com/0406-suhayl-saadi-psychoraag-in terview.php.

14 Suhayl Saadi, 'Infinite diversity in new Scottish writing'. http://asls.arts. gla.ac.uk/SSaadi.html.

15 Saadi, 'Infinite diversity in new Scottish writing'.

16 Suhayl Saadi, 'In Tom Paine's kitchen: days of rage and fire', in Berthold Schoene (ed.) *The Edinburgh Companion to Contemporary Scottish Literature* (Edinburgh: Edinburgh University Press, 2007), pp. 28–33. The most influential critique of this kind of linguistic exoticism remains Graham Huggan, *The Postcolonial Exotic: Marketing the Margins* (London and New York: Routledge, 2001).

17 Saadi, '*Psychoraag*: the gods of the door'.

18 Saadi's 2001 short story collection *The Burning Mirror*, for example, written in Glaswegian Scots mixed with standard Scottish English and Urdu, was published by independent Edinburgh publisher Polygon. He also publishes essays and other writing online, on his own and a range of other websites. 'Glaswegian-ish' ('first') and English ('second') versions of his short story 'Extra Time in Paradise', for example, are published online as part of the Stirling University/Newcastle University *Devolving Diasporas* project. www.devolvingdiasporas.com/writing_02.htm.

19 Ali Smith, 'Life beyond the M25', *Guardian*, 18 December 2004.

20 Saadi, 'In Tom Paine's kitchen', p. 31.

21 Suhayl Saadi, *Psychoraag* (Edinburgh: Chroma, 2004), p. 425.

22 Saadi, *Psychoraag*, p. 30.

23 Mitchell, 'Interview'.

24 Saadi, 'In Tom Paine's kitchen', p. 29.
25 Saadi, 'In Tom Paine's kitchen', pp. 29–30.
26 Saadi's glossary self-consciously recalls Diderot's encyclopedia not least in its refusal of the distinction between sacred and secular, an elision Doris Sommer has termed as itself a kind of 'bilingualism'. Doris Sommer, *Bilingual Aesthetics: A New Sentimental Education* (Durham, NC and London: Duke University Press, 2004), p. xx.
27 Saadi, *Psychoraag*, p. 60.
28 Saadi, *Psychoraag*, pp. 21, 199.
29 Saadi, *Psychoraag*, pp. 271, 233.
30 Saadi, *Psychoraag*, p. 75.
31 Saadi, *Psychoraag*, pp. 242–243.
32 Saadi, *Psychoraag*, p. 253.
33 Saadi, *Psychoraag*, p. 246.
34 Saadi, *Psychoraag*, p. 162.
35 Suhayl Saadi, *The Burning Mirror* (Edinburgh: Polygon, 2001), p. 3.
36 Saadi, *Psychoraag*, p. 227.
37 Saadi, *Psychoraag*, p. 199.
38 Saadi, *Psychoraag*, p. 66.
39 Saadi, *Psychoraag*, p. 109.
40 Saadi, *Psychoraag*, p. 384.
41 Saadi, *Psychoraag*, pp. 170, 58. Zaf here echoes the poet Imtiaz Dharker – a contemporary, and important point of comparison with Saadi – who has called herself a 'Scottish Muslim Calvinist'. James Procter, 'Imtiaz Dharker', *British Council* (2010). https://literature.britishcouncil.org/writer/imtiaz-dharker.
42 Saadi, *Psychoraag*, p. 60.
43 Saadi, *Psychoraag*, p. 260.
44 Saadi, *Psychoraag*, p. 70.
45 Saadi, *Psychoraag*, pp. 104–105.
46 Chow, *Not Like a Native Speaker*, p. 8.
47 Saadi, *Psychoraag*, pp. 132, 274.
48 Saadi, *Psychoraag*, p. 73.
49 Saadi, *Psychoraag*, p. 74.
50 Saadi, *Psychoraag*, p. 90.
51 Marie-Odile Pittin-Hedon, *The Space of Fiction: Voices from Scotland in a Post-Devolution Age* (Glasgow: Scottish Literature International, 2015), pp. 91–92.
52 Saadi, *Psychoraag*, p. 12.
53 Saadi, *Psychoraag*, p. 31.
54 Russell Potter, *Spectacular Vernaculars: Hip-Hop and the Politics of*

Postmodernism (New York: State University of New York Press, 1995), pp. 35–36.

55 Given my subsequent discussion of T. S. Eliot, it is worth noting his concern, in *Four Quartets*, with finding organisational parallels to counterpoint: 'the properties in which music concerns the poet most nearly, are the sense of rhythm and the sense of structure'. T. S. Eliot, 'The music of poetry' (1942) in *Selected Prose of T. S. Eliot*, ed. Frank Kermode (New York: Harcourt Brace, 1988), p. 113.

56 Saadi, *Psychoraag*, p. 5.

57 Saadi, *Psychoraag*, p. 283.

58 Saadi, *Psychoraag*, p. 282.

59 T. S. Eliot, 'London letter', *The Dial* 71:4 (1921), 452–455.

60 Saadi, *Psychoraag*, p. 428.

61 This is mentioned, for example, in Pittin-Hedon, *The Space of Fiction*, p. 84.

62 Saadi, *Psychoraag*, pp. 345–346.

63 Mladen Dolar, *A Voice and Nothing More* (Cambridge, MA and London: MIT Press, 2006), p. 30.

64 See Dolar, *A Voice and Nothing More*, p. 31.

65 Saadi, *Psychoraag*, p. 378.

66 Saadi, *Psychoraag*, pp. 8, 2.

67 Saadi, *Psychoraag*, pp. 51–52.

68 Saadi, *Psychoraag*, p. 418.

69 Saadi, *Psychoraag*, p. 419.

70 Saadi, *Psychoraag*, pp. 125–127.

71 Sommer, *Bilingual Aesthetics*, p. xxiv.

72 Sommer, *Bilingual Aesthetics*, p. xxiv.

73 Sommer, *Bilingual Aesthetics*, pp. 128–129.

74 Jan Blommaert, Sirpa Leppänen, and Massimiliano Spotti, 'Endangering multilingualism', in Jan Blommaert, Sirpa Leppänen, Päivi Pahta, and Tiina Räisänen (eds) *Dangerous Multilingualism: Northern Perspectives on Order, Purity and Normality* (Basingstoke: Palgrave, 2012), p. 9. See also, for example, Jens Normann Jørgensen, M. S. Karrebæk, L. M. Madsen, and J. S. Møller, 'Polylanguaging in superdiversity', *Diversities* 13:2 (2011). www.mmg.mpg.de/fileadmin/user_upload/Subsites/Diversities/Journals_2011/2011_13–02_art2.pdf.

75 Chow, *Not Like A Native Speaker*, pp. 14–15.

76 Raman Mundair, 'Sow, Reap and Slowly Savour', Centre for Contemporary Art Glasgow, June 2019. www.cca-glasgow.com/programme/raman-mundair-sow-reap-and-slowly-savour-workshop.

77 Raman Mundair, 'Mu Vich, Ajeeb Jeeb – In My Mouth, Strange and

Curious Tongue'. https://soundcloud.com/user-724492265/mu-vich-a
jeeb-jeeb?fbclid=IwAR2eicrgvp_kpz_Kgbnpq3paURkDb1qF-OP15zywk
K3SFt55K11ZElHK6Fg.

78 Raman Mundair, 'Losing my Tongue', Soundcloud. https://soundcloud.
com/user-724492265/losing-my-tongue-raphie?fbclid=IwAR38cydV9
QXh66TuKV6EFLWlotsJzKCYak2jro4Fv1I8ScN-WxW4TrfHZ1g.

79 Raman Mundair, 'Mu Vich, Ajeeb Jeeb – In My Mouth, Strange and
Curious Tongue'. www.facebook.com/ramanmundair/.

80 Chow, Not Like A Native Speaker, p. 47.

81 Chow, Not Like A Native Speaker, pp. 51–53.

82 Raman Mundair, 'Name Journeys', in Lovers, Liars, Conjurers and Thieves
(Leeds: Peepal Tree Press, 2003), p. 16.

83 Raman Mundair, 'About the author', in Lovers, Liars, Conjurers and
Thieves (Leeds: Peepal Tree Press, 2003).

84 Yildiz, Beyond the Mother Tongue, p. 12.

85 Raman Mundair, 'Osmosis', in Lovers, Liars, Conjurers and Thieves, p. 14.

86 Raman Mundair, 'The Folds of my Mother's Sari', in Lovers, Liars,
Conjurers and Thieves (Leeds: Peepal Tree Press, 2003), p. 12.

87 Mundair, 'The Folds of my Mother's Sari', p. 12.

88 Mundair, 'Name Journeys', p. 16.

89 Raman Mundair, 'Refractions', in Lovers, Liars, Conjurers and Thieves,
pp. 17–18.

90 Raman Mundair, 'The Meeting Point', in Lovers, Liars, Conjurers and
Thieves, p. 33.

91 A summary of 'A Choreographer's Cartography', arising out of Mundair's
collaboration with the artist Sean Clark, can be found at: www.seanclark.
me.uk/achoreographerscartography.

92 Raman Mundair and Lotte Petronella, 'Apnea'. www.youtube.com/
watch?v=dWmWGCDU5ak&t=277s.

93 In 2013–14, she again became Leverhulme Trust Writer in Residence for
Shetland; this is how the Incoming project came about.

94 Raman Mundair, 'The Rose of the Rock', in Linda Andersson Burnett,
Archipelagos: Poems from Writing the North ([n.p.]: AHRC/University of
Edinburgh, 2014). www.writingthenorth.com/wp-content/uploads/2014/
04/archipelagos-for-download.pdf.

95 Christopher Whyte, 'Nationalism and its discontents: critiquing Scottish
criticism', in J. Derrick McClure, Karoline Szatek-Tudor, and Rosa E.
Penna (eds) 'What Countrey's This? And Whither are we Gone?': Papers
Presented at the Twelfth Conference on the Literature of Region and Nation
(Newcastle: Cambridge Scholars Publishing, 2010), p. 27.

96 Roderick Watson, 'Living with the double tongue: modern poetry in Scots',

in Ian Brown (ed.) *The Edinburgh History of Scottish Literature. Volume 3. Modern Transformations: New Identities (from 1918)* (Edinburgh: Edinburgh University Press, 2007), p. 164.

97 Raman Mundair, 'The Incoming project', in Raman Mundair (ed.) *Incoming: Some Shetland Voices* (Lerwick: Shetland Museum and Archives, 2014), p. 17. www.shetlandamenity.org/the-incoming-project.

98 Raman Mundair, 'The Incoming project', p. 13.

99 Mundair discusses this as part of her dialogue with Penny Fielding about 'The Rose of the Rock'. www.writingthenorth.com/dialogues/rose-of-the-rock/.

100 Ian Tate, 'Mementoes of past lives', in Raman Mundair (ed.) *Incoming: Some Shetland Voices* (Lerwick: Shetland Museum and Archives, 2014), p. 28.

101 Raman Mundair, 'Blood Season', in *A Choreographer's Cartography* (Leeds: Peepal Tree Press), p. 31.

102 On Abas Amini's case, see Catherine Adams and Tania Branigan, 'Refugee sews up his lips, eyes and ears', *Guardian*, 27 May 2003. www.theguardian.com/uk/2003/may/27/immigration.immigrationpolicy; Tania Branigan, 'Kurdish poet finds a voice', *Guardian*, 31 May 2003. www.theguardian.com/uk/2003/may/31/immigrationandpublicservices.immigration.

103 Abas Amini, 2003; epigraph to Raman Mundair, 'Piercing Flesh', in *A Choreographer's Cartography*, p. 32.

104 Raman Mundair, 'Piercing Flesh', in *A Choreographer's Cartography*, p. 32.

105 Raman Mundair, 'Detox', in *A Choreographer's Cartography*, p. 33.

106 Chow, *Not Like A Native Speaker*, p. 14.

107 Raman Mundair, 'Your land is my land: perspectives from an immigrant', *Bella Caledonia*, 5 January 2018. https://bellacaledonia.org.uk/2018/01/05/your-land-is-my-land-perspectives-from-an-immigrant/.

108 H. Weinrich, 'Chamisso', quoted in Yildiz, *Beyond the Mother Tongue*, p. 203.

4

'Passing my voice into theirs'

In an increasingly diverse world, it is vital that we strengthen both
our sense of community belonging and the civic and political dimensions of British citizenship. In particular, we intend to offer language
teaching and light touch education for citizenship for those making
a home in the UK – with a view to a simple examination for citizenship applicants ... This will strengthen the ability of new citizens to
participate in society and to engage actively in our democracy. This
will help people understand both their rights and obligations as citizens of the UK, and strengthen the bonds of mutual understanding
between people of diverse cultural backgrounds. It will also help to
promote individuals' economic and social integration.

> 'Secure borders, safe haven: integration with diversity in
> modern Britain' UK Government White Paper, February
> 2002[1]

In terms of wanting people, encouraging people, to be part of British
society, they can't do that unless they have more than an understanding of English. If we don't get our resident population with
an understanding of English, then they become a sub-class that is
virtually unemployable or are stuck in a ghetto. We should not be
turning people out of our schools who aren't able to speak English
like a native.

> Eric Pickles, 9 March 2012[2]

Just for kicks I was well in with the English race,
my skin matched the beef of their ruddy skin
as one by one a walk-in sing-along of familiar faces

from the lark-about days of school chucked back chunks
of smoke to reveal their manhood, I shouldered the bulk
as they broadened like brick houses to broadly take me in,
we plundered up gulps of golden rounds for the great game,
united at our local, we booed at the mounted screen –
at the face of the anthem'd foreigner when we were at home.
Then we chanted with heart and soul for God and Queen!
I was one of us, at ease, so long as I passed
my voice into theirs – I didn't *bud-bud ding-ding*
on myself for dropping the asylum side to sign up
for the bigger picture. I wasn't Black or Latin or managed
by a turbaned ghost. No distant land forever
with rights to my name … At an own goal, I pitched up,
caught my mother on the screen, as keeper, in our net
gloving the ball with lard, from the Mutiny, launching it
into my hands, ticking, at the end of the day, as I walked alone
to my wife – outside on a sideline of frost, kicking off:
D-d-doze err shrubby peeepalll … !!!
D-d-deyy sprayyy all um ourrr valll … !!!
Venn hmmm veee g-go bbackkk … !!!
Lookk lookk ju nott British ju rrr blackkk … !!!
                    Daljit Nagra, 'The Man Who Would Be English!'[3]

In March 2012, the British Government's Communities Secretary, Eric
Pickles, announced the launch of a new 'integration strategy', 'encouraging' people from ethnic minority communities to speak English 'like
a native'. Pickles's pronouncement was couched in a liberal language
of inclusion and opportunity. Yet still, his invocation of a 'sub-class',
'unemployable or … stuck in a ghetto', undercut this apparent liberal-
ity by seeming to imply minority communities' culpability for their
own exclusion and revealed, uncommonly clearly, the way in which
arguments about language refract ideas about race, class, and national
belonging. This 'integration strategy' initiative might have been new,
but Pickles's pronouncement also sounded oddly familiar, as well it
might, being drawn from a long-established British political lexicon
associating languages other than English with a range of social ills and
threats to national cohesion. Over the preceding two decades, much of
the sense of menace once associated with 'black Englishes' and African
Caribbean inner-city youth had been transposed onto other, newer
immigrant communities, and other languages – particularly South

Asian languages – had supplanted Caribbean creole forms in focalising and making speakable in the realm of language anxieties about national integrity and belonging that have much to do with race, class, and ethnicity. As Adrian Blackledge discusses, in 2001, following riots in Oldham, Bradford, and Leeds in the north of England, politicians and the press associated the poverty, unemployment, and social divisions in these areas with the lack of 'a grasp of English' on the part of members of the South Asian community – often, specifically, wives from the Indian subcontinent.[4] Later the same year the British Parliament issued a White Paper, 'Secure borders, safe haven', which proposed 'the ability to speak our common language' as a commonsense response to 'an increasingly diverse world', laying the ground for the 2002 Nationality, Immigration and Asylum Act, which extended compulsory English language testing as a condition of citizenship to include spouses of existing British nationals.[5] That the supposed logic of the 2002 Act continues to be taken as read is evident from the fact that, since late 2010, proof of English language proficiency has been a condition for granting initial UK entry visas to the partners of British citizens, rules which were tightened still further in 2017.[6] Even so, in July 2019, at a hustings for the Conservative leadership, the MP Boris Johnson called for English to be mandatory for immigrants to the UK – indeed, arguing that there were 'too many parts of our country' where 'English is not spoken by some people as their first language'.[7] Public discourse in Britain persists in presenting English not just as the sole language of wider communication, but as the guarantor of culture, education, social cohesion, economic advancement, and moral order. South Asian languages, meanwhile, continue to be associated with a comprehensive range of social maladies: 'civil disorder, school underachievement, social segregation, societal burden, isolation, unhappy marriage, poor employment prospects, mental health difficulties, lack of social mobility, and threat to democracy, citizenship and nationhood'.[8]

That the poet Daljit Nagra should prove an astringent observer of language politics in Britain is, perhaps, not surprising. Born in London in the mid-1960s to Punjabi Indian parents, Nagra grew up in Yiewsley, near Heathrow Airport, on the outskirts of London, before moving to Sheffield in the north of England in his teens, and again back to London as an adult.[9] Punjabi was the language spoken at home, and he learned English at school; in common with many other second-generation

South Asians in Britain, Nagra speaks the language of his parents, but does not read or write it.[10] Memories of growing up in Britain in the 1970s and 1980s, and of the politics of race and language of that period, haunt many of his poems. In 'The Man Who Would Be English!', the speaker's longing for linguistic and racial assimilation is founded in memories of 'the lark-about days of school' in which the price of being 'one of us' is to 'pass ... | my voice into theirs' – including internalising the '*bud-bud ding-ding*' racist playground mimicry of South Asian voices. As Arvind Mandair has observed of his own upbringing in 1980s Britain, negotiating the relationship between Britishness and South Asianness took place predominantly at school and involved 'most of all the acquisition and politics of English enunciation, with or without accents and inflections of all sorts'.[11] Recalling Macaulayan scenes of colonial tutelage, Mandair reflects how this 'cannot but make one think of a similar scenario that would have been taking place in the so-called Anglo-Vernacular schools in late nineteenth-century colonial India'.[12] As Nagra's 'pass[ing]' reminds us, what is being called for is an act of racial self-effacement. Watching these colonial scenes on replay, who could miss how they also reinscribe the schism running through Macaulay's 'Minute on Indian Education', with its projection of Indian servants of empire whose perfect grasp of English would make them 'English in tastes, in opinions, in morals and in intellect' even as they would always remain visibly, racially different, still 'Indian in blood and colour'?[13] In this chapter, I look at how Nagra's poetry both enacts and worries at the politics of 'voicing' British Punjabis against a backdrop of linguistic racism, from the Macaulayan to the contemporary, including that internalised by British Asian speakers. The constant consciousness of using others' language extends between Nagra's performances of voice and his approach to 'English' as an object of knowledge and medium for poetry.[14]

In 1970s and 1980s Britain, the stigma attached to speakers of 'other' languages by the British media and in the education system was compounded, in many ways, by a broad strand of 'racial' mainstream comedy – regarded, as Charles Husbands observed at the time, as a benchmark of Britain's tolerance and capacity to examine questions of race through the lens of humour[15] – in which foreigners' voices were played for laughs. The long-running London Weekend Television sitcom *Mind Your Language* (1977–86), for example, was set in an adult education class of predominantly South Asian learners of English, and derived much of its comedy from their malapropisms and struggles with language.[16] British actors' mimicry of non-native speaker accents, particularly South Asian Englishes, meanwhile, were a staple of TV comedy, in the form of characters like Rangi Ram in the BBC's *It Ain't Half Hot Mum* (1974–81), or ITV's mercifully now long-forgotten *Curry and Chips* (1969), starring a blacked-up Spike Milligan as Pakistani Irishman 'Paki Paddy', or TV comedian Jim Davidson whose eponymous show ran from 1979 to 1982 and who was renowned for his performance of black and Asian 'characters'. The British comedian Peter Sellers's mimicry of South Asian Englishes in films like *The Millionairess* (1960) and *The Party* (1968), meanwhile, is so notorious that the British Asian BBC radio and TV comedy series *Goodness Gracious Me!* (1996–8; 1998–2001), its title taken from the Sellers song of the same name, started life as a stage show called *Peter Sellers is Dead!* Acknowledging his poetry's risk-taking relationship to this British history of linguistic mimicry, Nagra has observed:

> In terms of performance, I wanted to reference the racist television programming I grew up watching. The accent I use when I read is not supposed to be an authentic, representative Indian accent, but an attempt to enrich and reclaim those flat, one-dimensional Peter Sellers-type characters, so there's a backwards and forwards trajectory.[17]

This 'backwards and forwards trajectory' gestures to a complex language politics in which 'reclamation' takes place alongside and through avowedly *inauthentic* poetic voices, which are – perhaps even more riskily – connected to, and not entirely distinct from, those of Sellers et al. For while Nagra's poetry works to reclaim South Asian Englishes from the stigmas of linguistic racism, it is also haunted by that racism, as in the playground chant of '*bud-bud ding-ding*' in 'The Man Who Would Be English!'[18]

If Nagra writes in the context of linguistic racism directed at South Asian speakers, then he also writes in the consciousness of a different kind of stereotyping: the market-driven demands for certain kinds of 'authentic' Asianness, and what Sarah Brouillette calls 'creative-economy discourse' in arts policy, which promotes the 'benefits of cultural diversity' through initiatives to support the work of black and

Asian writers who are implicitly called upon to be 'representative' of a particular community.[19] Nagra started out publishing poetry under the pseudonym 'Khan Singh Kumar' – a South Asian everypoet persona combining typically Muslim, Sikh, and Hindu names, an impossible pastiche of 'authenticity' and a send-up of the supposed demands of an ignorant middle-class, liberal, white British readership for a representative 'British Asian' voice. In the poem 'Booking Khan Singh Kumar', the poet-narrator considers how the in-between space, the 'gooey' space between languages and cultures, is also a saleable space, 'the gap in the market'. Refusing to settle blame for his poetry's commodification firmly either with the audience or himself, he asks:

> Did *you* make me for the gap in the market
> Did *I* make me for the gap in the market[20]

On the one hand, the poet in the poem recognises the distance between his work and those it purports to represent – and the cachet he is able to claim by seeming to speak *for* them (while in fact speaking *past* them, to a mostly white, middle-class audience):

> Should I beat on my chest I'm a ghetto poet
> Who discorded his kind as they couldn't know it

On the other, he asks how far his language can travel and still remain marketable to readers in search of a tangible, but unthreatening, linguistic exoticism:

> Do you medal yourselves when you meddle with my type
> If I go up di spectrum how far can ju dye.[21]

This poem appears in Nagra's first collection, *Look We Have Coming to Dover!*, published by Faber in 2007 to much fanfare – and to the kind of high sales figures which are, as Brouillette observes, almost unheard of for a debut poetry collection.[22] Reviewers, of whom there were many, suggested that his was what BBC's *Newsnight Review* called a 'new voice for the Indian community', as well as a fresh take on English poetry.[23] Both the title poem and the collection itself won the Forward Prize, one of English-language poetry's most prestigious awards, and the book also won the high-profile 2007 *decibel*-Penguin prize, for writing addressing immigrant experience (in practice, usually awarded to black and minority ethnic writers).[24] Nagra's poetry has since become part of the British GCSE poetry curriculum (the poem 'Singh Song!', from *Look We Have Coming to Dover!*, has been included in two successive versions of the AQA poetry anthology) and been included in the *Norton Anthology of English Literature*.[25] From 2015 to 2017 he was BBC Radio 4's first ever Poet in Residence, at the same time as his fourth book with Faber, *British Museum* (2017), was published. As this all goes some way to suggest, from the beginning of his career to the present moment, Nagra has worked in a critical, self-conscious relation to the British Punjabi community and its intersections with other British Asian and ethnic minority communities; mainstream literary and cultural presumptions about 'Asianness'; English poetic traditions and poetic form; and the institutions of British – and indeed English – culture.

Look We Have Coming to Dover!, seeming to reclaim Punjabi Englishes as complex, creative media for poetry against the stigma of racist mockery, features dramatic monologues from a kaleidoscopic cast of poetic personae, predominantly working-class Indian Punjabi Sikhs. Highly diverse, Nagra's poetic 'voices' range from middle-class varieties of standard English, to pastiche urban vernacular, to highly stylised orthographic approximations of various kinds of Punjabi Englishes. Some poems switch between English and Punjabi, while others dramatise their own self-translation in which varieties of English are made to stand in for varieties of Punjabi. Subverting notions not only of a stable 'language' but also of a homogeneous 'speech community', his poetry traces the complex interplay, variation, flux, and conflict between languages and speech forms, discontinuous across context, caste and class, gender and generation. In 'The Man Who Would Be English!', for example, the speaker's would-be assimilationist English is disrupted by the orthographically and grammatically marked Punjabi English of his wife, while in 'The Furtherance of Mr Bulram's Education', the Anglophile English teacher Bulram is full of disdain for the working-class Punjabi 'onion-breath Calibans' next door, whose desire is for 'Queen's | quick "shop-keeper" English!!!'[26] The unsettling and generative collisions between English and Punjabi are announced in the title of the collection's eponymous 'Look We Have Coming to Dover!', which uses the mismatch between English and Punjabi tense formations to create an uncertain slippage between past, present, and future time. Referencing 'Dover Beach', Nagra deploys this alternate, disjunct temporality to reroute Matthew Arnold's Victorian lament of imperiled Englishness onto an imaginative terrain which splices past, present, and future narratives of immigrant arrival. Here and elsewhere, Nagra engineers productive collisions between languages that, as I'll go on to discuss, produce dazzling arrays of meaning. Yet the exchange between languages can also be the site of loss, and Nagra's poems also dwell on the intergenerational effects of language stigmatisation and attrition. In 'In a White Town', the narrator is ashamed of his mother's 'illiterate body', while she 'duck[s] at my stuttered Punjabi | laughing', and the son realises all too late what is lost in this transit:

> Nowadays, when I visit, when she hovers upward,
> hobbling towards me to kiss my forehead
> as she once used to, I wish I could fall forward.[27]

'Cane', in Nagra's most recent collection, *British Museum*, returns to the theme, though this time it is the mother whose position remains the more intransigent: '*No English talk at home!* my mother booms | in Punjabi'.[28]

Yet, as I've already suggested, voice in Nagra's poetry is anything but 'authentic', and in his staged poetic scenes of language mixing, code-switching, and linguistic appropriation, the line between solidarity and mockery, resistance and complicity, is often very hard to call. The ethics of voice, of writing and performing in a punning 'Punglish' that is not strictly his, are recurrent themes.[29] In 'Kabba Considers the Ontology of Representation, the Catch-22 for "Black" Writers ...', the speaker Kabba rears up out of the poem to indict his creator for cynical linguistic minstrelsy, exploiting the comic associations of an exaggeratedly South Asian voice – a 'whitey "fantum" English, blacked | to make me sound "poreign"!' Kabba accuses the poet of playing him for cheap laughs, while also pursuing consecration in 'British antologies'; though at the same time, the poem slyly points out, he is precisely the kind of reductive reader produced by assumptions that poetry should be 'authentic' and 'representative' when it comes to black and Asian communities.[30] In this poem Nagra anticipates criticism which has followed, that his relentlessly ironic approach to 'doing voices' provides cover for precisely the instrumentalisation and internalised racism he appears to critique.[31] This double-bind for the non-white poet is one which Nagra's poetry wittily and sometimes angrily anatomises, caught between celebration on grounds of being 'exotic' or an 'IMMIGRANT'S SON' on the one hand, and accusations of being 'too English' and therefore 'a mimic' on the other.[32] As Nagra puts it in 'Informant',

> whatever voice i put on
> i know i'm heading for bother.[33]

Coming from his particular angle as a Punjabi English poet (too Punjabi to make an unproblematic claim on English, too English to pass as Punjabi, keenly aware of how both 'English' and 'Punjabi' dissolve as coherent designations in any case under pressure) such instances of self-accusation form part of a wider view of language whereby linguistic provenance – where words come from, whose words they are, how they come to be used, and what that use might mean – is unsettlingly to the fore, and where all acts of poetic enunciation are acts of mimicry and to a certain degree compromised. In Bakhtin's terms, the 'word in language' is always 'half someone else's', as we struggle to capture language that 'exists in other people's mouths, in other people's contexts, serving other people's intentions: it is from there that one must take the word, and make it one's own'.[34]

In 'The Man Who Would Be English!', we find the poem's would-be assimilationist narrator watching the football in the pub, eager to belong with the 'familiar faces | from the lark-about days of school' as they cheer on the English national side (sporting loyalty's equivalence to national belonging evoking Norman Tebbit's famous 'cricket test').[35] The speaker's strained Estuary slang is both evocative and awkward: 'Just for kicks I was well in with the English race'. To speak this English is to 'pass my voice into theirs': an act of attempted 'passing', through which, by erasing all difference marked in his voice, he may be able to bring about his own racial invisibility. Yet even this transient and ambivalent moment of acceptance is achieved only by an act of willed amnesia: forgetting both the difficult truth behind the 'lark-about days of school' (from which the racist playground taunt of *bud-bud ding-ding* surely resonates) and the 'distant land forever | with rights to my name'. As the narrator works at his deliberate forgetting, his efforts

are undone by the histories which surge through the poem, revealing the covert imbrications of language and race in the imagining of
Englishness. Caught in unsteady identification between 'us' and 'them',
he internalises and reiterates the racist mimicry of '*bud-bud ding-ding*'
in order to lay claim to a language whose contemporary relationship
with British xenophobia is replayed in the word 'asylum' – that sign
central to what Paul Gilroy calls the 'quietly racialized code' of contemporary discourses on immigration.[36] The multiple betrayals and
self-betrayals consequent upon 'pass[ing] my voice into theirs' threaten
to engulf the poem. The history of the Empire cannot be evaded: in a
hallucinatory moment, the narrator sees his own mother on the TV
screen, 'gloving the ball with lard, from the Mutiny', pointing out how
his attempt at escaping history is just another 'own goal'. Meanwhile,
the effort at 'passing' cannot erase the presence of his wife 'on the
sidelines'. On the one hand, she is the kind of proletarian, subcon-
tinental spouse routinely denigrated in the British media and legislated against in the 2002 Nationality, Immigration and Asylum Act,
required to demonstrate 'sufficient knowledge' of English before she
might qualify for British citizenship, and as such, she represents the
disavowed, unassimilable linguistic 'other' of his claim on Englishness.
On the other, the italics connecting her words and the '*bud-bud ding-
ding*' of the preceding stanza, as well as the exaggerated orthographic
markedness of her grammatically 'incorrect', Punjabi-inflected speech,
invite readers to question whether this is 'her' voice we are hearing or
the narrator's racist mimicry of his own wife. And, with a final, ironic
spin on the notion of English as guarantor of national belonging, she
accuses him in the language of the racist graffiti sprayed on her wall:
'*Lookk lookk ju nott British ju rrr blackkk ... !!!*'
     The poem exposes and points at the disavowed politics of race
which underlie the notion of 'speaking English like a native', and it is
in this context that it addresses the risks, the compromises, and the
complicities involved in adopting a particular 'voice'. Nagra's ambivalent orientation to English combines a playful experimentalism with an
etymological attentiveness to the histories playing out in language, and
a propensity for playing its conventions against itself. He has argued in
interview, for example, that 'the noun is the basis of English writing',
and that to unsettle this – by making nouns into adjectives and verbs,
as he often does – is to make the reader feel that they are no longer in

'distinctly English territory'.[37] He defines himself, though not without reservation, as 'an English poet',[38] laying claim to Robert Browning as a model for the dramatic monologue. (Browning was also, we could note – given Nagra's interest in recording and playback – the first poet to record his voice onto Edison wax cylinder, in 1889.) He returns often to Anglo-Irish poets, particularly Seamus Heaney, and there are resonances, in his vision of language, of Tom Paulin's 1983 Field Day pamphlet 'A New Look at the Language Question', which begins: 'The history of a language is often a story of possession and dispossession, territorial struggle and the establishment or imposition of a culture.'[39] Paulin considers the history of English, as a language of power and as the carrier of beliefs in 'a chimerical idea of racial purity', yet at the same time holds out hope for Irish English that resides specifically in its energetic *impurity* in terms that find corresponding echoes in Nagra's work, the strands of dialect that provide a 'hoard of relished words'.[40] Nagra has also described his poetry as influenced by 'that first genera-tion of Caribbeans that came over', who 'were a bigger influence on me than Indians writing in English':

> They were here, writing in Britain, being influenced by the local voice, whereas quite a lot of the Indians – for example Anita Desai, and even V.S. Naipaul – didn't sound British to me. It sounded like the English of certain well-read Indians I knew, who'd come over from India, but people such as LKJ, John Agard and Grace Nichols had a distinctly English voice, they picked up some of the local lan-guage of London living, which was the life I was living too. This was also reflected in their phonetic spelling – instead of 'the', they used 'di' or 'da'. I wanted to allude to that voice but reflect an Indian ver-nacular. The significant thing in both cases is the movement away from 'the': you're still in the tradition of Englishness but with one foot in another practice too.[41]

Though Nagra's relationship to writers of South Asian heritage is ambivalent (there is no missing the sardonic tone in 'the stallion | black power of Sir Vidia and Sir Salman' in 'GET OFF MY POEM WHITEY', from *British Museum*),[42] his assaults on the mythic constructions of English are undoubtedly also shadowed by the brutal histories of eth-nolinguistic nationalisms in South Asia. In the poem 'The Punjab', for example, the contested history of the region plays out in inter-

and intralingual conflict between multiple, diasporic voices: 'Yoo say
"Púnjab" vee say Punjaaab'.[43] Across Nagra's poetry, the connected
histories of India and Britain, as well as the resonances and repetitions
between past and present, reflect mutually upon one another, together
offering a finely textured reflection of the danger and brutality, as well
as the absurdity, inherent in monolingual ideologies. Yet it is English
which is his central concern – in particular, how the English language
and the contemporary British multilingualism against which it is often
antagonistically pitted are equally products of a shared colonial and
imperial history. In 'The Gob-Smacking Taste of Mine Inheritance',
xenophobic Brit and immigrant 'Punjabi shop-wallah' are locked
together in a shared inheritance of misery handed down through the
Empire, their 'battle for turf' an analogue of the poet's struggles over
his own 'inheritance' of 'the English line', 'franchised' through the
Empire. As 'native poet' – freighted with all the ambivalence of that
phrase's double meaning – his claim to ownership is an uncertain one,
his task to 'graft my Heathen-word on our old soil'. Yet the poem's
conclusion is emphatically assertive, making of shared history a claim
to shared ownership: 'Henceforth the stock of the store is the fruit of a
mutual realm!'[44]

The glossary to Nagra's second collection, *Tippoo Sultan's Incredible
White-Man-Eating Tiger-Toy Machine!!!*, makes precisely such an
assertion of historical interconnectedness, revealed through the workings of language. The glossary's title, 'Bolly Bhaji', is a play on the
Punjabi term 'baar di boli' (ਬਾਹਰ ਦੀ ਬੋਲੀ, باہر دی بولی – approximately,
'language from the outside'), referring to the mixed, diasporic varieties of Punjabi spoken in Britain, characterised by grammatical influence and lexical borrowing from English. 'Bhaji', meanwhile, is a
nineteenth-century loanword into English from Hindi, so thoroughly
domesticated by now as to need no translation. Neither English nor
Punjabi, the 'Bolly Bhaji' points out by its title alone, can be conceived
of as stable, pristine, or independent of the other. Theirs is a shared
history of language contact, mixing and borrowing, between Britain
and South Asia, which persists into the present – a history invoked in
the glossary's omnivorous entries, which include references to both
the nineteenth-century Anglo-Indian glossary *Hobson-Jobson* and contemporary 'Yorkshire Punjabi'. But the 'Bolly Bhaji', delighting as it
does in linguistic melange, is at the same time highly conscious of the

colonial histories out of which its tasty mix of language emerges.[45] *Hobson-Jobson*, an important touchstone both for the 'Bolly Bhaji' and for the collection as a whole, was compiled by its authors, Henry Yule and A. C. Burnell, as a glossary of the mixed language, 'Anglo-Indian', spoken by the British in eighteenth- and nineteenth-century India, full of borrowings and adaptations from languages across South Asia and beyond, and – in Yule and Burnell's view – the defining feature of East India Company-era British identity in the Raj. As Nagra himself argues in a radio programme he made on *Hobson-Jobson* for the BBC, this mammoth work of lexicography is remarkable for its delight in language and in the sounds of words, revelling in linguistic impropriety as a source of pleasure and creative possibility – and in that sense, a model of multilingual poetics.[46] It also, and just as significantly, stands for a kind of language mixing which is anything but innocent: lexical borrowing in the service of, and as a metonym for, colonial power. At the same time, *Hobson-Jobson* is also a fascinatingly anxious text: it worries at the slipperiness of language and the mutability of signs; it reveals, while trying to evade, imagined connections between linguistic and racial hybridity; and it asks itself over and again what the processes of language mixing have to say about the nature of English and English national identity. Something of this anxiety can be seen in one of its most well-known passages, considering the long-standing impact of Indian languages on the domestic properties of English:

> Words of Indian origin have been insinuating themselves into English ever since the end of the reign of Elizabeth and the beginning of that of King James, when such terms as calico, chintz, and gingham had already effected a lodgement in English warehouses and shops, and were lying in wait for entrance into English literature.[47]

Nagra's 'Bolly Bhaji' – like Yule and Burnell's *Hobson-Jobson* – undermines the notion of languages as pure and distinct entities. It also uses the contiguity of the glossary form to suggest connections between its entries, such as that between '*nautch* – "ballet dance performed by women" (from Hobson Jobson)' and '*fettlin'* – (Yorkshire Punjabi) cleanin'.[48] Both *nautch* and *fettlin'*, as examples of language contact and lexical borrowing, imply a shared history, a 'backwards and forwards trajectory' and a commonality of process between Raj-era British India and contemporary Punjabi Yorkshire. Yet both their ostensible similarity and their glaring differences are instructive, suggesting how apparently similar kinds of language practice can have very different politics. *Nautch* is a highly charged word with a complex history: to the British in India the *nautch* dancer was, as Pramod Nayar puts it, 'after the fakir and the cruel Indian monarch, the key icon of the colonial exotic: mysterious, seductive, tantalising, and dangerous'.[49] In other words, the adoption of *nautch* into the lexicon of the British in India bespeaks something of the complex linguistic, erotic, and symbolic economies of the Raj – and its transformation into 'ballet dance' in *Hobson-Jobson*, something of the concealing power of cultural translation. But if *nautch*'s etymology opens out into a complex story about linguistic exchange and its relationship to power, and how language travels, then so too does that of *fettlin'*: a quotidian loanword, suggesting a domestic, largely unregarded (no colonial glossary exists to dignify its translation into standard English with a final 'g') traffic between marginalised language forms in the contemporary north of England. The two words appear in two different poems in the collection which attend to the cultural processes and human interactions of which they are products. 'This Be the Pukka Verse', a poem which speaks in a *Hobson-Jobson* voice, invokes in its title Larkin's famously bleak spin on questions of parenthood and inheritance ('they fuck you up, your mum and dad | they may not mean to, but they do'). Nagra moves Larkin's drama of familial misery into the realm of colonial history, dramatising the Raj's project of linguistic borrowing as just another instance of colonial exploitation – like its material acquisitiveness and sexual rapaciousness – and making a sustained metaphorical connection between the 'fucked up' children and 'fucked up' language which are both legacies of the 'mother incarnate | Victoria Imperatrix'.[50] In 'Raju t'Wonder Dog', meanwhile, 'Yorkshire Punjabi' thrives in a Huddersfield corner shop run by Avtar and Sapna, whose love for the hapless 'Wonder Dog' of the poem's title is a displacement of that which they long to lavish on the child they cannot have. These two very different poems' association via the 'Bolly Bhaji' invites their comparative reading, as two connected scenes of language contact and change with very different valency. The former is empowered, rapacious, and brutally productive of 'bastard' progeny; the latter mutual, intimate, kindly, yet unable to reproduce itself beyond the confines of the corner shop.

In 'Darling & Me!', the opening poem of *Look We Have Coming to Dover!*, complex layering of neologism, allusion, malapropism, and mimicry works to both exhilarating and discomforting effect, in the interpretation and attribution of words and voices. The poem is narrated by a male factory worker, recently married and very drunk, in a poetic fabrication of a 'learner's English' acquired from the TV and the factory floor, an interlanguage in which Punjabi operates on English at the level of grammar and syntax. He returns home from the pub to his wife, whose role in this marriage is to have 'disco of drumstick in pot. | Hot. Waiting for me'.[51] The poem's language is characterised by malapropisms and coinage – the noun-into-adjective neologism 'pirouetty' in the penultimate stanza – out of which complex chains of signification are generated. The *Guardian* critic Sarah Crown, in her review of Nagra's first collection, focuses on this poem in particular for its linguistic virtuosity, suggesting that the coining of 'pirouetty' 'gives a rapturous lift to the line, its freshness reflecting the startling joy the newly married couple have discovered in each other' (it will be clear in what follows that I find this 'startling joy' harder to locate).[52]

The poem layers intertextual allusion to T. S. Eliot's *The Waste Land* (the barman's bell ringing, the putting on of a record) with cultural references – Hilda Ogden berating her husband Stan in the TV soap opera *Coronation Street* (1960–), Torvill and Dean skating to Ravel's 'Bolero' – that place it in the Britain of 1984. This was the year of the miners' strike in Britain, emblematic of the 1980s Conservative government's decimation of British industry and manufacturing, a fate perhaps lying in wait for the factory where the poem's speaker works. It is also that cultural and political moment anatomised by Paul Gilroy in *There Ain't No Black in the Union Jack*, in which the 'racist television programming' alluded to by Nagra – the joke of the Indian man who can't speak English properly – helped to police the imagined boundaries of a nation conceived of as white, culturally homogeneous, and speaking English.[53] It is against this backdrop that Nagra's poem subverts the comedic associations of South Asian English speech forms with racist mockery, insofar as it demonstrates the creative possibilities of an improper English. At the same time, it stages a recalibration of the language politics of that period, by dramatising the everyday forces of postcolonial conviviality at work: in language, in food, in music; in the accommodations of the pub and the factory floor. Meanwhile, however, the poem's setting in 1984 plots an inescapable backwards-and-forwards trajectory between Britain and India. The terrible events of 1984 in India – the storming of the Golden Temple, the assassination of Indira Gandhi, and anti-Sikh riots which left thousands dead – are inextricable from the ethnolinguistic nationalisms which fuelled them. As the poem's broken-English-speaking Indian Punjabi narrator dances tango and rumba to the soundtrack of *Pakeezah* (a film about North Indian Muslims, recorded not in Hindi, as is conventional, but in Urdu), the poem's heteroglossia faces several ways at once, assaulting the pieties not just of English but also Hindi and Punjabi monologisms.[54]

At the same time, the poem's reference to *Pakeezah*'s soundtrack – in Bollywood style, recorded by playback artists, for lipsynching by the film's actors – raises questions about voice and provenance which equally lie at the heart of the poem. Nagra's invocation and subversion of racist linguistic stereotyping do not substitute an 'authentic' for an 'inauthentic' Indian voice; instead they form part of the poem's overlapping network of mimicries, from the allusion to *The Waste Land* and Eliot's 'doing voices', to the narrator's own impersonation of *Coronation Street*'s Hilda Ogden: '*heeya, eaht yor chuffy dinnaaah!*'.[55] Overlaying mimicry, repetition, and echo, the poem makes us ask whose words, and whose voice, we are hearing. In the fifth stanza – just after the narrator's Hilda Ogden impression – the poem takes a revealing turn:

We say we could never eat
in publicity like dat, if we did
wife advertisement may need
of solo punch in di smack.[56]

The malapropisms – 'publicity', 'advertisement' – play on the narrator's oscillation between object and consumer of popular culture. And, at a slight angle to English semantic propriety but making their own kind of perfect sense, they also suggest a process of linguistic appropriation, substitution, and approximation, by which a new learner may not so much learn as assemble a language from heterogeneous, found materials. But when the threat of violence – 'punch in di smack' – emerges out of this linguistic freewheeling, the lack of clarity as to who is 'doing' whose voice, whose these words are and where they come from, becomes suddenly pressing. So too, perhaps, does the sense that a reader might be beguiled by the established comic associations of non-standard language into missing the sudden note of threat. Is this a learner, delighted with the sound of his new language, 'trying out' a recently acquired phrase? A phrase which surely recalls the lexicon of casual, violent misogyny so prevalent, like the language of racism, in 1980s Britain – all of it, perhaps, language to be learned on the factory floor. The poem's other 'voices' resonate too. The queasy combination of working-class comedy with drinking and domestic violence recalls Stan and Hilda Ogden's relationship in *Coronation Street*. There are, too, the lingering notes of Eliot: precisely those moments in *The Waste Land*, in 'A Game of Chess' and at the end of 'The Fire Sermon', where the vision of relations between the sexes is at its most corrosive. And also, in this sudden, possible eruption of violence, might be heard echoes of 1984 in Punjab. Yet, at the same time, the poem also plays on the comedic associations of its poetic voice, making it possible (perhaps) to pass the threat off as a 'joke'; while of all the voices which this densely layered poem includes, the one it excludes is that of the wife who might be able – if we could hear her – to tell us the truth behind that 'pirouetty' move. 'Darling & Me!' assaults the pieties of English with an infinite regression of voices haunted by other voices, and in doing so, emphasises that linguistic hybridity and semantic transgression are not, in and of themselves, to be trusted as politically liberating.

In contrast to 'Darling and Me!', a poem that delights in the speaker's linguistic imprecision which is at the same time the source of its kaleidoscopic unease, the narrator of 'Yobbos!' is a study in apparently tight linguistic control. The poem is a dense collage of homage, allusion, and mimicry, starting from the opening epigram, an 1899 Pears soap advert which is itself an appropriation of Kipling: '*The first step towards lightening THE WHITE MAN'S burden is through teaching the virtues of cleanliness*'. The poem's narrator opens with a knowingly self-ironising mimicry of imperialist discourse:

> A right savage I was – sozzled
> to the nose with sprightly Muldoon, squeezed into the communal
> sweat of a Saturday tube home –
> I'm up to p. 388 of his sharp lemon-skinned
> Collected Poems[57]

This vernacular Londoner's postcolonial self-mockery as a 'right savage' is overwhelmingly confident: soaked in cultural capital, 'sozzled' not on drink but on difficult poetry, he is, after all, the sort of person who reads the collected poems of Paul Muldoon on the London Tube. Yet this assertive self-positioning is set up only to be undone in a moment:

> when some scruffy looking git pipes to his crew –
> *Some Paki shit, like,*
> *eee's loookin into!*[58]

The pain and discomfort of this moment of racial overdetermina-tion, recalling Fanon's train carriage encounter with a child in *Black Skin, White Masks* ('look, a Negro!'),[59] is played off against a joke at the semi-literate racism of the 'scruffy-looking git', with his northern English long vowels (*'eee's loookin'*), who assumes that a 'Paki' will be reading 'Paki shit', and doesn't recognise the poet's name as Irish (the 'sharp lemon-skinned' yellow Faber edition has Muldoon's name emblazoned in large letters on the cover). Belonging, in other words, cuts two ways: a claim to ownership of an unquestioned Britishness on grounds of racial whiteness, made in an undeniable act of racist aggres-sion, undercut by the implication of exclusion from a literary culture defined by region, class, language, and education.

Yet the speaker has more in common with the 'scruffy looking git' than he knows. Frustrated – as much by Muldoon's wilful, multilingual opacity, the '"Badhbh" ... "Cailidin" ... "Salah-eh-din"' of the poem he is reading, 'Yarrow', as by the racist taunting – he mimics both of their 'voices' at the same time as he protests silently to himself

> *Well mate, this Paki's more British than that inde-*
> *cipherable, impossibly untranslatable*
>
> *sod of a Paddy --*[60]

Couched within a formal pastiche of Muldoon (the caesura of 'inde- | cipherable'), the stanza break before 'sod of a Paddy' brings it into sharp relief, while the rhyme with 'Paki' restores to 'Paddy' its full freight of racist vitriol. This association is not lost on the narrator, shocked into self-recognition. It should also perhaps make the reader notice, if we did not do so before, the language of English *class* disdain in the poem: the 'yobbos' of the title, the 'scruffy looking git', the narrator's mimicry of his assailant's working-class northern accent. Suddenly overwhelmed by the overdetermined nature of his 'own' words, the need to wash the language of imperial history out of his mouth, the speaker ends the poem in the choked silence of an ellipsis:

> I catch my throat gungeing
> on its Cromwellian vile, my tongue foaming for soap ...[61]

The English language is, in Nagra's poetry, laden with the legacies of inequality and oppression, particularly (but not uniquely) of empire, which constitute a trap of 'Cromwellian vile' for the unwary. The speaker of 'Yobbos!' mimics the racists who assault him, only to find his own language also compromised. Sometimes explicitly acknowledged, sometimes not, the English spoken by Nagra's poems is freighted with histories of prejudice, with Powellian 'rivering[s] of blood'.[62] Even Kabba, when he accuses his poet-creator of racist 'mickeying', is not immune from this sedimented history.[63]

In such an etymological calling-to-account, the poem 'A Black History of the English-Speaking Peoples' (the one chosen by Jahan Ramazani for the 2018 *Norton Anthology of English Literature*)[64] casts its titular language as a dense fabric of lexical borrowing and allusion staggering under the weight of its own history. The poem's title itself is a reworking of Winston Churchill's *History of the English-Speaking Peoples* (1956–8) which, completed and published as the Empire was collapsing, envisions an Anglospheric commons, grounded in language, race, and history, between Britain and its former white settler colonies of the United States, Canada, Australia, and New Zealand. Nagra's poem is concerned to turn over that ground, which makes whiteness the defining property of English, and to think about what it would mean to restore to the language all of its 'black history'. The poem's narrator, watching a performance of one of Shakespeare's history plays at the Globe Theatre on London's South Bank, is '[spun] from my stand' into a reflection on the discursive systems that have sustained and reproduced imperial and racial power old and new:

> Between the birth and the fire and rebirth of the Globe
> the visions of Albion led to a Rule Britannia
> of trade-winds-and-Gulf-Stream
> all-conquering fleets that aroused theatres
>
> for lectures on Hottentots and craniology,
> whilst Eden was paraded in Kew.
> Between *Mayflower* and *Windrush*
> (with each *necessary murder*) the celebrated
>
> embeddings of imperial gusto where jungles
> were surmounted so the light of learning be spread
> to help sobbing suttees
> give up the ghost of a husband's flaming pyre.[65]

The poem's English is made to show not only its saturation with imperialism, but also the mobility and mutability of that imperialism across time and to suit new modes of power. The hyphenated connection between 'trade-winds-and-Gulf-Stream' is echoed in semantic chains which link 'sobbing suttees' to 'book burning', and connect Churchill (whose legacies to the English language, lest we forget, also include the phrase 'keep Britain white') with 'shock and awe'.

The position of the narrating poet within this linguistic order is an uncertain one. He asks,

> So does the red of Macaulay's map run through
> my blood? Am I a noble scruff who hopes a proud
> academy might canonise
> his poems for their faith in canonical allusions?
>
> Is my voice phoney over these oft-heard beats?
> Well if my voice feels vexatious, what can I but pray
> that it reign Bolshie
> through puppetry and hypocrisy full of gung-ho fury![66]

The distinction between Macaulayan comprador on the one hand and 'gung-ho' rebel on the other is, at least on an etymological level, fuzzy. 'Gung-ho' is a loanword introduced into English from Mandarin by US marines in World War Two in the South Pacific; 'Bolshie' a modified borrowing turned against its Russian original. In section III, the poet-narrator lays out the problem:

> Perhaps to aid the succession
> of this language of the world,
> for the poet weeding the roots, for the debate
>
> in ourselves, now we're bound to the wheels
> of global power, we should tend the manorial
> slime – that legacy
> offending the outcasts who fringe our circles.[67]

The poet-as-etymologist is tasked with exposing the 'roots' of the language, digging down and removing corruption in order to facilitate new growth. The 'manorial slime' carries an echo of Derek Walcott's 'On the Ruins of a Great House' – 'some slave is rotting in this manorial lake'[68] – while its ambivalence about English recalls the well-known lines from the final stanza of 'A Far Cry from Africa':

> I who have cursed
> The drunken officer of British rule, how choose
> Between this Africa and the English tongue I love?
> Betray them both, or give back what they give?[69]

Any attempt at reconciling the language to its 'black history' seems almost fatally compromised by the sheer density and proliferation of the poem's borrowings and allusions: from Macaulay to US forces in the South Pacific to 'shock and awe', from Tennyson to Churchill to the Rushdie affair, its English words generated by, and reproducing in their reiteration, the operations of imperial and neoimperial power. Yet at the same time, the poem's allusions also point to the porousness and mutability of English and gesture hopefully to how writers' struggles with the language can effect change. The properties of English poetry carry the influence of Walcott, as well as Kipling. '*Necessary murder*' comes from W. H. Auden's 'Spain', but also from Orwell's outraged attack on Auden's use of the phrase (memorably: 'Mr. Auden's brand of amoralism is only possible if you are the kind of person who is always somewhere else when the trigger is pulled') in 'Inside the whale'.[70] The poem's ending implies that the greatest danger comes not from the linguistic residues of history, but their sanitisation and erasure:

And how swiftly the tide removes from the scene
The bagpipe clamouring
Garrisons with the field-wide scarlet soldiery

And the martyr's cry: Every man die at his post!
Till what's ahead are the upbeat lovers who gaze
From the London Eye
At multinationals lying along the sanitized Thames.[71]

Thus when Nagra's poems take an etymological perspective, they do so not only to draw attention to the 'manorial slime' at the roots of English, but also to underscore the language's historical construct-edness and therefore its capacity to be reshaped. In this attentiveness to the historicity and mutability of English, as a willed position of insisting on its availability for use, Nagra's poetic etymologies recall Raymond Williams's insistence in *Keywords* that English not be seen as

> a tradition to be learned, nor a consensus to be accepted, nor a set of meanings which, because it is 'our language', has a natural authority; but as a shaping and reshaping, in real circumstances and from pro-foundly different and important points of view: a vocabulary to use, to find our own ways in, to change as we find it necessary to change it, as we go on making our own language and history.[72]

Yet Nagra's English, 'franchised' through the empire, belies the isomor-phic relationship of language and community implied by Williams, the implicit definition and the limits of the 'we' to whom he refers, just as it rejects the limits of Churchill's Anglospheric commons. The work of 'shaping and reshaping', agential and radical, needs to be underpinned both by etymology (as in Williams's *Keywords*), to trace language as a site of ceaseless struggle and as a living practice, and by multilin-gual disruption, by which English is made foreign to itself. In 'Tippoo Sultan's Incredible White-Man-Eating Tiger-Toy Machine!!!', the title poem of Nagra's second collection, the grown-up poet-speaker's child-hood was spent as 'foreign | kid of the class',

who chewed the fat
of the raw meat minty
tongue that English
is[73]

English is hard to reach, approached by jagged syntax, evoked grotesquely and viscerally as alien words in the mouth, all raw meat and mint, a tongue to be chewed. The poet's ambivalent triumph over the process has been to acquire a 'hoard' of words, 'swotted' in class, a 'stash | of coolly imperial diction' out of which to contrive a 'career | in poems'. Insisting on language for the 'foreign | kid' as anything but the organic emanation of self, it is instead something indigestible, awkwardly and uncomfortably ingested, or a commodity, laboriously acquired. The phrase 'coolly imperial diction' on the one hand signifies the dispassionate, disinterested, composed relationship to the language's 'imperial' nature that the poet can never cultivate and on the other, in the homophonic play of 'coolly'/'coolie' (a hired colonial labourer), suggests that the price of English, and of being a 'foreign | kid' English poet, may be ongoing indentureship to the history of empire. But this homophony is also there to attune the eye and ear to a third sign, the romanised Punjabi homonym given in the 'Bolly Bhaji' glossary: '*coolly* – loose (morally or materially)'.[74] This interlingual homonym, with its two possible interpretations, either indicts the poet further, his 'imperial diction' a sign of his morally suspect complicity, or (perhaps and/or) suggests how his 'hoard' is multiplied, and how Punjabi is able to unsettle English signification and 'loosen' the binding ties of its history.

'Tippoo Sultan's Incredible White-Man-Eating Tiger-Toy Machine!!!' shows how Punjabi operates as a sometimes unannounced presence, to the non-Punjabi-speaking reader, as a substratum in Nagra's poetry which is angled at English and working to effect its disruption from the inside. Dramatising the struggle to find a usable language, the effect is often to make all language appear suspect and unreliable. In the poem 'Raju t'Wonder Dog!', 'Yorkshire Punjabi' flourishes in a shop in Huddersfield run by the narrator Avtar and his wife Sapna. Avtar is a welcoming narrator whose language is equally accommodating: an exaggerated page-dialect that combines Yorkshire ('Tha gret wazzock!', 'fettlin'') with Punjabi ('soofna', 'sweet-as-ladoos'). The poem begins:

> First good penny I spent in 'uddersfield,
> after t'shop, were on a sweet-as-ladoos
> alsatian, against me wife, Sapna's wishes.

> Reet from t'off there were grief cos Beena,
> what's Sapna's friend, were visitin' –
> showin' off her reet bonny aubergine sari
> t'spit o'Meera Syal. Appen t'cage fer Raju
> weren't locked … I were fettlin' stuff
> on t'other aisle when I 'eard him skatin'
> towards t'till fer Beena![75]

The poem exploits the comic potential of this performatively mixed language, splicing the two British comedic staples of working-class northern life and the Asian-owned corner shop (the kind of comic juxtaposition which was the stock-in-trade of the British Asian comedy series *Goodness Gracious Me!*, one of whose writers and stars was the actor Meera Syal), even as it proceeds to confound the expectations engendered by both, in a sympathetic evocation of romantic love and the pain of unwanted childlessness. Avtar translates the couple's loving, multilingual in-jokes by addressing the reader:

> By t'way 'soofna' means 'dream' –
> a bit like Sapna in't it? That's why Raju
> and me'll stoop and I'll say: *Sapna,*
> *you're me soofna. Why would I do*
> *owt like to upset me soofna?* Chucklin'
> she'll add: *Aah Avtar, you're me avatar.*
> T'customers'll coo or look reet confused.[76]

In the confines of Avtar's shop, we see the operations of what Paul Gilroy terms 'conviviality' – an openness and hospitality born of Britain's 'unkempt, unruly, and unplanned multiculture' – played out in and through language.[77] Yet while Gilroy largely privileges London as the laboratory of conviviality, Nagra sets this scene of multilingual generosity and openness in the working-class north of England, where two of Britain's disenfranchised language forms, Yorkshire English and Punjabi, combine in the everyday accommodations of 'Yorkshire Punjabi'.

This is not, of course, the whole story. Avtar's Yorkshire Punjabi is just as flamboyantly inauthentic as the language of 'Darling and Me!' and, like that poem, this one trades on the comedic assumptions accru-ing to its poetic voice – here doubled between linguistic stereotypes of working-class Yorkshire and South Asians in Britain (in the key slap-stick scene, Raju crashes into a towering 'pink wafer display' and the ensuing chaos leaves 't'queue of 'ouse weefs near weein"), before giving way to the more humane and melancholy detailed texture of Avtar's relationship with Sapna. Leaving questions of authenticity aside, the poem's staging of conviviality is notably fragile, uneven, and provi-sional. Some of Avtar's customers 'coo', others look 'reet confused'; all may eventually desert this space of encounter for the local supermar-ket, the 'bright lights | o' Morrisons'. Avtar and Sapna's 'failing IVFs', meanwhile, as well as the poem's confinement within the space of the shop, caution against any implication that the scene stands for a readily reproducible conviviality. Nevertheless, in its refusal of the distinc-tion between endogamous and exogamous, Yorkshire dialect as 'local' and Punjabi as 'exotic', the poem offers a kind of consensual, convivi-al restaging of *Hobson-Jobson* – performing in language what James Procter has called the 'postcolonial everyday', a quotidian encounter where the relationship between 'Asianness' and 'Englishness' becomes 'commonsense' and 'taken-for-granted'.[78]

'Raju t'Wonder Dog' offers Nagra's trademark ambivalence as to how far, and how seriously, we are to take its proffered vision of welcome and conviviality, when its language, as with much of Nagra's language, is so weighed down by a consciousness of its own construct-edness. As this chapter has argued, he is a poet engaged with English as a whole cultural system – its structures, sounds, conventions, histo-ries, ideological underpinnings, literary conventions – including asking what its mainstream poetry markets demand of 'British Asian' poets. Nagra's insider/outsider position with regard both to English and to the British Punjabi community he incorporates as speakers in his poems, in relation to his studied disavowal of sentimental attachment to the idea of origins, is one which courts danger: on the one hand, of reductive readings which take his to be an 'authentic' voice; on the other, accusa-tions of self-colonisation, betrayal, minstrelsy. But in fact, in the world-view of his poetry, there is *no* uncompromised language – only infinite regress by which all words carry their own ghosts on their backs. Using etymology and intertextuality, Nagra compels English to confess to its histories of empire and oppression and, at the same time, to show how it has always been open and vulnerable to other forms of language even when most strongly disavowing them. His poetry calls for a reckoning with how the English language, and Britain's postcolonial multilingualism, are after all effects and legacies of the same history of empire. But Nagra's insistence on English's imbrication in colonial and postcolonial scenes of languaging also produces a more general position on language: that by its very nature it always comes to us from somewhere else.

Notes

1 Home Office, 'Secure borders, safe haven: integration with diversity in modern Britain, February 2002, p. 11. https://assets.publishing.service.gov. uk/government/uploads/system/uploads/attachment_data/file/250926/ cm5387.pdf.

2 Tony Grew, 'Eric Pickles: keep the faith', *The House*, 9 March 2012. http:// www.politicshome.com/uk/article/48272/?edition_id=998.

3 Daljit Nagra, 'The Man Who Would Be English!', in *Look We Have Coming To Dover!* (London: Faber, 2007), p. 15.

4 Adrian Blackledge, *Discourse and Power in a Multilingual World* (Amsterdam and Philadelphia: John Benjamins, 2005). On this issue in particular, and on the sea change in language discourses in British politics and culture after 2001, see also Deborah Cameron, 'The one, the many and the Other: representing multi- and monolingualism in post-9/11 verbal hygiene', *Critical Multilingualism Studies* 1:2 (2013), 59–77.

5 Blackledge, *Discourse and Power in a Multilingual World*. It is worth noting the different statuses accorded to so-called 'indigenous' and 'immigrant' languages; the Act does in fact enshrine both Welsh and Gaelic, alongside English, as alternate languages of national belonging.

6 United Kingdom Border Agency, 'SET17 – English Language Requirement', 2010. www.ukba.homeoffice.gov.uk/policyandlaw/guidance/ecg/set/set 17/.

7 Josh Halliday and Libby Brooks, 'Johnson pledges to make all immigrants learn English', *Guardian*, 5 July 2019. www.theguardian.com/politics/2019/ jul/05/johnson-pledges-to-make-all-immigrants-learn-english.

8 Blackledge, *Discourse and Power in a Multilingual World*, p. vii.

9 Claire Chambers, '"Meddl[ing] with my type": an interview with Daljit Nagra', *Crossings: Journal of Migration and Culture* 1 (2010), 87.

10 Patrick Barkham, 'The bard of Dollis Hill', *Guardian*, 18 January 2007. www.theguardian.com/books/2007/jan/18/poetry.race.

11 Arvind Mandair, *Religion and the Specter of the West: Sikhism, India, Postcoloniality, and the Politics of Translation* (New York: Columbia University Press, 2009), p. 21.

12 Mandair, *Religion and the Specter of the West*, p. 21.
13 Thomas Babington Macaulay, 'Minute on Indian Education', [2 February 1835], in *Selected Writings*, ed. J. Clive and T. Pinney (Chicago: Chicago University Press, 1972), p. 249.
14 Mikhail Bakhtin, 'Discourse in the novel', in *The Dialogic Imagination: Four Essays*, trans. Caryl Emerson and Michael Holquist (Austin: University of Texas Press, 1981), p. 293.
15 Charles Husband, 'Racist humour and racist ideology in British television, or I laughed til you cried', in Chris Powell (ed.) *Humour in Society: Resistance and Control* (London: Macmillan, 1988), pp. 149–178. For more on 1980s debates around this question, see also P. Cohen and C. Gardner, *It Ain't Half Racist Mum: Fighting Racism in the Media* (London: Comedia, 1982).
16 As Susanne Mühleisen observes of the Spanish waiter Manuel in *Fawlty Towers*, 'for decades, an imitation of the central features of the speech of this television figure – a "Spanish accent" or even a simple "Que?" – has been sufficient as a cue to set generations of British television viewers laughing'. Susanne Mühleisen, 'What makes an accent funny, and why? Black British Englishes and humour televised', in Susanne Reichl and Mark Stein (eds) *Cheeky Fictions: Laughter and the Postcolonial* (Amsterdam: Rodopi, 2005), p. 226.
17 Chambers, '"Meddl[ing] with my type"', p. 92.
18 Zadie Smith, in *White Teeth*, also plays the phrase for its comedic association with a racist version of South Asianness that is in fact distinctly British:

> 'Oh,' said Millat, putting on what he called a *bud-bud ding-ding* accent. 'You are meaning where from am I *originally*.'
> Joyce looked confused. 'Yes, *originally*.'
> 'Whitechapel,' said Millat, pulling out a fag. 'Via the Royal London Hospital and the 207 bus.'

Zadie Smith, *White Teeth* (London: Penguin, 2001), p. 319.
19 Sarah Brouillette, *Literature and the Creative Economy* (Stanford: Stanford University Press, 2014), pp. 116, 120.
20 Daljit Nagra, 'Booking Khan Singh Kumar', in *Look We Have Coming to Dover!* (London: Faber, 2007), p. 6.
21 Daljit Nagra, 'Booking Khan Singh Kumar', p. 7.
22 Brouillette, *Literature and the Creative Economy*, p. 123.
23 *Newsnight Review*, 19 January 2007, http://news.bbc.co.uk/1/hi/progra mmes/newsnight/review/6280089.stm.
24 On the *decibel* prize, see Brouillette, *Literature and the Creative Economy*, p. 117.
25 For discussion of the inclusion of Nagra's 'A Black History of the English-

Speaking Peoples' in the 2018 *Norton Anthology of English Literature* – and the poem's framing by paratexts which seem to neutralise its postcolonial politics – see Tabish Khair, 'The Nortoning of Nagra', *Massachusetts Review* 60:2 (2019), 325–335.

26 Daljit Nagra, 'The Furtherance of Mr Bulram's Education', in *Look We Have Coming to Dover!*, p. 38.

27 Nagra, 'In a White Town', in *Look We Have Coming to Dover!*, pp. 18–19.

28 Daljit Nagra, 'Cane', in *British Museum* (London: Faber, 2017), p. 11.

29 See Dave Gunning, 'Daljit Nagra, Faber poet: burdens of representation and anxieties of influence', *Journal of Commonwealth Literature* 43:3 (2008), 100.

30 Daljit Nagra, 'Kabba Questions the Ontology of Representation, the Catch 22 for "Black" Writers', in *Look We Have Coming to Dover!*, p. 43. I've discussed this poem in detail in Rachael Gilmour, 'Doing voices: reading language as craft in black British poetry', *Journal of Commonwealth Literature* 49:3 (2014), 343–357.

31 Sandeep Parmar, in an essay for the *Los Angeles Review of Books*, presents Nagra as a poet knowingly complicit with a 'mostly white poetic establishment prevail[ing] over a patronizing culture that presents minority poets as exceptional cases', engaged in 'deft ventriloquizing of Imperial fantasies': 'Voiced in the hysterics of "Punglish," a faux parodic mix of English and Punjabi, Nagra's poetry trots out old stereotypes of the awkward, cheerful Indian interloper, that Other of post-1960s Britain'. Sandeep Parmar, 'Not a British subject: race and poetry in the UK', *Los Angeles Review of Books*, 6 (December 2015). https://lareviewofbooks.org/article/not-a-british-subject-race-and-poetry-in-the-uk/.

32 Daljit Nagra, 'GET OFF MY POEM WHITEY', in *British Museum*, pp. 38–39.

33 Daljit Nagra, 'Informant', in *Look We Have Coming to Dover!*, p. 45.

34 Bakhtin, 'Discourse in the novel', pp. 293–294.

35 In 1990, the Conservative MP Norman Tebbit suggested that the loyalty of British Asians should be judged according to who they supported in international cricket matches.

36 Paul Gilroy, *There Ain't No Black in the Union Jack*, revised edition (London: Routledge, 2002), p. xxxv.

37 Chambers, '"Meddl[ing] with my type"', p. 91.

38 Chambers, '"Meddl[ing] with my type"', p. 91.

39 Tom Paulin, *A New Look at the Language Question* (Derry: Field Day, 1983), p. 5.

40 Paulin, *A New Look At The Language Question*, pp. 5, 18.

41 Chambers, '"Meddl[ing] with my type"', p. 90.

42 Nagra, 'GET OFF MY POEM WHITEY', p. 39.
43 Daljit Nagra, 'The Punjab', in *Tippoo Sultan's Incredible White-Man-Eating Tiger-Toy Machine!!!* (London: Faber, 2011), p. 34.
44 Daljit Nagra, 'The Gob-Smacking Taste of Mine Inheritance', in *Tippoo Sultan's Incredible White-Man-Eating Tiger-Toy Machine!!!*, p. 6.
45 The OED gives the first English usage of 'bhaji' as 1832; by 1888, it had made its way into the *Wife's Help to Indian Cookery: being a practical manual for housekeepers*.
46 Daljit Nagra, '*Hobson-Jobson*: a very English enterprise', BBC Radio 4, 13 July 2012. www.bbc.co.uk/programmes/b01kksr0.
47 Henry Yule and A. C. Burnell, *Hobson-Jobson: A Glossary of Colloquial Anglo-Indian Words and Phrases* (London: John Murray, 1886).
48 Daljit Nagra, 'Bolly Bhaji', in *Tippoo Sultan's Incredible White-Man-Eating Tiger-Toy Machine!!!*, p. 55.
49 Pramod K. Nayar, *Colonial Voices: The Discourses of Empire* (Oxford: Wiley-Blackwell, 2012), p. 69.
50 Daljit Nagra, 'This Be the Pukka Verse', in *Tippoo Sultan's Incredible White-Man-Eating Tiger-Toy Machine!!!*, pp. 16–17.
51 Daljit Nagra, 'Darling & Me!', in *Look We Have Coming to Dover!*, p. 4.
52 Sarah Crown, 'A flighty mix-up country', *Guardian*, 24 February 2007. www.guardian.co.uk/books/2007/feb/24/featuresreviews.guardianreview25.
53 Gilroy, *There Ain't No Black in the Union Jack*. On comedy and linguistic racism, see Mühleisen, 'What makes an accent funny, and why?'.
54 On Hindi as the dominant language of Bollywood, see Mihir Bose, *Bollywood: A History* (Stroud: Tempus, 2006).
55 Nagra, 'Darling & Me!', p. 3.
56 Nagra, 'Darling & Me!', p. 3.
57 Daljit Nagra, 'Yobbos!', in *Look We Have Coming to Dover!*, p. 11.
58 Nagra, 'Yobbos!', p. 11.
59 Frantz Fanon, *Black Skin, White Masks*, trans. Charles Lam Markmann (London: Pluto Press, 1986), pp. 111–112.
60 Nagra, 'Yobbos!', p. 11.
61 Nagra, 'Yobbos!', p. 11.
62 Daljit Nagra, 'Digging', in *Look We Have Coming to Dover!*, p. 39.
63 Nagra, 'Kabba Questions the Ontology of Representation', p. 43.
64 On the poem's inclusion in the *Norton Anthology*, see Khair, 'The Nortoning of Nagra'.
65 Daljit Nagra, 'A Black History of the English-Speaking Peoples', in *Tippoo Sultan's Incredible White-Man-Eating Tiger-Toy Machine!!!*, p. 50.
66 Nagra, 'A Black History of the English-Speaking Peoples', p. 51.

67 Nagra, 'A Black History of the English-Speaking Peoples', p. 52.
68 Derek Walcott, *Collected Poems 1948–1984* (New York: Noonday, 1986),
    p. 20.
69 Derek Walcott, 'A Far Cry from Africa', in *Collected Poems 1948–1984*,
    pp. 17–18.
70 W. H. Auden, *Spain [A Poem]* (London: Faber, 1937); George Orwell,
    'Inside the whale', in *Inside the Whale and Other Essays* (London: Gollancz,
    1940), pp. 9–50.
71 Nagra, 'A Black History of the English-Speaking Peoples', p. 53.
72 Raymond Williams, *Keywords: A Vocabulary of Culture and Society*
    (London: Fontana, 1976), pp. 21–22.
73 Nagra, 'Tippoo Sultan's Incredible White-Man-Eating Tiger-Toy
    Machine!!!', in *Tippoo Sultan's Incredible White-Man-Eating Tiger-Toy
    Machine!!!*, p. 9.
74 Nagra, 'Bolly Bhaji', p. 55.
75 Nagra, 'Raju t'Wonder Dog!', in *Tippoo Sultan's Incredible White-Man-
    Eating Tiger-Toy Machine!!!*, p. 18.
76 Nagra, 'Raju t'Wonder Dog!', p. 19.
77 Paul Gilroy, *After Empire: Melancholia or Convivial Culture?* (New York
    and London: Routledge, 2004), p. x.
78 James Procter, 'The postcolonial everyday', *New Formations* 58 (2006),
    62–80.

5

Living in translation

Write in a western language, publish in the west and you are constantly translating, back and forth – this is like this here but not there.
A thing has a high value here, a certain weight, move it to another
place and it becomes nothing.

Leila Aboulela, 'Moving away from accuracy'[1]

Words are incapable, words are weak, words are burdened, words are
manipulated, words are misinterpreted, words are obscure.

Xiaolu Guo, 'Visions in a whirling head'[2]

In the essay about her genesis as a writer from which the above quotation is taken, Leila Aboulela defines herself – a Sudanese Muslim writer
writing novels in English, publishing in Britain – as inevitably a translator. She finds the origins of her 'writing life'[3] in distance: in the need
to make connections between Britain and Khartoum, and to offer a
counternarrative to the 'stereotypical images of famine and war' which
dominate Western representations of Sudan.[4] In particular, she sets
out to make 'their language' – English – bear the weight of her perspective, rooted in a particular view of Islam, on life in Britain and to use
it to explore the emotional and spiritual lives of her Sudanese Muslim
women protagonists.[5] For Aboulela, translation is a question of fidelity,
of how to transfer 'value' without diminution, but she suggests that loss
in such transfer is inevitable, particularly across the power differential
between Sudan and the West: 'move it to another place and it becomes
nothing'. By way of illustration, she discusses the emotional valency of
'bahdala', 'an Arabic word I have tried to translate but I can't':

> There is no equivalent to it in English, no word comes close enough: dishevelled, no, undignified, no, harassed, also no. A friend would tell me about her bad day, a raw searing day, child rushed to hospital, husband God knows where, other children screaming in the background, she has had a rough time and she would say, in a Sudanese accent 'Itbahdalta yaa Leila,' or in an Egyptian accent 'Itbahdilt ya Leila.' And I would wish that she wasn't saying that. ... For I don't want that word. It frightens me.[6]

Bahdala is, in Aboulela's account, specifically connected to the experience of migrancy: 'I travel from home and blows to my pride knock some sense into me, some sense'.[7] It is an expression of a frightening dissolution which triangulates yet exceeds its closest English equivalents, 'dishevelled', 'undignified', and 'harassed'; but it is also a spiritual education, a 'medicine' which can 'cure the ego's badness, lead to wisdom'.[8] It is the kind of crisis which precipitates, in different ways, the spiritual journeys of the protagonists of her first two novels, *The Translator* (1999) and *Minaret* (2005). It is the lesson, Aboulela implies, which 'travel from home' has to teach the women migrants who people her fiction, yet it represents the part of that experience that resists translation. The act of writing in English about Arab Muslim women's lives becomes, then, an act of translation in which the writer is ceaselessly trying to guard against distortion or diminution, which appears at the same time inevitable. For the writer Xiaolu Guo, meanwhile, already established as a novelist and film-maker in China before moving to London and publishing her first novel in English, the movement between languages reveals not only the limits of translation, but problems with any language: 'Words are incapable, words are weak, words are burdened, words are manipulated, words are misinterpreted, words are obscure.'[9] Where operating within the parameters of any one conventional system of meaning is liable to let you down, Guo establishes an artistic practice that aims to put them into dynamic and mutually critical relation with each other – the better to see their weaknesses and dangers, but also to realise their revolutionary potential: 'the day literature dies, that will be the end of the world'.[10]

Women as translators figure in both Aboulela's and Guo's writing. This is the case in a literal sense in Aboulela's *The Translator* and Guo's *I Am China* (2014), both of which feature women protagonists who earn their living as translators – the former Sammar, a Sudanese

Arabic–English translator working at Aberdeen University, the latter Iona, a Scottish freelance Chinese–English translator working in London. Beyond this, both novelists write novels that are *about* translation in the self-conscious sense, dramatising what it means to move between different kinds of language or systems of meaning.[11] Guo's *A Concise Chinese-English Dictionary For Lovers* (2007) is narrated by a young Chinese woman who has come to London for a year to learn English, and is rendered in a stylised register of 'learner's English' which develops and changes through the course of the novel, in an extended meditation on the possibilities of accommodation and mutual understanding between languages, and also between fallible human beings. Aboulela's *Minaret* features a bilingual protagonist, Najwa, a Sudanese exile living in London, whose fluent movement between English and Arabic – a function of an elite Anglophone education, as the daughter of a now-deposed and executed Sudanese politician – is no salve for her loneliness and poverty, which in the end is to be found in a language that exists beyond translation or interpretation, in the sacred Arabic of the Qur'an.

These novels, in 'performing acts of cultural translation in the original itself' – in other words, in appearing to be already translated, in reflecting on acts of translation, in considering what is gained, what is lost, and what happens in the transit between different kinds of language – represent what Waïl Hassan has called 'translational literature', 'at once foregrounding, performing, and problematizing the act of translation', and in doing so raising 'many of the questions that preoccupy contemporary translation theory'.[12] Even more than this, for Guo's and Aboulela's protagonists translation is the lived experience of communication and consciousness, a permanent and inevitable state of existence. In Aboulela's case, she writes in the conscious recognition of a global Islam in which the majority do not speak the language of the Qur'an, Arabic, and about Muslim communities in Britain in which multilingualism and transnational connectivity are the everyday reality. In an essay entitled 'Barbie in the Mosque', the opening chapter in Tom Devine and Paddy Logue's *Being Scottish*, Aboulela writes of the community of her Aberdeen mosque: her friend Aisha, a Scottish Muslim convert brought up Catholic, who has 'never been outside Britain' yet is 'closer to the world than those who go abroad On Holiday every year', as well as children who are 'Sudanese, Lebanese and half-Bengali, speaking in the Scottish accent of Froghall and Tillydrone'.[13] For Guo, the back-and-forth transit between English and Chinese is at the centre of a 'multimodal' way of seeing in which different systems of meaning – the linguistic and the visual, the formal conventions of literature and film – are in dynamic, mutually energising relation and tension with one another.[14] Guo's work is at pains to acknowledge how translation serves dominant ideologies, from the power of global English and its relationship to global capitalism, to the Chinese state's manipulation of translation to serve its own ends. But it nevertheless invests in an idea of translation that can offer resistance to such power, whether that is to be found in the subversive capabilities of everyday heteroglossia or in radical experimental art.

Whereas the writers discussed in preceding chapters write from the perspective of the multilingual local, contesting language politics that have to do with Englishness, Scottishness, or Britishness even while claiming different kinds of internationalism or transnational connectivity, for both Aboulela and Guo, multilingualism in Britain appears simply as part of a global pattern whereby living in translation is the norm. Theirs is writing set in Britain that travels through multiple locations: Khartoum, Beijing, Aberdeen, London. Both writers are interested in the affective, social, and political dimensions of being Chinese or Arab women speakers of English as a second language in Britain, but their primary focus is on the interior, psychic dimensions of living in translation, and on the different kinds of connection or community that this makes possible – outside of, and indeed opposed to, what might more conventionally be termed 'language community'. Bearing the traces of multiple languages, both Aboulela's and Guo's writing foregrounds and dramatises the processes of translation of which it is both product and representation. Nevertheless, translational literature is like translation theory in offering no consensus on the practice of translation: how it works, what it is for, what its risks are, and what its possibilities might be. Aboulela emphasises the ideal of translation as equivalence and fidelity. Taking into account the meaning of translation as 'carrying across', in this view of things, both the act of migration and the process of translation are made possible by investment in the notion of stable meanings which can be transmitted intact and unchanged into new contexts. At the other end of the spectrum, meanwhile, lies a view of translation as iconoclastic and transformative, both violent and creative – as for Homi Bhabha, going via Rushdie to cast its inevitable distortions and infidelities as the site where 'newness enters the world'.[15] In both Aboulela's and Guo's work, translation is on one level an inevitable and permanent state of existence – in Aboulela's case both because of her interest in migrant women's lives and because of her commitment to a global, transnational Islam; in Guo's case because, as Fiona Doloughan observes, as an artist who moves between film and writing and between Chinese and English, her work constantly cross-cuts between different kinds of linguistic and visual meaning-making as a way of reflecting how, in a contemporary globalised world, such constant experience of translation is not the exception but the norm.[16] The central question this chapter will explore is what it means, and what it costs, in each writer's work, to move between languages, and the conclusions to which this leads them about the nature of language.

'Teach me something old. Shock me. Comfort me': Leila Aboulela translating Islam

Leila Aboulela writes what she has called 'Muslim immigrant fiction' – set in Scotland, England, and Sudan – exclusively in English.[17] Aboulela herself, born in Cairo and raised in Khartoum, was educated in English from the age of seven; her bilingual female protagonists, like their author, show little outward sign of a struggle to express themselves in English.[18] Nevertheless, as we've seen, Aboulela has suggested that a writer in her position is inevitably a translator, moving back and forth between languages, cultures, systems of belief, ways of life, and that this movement is inevitably difficult partly because of the radical differences involved in translating Sudan into Britain, Arabic into English, Islam into Western secularism. There is an obvious concern with power differentials at play in the notion that something with 'a high value', 'a certain weight', can easily 'become nothing' in the transit, specifically in relation to contemporary Western perspectives on Islam. But beyond this, what Aboulela also suggests is a perspective on translation, more broadly, as risk, and concern not only about Arabic and English, and the possibilities or not of translation between them, but also with the ways in which one might be able to get away from the whole difficult business of linguistic signification altogether.

Aboulela's first novel, *The Translator* (1999), set in Edinburgh, recounts the love story of a Sudanese Muslim widow, Sammar, and the Scottish 'Middle-East historian' and 'lecturer in Third World Politics', Rae, for whom she works as an Arabic–English translator.[19] Devastated by the death of her husband Tarig, unable to cope with the care of her son, whom she has left with Tarig's mother in Sudan, Sammar's life in Edinburgh is a lonely one lived sparsely in a bare flat, only tenuously connected to her surroundings, consumed by 'the feeling this has nothing to do with me, these shops, these people have nothing to do with me, this sky is not for me'.[20] As a translator, Sammar expresses a doctrinaire view of her work as finding precise linguistic equivalence: 'moulding Arabic into English, trying to be transparent like a pane of glass not obscuring the meaning of any word'.[21] Yet in fact, as both Waïl Hassan and Tamar Steinitz point out, this is a version of inter-lingual translation that does not exist in the world of the novel. Even when Sammar is not mechanistically 'pushing Arabic into English, English into Arabic', she is otherwise revealing the myriad ways in which the kind of 'transparent' direct translation she espouses is out of the question.[22] As she reflects, even her own name has gained a false etymology in the transit into English by being pronounced 'like the season, summer', while losing its Arabic signification: 'It means conversations with friends, late at night. It's what the desert nomads liked to do, talk leisurely by the light of the moon, when it was no longer so hot and the day's work was over.'[23] Part of the problem being gestured to here is the need for what Kwame Appiah calls 'thick translation': it is one thing to learn to pronounce someone's name, quite another to learn its meaning and history and activate them imaginatively in a new linguistic setting.[24] In an interlude at the start of the novel which asks readers to consider what we mean by 'meaning', Sammar is asked to translate a manifesto written by Al-Nidaa, an extremist group in the south of Egypt, in order to ascertain whether they pose a terrorist threat.

> The document was handwritten, badly photocopied and full of spell-ing mistakes. It was stained with tea and what she guessed to be beans mashed with oil. Last night she had stayed up late transforming the Arabic rhetoric into English, imagining she could smell beans cooked in the way she had known long ago, with cumin and olive oil.[25]

As Sammar hands Rae the folder that contains her translation of the manifesto itself (which the reader never sees), he asks her what she thinks of it, and it is these extralinguistic yet signifying aspects of the document – its poor reproduction, the handwriting and spelling mistakes, the food stains and the associations they provoke in her – that she invokes, not its written contents, to describe it as 'pathetic', 'in spite of the bravado', written by 'people overwhelmed by thinking that nothing should be what it is now'.[26] These are precisely the aspects of the manifesto, however, which can have no place in Sammar's literal translation, a document commissioned – as much of her work is, through the course of the narrative, such as the interrogation records she later translates – for the purposes of assessing a terrorist threat. Where does the meaning of something like the Al-Nidaa manifesto reside, the novel perceptively asks – in its literal, written contents (which we, as readers, never see) or in its extralinguistic semiotics? What does translation mean in the case of this – or any – text?

Sammar's life in Edinburgh, meanwhile, is also experienced as a bad translation. She still notices, though her alarmed responses have been dulled over the years, the 'things that jarred – an earring on a man's earlobe, a woman walking a dog big enough to swallow the infant she was at the same time pushing in a pram, the huge billboards on the road: Wonderbra, cigarette ads that told people to smoke and not to smoke at the same time, the Ministry of Sin nightclub housed in a former church'.[27] In intense, disorienting interludes, she experiences the incommensurability of one reality overlaying another:

> Outside, Sammar stepped into a hallucination in which the world had swung around. Home had come here. Its dimly lit streets, its sky and the feel of home had come here and balanced just for her. She saw the sky cloudless with too many stars, imagined the night warm, warmer than indoors. She smelled dust and heard the barking of stray dogs among the street's rubble and pot-holes. A bicycle bell tinkled, frogs croaked, the muezzin coughed into the microphone and began the azan for the Isha prayer. But this was Scotland and the reality left her dulled, unsure of herself.[28]

With Rae, who seems to understand how Sammar's consciousness is split between places, languages, and cultures, she discusses her sense of the multi-layered untranslatability of Sudan into Scotland:

She said that colours made her sad. Yellow as she knew it and green
as she knew it were not here, not bright, not vivid as they should be.
She had stacked the differences; the weather, the culture, modernity,
the language, the silence of the muezzin, then found that the colours
of mud, sky and leaves, were different too.[29]

Through the figure of a struggling translator, Aboulela asks whether
there is ever any kind of accommodation between ordinary human
languages which will not, inevitably, one way or another, fall short.
Crucially, this question is framed in relation to a religious conception
of translation: the novel's problems with translation are grounded in
what Rae observes, midway through the novel, about the Qur'an.[30]
Though the holy text has of course been translated, he says, those translations 'don't do it justice. Much is lost'. Agreeing, Sammar replies:
'Yes, the meaning can be translated but not reproduced. And of course
the miracle of it can't be reproduced.'[31] This is a view which takes the
Qur'an as a work of divine revelation that exists outside the parameters
of human signification, beyond human agency, and is thus fundamentally untranslatable, in a meaningful sense. This 'miracle' of a language
that exists – in this view of things – as outside time and space and in a
sense beyond hermeneutics, contrasts with a worldly experience of language as flawed, difficult, and insufficient. As the novel moves towards
its one, divinely ordained, successful act of translation – Rae's conversion to Islam – it proffers a resonant image of the material and fallible
nature of human language, and its oblique relationship to the divine.
Sammar learns of Rae's conversion in a letter from his friend Fareed,
which she treasures and rereads endlessly, until it is 'worn and crum-
pled: stained with kitchen water, egg from the children's sandwiches,
Amir's fingerprints when he had tried to snatch it from her hands while
she was helping him with his multiplication homework'.[32] Like some
kind of redeemed analogue of the Al-Nidaa manifesto, the letter trans-
mits the kernel of a miracle that lies beyond human signification – the
perfect act of translation that is Rae's conversion to Islam – while it also
accrues meanings that make it seem ever more earthbound and domestic, in stains that commemorate meals cooked, children fed, homework
completed.

For a reader already familiar with *The Translator*, the prologue
to Aboulela's second novel, *Minaret*, opening as it does with the

transliterated first surah of the Qur'an, suggests related questions about translation and translatability: '*Bism Allahi, Ar-rahman, Ar-raheem*'. The surah hangs over a vision of London, seen from Regent's Park, in the early morning light – a cityscape which is defined by the minaret of the nearby mosque, and which is also a reflection of the narrator's psychological state:

> The trees in the park across the road are scrubbed silver and brass. I look up and see the minaret of Regent's Park mosque visible above the trees. I have never seen it so early in the morning in this vulnerable light. London is at its most beautiful in autumn. In summer it is seedy and swollen, in winter it is overwhelmed by Christmas lights and in spring, the season of birth, there is always disappointment. Now it is at its best, now it is poised like a mature woman whose beauty is no longer fresh but still surprisingly potent.[33]

As a medium of translation, this city scene offers oblique, defamiliarised glimpses of the narrator – overwhelmed, disappointed, beautiful – that reveal a different perspective to the one we see in Najwa's momentary reflection in a mirror a little later: 'a woman in a white headscarf and beige, shapeless coat'.[34] These alternate angles of vision on Najwa, personalised and depersonalised, interior and exterior, key into the novel's concern with how its Muslim protagonists are perceived, and British Islamophobia is a constant if unemphasised presence, here as elsewhere in Aboulela's writing. One night on a bus, a group of drunken youths call Najwa 'Muslim scum' and throw a can of Tizer at her (an almost absurdly British choice of drink; the fact that she recognises its taste immediately is a reminder that she has known British culture intimately since childhood).[35] Later, out walking with Tamer, the devout Muslim son of her employer, Najwa senses 'the slight unease he inspires in the people around us. I turn and look at him through their eyes. Tall, young, Arab-looking, dark eyes and the beard, just like a terrorist'.[36]

Translation is not, at least overtly, a problem for the novel. Najwa's innermost thoughts, her doubts and strivings, her developing personal engagement with Islam, are expressed in an English-language narrative in which translation is mostly unmarked, save for a few embedded words of transliterated Arabic, and – unlike in *The Translator* – translatability is rarely explicitly brought into question. But what Aboulela dwells on in *Minaret*, as in *The Translator*, is the inner life of a subject whose fluent bilingualism in English and Arabic is offset by a kind of pervasive sense of discomfort with secular languages altogether. As a teenager in 1980s Khartoum, Najwa's bilingualism is a mark of her elite status as the privileged daughter of an influential politician, a product of her English-medium private education. Sudanese Arabic is the language of Sudanese nationalism[37] but English holds power both as the former colonial language in Sudan and as the language of US-led international communication. When the family are forced into exile after the Sudanese President's overthrow, at first Najwa's excellent English contributes to her feeling largely at home in a London familiar from childhood holidays. But, as she begins what she describes as her 'fall' – her father is executed, her mother dies, her brother Omar is imprisoned for stabbing a policeman during a drugs raid, the family's money runs out – Najwa's isolation intensifies despite her familiarity with the city and command of English. She rediscovers an old flame, the secular political radical Anwar who is also seeking asylum in London, and they rekindle their romance into what eventually becomes a sexual relationship. But their fraught alliance is symbolised by the way Anwar simultaneously admires, covets, and resents Najwa's bilingualism; he comments on her excellent English to his friends, and insists that she act as both his editor and cheerleader as he attempts to break into English-language journalism, while seeking to undermine her intellectually and reacting angrily whenever she corrects his writing in English. Their intimate language with one another, meanwhile, is a code-switching, rule-breaking mix of English and Arabic – 'It made us laugh, mixing the two languages, Arabic nouns with English verbs, making up new words that were a compound of both'[38] – which, associated as it is with their troubled and doomed relationship, is not a language to be trusted. The words which Anwar particularly favours – 'frustrated, inevitable, sexy'[39] – foreshadow the sexual relationship that they will soon embark on, which will reveal finally to Najwa that the 'freedom' she possesses in London is indistinguishable from a dizzying, amoral anonymity.

Having a shared language is no prerequisite for a shared understanding in the novel, a fact abundantly demonstrated in Najwa's failed relationship with Anwar. At cross-purposes to contemporary British political and popular discourse – which has, certainly since 2001, ascribed a whole raft of social ills specifically to Muslim women's

isolation through their lack of English – for Aboulela's bilingual protagonists there is no causal relationship between fluency in English and
a sense of British belonging.[40] Despite having been educated in English,
Najwa's experience in London is circumscribed by her poverty, her
status as a refugee, and her visibility as an observant, *hijab*-wearing
Muslim woman: 'it is safe for us in playgrounds, safe around children.
There are other places in London that aren't safe, where our very presence irks people'.[41] And English can be a medium of hatred, as when
the boys on the bus shout 'Muslim scum!' Nevertheless, the novel and
Aboulela's work more generally take no particular issue with English,
though they are certainly suspicious of monoglot nationalisms – be
they Sudanese, British, or the Iranian revolution which so fascinates
Najwa on TV as a teenager. Rejecting linguistic, ethnic, and national
affiliations, Aboulela's angle of vision takes in a transnational, and thus
by definition polyglot, Islam to which English is a vehicular language.[42]
As Tamer says, "My mother is Egyptian. I've lived everywhere except
Sudan: in Oman, Cairo, here. My education is Western and that makes
me feel that I am Western. My English is stronger than my Arabic.
… I guess being a Muslim is my identity. What about you?' Najwa
replies, 'I feel that I am Sudanese but things changed for me when I
left Khartoum. Then even while living here in London, I've changed.
And now, like you, I just think of myself as a Muslim'.[43] The English
language is associated in the novel as much with the international reach
of American popular culture – for example in Najwa and her brother's
teenaged obsession with Michael Jackson's *Off the Wall* – as it is with
the legacies of British colonialism. The ending of the novel has Najwa
renouncing her romantic claim on Tamer so that he can go to read
Middle Eastern Studies, in English, at an American university in Cairo.
And, as with English, so with modern Arabic, as Najwa sits in London
watching Arabic satellite TV channels from across the world, a deterritorialised medium for a global Islam.

The locus of Najwa's transformation into a devout Muslim –
attending prayers, wearing the *hijab* – is the Regent's Park mosque, to
which she is drawn by the sight of the minaret over the centre of the city.
The mosque is a space in which Muslims from all over the world come
together, and many languages are spoken: as Najwa first enters, she is
initially discomforted to hear women whispering about her in a language she doesn't understand, which she identifies as perhaps Turkish,

perhaps Urdu.[44] English is a lingua franca for the mosque's diverse congregation, but the sense of community which Najwa discovers there is not premised on having a (secular) language in common. When she meets the Syrian teacher Um Waleed in the mosque, she is immediately described in terms of her linguistic proximity to Najwa, both of them Arabic speakers – but although Najwa admires Um Waleed, she feels no close connection to her: 'she is not my friend, I can't confide in her and when we are alone the conversation hardly flows. Our natures are not harmonious; we orbit different paths'. [45] When she meets the Senegalese ambassador's wife at the mosque during Ramadan, by contrast, the immediate closeness she feels is not dependent on language: 'I didn't tell her any more than my name and what I did. There was no need – we had come together to worship and it was enough.'[46] Instead, sitting in the ambassador's wife's car, 'I used to doze to … her voice speaking on a mobile phone in Senegalese. I would dive in dreams to become small again, pampered by my parents.'[47] Later, near the end of the novel, Najwa experiences something similar listening to the meaningless chatter of her friend's baby:

> Ahmed is babbling away: words that don't make sense, strung together with inflections and exclamations of surprise, as if he is talking in a foreign language. His voice is lovely. I close my eyes. There is nothing to work out, just memories, impressions.[48]

This sense of comfort derived from the experience of being in the presence of other, unfamiliar languages is one which reappears in Aboulela's writing. In her essay 'Barbie in the Mosque', she describes the soothing sounds of voices which come to her ear not as meaningful utterances but as sound only:

> I hear the children and the tinkling blur of Turkish; one woman is breastfeeding a huge baby, the other has a mole on her cheek. They are louder than the Bengali woman and her sister. I can understand neither Turkish nor Bengali, and this soothes me. It is as if I am a child, too young to understand what my mother is saying to her friends.[49]

Here Aboulela describes a comfort derived from a feminised and spiritual homeliness which resides in the mosque as a polyglot space, but which is independent of her ability – or perhaps more properly, dependent on her *inability* – to understand what is being said around her. To move outside language as a system of signification, to experience human voices as sound, rhythm, and cadence without the hermeneutic demand to interpret, is a 'soothing' experience she associates with childhood, the prelinguistic experience of hearing voice without meaning.[50] In *Minaret*, Najwa longs to be soothed in such a way too.

At moments such as these, Aboulela's writing seems to fantasise a freedom from the vagaries of ordinary linguistic signification – freedom from the slippage of meanings, the need to 'work [things] out'. Such freedom is to be found in the prelinguistic: in the babbling of baby Ahmed, which allows Najwa to move freely in 'memories, impressions'. But most significantly, it is to be found at the point from which the novel begins, in the immutability of the Qur'an. The Islam which becomes Najwa's solace and refuge is an Islam premised on the miracle of direct revelation, a miracle which inheres in the word-as-divine-truth, absolutely stable, atemporal, and unchanging:

> The words were clear, as if I had known all this before and somehow, along the way, forgotten it. Refresh my memory. Teach me something old. Shock me. Comfort me. Tell me what will happen in the future, what happened in the past. Explain to me.[51]

In Najwa's case, the power of such a vision of language provides a sense of stability amid displacement and a salve for traumatic remembering. It is this she wants, rather than critical engagement: she is careful to avoid 'discussion' and the expression of 'opinion'.[52] Instead, Najwa's life at the mosque revolves around the language-work of *tajweed*, the rules of recitation of the Qur'an, which she learns and practises in the exclusively feminised space of the women's classes. David Farrier, writing about *Minaret* as 'asylum fiction', considers how Najwa's experience of uprootedness, isolation, and trauma lead her to value 'repetition', such as the recitation of *tajweed*, 'as a pathway to being-in-stasis'.[53] In a *tajweed* class all differences of language, history, class, culture are erased in recitation that aspires to one voice:

> The Tajweed class is my favourite. I learn how to pronounce the letters correctly, when to blur two letters together, when to pronounce the n in a nasal way, for how many beats to prolong a certain

letter. This concentration on technique soothes me; it makes me forget everything around me. … Here in the Tajweed class, all is calm and peaceful. We practice and practice until we get the words right. I want to read the Qur'an in a beautiful way.[54]

As Peter Morey observes, Najwa's approach to *tajweed* 'draws our attention to an embodied engagement with textual material quite different from hermeneutic protocols of reading that are concerned with extracting meaning'.[55] Ritual performance of phonological homogenisation – technique, pronunciation, 'get[ting] the words right' – stands metonymically for the fixity of the sign, in a language of revelation which exists outside time and space and beyond interpretation.

Coming to Aboulela's writing thinking about translation is unsettling, insofar as she both insists on its ubiquity and makes a case for its impossibility. Translation is, in her writing, an inevitable state of existence; the pivot for transnational, multilingual Muslim communities whose sense of global belonging in Islam supersedes secular, monoglot nationalisms; and an experience with the power to teach. Islam is, moreover, a faith into which one is translated – hence her focus on converts and reverts, and what she casts as the divine miracle of coming into Islam. Yet the instabilities and infelicities of ordinary human language and signification are underlined in her writing, with its scenes of partial and mis-translation, its scepticism about human communication in language and how 'value' is lost in the shuttling of translation 'back and forth'. Her polyglot, feminised, global vision of Islam, superseding other modes of national, cultural, linguistic, and ethnic affiliation, is forged in translation yet paradoxically beyond it, guaranteed by the untranslatability of the Qur'an itself, impervious to historical change, given in a language of revelation representing the 'miracle' of absolute correspondence between sign and referent, divided by an unbridgeable ontological distance from ordinary human language.

'Sorry of my English': Xiaolu Guo travelling between languages

Unlike Aboulela, who has always written in English, Xiaolu Guo was established as a novelist, film-maker, and critic in Chinese, in

China, before moving to London in 2002 to take up a British Council film-making scholarship, since which time she has written in and translated her work into English. Her first novel in English, *A Concise Chinese-English Dictionary for Lovers* (2007), is structured formally, thematically, and linguistically around the movement between languages. Its female protagonist and narrator, Zhuang Xiao Qiao – or Z, as she becomes known to the English people around her who can't pronounce her name – is a young woman from rural China, sent to London by her peasant-turned-shoe-factory-owner parents for a year to learn English at one of the city's many private language schools. Laid out as a journal, each chapter recounting a month of the year she spends in London, the novel marks her shifting relationship to English and Chinese as it charts her affair with an older British man – whose 'beautiful language' she falls for – exploring the possibilities and limitations of translation as a metonym for human relationships.[56] Tellingly, Z's love affair is founded upon a mistranslation: he says 'be my guest' and she, interpreting the phrase literally, packs her suitcase and moves into his Hackney home. Since then Guo has self-translated and adapted her earlier Chinese novel *Fenfang's 37.2 Degrees* into English as *Twenty Fragments of a Ravenous Youth* (2009), and published a collection of short stories, *Lovers in an Age of Indifference* (2010), and a memoir, *Once Upon a Time in the East* (2017), as well as two more novels in English. *UFO in Her Eyes* (2009) is constructed as the interrogation log of a Chinese peasant woman, Kwok Yun, who claims to have seen a flying disc-shaped object over her home village, and becomes a sharp satire of both the all-encompassing power of the Chinese state and the dubious benefits of capitalist modernity. *I Am China* (2014), meanwhile, picks up the thread of translation again in following the interplay between a Scottish translator of Chinese into English, Iona, and the material she is translating: a sheaf of letters and documents charting the relationship between a Chinese musician, Jian, and poet, Mu, spanning the period from the student revolution and massacre in Tiananmen Square in 1989, through their early relationship at Beijing University, to Jian's involvement in the Jasmine Revolution after the Arab Spring in 2011, to his forced exile and life as a political refugee and undocumented worker in Europe. Translation becomes, for Iona, a mode of human connection – and her own salvation – even as the letters she translates reveal Jian's experiences, shuttling between the regimes of postsocialist China and Fortress Europe, as the dark reverse of a vision of liberating, cosmopolitan translation.

Perhaps the most distinctive feature of *A Concise Chinese-English Dictionary for Lovers* – certainly, that feature most commented upon by reviewers and critics, of whom I am of course destined to be one – is Z's narrative voice, which is an astonishing literary performance of Chinese 'learner's English'. At the outset, it is extremely unpredictable and fragmented, characterised by calques (where she is thinking in Chinese and translating word-for-word into English), malapropisms, mishearings, and misinterpretations. As the narrative progresses, Z's English becomes more complex and more stable, developing into a flexible and expressive interlanguage, inflected by Chinese grammar and peppered with east London slang, which remains uniquely her own. Guo's risky literary experiment with narrative voice attracted some criticism – Jonathan Mirsky, writing in the *Spectator*, concluded a dismissive review by remarking that he looked forward to reading her next novel, 'written in grown up English'.[57] Certainly, issues of language and problems of translation are the source of much of the novel's humour, which at times plays to stereotypes of Chinese English: Z writes of 'Heathlow Airport', the 'Loyal Family'. Yet at the same time, the text works to subvert the kind of British comic norms which would make the language-learner a figure for mockery, while Z herself becomes increasingly aware of how her English fits with, or contradicts, British stereotypes of the 'typical Chinese'.[58] It is to be expected that she 'cannot pronounce the difference between "r" and "l", and request people without using *please*' – far less so, that she will sit alone in a Hackney cafe studying a porn magazine for three hours, with the aid of a dictionary, as a means to learn English.[59] In the end, the novel flouts English linguistic and literary norms to aesthetic and existential, as well as comic, effect. Z's shifting English becomes a medium to consider how languages create worldviews, and how a self is constructed in and between languages.

Z arrives in London armed with her *Collins Concise Chinese-English Dictionary* and an attendant faith in what it seems to represent: language as a stable system of one-to-one correspondences between word and referent; translation as a straightforward process of substitution between different yet at the same time commensurable systems. As Z puts it: '*Concise* meaning simple and clean'.[60] Guo's novel works swiftly to destabilise such a way of thinking by exposing growing tensions between the apparent certainty of the dictionary definitions which begin each chapter (the slipperiness of signification again evident when the *Dictionary* is partially supplanted by *Roget's Thesaurus*) and the complicated nature of Z's lived experience of English, particularly her experience of love. The novel's title points us to one of the narrative's central ironies: the insufficiency of the dictionary's model of translation as a vision of interpersonal relationships. In the end, it is Z and her lover, rather than Chinese and English, that prove to be incommensurable.

Although Z arrives full of expectations about a London comprised of 'important places including Buckingham Palace, or Big Stupid Clock', in fact her experience of the city remains largely limited to its impoverished seams: Tottenham Hale, Hackney, the red light district of Soho.[61] The London of the novel is also a city largely populated by immigrants, second-language speakers of English; even when Z meets fellow Chinese people, they are Cantonese speakers whom she cannot understand. Incomprehensibility is a repeated theme: for example, while in Aboulela's *Minaret* Anwar and Najwa find the Tube map to be a reassuring representation of the city's 'system' and 'structure', to Guo's Z it is 'like plate of noodles'.[62] The linguistically complex, baffling, demotic London in which she finds herself adrift is further signalled in the novel's patchwork of registers, languages, and scripts. Embedded in Z's narrative are Collins English dictionary entries; scrawled cafe menus; condom and vibrator instructions; scraps of handwritten letters, notes, and maps; the utterances of other second-language speakers of English as well as surly London cab drivers; poetry and song lyrics; and both transliterated Mandarin and written Chinese.

In the face of such incomprehensibility, Z is swiftly led to begin compiling her own, piecemeal 'dictionary' which, in its heterogeneity (in common with the heterogeneity of her narrative itself), charts a more complex, provisional, and idiosyncratic route between languages. In Whorfian mode, the novel probes disjunctures between Chinese and English at the level of syntax, grammar, and lexis, in order to consider how languages construct reality differently.[63] At the same time, however, Guo rejects a deterministic view of the relationship between language and individual consciousness. To give the most striking, if the most obvious, example: one repeated refrain, in the novel, is the problem of grammatical temporality and English tense construction for speakers of Chinese. Yet while it may be Z who has difficulties with the future tense, it is her commitment-phobic English lover who finds it impossible to talk about the future.[64]

The idealised vision of language and translation represented by the Chinese–English dictionary is replicated in the breezy ESOL-speak of Z's language school brochure:

> Dear Student, Welcome to London! On finishing our course, you will find yourself speaking and thinking in your new language quite effortlessly. You will be able to communicate in a wide variety of situations, empowered by the ability to create your own sentences and use language naturally.[65]

In the context of Z's narrative, the brochure's assurance sounds parodic. Speaking and thinking, this novel suggests, can never be 'effortless'; the movement between languages and the business of human communication are complex and exhausting negotiations from which Z at times longs to be free. In a Soho peep show, her momentary fantasy of becoming a prostitute is simultaneously a fantasy of escape from the constraints of language: 'I want be able to expose my body, to relieve my body, to take my body away from dictionary and grammar and sentences, to let my body break all disciplines'.[66] For a woman from the global South – for impoverished women from all over the world, including the women from Eastern Europe whose labour keeps the Soho sex industry running – the struggle with English is enmeshed with socioeconomic and gendered, as well as racial, structures of power. For Z, too, these are indivisible from the complex power dynamics of her relationship with her lover. In one moment of crisis in their relationship, Z reverts to written Chinese, in a passage which is then given in an English 'Editor's translation' (the 'editor' being Guo herself) as follows:

> *I am sick of speaking English like this. I am sick of writing English like this. I feel as if I am being tied up, as if I am living in a prison. I am scared that I have become a person who is always very aware of talking, speaking, and I have become a person without confidence, because I can't be me. I have become so small, so tiny, while the English culture surrounding me becomes enormous. It swallows me, and it rapes me. I am dominated by it.*[67]

English is cast as a masculine aggressor, out to consume her, out to violate. Translation is, here, a process of which she feels far more victim that agent; as if to corroborate her view, even Z's resistant refusal of translation in temporarily reverting to Chinese is overridden by the operation of the 'editor'.

Desperately, Z continues, '*I wish I could just go back to my own language now*'. Yet the novel does not countenance the possibility of return to a pristine monolingualism. For one thing, Z's 'Chinese' is already not one but several, split between Mandarin and written Chinese, as well as between national standard and local dialect.[68] Moreover, while the 'homeliness' of the 'mother tongue' may be a staple of some translingual writing, in this novel it is an excoriating presence: Z is haunted by her 'mother's harsh local dialect', in a voice which tells her over and over, 'You are ugly peasant girl'.[69] Thus on one level, English comes to represent a language of love and beauty, displacing the castigating sound of her mother('s) tongue:

> When I badly communicating with others, my mother's words becomes loud in my eardrum. I am ugly peasant girl. I am ugly peasant girl.
> 'My body is crying for you,' you say.
> Most beautiful sentence I heard in my life.[70]

In this sense, the novel narrates a flight from origins and casts language-learning, alongside love, as the site of a self-remaking which is both tortuous and liberating. To acquire a new language, as Stephen Kellman argues, is to acquire a new way of seeing the world and oneself.[71] In particular, Guo traces a nexus between language-learning, gender, sexuality, and self-authorship – as, for example, in her repeated riffing on the double signification of 'lips' as the site both of articulation and of female sexuality.[72] Sitting in a cafe one day, Z reads a newspaper article about the death of a 90-year-old Chinese woman, the last speaker of a 'womans-only language: "Nushu". This four-hundred-year-old secret language being used by Chinese womans to express theys innermost feeling.' Z continues:

> I want create my own 'Nushu'. Maybe this notebook which I use for putting new English vocabularies is a 'Nushu'. Then I have my own

privacy. You know my body, my everyday's life, but you not know my 'Nushu'.[73]

Z's imagined 'Nushu', created in the space *between* the languages of the Chinese–English dictionary, stands at the other end of the spectrum to the model of language which the dictionary represents: a language which is intensely interior, feminine, covert. In Z's 'Nushu', the learner does not so much acquire as *make* language, creatively and idiosyncratically, filling it with her own meanings. For all her confusion, Z is alive to the workings of language, as, for example, when she grapples with the meaning of 'drifter', and the dead metaphor comes alive in her hands:

> Something is very important about this word *drifter.* …
> I have to learning this word first, then to learning something about you.
> …
> *Thesaurus* only make me more confusing. Drifter like fishing boat? Drifter goes fishing on fishing boat? Or situation of a fishing boat swing in the sea is like situation of drifter?
> I think of that picture you are on the boat wearing the shorts, holding the paddle, smiling at the camera. Behind you is brown colour sea. You a drifter, I believe.[74]

Her study visa and her love affair both expired, the novel ends with Z's return to China, although not to her village. Instead, she opts to move to Beijing – perhaps to become a writer, in spite of her mother's desperate, joyless protest that 'Writing on paper is a piece of nothing compared with a stable job in a government work unit!'[75] The Beijing she finds, however, is 'unrecognizable', a postsocialist megalopolis dominated by ceaseless construction and consumption:

> I am sitting in a Starbuck's cafe in a brand new shopping centre, a large twenty-two-storey mall with a neon sign in English on the roof: *Oriental Globe*. Everything inside is shining, as if they stole all the lights and jewels from Tiffany's and Harrod's. In the West there is 'Nike' and our Chinese factories make 'Li Ning', after an Olympic champion. In the West there is 'Puma' and we have 'Poma'. The style and design are exactly the same.[76]

This sudden sequence of brand-names is as arresting, in its own way, as the broken English at the start of Z's narrative; as Emily Apter puts it, 'trademark language is perhaps the last taboo, ushering in what is strictly speaking profoundly exogamous to literature'.[77] Beijing has become a vast, febrile, transnational contact zone, crossed and recrossed by ceaseless processes of translation in the service of capital. We see here not only what Apter calls 'CNN creole' – the incursion of global brand names – but also other complex processes of translation and indigenisation, whereby 'Puma' becomes 'Poma' but remains in other senses 'the same'. The moniker of the *Oriental Globe* is overlaid with irony, signalling as it does not only the ongoing cultural power of the West, but also China's aggressive ambition to make the globe '*Oriental*'.

The novel's vision of capitalist globalisation, like its vision of love and of creativity, rests on translation. As Z continues:

> I feel out of place in China. Wherever I go, in tea houses, in hotpot restaurants, in People's parks, in Dunkin Donuts, or even on top of the Great Wall, everybody talks about buying cars and houses, investing in new products, grabbing the opportunity of the 2008 Olympics to make money, or to steal money from the foreigner's pockets. I can't join in their conversations. My world seems too unpractical and nonproductive.
>
> 'But you can speak English, that alone should earn you lots of money! Nowadays, anything to do with the West can make money.' My friends and relatives keep telling me this.[78]

Shifting perspective from the personal to the global, Guo concludes with a vision of deterritorialised language in a world characterised by constant linguistic flux and transfer. Z is indeed 'out of place', in relation to a commodified translation which promiscuously and indiscriminately subsumes all cultural material, from the Great Wall to Dunkin Donuts, in the pursuit of profit. Yet this dystopian view of Beijing as a contact zone, in which translation is the instrumentalised medium of capitalist exchange, serves as a foil for the novel's alternate and ultimately redemptive vision of translation as defiantly 'unpractical and nonproductive'. In the last scene of the novel, Z receives her lover's final letter. Written in English, but also invoking Britain's own always-existing language diversity in its Welsh point of origin at Carningli, 'Mountain of the Angel', it is precisely the handwritten letter's low-tech materiality which allows it to embody the transnational and transcendent power of language. The words, 'soaked in great peace and happiness', are in the end 'the best gift you ever gave me':

> I kiss the letter. I bury my face in the paper, a sheet torn from some exercise book. I try to smell that faraway valley. I picture you standing on your fields, the mountain behind you, and the sound of the sea coming and going.[79]

Guo's 2014 novel, *I Am China*, also begins with a letter. Dated '29 December 2011', its opening phrase, unidiomatic in English – 'the sun is piercing, old bastard sky' – immediately suggests the direct, foreignising translation which it subsequently turns out to be: a translation of a letter between a Chinese punk musician and dissident, Kublai Jian, and his partner, a poet called Mu, recalling his emergence as a 'punk musician' in Beijing in 1989 and his response to the massacre of protesting students by government forces in Tiananmen Square. The translator of the letter is the novel's protagonist – or more properly, one of the novel's three protagonists, the others being Jian and Mu – a London-based Scottish translator of Chinese called Iona Kirkpatrick. For Iona, as for Z, entry into another language has provided the means to escape an isolated and difficult childhood. As a teenager, living on Mull with her emotionally repressed parents and 'driven crazy by the boredom of living on a small Scottish island', she 'found herself longing for foreign words: the alien sound, the unknown syllable, the mysterious sign', following the lure of a new language which 'might offer her an escape'.[80] In London she becomes a stellar student of Chinese at the School of Oriental and African Studies (SOAS) before turning her back on academia to work as a freelance translator, living an isolated life punctuated by occasional sex with strangers, which she both values for the freedom it affords her and recognises as a means to avoid the intimacy she finds difficult. Commissioned by a literary editor to translate a mysterious bundle of documents handed to him in Beijing – which turn out to be journal entries from Jian and Mu and letters between them, charting in a gradually unfolding but not chronological order their relationship, Jian's arrest and political exile over a mysterious 'manifesto' (with which the novel concludes), his experiences in

Europe's exclusionary regimes of asylum, Mu's emergence as a poet and punk musician in her own right and her travels to the US and Britain – translation becomes for Iona a means to reflect on the priorities of her own life and the meaning of intimacy, and ultimately to achieve something approaching it herself by the end of the novel, with her editor, Jonathan.

The novel intersperses third-person narration with Iona's translations of letters and diary entries. She doesn't order them in advance (although many are dated), preferring to translate them in the order in which she finds them, into which they have been put by unknown hands (perhaps by Mu, perhaps someone at Jonathan's agency, perhaps somebody else). The novel preserves a sense of the materiality of the documents which it purports to be translating, not only in the disordered sequence in which they appear but in reproduced passages of handwriting, complete with scribblings and crossings out, lines and creases in the paper, the marks of prior photocopying; and Iona dwells, in the narrative, on the material particularity of the sources she is trying to translate:

> The page she is holding with one dry hand is covered with doodles, black ink mixed with blue. Large characters. She recognizes Kublai Jian's scrawl. Here and there the words have been furious crossed out:[81]

At certain points – in a pseudotranslational move that draws attention to the contingent and material practice of translation – the writing peters out or becomes unreadable.[82] Guo upends conventions of narrative temporality and legibility in general, and those specific to the epistolary novel, in contrast to the 'book' that Jonathan is concurrently 'mapp[ing] out' within the narrative itself, which – for all of his progressive views – threatens to schematise Jian and Mu as representative figures, two 'contrasting voices' in a dialogue standing for 'two facets of the great contemporary enigma: China'.[83] The notion of schismatic distinctions between 'East' and 'West', 'North' and 'South' is ceaselessly undone in the novel's translational perspective. The letters Iona translates reveal Jian in Beijing wearing a Sex Pistols' 'Never Mind the Bollocks' t-shirt while Mu reads Chinese translations of Pablo Neruda and Leo Tolstoy, and they quote Mary Shelley's *Frankenstein*

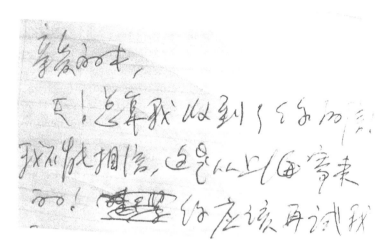

1 Image from Xiaolu Guo, *I Am China*
(London: Chatto & Windus, 2014), p. 70.

to one another and sing 'La Marseillaise'. Later Jian, in an immigration
detention centre in Dover, finds an English translation of Marx's *Das
Kapital*, and reflects to Mu:

> I tried to make out the English by picturing that Chinese translation
> we read at school. What a different book it is in English! Now I feel
> like I never understood Marx, and maybe all of China doesn't under-
> stood [sic] what *Das Kapital* is really about.[84]

Translation serves, in the novel, as a model for perpetually open-ended
meaning (just as *Das Kapital* appears, to Jian, as 'a different book' in
English, and which of course is not the 'original' either but another
translation) – a process that is always in train, never completed.

Guo's section headings, giving dates and locations, underline the
narrative's zigzag movement between Iona in London in 2013, under-
taking the work of translation along a timeline between April and
November, and the various places and past times in which it finds Jian
and Mu, largely in the preceding year – Jian travelling as an asylum
seeker across an unaccommodating Europe, while Mu struggles with
her dying father in Shanghai and crisscrosses the US with her band,
having been spotted by a Chinese American manager who rapes her

while on tour – while via letters and diary entries the narrative travels analeptically to scattered earlier points in their lives and relationship. All of the novel's three protagonists are separated in the main narrative by time and space, yet both Iona's work of translation and the omniscient third-person narration serve to draw them together into one frame. As Iona sits at home translating, she feels 'her flat dissolv[ing] at the edges of her consciousness. All she can feel around her are the blank faceless rooms of the letters: one lined with dying cancer patients, the other with immigrant refugees in limbo'.[85] Just as translation 'dissolves' the distances between the spaces and times of the novel, so too does the narration: 'Iona doesn't know it yet, as she walks along Regent's Canal in Camden Town, but just a year and three days ago, Jian was caught up in his own waterway'; 'As [Mu] and the band leave Wisconsin, heading for Minnesota, on the other side of the Atlantic, Jian is writing to his lost lover'.[86] On another tack, there are connections between the ways in which all three characters perceive and conceptualise the world: each is, in their own way, a translator. Iona, living in her flat above the noise and bustle of Chapel Market, is always attuned to sound – 'the roar of the city', 'traffic, church bells, buses, gulls, sirens' – just as it is the acoustic experience of difference that drew her originally to Chinese: 'the alien sound, the unknown syllable'.[87] Meanwhile, on another continent, Mu uses a small Dictaphone to record her conversations and street sounds as she travels from Milwaukee to Minneapolis, in found sound-collages of human voices, natural sounds, mechanical noise: 'Some people take photos, others record sounds. I choose sound', she says. 'You never know, maybe one day I will transcribe all these sounds and conversations into a book.'[88]

The novel's structuring emphasis on synchronicity and connection gives a space–time compression effect: things that appear to be distant and separate are suggested to be proximal and related. This sense of a networked and connected world mirrors Iona's fantasy as a translator of order and convergence: she wants to believe that Jian and Mu can be reunited by the power of her translation.

> Both of them trying to build a bridge on which to meet. And it's like Iona is building this bridge again, through her reading, her translation. Building a bridge of meaning from their letters, and she has to choose the right words to keep the structure standing. And it is so hard.[89]

Guo represents Iona's work of translation in terms which emphasise its deep interiority and emotional intensity. At times she feels as if her own boundaries as a self-identical subject are dissolving, Jian's and Mu's words and inner lives more vivid to her than her own. Translating one of Mu's poems, she 'chews on the words, gets tangled up in their meaning until she cannot tell what is her meaning and what is Mu's'.[90] What can feel close to authorial control – 'like she herself owns these diaries. Or she now has a right to reshape them, or even a duty to do so' – is also felt as a kind of invasion of her inner self by someone else's words: 'Or is it that the words have lodged in her mind and they are now reproducing themselves in a different way, like viruses in a new host, shaping their own structure?'[91] The intensity of the experience leaves her hollowed out by the recognition that it is one-way only: 'she does not exist in their lives, in the way that they do in hers. She is at best a voyeur. She has fed on their life's meaning, but it has left her feeling empty, famished.'[92] But translation is, by the end of the novel, the means by which she has translated herself into being and learned enough about love and intimacy that she and Jonathan, her editor and eventual lover, are able to end up 'on the same page' – the novel's reso-nant motif for human connection.[93]

The novel courts this idea of translation as narrative closure, but it also foils it. In the novel's closing pages, Iona's and Jian's timelines finally converge in November 2013. Translating Jian's final, cryptic diary entry, Iona deduces that he has gone to Crete, and that he is planning to die there. She pursues him to the island, but is nevertheless unable to avert his suicide: Jian drowns himself at precisely the same time as she, only a couple of miles away, is getting settled in her hotel room and having a drink at the bar. It is she, in the end, who must iden-tify Jian's body (though she cannot identify him with certainty because she has never met him). It is she, too, who must be the one to inform Mu of his death – Mu who, it turns out, has been living right nearby in prosaic east London for the whole time Iona has been translating.

In a novel full of analogues and echoes, Iona, the figure of the trans-lator coming into existence between languages, is doubled in the novel by Jian, caught between China's coercive repression and European regimes of exclusion. Jian's whole lived experience, like Iona's, has been structured through translation, but as an asylum seeker and illegal worker in Europe he experiences it in its far less liberating,

cosmopolitan articulations. The British asylum system he encounters is a regime with strict linguistic and discursive limits. As Fiona
Doloughan points out, it is his rage at 'his inability to articulate his situation (he is after all a Chinese man from Beijing) in language that the
authorities understand' which ends with him being sent to a psychiatric
ward and heavily sedated.[94] Ultimately, this inability to use 'language
that the authorities understand' leads to his claim for asylum being
denied. Language, meanwhile, is carefully managed to provide cover
for the system: on his release from the hospital Jian is sent to a '*Removal
Centre*', which is rebranded as a '*Detention Centre*' just at the same time
as the law changes to escalate 'removals'.[95] And language is also used
to withhold the status of personhood from those claiming asylum; Jian
finds himself classified as 'a "non-person"', 'a man of nothing. Merely a
registration number: UK66034-GH568. I've even learned to recite it.'[96]
Even in Switzerland, under a more accommodating regime in which
Jian is granted asylum, the 'welcome' which he receives is nothing
if not ambivalent: 'Now you are entitled to be part of our country!
But don't forget you must register your address with the police within
eight days.'[97] In the multilingual world of European asylum reception
and detention centres, Jian is isolated through language both within
the system itself and among his fellow asylum seekers.[98] As immigration detention particularly strikingly demonstrates – and as will be the
concern of my next chapter – not all kinds of language diversity can
be conceived of as liberating. Indeed, the French classes in the Centre
d'Assistance in Switzerland are in many respects a parody of an accommodating European multilingualism:

> Monsieur Godard asks everybody in the class to change the last word
> according to their origin and to say the sentence out loud:
> 'Réquérant d'asile, je suis venu de Somalie.'
> 'Réquérant d'asile, je suis venu d'Angola.'
> 'Réquérant d'asile, je suis venu de Libye.'
> 'Réquérant d'asile, je suis venu d'Égypte.'
> 'Réquérant d'asile, je suis venu de Syrie.'[99]

The statement the class repeats in French is the request for asylum – a
legal request for sanctuary under the 1951 UN Refugee Convention. It
is a request uttered from what Jian calls 'a limbo space between arrival
and departure', and for many it is one which will be refused – as it is

for Jian's Libyan friend Mahmud.[100] Asylum seekers spend an average of two weeks in the Centre, hardly enough time to learn much more French than this one phrase, before in many cases being deported back to 'Somalie ... Angola ... Libye ... Égypte ... Syrie'.

Iona imagines her work of translation as a kind of salvation, rebuilding the 'bridge' to bring Jian and Mu together; but translation in the novel does not offer this kind of rescue. Jian's final diary entry is a blank page with only two lines 'scribbled with big characters', reproduced as an image in the text as a page which looks as though it has been soaked with water. Iona has to struggle to make out the characters and 'has to hold the page at odd angles to try and decipher the words'. In the end, she comes up with a translation:

> The sea there is the bluest and purest. It's the last blue I will see.[101]

Unsure as to its meaning, she tries to translate it a different way:

> The sea there is the bluest and purest. And this is the last blue I can see.

Without verb tense marking, Iona is unable to work out what is most crucial to her translation,whether Jian is writing about the present or the future, and so she comes up with two more versions:

> The sea there was the bluest and purest. It was the last blue I have ever seen.
> ...
> There, that sea, the bluest and purest sea. It will be the last blue I shall ever see.[102]

The issue of grammatical tense in Chinese and English is not, as it is for Z in Dictionary, a matter of a learner trying to make herself understood or to reflect on the different ways of interpreting the world each system implies, but instead of trying to work out whether an event has yet happened. It is only later, when it is too late, that Iona reads the letter Jian has left for Mu in which, from context, tense becomes finally and devastatingly clear (and it appears that Iona's first translation was the 'right' one):

To the ones in this world who will eventually read my words:
And to Mu:
The sea here is the bluest and purest I have ever seen. It's the last blue
I will see. They say planet Earth is a blue planet when you see it from
space. So I want to go out with the blue.[103]

Jian's fate, as a refugee drowned and washed up on a Greek beach, calls
to mind the thousands who drown in their efforts to reach Europe
fleeing war, crisis, and poverty. In another instance of the novel's 'synchronicity', Jian's death takes place in November 2013, the point at
which the death toll from the 'refugee crisis' in the Mediterranean
began its most rapid escalation, at least 550 people having drowned off
the coast of Lampedusa only the preceding month.

Translation, around which *I Am China* revolves at levels of form,
narrative, language, and theme, is the novel's governing metaphor for
the experience of contemporary, global late modernity, in which *everything*, more or less, is translation. More than this, a particular mode of
translation is held out in the novel as a kind of radical politics, insofar
as it constitutes a form of solidarity: the means to connect, understand,
and engage with others' realities in all of their messy complexity. This is
no fully idealised vision of translation, which as the novel makes clear
can just as easily be alienating, manipulative, or co-opted to the service
of power. Nowhere is this more obvious than when Mu, travelling with
her band performing her own radical version of Ginsberg's 'America'
which she has translated and transformed as 'China', discovers that the
Atlanta leg of the tour is being sponsored by Coca-Cola.[104] Yet in spite
of these vulnerabilities, it is radical art forms – film, poetry, punk music
– which operate as analogues of one another in the novel, as experimental, inherently translational forms in which meaning remains fluid
and contingent as they travel globally.

The novel concludes with a translation of Jian's manifesto, for
which he has been imprisoned and deported: a manifesto for the power
of revolutionary art, for the artist as revolutionary, to counter the
'myths' of power and the state as instruments of coercion and control.
Although its explicit revolutionary medium is art, what is titled in
the book 'Translation of the Manifesto' could just as easily be read
as 'Manifesto for Translation' – insofar as the novel's most sustained
analogy, ultimately, is between art and translation in their radical

forms. As Guo's novel contends, it is art and translation that each in their way have the liberating power to make us see from new perspectives. Iona recalls, at one point, a 'little Zen story' her mother used to read to her: 'two young fish are swimming along in the water and they meet an older fish swimming the other way who nods to them and says: "Morning, how's the water?" And the two young fish swim on for a bit, and wonder: "What the hell is water?"'[105] In his manifesto, Jian turns to an analogous image:

> I am a drop in the ocean, in an ocean I cannot see.
> I am a brick in a wall I cannot feel.
> I am a citizen of a state, but of a state that is everywhere.[106]

Translation, as the necessary effort to go beyond oneself and to see from another perspective, becomes the means to see the water (the ocean, the wall, the state). It is not, therefore, anything like a closed system of equivalence, but a perpetual process. This is the kind of energy ascribed to translation by Barbara Cassini's 2014 *Dictionary of Untranslatables*, in which 'the untranslatable' stands for the irreducible supplementarity of translation, how it is always possible yet never finished: 'what one keeps on (not) translating'.[107] Thought of this way, translation becomes a model of the kind of revolutionary art Jian calls for in his manifesto, art which is 'the politics of perpetual revolution', 'the purest political form there is', revelatory in the sense that:

> Revolution happens when the water in which the citizens swim is frozen. The ice breaks and shatters and the fish are cast out onto the dry land, gasping for air.[108]

The manifesto was published again, and separately, as the concluding entry in a 2016 special issue of *ARIEL*, titled 'experimental writing in a globalizing world'. As Guo told the special issue editors Wendy Knepper and Sharae Deckard, she had originally written it as an independent text, but could find no publisher for it – 'a fact', as they observe, 'that is not especially surprising in an era of publishing dominated by commercial imperatives'.[109] And again, what holds for revolutionary art in Guo's vision also holds for revolutionary translation, as *I Am China* tries to imagine it:

There is no PLACE of perfect revolution since it's not a place. It's a
process. It's not something we arrive at, but an imperative. It's an
arrow. It always moves beyond itself.[110]

Guo's arrow-shaped vision of revolution has in common with
Aboulela's writing its property of being decentred, coming from multiple starting points in space, time, and language. In part, this is bound
up with a vision of English as thoroughly globalised: dominating literary markets, international commerce, and digital media, and spread
by the global big business that is English language teaching. But the
corollary of this is a deterritorialised English, always being translated
into and out of, always in the presence of other languages. Aboulela's
is an unmarked, standard English that points narratively to its own
relation to other languages; Guo plays with a glitchy, self-consciously
material and visual language that shows itself in the process of being
translationally made and remade. Both use the idea of translation as a
way to imagine transnational models of exchange and relationality that
evade the forces that drive 'global English': 'the expansion of capital,
new financial circuits, technoglobalism'.[111] Translation is the key to the
vision of revolutionary creativity around which Guo's novel revolves,
just as Aboulela's concept of translation is fundamental to her view of
Islam.

    Both Aboulela and Guo write about language and translation as
practised by women, and how different women's sense of selfhood
takes shape in the space between multiple forms of language. Aboulela
points to different kinds of transnational spaces – particularly within
mosques and Muslim communities – where women come together,
practising a feminine sociality in multiple languages but also sharing
in an experience of faith that transcends language difference altogether.
Her protagonists often seem to fall apart in transit between languages,
but the dissolution in translation is a spiritual education, a route to a
new order (though one which is in fact not new at all) that recognises
the Qur'an as divine revelation, in language that is eternal and directly
created by God. Aboulela's writing is thus translational literature that
is not just deeply suspicious of translation as it is conceived in the
Western tradition – as neutral cultural brokerage, operating transpar-
ently between equal systems, as Steinitz observes[112] – but that decentres
the individual interpreting subject altogether. Guo's female characters,

on the other hand, come into being between languages, eluding the 'mother tongue' for another tongue and using the perspective of linguistic estrangement as a means of self-reflection. But above all – and this will be the central concern of my final chapter, too – Guo's writing insists on this as not just pertaining to individual subjectivity, but as relational and ethical. Translation is, in Guo's work, that which undoes the fundamental narcissism of monolingualism, forcing us to recognise our own being in relation to (different) others.

Notes

1 Leila Aboulela, 'Moving away from accuracy', *Alif: Journal of Comparative Poetics* 22 (2002), 200–201.

2 Xiaolu Guo, 'Visions in a whirling head' (2008), n.pag. Available at: www. guoxiaolu.com/WR_visions_whirling_head.htm.

3 Aboulela, 'Moving away from accuracy', 203.

4 Aboulela, 'Moving away from accuracy', 204–206.

5 Aboulela, 'Moving away from accuracy', 206.

6 Aboulela, 'Moving away from accuracy', 202.

7 Aboulela, 'Moving away from accuracy', 202.

8 Aboulela, 'Moving away from accuracy', 202.

9 Guo, 'Visions in a whirling head'.

10 Guo, 'Visions in a whirling head'.

11 It is worth noting that both Aboulela's *The Translator* and Guo's *Dictionary* make oblique connections with other, earlier texts also interested in matters of translation. For discussion of Aboulela's relationship to Tayeb Salih's *Season of Migration to the North*, see Stephan Guth, 'Appropriating, or secretly undermining, the secular literary heritage? Distant echoes of *Mawsim al-Hijra* in a Muslim writer's novel: Leila Aboulela, *The Translator*', in Luc Deheuvels, Barbara Michalak-Pikulska, and Paul Starkey (eds) *Intertextuality in Modern Arabic Literature since 1967* (Durham: Durham Modern Language Series, 2006), pp. 65–82; Brendan Smyth, 'To love the Orientalist: masculinity in Leila Aboulela's *The Translator*', *Journal of Men, Masculinities and Spirituality* 1:2 (2007), 170–182; Waïl Hassan, 'Leila Aboulela and the ideology of Muslim immigrant fiction', *Novel: A Forum on Fiction* 41:2/3 (2008), 298–319. Bachner notes, albeit rather dismissively, Guo's relationship to Han Shaogong's radically experimental *Dictionary of Maqiao* (1997); Andrea Bachner, '"Chinese" intextuations of the world', *Comparative Literature Studies* 47:3 (2010), 318–345.

12 Waïl Hassan, 'Agency and translational literature: Ahdaf Soueif's *The Map of Love*', *PMLA* 121:3 (2006), 754.

13 Leila Aboulela, 'Barbie in the Mosque', in Tom Devine and Paddy Logue (eds) *Being Scottish: Personal Reflections on Scottish Identity Today* (Edinburgh: Polygon, 2002), p. 2.

14 Fiona Doloughan, *Contemporary Narrative: Textual Production, Multimodality and Multiliteracies* (London and New York: Continuum, 2011), p. 2.

15 Homi Bhabha, 'How newness enters the world. Postmodern space, post-colonial times and the trials of cultural translation', in Homi Bhabha, *The Location of Culture* (London and New York: Routledge, 1994), pp. 223–229.

16 Fiona Doloughan, 'Translation as a motor of critique and invention in contemporary literature: the case of Xiaolu Guo', in Rachael Gilmour and Tamar Steinitz (eds) *Multilingual Currents in Literature, Translation and Culture* (London and New York: Routledge, 2018), p. 151.

17 For Aboulela's views on being regarded as a 'British Muslim writer', see Claire Chambers, 'An interview with Leila Aboulela', *Contemporary Women's Writing* 3:1 (2009), 91.

18 Aboulela, 'Moving away from accuracy'.

19 Leila Aboulela, *The Translator* (Edinburgh: Polygon, 1999), p. 5.

20 Aboulela, *The Translator*, p. 103.

21 Aboulela, *The Translator*, p. 164.

22 Aboulela, *The Translator*, p. 143; Hassan, 'Leila Aboulela and the ideology of Muslim immigrant fiction', 305; Tamar Steinitz, 'Back home: translation, conversion and domestication in Leila Aboulela's *The Translator*', *Interventions: International Journal of Postcolonial Studies* 15:3 (2013), 365–382.

23 Aboulela, *The Translator*, p. 5.

24 Kwame Anthony Appiah, 'Thick translation', *Callaloo* 16:4 (1993), 808–819.

25 Aboulela, *The Translator*, pp. 5–6.

26 Aboulela, *The Translator*, p. 26.

27 Aboulela, *The Translator*, p. 70.

28 Aboulela, *The Translator*, pp. 20–21.

29 Aboulela, *The Translator*, p. 44. This imperfect translatability cuts both ways: when she is back in Sudan, she finds herself at a loss to trans-late Scotland in a way that makes meaningful sense: '"If we were in Scotland", she said to them as they crossed the road, "you would have had to sit in the back and wear seat-belts." What she said made no sense to them. They had never seen anyone wear a seat-belt; they could not

imagine a place far away called Scotland.' Aboulela, *The Translator*, p. 145.

30 Hassan, 'Leila Aboulela and the ideology of Muslim immigrant fiction'; Steinitz, 'Back home'.

31 Aboulela, *The Translator*, p. 124.

32 Aboulela, *The Translator*, p. 190.

33 Leila Aboulela, *Minaret* (London: Bloomsbury, 2005), p. 1.

34 Aboulela, *Minaret*, p. 3.

35 Aboulela, *Minaret*, pp. 80–81.

36 Aboulela, *Minaret*, p. 100.

37 Aboulela, *Minaret*, p. 16.

38 Aboulela, *Minaret*, p. 163.

39 Aboulela, *Minaret*, p. 163.

40 See Adrian Blackledge, *Discourse and Power in a Multilingual World* (Amsterdam and Philadelphia: John Benjamins, 2005).

41 Aboulela, *Minaret*, p. 111.

42 This can be seen, for example, in the emphasis Aboulela places upon British Muslim converts in her writing, who as Hassan says, serve to 'demonstrate the universality of Islam' ('Leila Aboulela and the ideology of Muslim immigrant fiction', 312). It could be argued, though, that Aboulela's vision of the transcendental Islamic faith group or *ummah* 'downplays the very real tensions between different Muslim groups' across the world, as well as 'within an in any case divided Britain'; Claire Chambers, 'Recent literary representations of British Muslims', in Michael Bailey and Guy Redden (eds) *Mediating Faiths: Religion and Socio-Cultural Change in the 21ˢᵗ Century* (Farnham: Ashgate, 2011), p. 182.

43 Aboulela, *Minaret*, p. 110.

44 Aboulela, *Minaret*, p. 238.

45 Aboulela, *Minaret*, pp. 76, 185.

46 Aboulela, *Minaret*, p. 188.

47 Aboulela, *Minaret*, pp. 188–189.

48 Aboulela, *Minaret*, p. 274.

49 Aboulela, 'Barbie in the Mosque', pp. 1–2.

50 For discussion of the role of religion in the novel as 'substitute for parental care', see Chambers, 'Recent literary representations of British Muslims', p. 184.

51 Aboulela, *Minaret*, p. 240.

52 Aboulela, *Minaret*, pp. 77, 79. Notably, like other of Aboulela's female protagonists, Najwa rejects the kind of critical engagement central to many strands of Islamic, and Islamic feminist, thought. See Hassan

'Leila Aboulela and the ideology of Muslim immigrant fiction', 314–316; Miriam Cooke, *Women Claim Islam: Creating Islamic Feminism Through Literature* (New York: Routledge, 2001); Asma Barlas, *'Believing Women' in Islam: Unreading Patriarchal Interpretations of the Qur'an* (Austin: University of Texas Press, 2002).

53 David Farrier, *Postcolonial Asylum: Seeking Sanctuary Before the Law* (Liverpool: Liverpool University Press, 2011), p. 112.

54 Aboulela, *Minaret*, pp. 78–79.

55 Peter Morey, ' "Halal fiction" and the limits of postsecularism: criticism, critique, and the Muslim in Leila Aboulela's *Minaret*', *Journal of Commonwealth Literature,* 53:2 (2018), 301–315.

56 Xiaolu Guo, *A Concise Chinese-English Dictionary for Lovers* (London: Vintage, 2007), p. 59.

57 Jonathan Mirsky, 'Cute pidgin pie', *Spectator,* 15 February 2007, n.pag. http://archive.spectator.co.uk/article/17th-february-2007/25/cute-pidg in-pie. See also the (rather more sympathetic, despite the title) review by Carole Cadwalladr, 'Heathlow airport? Oh how we laughed', *Observer,* 11 February 2007. www.guardian.co.uk/books/2007/feb/11/fiction.feat ures2.

58 As I discuss in the preceding chapter as well, from Sheridan's Mrs Malaprop to the 1970s British TV comedy *Mind Your Language* and beyond, the speaker who attempts unsuccessfully to master English norms has served as an object – but rarely the subject – of British comedy. For discussion of the comedic exploitation of racialised 'linguistic deficiency' in modern British literature, see Michael Ross, *Race Riots: Comedy and Ethnicity in Modern British Fiction* (Montreal and Kingston, London, Ithaca: McGill-Queen's University Press, 2006).

59 Guo, *Dictionary*, pp. 187, 118–119.

60 Guo, *Dictionary*, p. 10.

61 Guo, *Dictionary*, p. 14.

62 Aboulela, *Minaret*, p. 149; Guo, *Dictionary*, p. 19.

63 'We ascribe significances as we do, largely because we are parties to an agreement to organize it in this way – an agreement that holds throughout our speech community and is codified in the patterns of our language. The agreement is, of course, an implicit and unstated one, but its terms are absolutely obligatory; we cannot talk at all except by subscribing to the organization and classification of data which the agreement decrees'; Benjamin Lee Whorf, *Language, Thought and Reality* (Massachussetts: MIT Press, 1972), p. 214. Or in Edward Sapir's famous formulation, 'human beings are very much at the mercy of the particular language which has become the medium of expression for their society'; Edward

Sapir, 'The status of linguistics as a science', *Language* 5 (1929), 207–214. See, for example, Guo, *Dictionary*, pp. 26–27, 125–126, 153, 299, 301.

64 Guo, *Dictionary*, p. 319.

65 Guo, *Dictionary*, p. 342.

66 Guo, *Dictionary*, p. 138.

67 Guo, *Dictionary*, pp. 179–180.

68 Guo, *Dictionary*, p. 180. As Rey Chow observes: 'Because the traditionally written Chinese language does not operate with an alphabet (which allows one to learn words by spelling), even a seemingly monolingual Chinese speaker typically picks up two systems at once – one through sound and the other through written characters – in the process of learning Chinese'; Rey Chow, *Not Like a Native Speaker: On Languaging as a Postcolonial Experience* (New York: Columbia University Press, 2014), p. 45.

69 Guo, *Dictionary*, pp. 18, 60. On the 'homeliness' of Chinese in Chinese migrant writing in Britain, see Diana Yeh, 'Contested belongings: the politics and poetics of making a home in Britain', in A. Robert Lee (ed.) *China Fictions/English Language: Literary Essays in Diaspora, Memory, Story* (Amsterdam and New York: Rodopi, 2008), pp. 299–325.

70 Guo, *Dictionary*, p. 60.

71 Stephen G. Kellman, *The Translingual Imagination* (Lincoln and London: University of Nebraska Press, 2000), pp. 20–21.

72 Guo, *Dictionary*, pp. 38–39, 137, 245.

73 Guo, *Dictionary*, pp. 121–122.

74 Guo, *Dictionary*, p. 92.

75 Guo, *Dictionary*, p. 351.

76 Guo, *Dictionary*, p. 352.

77 Emily Apter, *The Translation Zone: A New Comparative Literature* (Princeton and Oxford: Princeton University Press, 2006), p. 167.

78 Guo, *Dictionary*, pp. 352–353.

79 Guo, *Dictionary*, p. 354.

80 Xiaolu Guo, *I Am China* (London: Chatto & Windus, 2014), p. 11.

81 Guo, *I Am China*, p. 70.

82 See, for example, Guo, *I Am China*, p. 77.

83 Guo, *I Am China*, pp. 264–265.

84 Guo, *I Am China*, p. 72.

85 Guo, *I Am China*, p. 82.

86 Guo, *I Am China*, p. 105.

87 Guo, *I Am China*, pp. 143, 11.

88 Guo, *I Am China*, p. 136.

89 Guo, *I Am China*, p. 78.

90 Guo, *I Am China*, p. 180.

91 Guo, *I Am China*, p. 256.
92 Guo, *I Am China*, p. 320.
93 Guo, *I Am China*, p. 246.
94 Doloughan, 'Translation as a motor of critique and invention', p. 158.
95 Guo, *I Am China*, p. 63.
96 Guo, *I Am China*, pp. 55, 72.
97 Guo, *I Am China*, p. 211.
98 Doloughan, 'Translation as a motor of critique and invention', p. 158.
99 Guo, *I Am China*, p. 154.
100 Guo, *I Am China*, p. 161.
101 Guo, *I Am China*, p. 312.
102 Guo, *I Am China*, p. 313.
103 Guo, *I Am China*, p. 342.
104 Guo, *I Am China*, p. 177.
105 Guo, *I Am China*, p. 256.
106 Guo, *I Am China*, p. 361.
107 Barbara Cassin and Michael Wood, 'Introduction', in Barbara Cassin (ed.) *Dictionary of Untranslatables: A Philosophical Lexicon* (Princeton: Princeton University Press, 2014), n.pag.
108 Guo, *I Am China*, p. 362.
109 Wendy Knepper and Sharae Deckard, 'Towards a radical world literature', *ARIEL: A Review of International English Literature* 47:1–2 (2016), 19.
110 Xiaolu Guo, personal interview. Quoted in Knepper and Deckard, 'Towards a radical world literature', 19.
111 Walter Mignolo, *Local Histories/Global Designs: Coloniality, Subaltern Knowledges, and Border Thinking* (Princeton: Princeton University Press, 2000), p. 229.
112 Steinitz, 'Back home'.

'The language is the border'

The BBC World Service ... advises that a genuine Rwandan national from any of the ethnic groups will normally be able to speak Kinyarwanda and/or French.

...

Reasons to doubt your nationality can be drawn from the fact that you are unable to speak Kinyarwanda and/or French. As already stated ... you were screened for the main part in the Ugandan dialect [sic] and then were substantively interviewed in English. It is noted that you were able to answer a few questions asked in Kinyarwanda at the start of your screening interview. However, in your substantive interview you were asked to state the numbers one to ten in Kinyarwanda ... and also asked for the phrases 'Good Morning' and 'Goodbye', you wrote your answers down phonetically because you could not write in the language ... it has been decided that although written phonetically you did not get all of them correct ... Your lack of basic knowledge of the Kinyarwanda language suggests that you are not a genuine national of Rwanda.[1]

In 2005, a young Rwandan refugee, known in Jan Blommaert's account of his case as Joseph Mutingira, had his claim for UK asylum refused on grounds of language. His linguistic repertoire – speaking English, Runyankole, a few words of Swahili, and only a smattering of Kinyarwanda – suggested, in the words of the decision letter, that he was 'not a genuine national of Rwanda', and as a consequence the whole of his story was dismissed as fraudulent. His sociolinguistic profile may have been consistent with the horrific account he gave, of a peripatetic early childhood spent speaking English in a household always in readiness to flee, a life dislocated by violent conflict in the period surrounding the 1994 genocide, but it did not conform to the Home Office's interpretation of what constituted Rwandan 'sociolinguistic normalcy'.[2] Not the content, but the medium of Joseph's narrative became in the end the deciding factor in denying him asylum and 'returning' him to Uganda, a country which he had never visited.

As Joseph's case suggests, in some fundamental ways the UK asylum system is a regime of language. Its material is narrative: the 1951 UN Refugee Convention founds the right to asylum on 'justifiable' fear of persecution, thereby placing the onus on individual refugees to prove the authenticity of their claim through the 'credibility' of their story.[3] In David Farrier's words, 'seeking sanctuary is an act of storytelling'.[4] It is also almost always, in a literal as well as a metaphorical sense, an act of translation. Asylum seekers in Britain can choose either to give their story in English, which may be their second, third, or fourth language, or to depend on a Home Office-approved interpreter to mediate between English – specifically, the English of governmental administrative procedure and asylum law – and another 'language/dialect' from their repertoire (which may itself, as in Joseph's case, be considered a form of evidence).[5] According to UNHCR guidelines used within the UK system, criteria for assessing the authenticity of asylum testimony include: internal consistency, agreement with known facts, 'logical and consistent' chronology, 'fluency of the testimony (that is, the incidence of hesitation)', clarity, and detail.[6] Throughout all of the mediating processes of the asylum system, the narrative fragments of an individual's story – of home, family, friends, trauma, loss, dislocation, travel, detention – have to appear as orderly, sequential, evidential, measured, detailed, and consistent.[7] These are the narratological criteria which are taken to constitute 'evidence' on the one hand and 'truth' on the other, and the grounds on which a decision is made as to a person's right to protection under the law.[8] As Blommaert points out, 'narrating in a second, third or other foreign language' in the giving of asylum testimony is risky, reducing the resources available for structuring a story and the precision with which meanings can be conveyed.[9] The mediation of interpreters carries other risks, as Katrijn Maryns discusses: ambiguity leads to misinterpretation, important polysemic subtleties are flattened out, meanings can be distorted.[10] The same interpreter may not translate the same way twice; often, several interpreters may be involved at different points in an asylum seeker's case.[11] Either the mediation of even the most diligent interpreter or the use of a second, third, or other foreign language can carry terrible costs where detail, consistency, and precision are under constant scrutiny. Where decisions hang on the nuance of a word, language itself becomes a primary object of suspicion.

If the asylum seeker is perhaps the pre-eminent multilingual figure of our globalised times, then, as the example of Joseph Mutingira demonstrates, this is 'dangerous multilingualism' with serious, even life-or-death consequences.[12] On the other side of the coin from dreams of global mobility – people, information, ideas, money, goods, language travelling physically and electronically as never before – stands the deterritorialised mobility of the displaced. Reaching Britain from situations of conflict and oppression, via multiple dislocations, refugee camps, and dangerous, often circuitous clandestine routes, asylum seekers arrive only to be assessed, perversely, and with sometimes devastating consequences, according to language ideologies of the nation state. Within the asylum system, invested in the idea of stable, homogeneous language communities contained by national borders ('a genuine Rwandan national … will be able to speak Kinyarwanda'), 'inconsistent' language practice becomes an object of suspicion.[13] There is some unintended late-colonial irony in the fact that Joseph's 'reason for refusal' letter cites the authority of the BBC World Service in turning his language against its speaker. In other instances, Home Office officials call on the expertise of privately contracted firms based in Switzerland to carry out 'language analysis' intended to assess an asylum applicant's 'true place of origin'. Indeed, as the *Guardian* recently reported, almost two in five Syrian asylum seekers in the UK – including those who had plentiful documentation proving their identity – were subject to language analysis tests administered by private firms Verified AB and Sprakab between 2011 and 2018.[14] A pro forma Home Office 'reason for refusal' letter reads:

> You took part in a language analysis interview on [date] to ascertain your linguistic origin. You claimed to come from [place or clan or group] and to be of [nationality]. The language analysis considered the hypothesis [state the hypothesis of the claimed origin]. The

language analysis conclusion to this was that [state the conclusion]. Language analysis also considered the hypothesis [state the second hypothesis]. The language analysis conclusion to this was that [state the conclusion].

Giving full consideration to this and the other evidence in your case, it is not accepted that you come from [place or clan or group]. It is considered that you actually come from [place or clan or group].[15]

Language diversity vs. Lunar House

Lunar House, a twenty-storey office block in Croydon, south London that is the headquarters of the Home Office's Visas and Immigration Service, is a distinctive kind of multilingual space. Completed in 1970, its name and design a testament to the excitement of the recent moon landings, the building's architectural motifs of limitless space-age travel stand in ironic counterpoint to its current status as home to the Asylum Screening Unit, the only place from which people can claim asylum within the UK, and thus the point of entry into a system which is precisely defined by the restriction of movement: from the 'asylum dispersal' policy which determines where asylum seekers can live and prepaid payment cards which determine where they can shop, to electronic tagging, indefinite immigration detention, and forced removal. In terms of the range of language varieties spoken within a single building, it is one of the most densely multilingual spaces in Britain and its procedures reflect the British state's efforts to devise means for the orderly management of language diversity across the UK's 'dispersed border'. People claiming asylum have the legal right to choose the language in which they are interviewed.[16] Yet a persistent monolingualist logic of either/or governs a system which continues to insist that languages are separate and discrete within particular domains, and compels an asylum seeker in choosing to 'isolate one language from their linguistic repertoire – *either* Krio *or* English' while other parts of their language repertoire are 'disqualified or suppressed'.[17]

It is interpreters, primarily, who serve as intermediaries between asylum applicants and their language repertoires, and the fundamentally monolingualist operations of British asylum law. The task of the interpreter is to provide 'exact translation' – and the lack of detailed commentary on what this might mean, in Home Office documentation on asylum procedures, speaks volumes about the assumptions about language and translation on which the system is built.[18] Home Office guidelines on the asylum interview emphasise that interpreter and interviewee should be able to understand one another clearly in 'the same language/dialect' and, this being said, go on to assume the role of the interpreter to be that of a neutral conduit for the one-to-one transmission of meaning without impediment between languages.[19] This approach is typified in the UK Visas and Immigration 'Interpreter's Code of Conduct', which directs:

> You must ... retain every single element of information that was contained in the original message, and interpret in as close verbatim form as English style, syntax and grammar will allow.
> ...
> Your duty is to interpret *everything* that is said.[20]

As Gibb and Good argue, and in spite of this fantasy of 'retain[ing] every single element of information', not only does the mediation of even the most competent interpreter create 'barriers to communication' at every stage of the asylum adjudication process, but it also conditions the shape of the asylum interview itself, on which asylum determinations are made.[21] The interview is structured around a sequence of questions: asylum applicants are instructed to answer these in short phrases or sentences so that they can be fully translated. The effect is to interrupt, disjoint, and break up the flow of narrative. As one Home Office interpreter observed,

> People are discouraged from talking, and the interpreter is always made the excuse for that; you know, that you need to give short answers so that the interpreter can translate? That is another constraint brought on by the interpretation process itself ... and it works in the favour of the Home Office because people do not speak like that naturally, and they will lose track; they will say less than they mean to say simply because they have to break it down. I've seen it on their faces; they just give up, you know? They try to do it for a bit and then they give up. And let's not forget, the interpreter has practice at doing this, so do the Presenting Officers, so do the judges, so do the lawyers, but the asylum applicant doesn't. He's the only one who comes to this all fresh and raw and natural, and the flow of speech, when it's constrained like that, very often dries up.[22]

The oral exchanges on which an asylum adjudication is based – this necessarily dialogic process, this 'flow of speech', mediated by an interpretation process, governed by a question-and-answer structure, 'drie[d] up' by its repeated stopping and starting – are converted by the adjudicating officer into a written record summarising the asylum seeker's story and detailing the decision made. Asylum interviews in Britain are not recorded and so the written account becomes not only the official, but the only, record. Interviewing, interpretation, the conversion of spoken dialogue into written text, the conformity of that written text to established formal and procedural conventions, are elements in an administrative network of narrative shaping and reshaping – noting, summarising, filling in forms, making 'files'. Across all of these processes, as Blommaert has argued, every new version continues to be considered as another iteration of the 'same' narrative:

> [T]he difference between the 'original' and its 'copies' are assumed to be minimal (hence in which it is assumed that every translation, summary, quotation, reading of the story is correct and accurate) because 'procedurally correct text' (i.e. text produced or collected according to standard procedures) is supposed to be a transparent, unambiguous set of signs. The story of the asylum seeker is remoulded, remodelled and re-narrated time and time again … at the same time, the story is treated as a singular text, and responsibility for that text … is attributed to the asylum seeker … as the responsible author for the whole intertextuality complex.[23]

'The Interpreter's Tale'

The asylum system, as a regime of language, is double-faced. It revolves around the figure of the individual speaking subject – the one who testifies, the one who recounts – while its narrative protocols move that testimony, that act of speaking, ever further away from the speaker's own control. This is the perversity which Carol Watts probes in her poem 'The Interpreter's Tale'. Opening with an epigraph which is a fragment of the Home Office guidelines – 'Your duty is to interpret *everything* that is said' – Watts's poem weighs the injunction: duty to whom? What can it mean to 'interpret *everything*'? She pivots the poem on a fundamentally ethical translation of the depersonalised, mechanistic 'interpret *everything* that is said' into the intimate transaction of giving 'my word for hers'. Still, her scene of translation is haunted by what 'remains unsaid':

> Fear. Absence. Oxygen. Children. Mothers. Clandestine.
> Freedom. Risk.
> Better life. I miss you.[24]

Watts's interpreter is imprecated by an asylum system that believes in translation as a mechanical process of transference without loss: 'translate everything', 'embellish nothing';[25] in which the necessary mismatch between that belief and language's reality – the imprecision of equivalence, the weight of implication – can destroy hope of sanctuary, is a matter of life or death, where every word is an object of judgement.

> Let me give you a word.
> Let's say: brother.
>> My brother gave me money to leave.
>> My brother sent me money to leave.
> Between giving and sending are continents.
> …
> In giving, you might understand some closeness, as if he had come
>> into the house that morning.
> Pressed into my hand.
> Take this.
> Go now.
> In sending, a necessary distance.
> …
> Mobile contact.
> A choice of two words her story relies on, in me.
> Giving and sending.[26]

Caught in 'a choice of two words' and all that they imply – giving or sending, closeness or distance – the asylum seeker is hostage to an impossible demand for words-as-labels and translation as one-to-one equivalence:

> I say brother. That is, uncle.
> *So it was not her brother who helped her?*
> *Her story isn't stacking up.*
> I say brother, meaning the brother of my father.[27]

This demand for a story that 'stacks up' reveals itself as a fantasy about words that can be interpreted singularly, without ambiguity; which in turn reveals precisely its opposite: that even at its most starkly brutal, language is still inescapably metaphorical (and how, we might ask, would one adequately translate the phrase *'isn't stacking up'*?). The interpreter in Watts's poem uses the first-person voice instructed by the Home Office guidelines: 'use direct speech when interpreting. You should not say, "he said he…" this should be interpreted as, "I…"'.[28] These translated first-person phrases and fragments 'stack up' in the poem, not as the sequential individual narrative which is required by the system but as an accumulating tally of loss and suffering. Interrupting this litany, the language of asylum adjudication appears jarringly in parentheses to reveal how every phrase is the object of an interpretive system which has already marked it 'criminal':

> I heard them threaten to take her organs.
> I was shot at by snipers.
> I waited in the house of a man with a tank in his garden.
> I was packed in cartons of washing powder.
> I saw people taken from containers and hung by the side of the
>   road.
> I was detained.
> I was mobile (and therefore a criminal)
> I was immobile (and therefore a criminal)
> I wrapped my phone in plastic.
> I flew over sand and now I meet the shore.
> Now a leaky boat. Now a port. Now a train. Now a lorry.
> Now you.[29]

'The Interpreter's Tale' forms part of *Refugee Tales*, a project begun in 2014 with the aim of drawing attention, and calling for an end, to indefinite immigration detention in the UK. Each 'tale' is the product of a collaboration between a creative writer and an individual with direct experience of the UK asylum system, echoing both the structure and the vernacular impulse of Chaucer's *Canterbury Tales*: 'The Migrant's Tale', 'The Unaccompanied Minor's Tale', 'The Lorry Driver's Tale', 'The Detainee's Tale'. Organised by Gatwick Detainees Welfare Group, the project is subtitled '*A Walk in Solidarity with Refugees, Asylum Seekers and Detainees*'. Each walk, taking place every year since 2015, has traversed the south-east of England along routes that themselves contextualise the project and Britain's system of immigration detention: along the North Downs Way from Dover Immigration Removal Centre to Brook House and Tinsley House Immigration Removal Centre at Gatwick Airport; from Canterbury to Westminster via Dartford; from Westminster to Runnymede, site of the signing of Magna Carta. The walks are punctuated by the public telling of tales: of people who have sought asylum in the UK and of people who work within the asylum system.[30] The process of producing the tales, through collaboration between an established writer and the person whose tale is being told, moving from dialogue to written text, echoes the praxis of the asylum process while attempting to invert its logic, by seeking to establish spaces for narrative – for the telling of 'refugee tales' – beyond implied structuring judgements of truth or plausibility, freed from the shadow of 'tribunals', 'lines of questioning', 'people present by video | answers mistranslated'.[31] At the heart of the project is consciousness of the violence done in and through language within the asylum system. This chapter's title comes from David Herd's 'Afterword' to the second volume of *Refugee Tales*: 'the language is the border'.[32]

The asylum system is, in many ways, a system of language geared to move the shape and meanings of an individual's own asylum account beyond their control. As Blommaert points out, the logic of the process is to abstract the story 'away from the local, away from the experiential, the affective, the emotional, the individual position of people in conflicts' and 'towards generalizable categories and space-time frames', using 'official version[s]' of conflicts that are common not only to asylum procedures but to international trade, development, law, and foreign policy. The particularised account of an individual's experience within a specific social context is replaced by a grid of 'general categorizations': '"In country X, human rights are consistently violated", "country Y is a democracy", "in country Z there is a peace agreement between the warring parties, hence the situation has been stabilized"'.[33] At all levels, an individual's story meets and is overtaken by a language of generality that is by no means innocent. The 2002 Nationality, Immigration and Asylum Act, for example, reintroduced the notorious so-called 'white list' of 'safe' countries of origin. As Imogen Tyler points out, since by its logic 'countries on the list are safe and democratic', it follows that 'nobody coming from these countries can be a "real refugee"; the almost irrefutable presumption being that claims to asylum from white list nationals must be "bogus".[34] This is 'the hostile language of immigration law', as Rachel Holmes describes it in 'The Barrister's Tale':

> Temporary indefinite detention. How do you measure time that's both temporary and indefinite? …
> Indefinitely temporary: temporarily indefinite. Holding people prisoners of language.[35]

Hostile language, coined to put people beyond the law's protection. Countries on the white list are safe and democratic. Detention can be indefinite, as long as it is temporary. Tyler gives the term 'asylum seeker' itself as an example of this kind of semantic manoeuvring – denoting a state of temporal and legal suspension, of deferred subjectivity, defining a person according to a status not yet arrived at:

> While the term 'refugee' has a specific international legal genealogy, the term 'asylum-seeker' gained political and popular currency in the UK in the early 1990s. In contrast to the term refugee, which names a (legal) status arrived at, 'asylum-seeker' invokes the non-status of a person who has not been recognized as a refugee. Asylum-seekers are literally pending recognition. Inscribing the category of asylum-seeker in British law through the enactment of a series of punitive asylum laws has enabled the British Government to manoeuvre around the rights of the refugee as prescribed by international law.[36]

Asylum seekers are held within a regime of 'hostile language' which serves to place them beyond the margins of the nation and the protection of the law. In British public discourse, Roger Zetter tracks a further fragmentation into subcategories, securing an ever-increasing marginality and infrahumanisation for those so defined: 'bogus asylum seekers', 'economic refugee/asylum seeker', 'overstayers', 'trafficked migrant', 'undocumented asylum seeker/migrant', 'illegal migrant'.[37] This is the marking in public discourse of the infrahuman figure whose exclusion secures the nation's imaginary borders and – in Paul Gilroy's tellingly linguistic metaphor – vouchsafes the 'syntax of British racism'.[38] A 2004 report by the Information Centre about Asylum and Refugees in the UK, examining how British news media and political reporting represent asylum seekers, gives a list of terms repeatedly used in newspaper accounts of asylum. The list reenergises the already-established lexicon of British racism – language of swamping, flooding, disorder, violence – while extending it with a newer vocabulary that emphasises both inauthenticity and a place beyond law – 'bogus', 'false', 'illegal':

> Crime, dirty, thieves, fraud, deception, bogus, false, failed, rejected, cheat, illegal, burden, drugs, wave, flood, influx, scrounger, sponger, fraudster, tide, swamp, flood, mob, horde, riot, rampage, disorder, race war, fight, brawl, battle, fighting machine, deadly, orgy of violence, fury, ruthless, monsters, destruction, ruin.[39]

'Do I come from a place, terrortory, is this a place where people are': James Kelman's *Translated Accounts*

In an Amnesty International debate on the 1992 UK Asylum Bill, James Kelman pointed out that the issue of asylum turns on questions of language. Foreign Secretary Michael Heseltine's proposal in the Bill to send asylum seekers back to 'international camps' and 'safe havens' in their countries of origin to have their claims assessed was language used as a weapon by the powerful against the weak: a semantic sleight-of-hand that, by the use of 'international' and 'safe', was able to conceal its cruelty beneath a veneer of legality, while conveniently resituating the problem of asylum beyond Britain's borders. In truth, says Kelman, 'They proposed this in the full knowledge of the mass murder that has taken place in "international camps" and "safe havens" from Beirut to Turkey'.[40] In the context of the British asylum system, Kelman returns to the question of language politics: how the language of power is used to marginalise and brutalise, how the disenfranchised become objects of discourse rather than its agents. As he suggests in his lecture on the work of Noam Chomsky, as I discussed in chapter one, for as long as language continues to be considered the possession of the powerful, it will continue to be a tool not only of symbolic, but of actual violence. In the realm of international politics and law, language provides 'unlimited opportunity' to sidestep the realities of atrocity and an alibi to avoid the human response they demand, when the words used to describe it are subjected to a 'slow

trudge through semantics' which abstracts them from the experiences
they denote and from the control of those who have suffered them:

> What do we mean by pain? What do we mean by suffering?
> Around this point the terms get surrounded, captured by inverted
> commas – e.g. what do we mean by 'torture' – thus throwing into
> doubt the very existence of the experience. A distinction is created
> between the actual experience and the 'concept of the experience'. In
> creating this distinction a closed system is put into operation: only
> those who specialise in discussing concepts will be admitted. The
> actual experience of atrocity becomes redundant.
>
> …
>
> When refugees' reports are heeded it is usually as an aid to appor-
> tioning blame, to discover which individual is responsible. During
> this the position of the victims will be brought into question: are they
> innocent or guilty, are they innocent victims or guilty victims.[41]

The violence done in language – prevaricating over the definition of
'torture' rather than acting to end its practice or to care for those who
have suffered, implying the existence of 'innocent victims or guilty
victims' so that the fact of victimhood need not call for our protection –
is answered, for Kelman, by a reading of Chomsky's linguistic thought
as a radically political vision of language as belonging to all people,
lived in the everyday practices of its speakers, to whom its definitions
belong.[42] What Kelman points to here, in effect, is a struggle over language which is at the heart of the asylum process: between the language
in which an individual may try to express experience and the 'hostile
language' of power.

In an interview with the *Guardian* discussing the publication of
Translated Accounts: A Novel (2001), Kelman associated its political
force with the plight of refugees internationally and their treatment
in Britain.[43] As Drew Milne observes, while studiously displaced from
any specific setting, *Translated Accounts* speaks to 'the administration
of language within unspeakable structures of human abuse' in a way
that has resonances both internationally and in British procedures of
asylum and the practices of immigration detention.[44] The novel stages
the struggle between the languages of authority on the one hand and of
the lived experience of atrocity on the other, in what resembles a heterogeneous archive of first-person accounts, coming from an unnamed

country under occupation. The accounts are pseudotranslations, claiming to be translated from unknown source language/s, given in an unsettling, defamiliarised English.[45] Emphasising their specific located-ness within a specific 'terrortory' while being impossible to locate, the accounts resemble testimony from Bosnia, Rwanda, or any other place where 'unspeakable atrocities' have been perpetrated against people. As Fabio Vericat argues, the emphatically textual, written language of *Translated Accounts* is not 'conceived to play the alphabetically-re-corded voice of a speaker' – as, arguably, much of Kelman's other writing might be said to – but, on the contrary, is written in such a way as to underline its mediated distance from an unreachable source.[46] Extending Kelman's language politics to scenes of atrocity across the world, the accounts' deterritorialised English stands for the unassim-ilated foreignness of languages in the coercive shadow of an inter-national English – of international law, international politics, global capital, electronic media, journalism, and human rights – which con-stantly threatens to engulf them.[47]

The fifty-four first-person narratives which make up *Translated Accounts* are preceded by a one-page 'Preface' which flags them up as 'translations', purporting to frame the accounts and describe the cir-cumstances in which they have been compiled. This Preface is written in an agentless passive tense in the third person, in the standard English officialese of administrative procedure: 'It is confirmed that these accounts are by three, four or more anonymous individuals of a people whose identity is not available'.[48] Underlining the accounts' hetero-geneity, it describes them as 'narrations of incidents and events', 'also reports, letter-fragments, states-of-mind and abstracts of interviews, some confessional', having been 'transcribed and/or translated' from an unspecified source language or languages into English, 'not always by persons native to the tongue'.[49] That they have passed through the hands of those with power is evident from the fact that a few 'have been modified by someone of a more senior office'; yet the motivation for these interventions is unclear and they have been neither wholesale nor systematic: 'If editorial control has been exercised evidence sug-gests inefficiency rather than design, whether wilful or otherwise.'[50] The Preface thus both emphasises the mediating procedures to which the accounts have been subject and flaunts their unsystematic nature and tenuous authority. Purposeful mediations in the form of translation, transcription, or modification have taken place in uncertain proportion to agentless, automated processes: 'computing systems of storage and retrieval' with their own 'variable ordering motions'.[51] And, though we are told that 'a disciplined arrangement of the accounts has been undertaken', we do not learn by whom, or according to what rationale.[52]

The accounts are related in an English the strangeness of which may, in part, be an effect of these mediating processes of transcription, translation, editing, storage, and retrieval. There are oddities of grammar and syntax, typographic glitches, repetitions, absences and negations, contradictory formulations, and jagged tense formations. Occasionally, accounts dissolve into strings of not-quite-meaningless computer code. Repeatedly, like a tic, conditional clauses are left hanging without defining their consequence or outcome ('If I may speak', 'if I am to say them', 'if he has had a limb taken') as if translated from a language from which war has stripped all sense of rational or grammatical causality ('if … then …'). These appear as glitchy, hard-to-interpret translated traces of a diverse language-world, one in which power includes the power to make others speak your language: 'This woman was familiar with their dialect, I have said, that language. They knew nothing of hers. Thus she had become the inferior.'[53] In account 25, 'history must exist for colleagues', apparently the transcript of a speech by a young member of a 'campaigning formation', a few exaggerated phonetic spellings appear, giving the sense of the voiced, accented mimicry of an occasional, foreign, imported English word: 'others remained in foreign institutes becoming meelionerrs', 'we may say meester presidente'.[54] This weird, untransparent English contributes to the sense of opacity and claustrophobia in these accounts in which everyday life is riven by suspicion, surveillance and oppression, rape and torture, random killing, state violence, and genocide. There are echoes, both in *Translated Accounts'* language and in its first-person narratives of human relations made and broken in a disorienting horrorscape of conflict, of Nigerian novelist Ken Saro-Wiwa's *Sozaboy*. As I discussed in chapter one, Kelman has recommended Saro-Wiwa's discussion of the politics and practice of language use in the author's note to the novel,[55] where he describes *Sozaboy*'s language as '"rotten English", a mixture of Nigerian pidgin English, broken English and occasional flashes of good, even idiomatic English', which is 'disordered and disorderly'.[56] Protagonist Mene's consciousness is refracted through his 'rotten English' narration as he struggles to grasp the nightmarish events unfolding around him and to interpret the exercise of power enacted through the language of obfuscation and tautology, which he – for all his naively confident assertions of mastering 'big big grammar' – understands no more clearly than the war into which he is thrown. *Sozaboy*'s Mene, 'knacking tory' (telling stories), resonates in Kelman's narratives from an unnamed 'terror-tory'; and what Emily Apter says of Mene's polysemic 'rotten English' is equally true of the language of *Translated Accounts*, in which 'ghostly aporias, double-entendres and mimetic effects' also conjure a hallucinatory world of perpetual war.[57]

In an even more pronounced way than elsewhere in his work, in *Translated Accounts* Kelman's narrators are often anxiously aware of the dangers of their language's co-option by others. In the narrative claustrophobia of account 10, 'lecture, re sensitive periods', the narrator's efforts to plainly challenge the operations of state terror are met by the generalising language of 'international legality' from experts claiming to speak for the 'universal'.[58] The narrator's focus – to communicate, to representatives of international authority, specific acts of violence carried out in a specific territory by agents of the state – is challenged by the language of legal example, a linguistic labyrinth of 'circles' and 'structures', the purpose of which is to distance violence into a generalisable abstraction:

> Legal circles, power structures, spheres of influence within these circles and structures. Lawyers and other moral people, all professors, assistants to the aides of political leaders, secretaries to charitable corporations over this planet Earth. They talk to us. They also are members of the human species. Yes. Thank you. They warn us of international legality inter as between the owner of one dog that has bitten one child and the parents of such child. The example offered to us, common to these circles, often used, often abused. We learn these examples thus to enter discourse. How else to talk. We can talk. Can we talk. Yes, we learn.[59]

The child bitten by the dog signifies two ways, in two forms of language fundamentally at odds. In the language of international legality, she is an idea: the site of a debate over how facts are determined and where responsibility should lie. In the language of 'the realistic natural world' of the narrator, she stands for the real experience of violence: 'such a

one sinking its teeth into the leg of the child, skinny little girl, blood
hardly appearing at the puncture'.

> So in this manner is signalled to ourselves the dragging into the
> streets of neighbours and relatives, elderly females, there having fire
> set to their nightclothes and hair, groups of elderly males who, being
> stripped naked, having their testicles tied link to link to link to link
> thus to be led around that others of the community might ridicule
> them, if not so themselves becoming liable to retributive action by
> security, by military or what other State operatives, some may exist.
>
> It is said to us such affairs are not to be discussed. Specialty indi-
> viduals and professional expert people, lawyers, doctors, all profes-
> sors and higher authoritys, these look to us, thinking to smile, smile
> at our matters.[60]

Language is a closed circuit: to be able to 'enter discourse' at all is
to forfeit the right to challenge the terms of that discourse, in which
'victim' becomes 'so-called victim' and 'horrors, atrocities, precedents
are of minimal value' in the deliberations of 'the State and wider community, international community', as it falls to them to 'determine …
what then should we designate evidence, what then is proof, how truth
can be so determined, whose burden might that become, tell to me a
victim, and is this consent'.[61]

Accounts appear constantly shadowed by their own erasure: any
speaker may disappear, any account may be erased on the one hand by
the violence, torture, rape, abduction, execution, murder, and genocide
which permeate the novel, and on the other by languages of power that
seek to dictate what is speakable and how. The violence, fear, uncertainty, and paranoia they contain is untranslatable into the language of
certainty, 'proof', legal example, or 'evidence', and they consequently
move in a no-man's-land between presence and absence, the living
and the dead, reality and unreality. In account 50, 'it is possible', the
fly-covered apparently dead body of a man unexpectedly and horri-
bly manifests the last signs of life.[62] In account 52, 'spectral body', the
material sensorial world appears in indistinct relation to that which is
spectral, 'not human', a 'dead thing', 'boys and girls' who 'may vanish
quickly'.[63] In account 2, 'the elderly woman died', the declarative language of witness ('the woman discovered early on the road, I know
who she was'; 'yes, in that section, by that staircase, that staircase') only

makes more ambiguous an account in which the subjects of inquiry – the narrator's relationship to the old woman, her fears and delusions (if that is what they are) about devils, thieves, and murderers, the circumstances of her life and death – are suffused with contradiction:

> She was not murdered, neither killed. She died.
> If she would think of herself as having been murdered. None may ask her opinion.
> …
> She was of an age that to die is natural but she died on the road. Natural unnatural, unnatural natural.[64]

Translated Accounts is riven with concern about who controls narrative, how perspective and interest dictate the shaping of stories, and how they may be distorted by the demands of others:

> No, she said, stories for our people and stories for foreign people will differ. The stories will be of a different kind. There are the stories, yes, they can be the stories one will recount but some will not. Some cannot recount stories, these stories any stories.[65]

Faced with such demands, the silences and breakdowns in language may be seen as what Agnes Woolley calls 'act[s] of narrative withholding' that resist the coercive demand for particular kinds of narrative recounted in particular ways – 'stories for foreign people' – in exchange for safety or justice.[66] In a number of accounts, the act of 'witnessing' itself appears as a form of violence. In account 34, 'if she screamed', the narrator attempts to recount the multiple rape of a girl by 'securitys' where the fact of enforced witnessing is an aspect of the atrocities being perpetrated, collectively, on a group of people held in detention: 'Another security shook his head, wagged his finger at the girl's father and said to us, He is able to bear this, he is not a man, a man would have killed himself. Instead he messes on the ground, messes in his trousers. What kind of people are you, you people.'[67] Being called on to witness brutality by its perpetrators, the narrative fragments into broken, traumatised phrases:

> each of us
> space

> each of us, the girl too
> …
> passage from my mouth, my stomach
> but how long since I had eaten, later
> it is also a numbness, below the jaw, upper neck
> our eyes are open.[68]

In account 5, '¿FODocument', an account of atrocity similarly emerges from and dissolves into shattered fragments. We are told in the Preface that this particular account has been retained 'in the form it emerged from computative mediation' and its intermittent strings of computer code suggest the breakdown of a signifying system – computational, linguistic – perhaps in its struggle to represent something almost unrepresentable. The account is given by an incomer to a town under curfew, who witnesses a foreign politician being chased and killed by 'securitys'. These 'securitys', volatile young men with guns and bayonets, confront the narrator, challenging him for being out so close to curfew, and demand to know where his 'home' is. He points out a house, one he has seen being entered by a trade unionist he recognises, and, having been sent on his way by the 'securitys', he runs there and demands to be let in. Conscious that the 'securitys' are likely to arrive any moment – they are watching the trade unionist as well as him, the witness to their recently committed murder – the narrator sees a baby among the group, and the narration lingers over the vision of the baby playing:

> I saw the baby on the floor by the fireside, the other baby was with it, the baby, now as in mid movement, its image forever there for me, laughing and on one hand, the other raised as if balancing itself, on its knees looking up to the child, its sister, brother, I cannot remember, girl I think, but the baby, the interested look that a baby gives, I see my own daughter, and its laughingand andto the guest in our country. SummaryInformationhatlanguageor@ifdotcom˛or@ ifdotcomiftildnottild[69]

The fragmented code suggests perhaps a breakdown in machine storage, perhaps in the process of telling or of translation – 'hatlanguage', 'whatlanguage pleas' – that loses the thread of the narrative, while containing its own compressed meanings. When the narrative

reasserts itself, the narrator is recalling a memory from military train-
ing (he too, perhaps, has been 'security'): a funny story about a friend
who could not march in rhythm, but also a story about the weaponry
which soldiers use.

> Bayonets, I remember too, old fashioned, design from years back.
> They could fix their bayonets and throw sacks of grain to one another,
> they could catch the sack on the bayonet and throw to the next man,
> this was practice for them, if they might use babies, of course.[70]

Through repeated dissolutions, we learn that the narrator – presumably
wanting to make this domestic scene look convincing – demands to
hold the baby, whom he has 'in the crook of my arm' when the securitys
arrive. The sense of threat is immediately palpable:

> Yes we can take the baby, said that same one also smiling, but babies,
> we have enough babies. What else do you have for us? Who is your
> wife? … What woman, who is yours, two of them. You people have
> many wives. The securitys smiled.[71]

As the securitys demand 'we do not want your jokes, give something
else to me' and the narrator repeats 'the baby was in the crook of my
arm', the account once again disintegrates into jumbled code, interrupted by fragments which attempt to retell other, earlier portions
of the story. When it is restored to some kind of order, the narrative
returns to the beginning, recounting the story again but differently,
yet still it can get no further in telling what happens to the baby: 'He
took the baby from me'. It is in the shattered portions of narrative, and
in the strings of apparently jumbled code, that recurrent, compressed
visions emerge of babies, bayonets, and sacks of grain: 'S, as a baby for
these babies I heard crying as of sacks one to another'; 'baybyonets';
'Items::hot:whatlanguage baynets'; and then, finally: '*baybybyeby-
nets'.[72] As Simon Kövesi puts it, 'we are never told clearly that the baby
and bayonet meet, but the language brings the two together anyway,
bidding a repressed bye bye to a murdered child'.[73]

In their difficulty, their ambiguity, their gaps and aporias, their
language pulled and distorted by unknowable layers of mediation and
the coercive operations of power as well as by the horrors they try to
convey, Kelman's accounts constitute both an exposure and a refusal of

the demands placed upon asylum testimony. In a broken language, in a shattered archive, Kelman's narrators struggle to narrativise and transmit their experiences of human life under conditions of suffering and atrocity, while fending off the deforming logic of an assimilative global English in which experiences of suffering are abstracted into generalisable lessons, in which victims become 'so-called victims'. Convulsed by the need to narrate, to transmit experience even when it seems inexpressible – like Mene in Saro-Wiwa's *Sozaboy*, 'knacking tory' as a means to assert his presence beyond the realm of ghosts to which he has been consigned – Kelman's narrators demand to speak, to be heard, to be listened to: 'if I may speak', 'I am to speak', 'ifimayspeak':

> What I am to say now, what account it is to be, I can speak if I should speak you can listen, I shall speak, speak now, let me speak, I wish to.[74]

'Them asylum-seeker eyes': Brian Chikwava's *Harare North*

The concern to speak, to give an account of himself, is shared by the unnamed asylum-seeking narrator-protagonist of Brian Chikwava's bleakly comic 2009 novel *Harare North* but, certainly on the face of it, strictly as a means to serve his own ends. Arriving in London from Harare, he has claimed asylum, alleging he has been persecuted as an opposition party supporter in Zimbabwe. In actual fact, he has been part of ZANU-PF's feared youth militia, the 'Green Bombers', and has come to Britain to raise the money he needs to pay off officials and avoid prison after – probably – torturing a suspected opposition party supporter to death. But though he makes grandiose claims about his narratorial powers to tell stories that people will believe, in fact he is someone whose self-knowledge and estimation of his own capabilities, including his own mastery of language, is tragically inadequate. And, seeking to control the meanings which are made about him and the narratives by which he understands the world, he is caught up in hostile regimes of language that are his endless undoing. The effect of Chikwava's narrative, by turns funny and horrifying, is to call into question categories of perpetrator or victim, 'real' refugee or 'bogus' asylum seeker, around which the demands of asylum testimony are constructed and, beyond that, to unsettle the idea of meaning and belonging in language altogether, in a linguistic nightmare-world of empty signs and semantic inversions.

The novel begins with an echo of the iconic opening image of Sam Selvon's classic novel of postwar immigrant experience, *The Lonely Londoners*: a vision of Brixton Tube station over which the 'white, ice-cold sun hanging in the sky like frozen pizza base', recalling Selvon's unnatural 'force-ripe orange' peeping through the London fog.[75] Later, Chikwava gives a knowing nod to Selvon's stream-of-consciousness evocation of 'coasting a lime' in the city in summertime: 'And the good weather in London, it now begin to change and put me in good mood as we coast into them unending English summer days'.[76] Chikwava's London is continuous with Selvon's insofar as it charts the precarious, labouring lives of black subjects who find themselves fixed into position by the city's linguistic and racial order, in which they are simultaneously erased from view and all too constantly visible. But in contrast to Selvon's synthesised pan-Caribbean literary vernacular, which facilitates a sense – though fragile – of collective belonging under the sign of creolisation, the linguistic fabrication that is Chikwava's narrator's language is a disorienting and dislocated idiolect that resists being read as a medium for collective identity (or indeed any kind of stable, coherent whole).

When the novel's narrator arrives at Gatwick airport from Harare, he greets the border officials: 'I mouth the magic word – asylum – and flash toothy grin of friendly African native. They detain me.'[77] The magical property of this word is not to grant him asylum but to turn him into an asylum seeker. Though swaggeringly confident about his powers of persuasion in telling the immigration authorities a 'story that … is tighter than thief's anus',[78] he is held in immigration detention for eight days and then released into a state of indefinite waiting, which in its vacantly atemporal endlessness stands for the 'uncertainty' that defines the condition of 'asylum seeking' in which the rest of the novel's whole circular narrative is suspended.[79] This sense of temporal indeterminacy is captured in the idea of 'the 44th of the month', written on visa applications, but also in the novel's hazy distinctions between day and night, its indistinct weeks, months, or seasons. The narrator ends up in a squat in Brixton, living with his childhood friend Shingi, whose asylum claim has been approved. Without papers allowing him to work and not entitled to any benefits, he earns money where he can in an attempt to accrue the $5000 he needs to pay off his debt.[80] These two, the narrator and Shingi, 'bogus asylum seeker' and 'legitimate refugee', are uneasy friends and doubles, the distinction between them hazy: often, the narrator looks at his reflection and sees Shingi looking back, and the house they live in feels to him like living inside Shingi's head. They are both part of the novel's underclass of impoverished, largely black immigrants who work in the city as cleaners, domestic workers, healthcare assistants ('BBC' – 'British Buttock Cleaners'), or construction labourers, and whose vulnerability or deportability is key to their cheapness and tractability as labour. Though forced to the city's peripheries, their integral role in its day-to-day running is underscored in grotesquely comic mode when Shingi gets a cleaning job in the Houses of Parliament, 'moaning about some big battle he have in the gents' toilet with one joist of poo. He swear it can support roof of the House of Commons'.[81] As black African immigrants in London they are on the one hand highly visible – women on the street give the narrator 'loud looks' – but, on the other, anonymous: the narrator is able to use Shingi's identification papers on the grounds that nobody can tell them apart. By the end of the novel, Shingi lies dying anonymously in hospital while the narrator has begun a disorderly psychic and physical dissolution whereby he and Shingi – never, in any case, completely distinct – are doubling and merging into one:

> Soft rain start and get the tarmac wet so that them street lamps reflect off the wet tarmac doubling up in numbers. Even me – there is my double image reflected on the wet tarmac. In the sky the moon struggle to come out of them clouds. Shingi's trousers is missing now, I am only in his underpants … I look down into puddle; the crack that is screaming out of corner of my glasses' left lens in all directions make things unclear; I can see Shingi looking straight back. My stump finger now feel cold and sore from carrying suitcase. I shake my head and Shingi shake his head until I start to feel dizzy. Why he want to shake me out of his head like so, me I don't know.[82]

In their strange narrative merging, the narrator and Shingi embody what David Farrier describes as the 'double-voicedness' of the term asylum itself, which 'articulates at once notions of sanctuary and illegitimacy' and in which 'the "genuine" refugee and the "bogus" asylum seeker converge'.[83] Asylum is the 'magic word' that marks the entry-point to the novel's perverse language-world in which meaning – like the narrator's vision through his cracked glasses lens – is rendered foggy and unclear. Chikwava has described *Harare North*'s narrative register as a 'patois', influenced by the relationship between African urban and Caribbean language forms. Its first-person narration draws on a heterogeneous mix of codes: Zimbabwean English, Shona, Jamaican Creole, London Cockney, and street slang, as well as what Emily Apter calls the 'CNN creole' of global brand names.[84] 'Everyone's troubled buttock holes get vex and now turn into likkle red knots', says the narrator on the opening page, using Jamaican Creole grammar and lexis to describe the effect on Zimbabwean bums of the toilet paper drought being reported in the *Evening Standard*; 'we have been stitch up, I know straight away', he says, splicing London Cockney phraseology with Zimbabwean English grammar, of the building site that closes without warning, leaving its paperless migrant labourers unpaid.[85] This stylised performance is the linguistic analogue of the novel's networked globe, crisscrossed by emails, mobile phone calls, print and digital news reporting, money remittances, people, resources, and goods. And just like the networked globe, there is nothing egalitarian or democratising about it: this is no welcoming cosmopolitan vernacular, still less a language of collective belonging in the manner of Selvon's literary creole. Offering a bleakly satirical take on the idea of a shared language as grounds for solidarity or community, language of all kinds, in *Harare North*, is rife with both misunderstanding and cruelty. When the narrator addresses Tsitsi, the young Zimbabwean mother who shares the squat, in 'deep Shona', for example, it is only the better to manipulate her. His own powerlessness, meanwhile, is evident in his tragicomic attempts to acquire 'proper culture' by learning a lexicon of global brand names:

> We talk heaps about how we now have to start getting familiar with them clothes labels if we want to acquire proper culture. All them names like Tommy, Diesel, Levi, iPod, Klein and all them such kind of people that stick they names on people's clothes.[86]

The irony which the novel ceaselessly hammers home is that, of course, the closest he is ever likely to get to this vision of consumerist belonging is via its shabbiest simulacra and its refuse: the fake, odourless 'Moschino Parfum' he buys for Tsitsi in Brixton Market, the broken-down electronic appliances which Shingi collects, or the discarded Marks and Spencer ready meals which they salvage from bins.

What the ceaseless flows of resources, money, and language in the novel have in common is that none can be trusted to hold their value and that their extraction, circulation, and depreciation is always at the expense of the already impoverished and marginalised. Like the hyperinflation which has made Zimbabwean currency worthless ('Me I only have Z$1,000,000 in my bag, which even if I change it will come to something like £4'),[87] or the unpredictable relationship between labour and wages, words too are debased and untrustworthy. In the Zimbabwe from which the narrator has come, violence comes couched in a perverse language of opposites. 'Forgiveness' has become code for the torture and death the Green Bombers dish out to opposition party supporters – 'for traitors, punishment is the best forgiveness', his commander tells him.[88] He distinguishes himself disdainfully from 'civilians' by the characteristics he possesses as a Green Bomber: 'discipline' (manifest, for example, in his strenuous efforts not to end up burying his cousin and his wife under the bathroom floor); knowing 'history' (largely an ill-assorted jumble of propaganda); and being a 'principled man'.[89] He, boasts that he, like other 'jackal boys', knows how to turn 'skill' into 'kill' and 'laughter' into 'slaughter'.[90] He is an agent in these manipulations of language, just as he is an agent of the violence they conceal, but much of the novel's humour and pathos comes from how little, in fact, he really understands, of language or himself. He carries a fearful 'secret' with him in his suitcase, one which, he says, confirms his view that 'life is never fair': it is a letter confirming his status as 'HIV negative', which he takes to mean that he has contracted HIV after being raped in prison. 'Who has ever hear of good news that is negative?'[91] In a weird, dislocated address to himself in the second person near the end of the novel, he reveals – in a semantic hall of mirrors in which touching becomes torturing, that perhaps recalls suppressed memories of his own rape – how the 'secret' of his supposed HIV status is connected to the killing he has perpetrated:

> Negative result. But you don't throw it away. It's proof that life is not fair. You keep it inside the pocket. You keep it inside the suitcase

where no one can see it. Right there. Life is not fair, you even tell that
traitor in Goromonzi when you give him your touch because you was
knowing that tomorrow you is going to be dead. And it's all because
life is never fair, you tell him, but he don't understand you is also
dying and it's not your fault. By the end he can only tell you apart
from everyone because of your touch; the skill and the laughter.[92]

This labyrinth of language merges seamlessly into a Britain in
which, too, words can mean their opposites, as in the term asylum
seeker itself, which has come to signify a system of calculated degrada-
tion and infrahumanisation:

> [T]hey also have them asylum-seeker eyes; them eyes with the shine
> that come about only because of a reptile kind of life, that life of sur-
> viving big mutilation in the big city and living inside them holes.[93]

The London of the novel is haunted by the ghosts of the narrator's
past in Zimbabwe – by the *mamhepo* or spirit winds which threaten to
send him mad, by all his memories and his guilt. But it is also haunted
by its own past, by the 'ghosting of colonialism', in Simon Gikandi's
terms.[94] The racialised colonial figure of the 'original native', which the
narrator so assiduously tries to evade, has merged seamlessly with that
of the 'asylum-seeker', as 'lived-in categor[ies]' from which it appears
impossible to escape.[95] As Paul Gilroy argues, the word 'asylum' in the
UK is central to a 'quietly racialized code' which 'supposedly uncouples
racism from debates over immigration' but in fact allows race to be
'calculatedly brought back to life' – such that there is to be, in this novel
at least, no escape from such racial reification ('original native', 'asylum
seeker', 'illegal immigrant').[96] At one point, Shingi discovers a scam for
buying fake French passports and fantasises about evading his position
as 'original native' by becoming a black Frenchman, calling himself
'President Chirac' and dreaming of ' "hitting French wine and wiping
my bottom with them butter croissants" '.[97] But the scam is blown, out
of fear of the immigration authorities, and 'President Chirac vanish.
Now the original native appear again'.[98] In a satirical swipe at the supposedly liberating potential of electronic communication, even Shingi's
email password is 'originalnative'.[99]

As Patricia Noxolo has argued, in *Harare North*'s inconsistent,
self-contradictory, self-deluding, elliptical, unsettling, and hallucinatory

narration, there is nothing that approaches credible testimony as it is defined within the asylum system.[100] Even more than this, the novel's narrative refutes both its very terms of engagement and the assumptions about the truth-value of language on which they are based. As words in the novel slip their moorings, the sets of definitions on which the legal apparatus of asylum depends – authentic and inauthentic, perpetrator and victim – begin to unravel. It is in a linguistic hall of mirrors that readers glimpse how the novel's narrator has been coerced through poverty, lack of education, and the perverse language of Green Bomber ideology into becoming an agent of state violence, how he is traumatised by the brutality he has both witnessed and inflicted on others, and how he is a victim of physical and sexual violence he can barely bring himself to name. He is also, in a broader sense, a victim of global systems of colonial power, which are not mitigated but if anything intensified in Britain, in the inescapable 'mutilat[ing]' circuits of a system which relegates poor black African immigrants to its margins as a precarious underclass of tractable, anonymous labour. This is what emerges in a narrative suspended in a period of waiting within an institutionalised system which will arrive, eventually, to erase all such complexity.

Language becomes an alien and alienating medium in *Harare North*, as it does in *Translated Accounts*: linguistic structure is unmoored, the meanings of words become suspect, 'truth' is elusive, particularly when framed by violent regimes of linguistic expropriation, of which the system of asylum law is primary exemplar. Moving away from any kind of naturalistic representation of actually occurring language, both writers respond with an odd and idiosyncratic English, born of cruelty and coercion, that stands for resistance to being reduced to 'examples', 'testimony', 'intelligibility' while they use it to point to the ways violence is carried out and covered for in language. At the same time, the denaturalised medium of both *Translated Accounts* and *Harare North* – languages that come out of multiple places, that can be ascribed to no one place – resist being co-opted into, or misrecognised as, a collective and bounded ethnolanguage into which or out of which to translate a regime of law or testimony.

Notes

1 Cited in Jan Blommaert, 'Language, asylum, and the national order', *Current Anthropology* 50:4 (2009), 420.

2 Blommaert, 'Language, asylum, and the national order', 424.

3 On the foundation of asylum law on narrative, see Agnes Woolley, 'Narrating the "asylum story": between literary and legal storytelling', *Interventions: International Journal of Postcolonial Studies* 19:3 (2017), 376–394; Agnes Woolley, *Contemporary Asylum Narratives: Representing Refugees in the Twenty-First Century* (Basingstoke: Palgrave Macmillan, 2014); David Farrier, *Postcolonial Asylum: Seeking Sanctuary Before the Law* (Liverpool: Liverpool University Press, 2011); Gillian Whitlock, *Postcolonial Life Narratives: Testimonial Transactions* (Oxford: Oxford University Press, 2015), p. 182.

4 Farrier, *Postcolonial Asylum*, p. 1.

5 Home Office, 'Asylum policy instruction: asylum interviews', version 6.0, March 2015. www.gov.uk/government/uploads/system/uploads/attach ment_data/file/410098/Asylum_Interviews_AI.pdf.

6 UNHCR, *Handbook on Procedures and Criteria for Determining Refugee Status under the 1951 Convention and the 1967 Protocol relating to the Status of Refugees* (Geneva, 1992), pp. 58–59.

7 See Katrijn Maryns, 'Displacement in asylum seekers' narratives', in Mike Baynham and Anna de Fina (eds) *Dislocations/Relocations: Narratives of Displacement* (Manchester: St Jerome, 2005), p. 179; Katrijn Maryns, *The Asylum Speaker: Language in the Belgian Asylum Procedure* (Manchester: St Jerome, 2006), p. 208; Jan Blommaert, 'Investigating narrative inequality: African asylum seekers' stories in Belgium', *Discourse and Society* 12:4 (2001), 414.

8 In *Human Rights Inc.*, Slaughter contends that formulations of human personhood – specifically, what it means to be a civic, rights-bearing individual – have emerged in the mutually constructing and defining relationship between literary fiction on the one hand, epitomised by the *Bildungsroman*, and legal discourse on the other. Out of this relationship has emerged ideas of the person, as 'a moral creature capable of bearing rights and duties', who is inculcated into a civic order and granted rights accordingly. Joseph R. Slaughter, *Human Rights Inc.: The World Novel, Literary Form, and International Law* (New York: Fordham University Press, 2007), p. 17. See also Woolley, 'Narrating the "asylum story"', 378.

9 Blommaert, 'Investigating narrative inequality', 418.

10 Maryns, *The Asylum Speaker*.

11 Robert Gibb and Anthony Good, 'Interpretation, translation and

intercultural communication in asylum status determination procedures in the UK and France', *Language and Intercultural Communication* 14:3 (2014), 385–399.

12 Jan Blommaert, Sirpa Leppänen, and Massimiliano Spotti, 'Endangering multilingualism', in Jan Blommaert, Sirpa Leppänen, Päivi Pahta, and Tiina Räisänen (eds) *Dangerous Multilingualism: Northern Perspectives on Order, Purity and Normality* (Basingstoke: Palgrave, 2012), p. 1.

13 Blommaert, 'Language, asylum, and the national order'. See also Jan Blommaert, *The Sociolinguistics of Globalization* (Cambridge: Cambridge University Press, 2010); Marco Jacquemet, 'Transcribing refugees: the entextualisation of asylum seekers' hearings in a transidiomatic environment', *Text and Talk* 29:5 (2009), 525–546.

14 Aamna Mohdin and Niamh McIntyre, '"Discredited" test used on two in five Syrian asylum seekers in UK', *Guardian*, 17 July 2019. www.theguardian.com/uk-news/2019/jun/17/discredited-test-used-on-two-in-five-syrian-asylum-seekers-in-uk.

15 Proforma 'reason for refusal' letter. Home Office, 'Language analysis', version 20.0, February 2017.

16 Katrijn Maryns, 'Multilingualism in legal settings', in Marilyn Martin-Jones, Adrian Blackledge, and Angela Creese (eds) *Routledge Handbook of Multilingualism* (London: Routledge, 2012), p. 310.

17 Marijns, 'Multilingualism in legal settings', p. 311.

18 See Gibb and Good, 'Interpretation, translation and intercultural communication', 390.

19 Home Office, 'Asylum policy instruction: asylum interview'.

20 UK Visas and Immigration, 'Code of conduct for the Home Office registered interpreters', December 2008.

21 Gibb and Good, 'Interpretation, translation and intercultural communication', 392.

22 Quoted in Gibb and Good, 'Interpretation, translation and intercultural communication', 392.

23 Blommaert, 'Investigating narrative inequality', 438.

24 Carol Watts, 'The Interpreter's Tale', in David Herd and Anna Pincus (eds) *Refugee Tales* ([Manchester]: Comma Press, 2016), p. 66.

25 Watts, 'The Interpreter's Tale', p. 66.

26 Watts, 'The Interpreter's Tale', pp. 64–65.

27 Watts, 'The Interpreter's Tale', p. 65.

28 UK Visas and Immigration, 'Code of conduct'.

29 Watts, 'The Interpreter's Tale', p. 67.

30 David Herd, 'Afterword', in Herd and Pincus (eds) *Refugee Tales*, p. 133.

31 David Herd, 'Prologue', in Herd and Pincus (eds) *Refugee Tales*, p. vii.

32 Herd, 'Afterword', p. 120.

33 Blommaert, 'Investigating narrative inequality', 442.

34 Imogen Tyler, '"Welcome to Britain": the cultural politics of asylum',
    European Journal of Cultural Studies 9:2 (2006), 189.

35 Rachel Holmes, 'The Barrister's Tale', in David Herd and Anna Pincus
    (eds) *Refugee Tales II* ([Manchester]: Comma Press, 2017), p. 55.

36 Tyler, '"Welcome to Britain"', 188–189.

37 Roger Zetter, 'More labels, fewer refugees: remaking the refugee label in
    an era of globalization', *Journal of Refugee Studies* 20:2 (2007), 183–184.

38 Paul Gilroy, *There Ain't No Black in the Union Jack* (London: Routledge,
    2002), p. 88.

39 Information Centre about Asylum and Refugees in the UK, *Media Image,
    Community Impact: Assessing the Impact of Media and Political Images of
    Refugees and Asylum-Seekers on Community Relations in London* (2004),
    pp. 49–50, quoted in Tyler, '"Welcome to Britain"', 191. See also Costas
    Gabrielatos and Paul Baker, 'Fleeing, sneaking, flooding: a corpus analy-
    sis of discursive constructions of refugees and asylum seekers in the UK
    press, 1996–2005', *Journal of English Linguistics* 36 (2008), 5–38.

40 James Kelman, 'On the Asylum Bill', in James Kelman, *Some Recent
    Attacks: Essays Cultural and Political* (Stirling: A K Press, 1992), pp. 64–68.
    Perhaps the most notorious example is the UN's cavilling – what Philip
    Gourevitch calls the 'semantic squirm' – over the definition of 'genocide'
    in the context of Rwanda and Darfur. Philip Gourevitch, *We Wish to
    Inform You that Tomorrow We Will Be Killed with Our Families* (London:
    Picador, 1999), p. 152. Joseph Slaughter also gives the example of the
    definition of 'enemy combatants' incarcerated at Guantanamo. Slaughter,
    Human Rights Inc., pp. 9–10.

41 James Kelman, 'A reading from the work of Noam Chomsky and the
    Scottish tradition in the philosophy of common sense', in Kelman, *Some
    Recent Attacks*, pp. 166, 169.

42 See, for example, Fabio L. Vericat, 'Letting the writing do the talking:
    denationalising English and James Kelman's *Translated Accounts*',
    Scottish Literary Review 3:1 (2011), 138.

43 Nicholas Wroe, 'Glasgow kith', *Guardian*, 2 June 2001. www.theguardian.
    com/books/2001/jun/02/fiction.artsandhumanities.

44 Drew Milne, 'Broken English: James Kelman's *Translated Accounts*',
    Edinburgh Review 108 (2001), 109.

45 On 'pseudotranslations', see Gideon Toury, 'Enhancing cultural changes
    by means of fictitious translations', in Eva Hung (ed.) *Translation
    and Cultural Change: Studies in History, Norms and Image-Projection*
    (Amsterdam: John Benjamins, 2005), pp. 3–17.

46 Vericat, 'Letting the writing do the talking', 141, 142.

47 Kelman, 'A reading from the work of Noam Chomsky', p. 166.

48 James Kelman, *Translated Accounts: A Novel* (Edinburgh: Polygon, 2009; first published Secker and Warburg, 2001), p. ii.

49 Kelman, *Translated Accounts*, p. ii.

50 Kelman, *Translated Accounts*, p. ii.

51 Kelman, *Translated Accounts*, p. ii.

52 Kelman, *Translated Accounts*, p. ii.

53 Kelman, *Translated Accounts*, p. 293.

54 Kelman, *Translated Accounts*, pp. 158, 159.

55 James Kelman, 'And the judges said', in *'And the Judges Said ...': Essays* (Edinburgh: Polygon, 2008), p. 43. For discussion of the relationship of Kelman's writing to that of Saro-Wiwa, see Iain Lambert, 'This is not sarcasm believe me yours sincerely: James Kelman, Ken Saro-Wiwa and Amos Tutuola', in Michael Gardiner and Graeme Macdonald (eds) *Scottish Literature and Postcolonial Literature* (Edinburgh: Edinburgh University Press, 2011), pp. 198–209.

56 Ken Saro-Wiwa, 'Author's Note', in Ken Saro-Wiwa, *Sozaboy: A Novel in Rotten English* (London: Longman, 1985).

57 Emily Apter, *The Translation Zone: A New Comparative Literature* (Princeton and Oxford: Princeton University Press, 2006), p. 147.

58 Kelman, *Translated Accounts*, pp. 68, 70.

59 Kelman, *Translated Accounts*, p. 70.

60 Kelman, *Translated Accounts*, p. 72.

61 Kelman, *Translated Accounts*, p. 79.

62 Kelman, *Translated Accounts*, pp. 285–289.

63 Kelman, *Translated Accounts*, p. 292.

64 Kelman, *Translated Accounts*, p. 5.

65 Kelman, *Translated Accounts*, p. 191.

66 Woolley, 'Narrating the asylum story', 387.

67 Kelman, *Translated Accounts*, p. 205.

68 Kelman, *Translated Accounts*, pp. 205–206.

69 Kelman, *Translated Accounts*, p. 27.

70 Kelman, *Translated Accounts*, p. 28.

71 Kelman, *Translated Accounts*, p. 31.

72 Kelman, *Translated Accounts*, pp. 36, 37, 39.

73 Simon Kövesi, *James Kelman* (Manchester: Manchester University Press, 2007), p. 177.

74 Kelman, *Translated Accounts*, p. 236.

75 Brian Chikwava, *Harare North* (London: Vintage, 2010), p. 1.

76 Chikwava, *Harare North*, p. 143.

77 Chikwava, *Harare North*, p. 4.

78 Chikwava, *Harare North*, p. 4.

79 See Farrier, *Postcolonial Asylum*, p. 6.

80 Chikwava, *Harare North*, p. 23.

81 Chikwava, *Harare North*, p. 190.

82 Chikwava, *Harare North*, p. 229.

83 Farrier, *Postcolonial Asylum*, p. 6.

84 Ranka Primorac, 'Making new connections: interview with Brian Chikwava', in JoAnn McGregor and Ranka Primorac (eds) *Zimbabwe's New Diaspora: Displacement and the Cultural Politics of Survival* (Oxford and New York: Berghahn Books, 2010), p. 260.

85 Chikwava, *Harare North*, p. 1.

86 Chikwava, *Harare North*, p. 147.

87 Chikwava, *Harare North*, p. 5.

88 Chikwava, *Harare North*, p. 19.

89 Chikwava, *Harare North*, pp. 19, 21.

90 Chikwava, *Harare North*, p. 69.

91 Chikwava, *Harare North*, p. 212.

92 Chikwava, *Harare North*, p. 212.

93 Chikwava, *Harare North*, p. 2.

94 Simon Gikandi, *Maps of Englishness: Writing Identity in the Culture of Colonialism* (New York: Columbia University Press, 1996), p. 3.

95 The quotation is from Andersson, drawing on the philosopher Ian Hacking's notion of 'making up people', in which categories such as 'illegal immigrant' or 'asylum seeker' are not just discursive categories but help to define 'new way[s] to be a person'. Ruben Andersson, *Illegality, Inc.: Clandestine Migration and the Business of Bordering Europe* (Berkeley: University of California Press, 2014), p. 16.

96 Gilroy, *There Ain't No Black in the Union Jack*, p. xxxv.

97 Chikwava, *Harare North*, p. 54.

98 Chikwava, *Harare North*, p. 62.

99 Chikwava, *Harare North*, p. 220.

100 Patricia Noxolo, 'Towards an embodied securityscape: Brian Chikwava's *Harare North* and the asylum seeking body as site of articulation', *Social and Cultural Geography* 15:3 (2014), 300–301.

Conclusions: 'Say Parsley'

How you speak will be used against you.

Caroline Bergvall, 'Say: "Parsley" '[1]

In her site-specific sound and language installation 'Say: Parsley' (2001–10), a collaboration with composer Ciarán Maher, the French-Norwegian poet Caroline Bergvall explores the force of the shibboleth, or 'the power of language to single out and denunciate speakers'.[2] The installation's title refers to the massacre of tens of thousands of Creole Haitians on the border of the Dominican Republic in 1937, and the version of this event in which, as Bergvall puts it, 'the criteria for execution was the failure to pronounce "perejil" (parsley) in the accepted Spanish manner, with a rolling "r" '.[3] Bergvall recalls the so-called Parsley Massacre, the acme of the modern-day shibboleth, specifically in the context of 'official and brutal unofficial responses to 9/11', including the intensification of regimes of linguistic border security. The 2004 Liverpool exhibition of 'Say: Parsley' revolved around the phrase 'Speak English at home'.[4] The phrase was commonly ascribed in the British press to then-British Home Secretary David Blunkett, from a September 2002 essay for the Foreign Policy Centre, in reference to Asian families in Britain in the wake of riots in Bradford, Burnley, and Oldham in the north of England in the summer of 2001, as well as 9/11. In the essay, Blunkett articulated a vision of citizenship, civil society, and the preservation of democracy underpinned by a seemingly fragile linguistic order demanding to be maintained at the level of the home, the family, the individual speaker. English was the means for British

Asians to access 'wider modern culture', as well as shared civic values; South Asian languages, even when spoken in the home, were associated with backwardness, disorder, even 'schizophrenia'.[5] Not long after Blunkett associated languages other than English with violence on the streets of England, the 2002 Nationality, Immigration and Asylum Act extended requirements for English language proficiency among applicants for British citizenship. Across the four site-specific iterations of 'Say: Parsley', various shibboleths threaten to 'denunciate' their speakers on grounds of race, class, or foreignness: a dropped /h/, a 'false friend' word, the substituting of /s/ or /t/ for the dental fricative /ð/. As Bergvall observes: 'The pronunciation of a given word exposes the identity of the speaker. To speak becomes a give-away. Are you one of us, not one of us?'[6]

Recordings of Bergvall's voice used as part of the installations give her carefully enunciating words in her own, French Norwegian accented English. She performs strings of words connected by their near-homophony, each one's difference in speech from the next resting on precise gradations and combinations of consonant and vowel: 'say: myrtle ... say: mortal ... say: portal ... say: portly ... say: paltry ... say: partly ... say: parsley'.[7] The crisp, highly defined recording of Bergvall's voice reveals the pauses, intakes of breath, the work she puts in to pronounce the words 'correctly': it is a performance of the labour of linguistic assimilation and the audibility of foreignness. In a recent interview, she describes her own writing as having been born in the transit between languages – specifically, from her 'own languages' into another, English:

> I would say that writing began, in all seriousness, when I began writing in English, when I moved from my own languages of French and Norwegian to working in my third language, English. In that choice, I situate some of the motifs of my practice as well – the consciousness of speaking, the acquisition of languages, the confusion of origins, the fact that everything is thrown into transit, that a language can be a passage to something else or from something else.[8]

Moving between languages, Bergvall suggests, makes language look and feel different. Even more than that, she places emphasis on the value of an experience of language that is not your 'own': what matters about English, as much as anything else, is that it is *not hers*. To be 'thrown

into transit' in this way underlines language's externality – becoming
something consciously acquired, something one experiences oneself
speaking – and thus it does away with the idea of language as interiority, as something inhabited fully and unselfconsciously. But at the
same time, it is an experience which throws into relief how language
acts upon us, individually and collectively, as a means of regulation and
exclusion. Language, writes Bergvall, is 'a dangerous, a lethal environment, one of the most infiltrated areas through which power structures
regulate, censor, and shape the social body or the individuated body'.[9]
These are the concerns that underpin 'Say: Parsley'. Nevertheless, as
Bergvall also acknowledges by invoking Blunkett and 9/11, her linguistic 'exposure' as a white middle-class speaker of French and Norwegian
is not of the kind that puts her directly at risk by racialised linguistic
border regimes.

Bergvall's *Drift* (2014) is a multilingual and multimodal assemblage
of image and text, drawn in part from collaborative performed work
begun in 2012, built around sources which include both the Anglo-
Saxon poem 'The Seafarer' and a contemporary human rights report by
the research group Forensic Architecture. 'The Left-To-Die Boat' documents the 2011 case of seventy-two African migrants, sixty-nine adults
and three children, who were left stranded in the Mediterranean when
their overcrowded boat ran out of fuel after they set off from Tripoli.
Despite their distress calls, they were left to drift for fourteen days
continuously without food or water, first towards Lampedusa, then
back towards the Libyan coast.[10] By the time they made landfall, all but
eleven of the people on board were dead; two more died soon after.
The report was produced by the ERC-funded, Turner Prize-nominated
research group Forensic Architecture, based at Goldsmiths, University
of London, whose stated commitment is to 'the reversal of the forensic
gaze, to ways of turning forensics into a counter-hegemonic practice
able to challenge state and corporate violence'.[11] The damning conclusion of 'The Left-To-Die Boat' is that the whole tragedy took place in
sight of a global arsenal of surveillance technology that was being used
to monitor the central Mediterranean Sea, as well as of boats and hel-
icopters that came to observe and photograph the stranded migrants
but did nothing to prevent them from dying. Located right at the centre
of *Drift*, 'Report' is a condensation of Forensic Architecture's account
which leaves aside linguistic experimentalism, adhering without embel-

lishment to the language of the original report. Its layout, in white type-script on a black page, visually recalls the radar images, oceanographic current maps, and drift maps used by Forensic Architecture in their analysis in 'The Left-To-Die Boat', and suggests that *Drift* is another piece of evidence, like these others, of the violence done in the name of regimes of border security.

In the rest of *Drift*, language appears as a boundless field across the North Atlantic: distinctions blur between supposedly discrete languages, from the archaic to the modern. In the sequence 'Seafarer', for example, words and sounds drift across oceanic space and time:

> Sailed on due north nord norþ norð norit norþe norh northt give or take a few transmission errors when steering by the sun.[12]

Bergvall seems to suggest that we think of language in terms of an oceanographic drift map – a matter of tracking intersecting currents, of following objects as they move – and that we do so in relation to Europe's historical relationship to the sea, from the Vikings, through colonialism and empire, to the undocumented labour of Chinese cockle-pickers dying on the English shore. In its construction *Drift* implies a remapping of Europe, linguistically, historically, and materially, by shifting the focus from fixed borders to sea routes. In alliterative, onomatopoeic streams of words, Bergvall mixes archaic and modern language forms, agglutinates Germanic prefixes with English verbs, blending the Anglo-Saxon of 'The Seafarer' with the modern reality of deadly migrancy by sea:

> Thats why he ah wat gets happily gedrunk
> laughs off dark nihtscua nightsky nightclouds
> shadowy northan snows earthless orphans
> hurdled in containers noodled on plastic beach
> in the corner coldest of the storm Days now
> clasping at my cracking scin noman to steer
> the failing structure Im a hostage of the waves
> floating in my coffin I have lost all my papers all
> I had with me Oneman gone thats all theyll say
> Oneman gone, thats all theyll say Blow wind
> blow, anon am I.[13]

'The forensic principle', as Bergvall reflects in *Drift*, is 'that every action or contact leaves a trace'.[14] The methodology of Forensic Architecture, the research group who produced 'The Left-To-Die Boat', uses technologies and apparatuses of border security and state power 'against the grain' in contexts of disaster and atrocity, shedding light on the regimes they help to police, as well as the alternate forms of knowing they can be turned to. Satellite surveillance, for instance, becomes a technology for humanitarian witnessing:

> Synthetic Aperture Radar (SAR) satellite imagery is routinely collected over the Mediterranean Sea for various purposes, including the policing of illegalised migration. Using these media to document the crime of nonassistance of people in distress at sea thus involved a strategic repurposing of these images and the use of surveillance technologies 'against the grain'. In this we exercised a 'disobedient gaze', one that refuses to disclose clandestine migration but seeks to unveil instead the violence of the border regime.[15]

In like manner, Bergvall's approach to English embraces it as a vantage point from which it is possible to see the contingency and connectedness of all language, while pointing to the violent, exclusionary border regimes it helps to shore up. In its final sections, *Drift* reflects on how the Old English voiceless þ (thorn), left over from the ancient runic alphabet and distinct from the voiced ð (eth), was lost in the development of the letterpress that replaced both in English with the digraph ‹th›. To Bergvall, the 'success and ultimate demise' of thorn in English shows 'the contingencies and accidents of writing', and provides a 'compressed reminder' of the dense and entwined linguistic histories that have produced language that now pretends to be a bordered and stable thing.[16] But it is in this capacity, too, that thorn has also bequeathed the English language one of its shibboleths: '[f]amously, the sound itself is one of the tings which makes English so difficult to get right'.

> This local difficulty might well account for the historically fascinating state of the English dental apparatus. At any rate, it is no small wonder that this 'theta' sound finds substitutes such as the short voiceless sibilant /s/ or the voiceless alveolar stop /t/ not only in its language variants but especially among late learners of the language, for whom it remains a vexing and more or less chronic obstruction.[17]

The example of thorn reveals some of the ways in which the idea of standard language operates: how what is contingent is made to appear permanent, given, self-evident, and how that givenness and self-identity is built on the exclusion of those who do not or cannot comply with its rules. In this sense, it is an analogue for all regimes that sanction certain kinds of identity and disbar others; being 'in transit' or 'lost' in language is also associated, in Bergvall's work, with gender non-conformity and sexual dissidence. As the chapters in this book have shown, diverse experiences of multilingualism and linguistic outside-ness have led writers to probe the idea of 'a shared language' and the several kinds of ideologies – of aesthetics, social formation, or political belonging – which it helps to shore up. In place of this idea, Bergvall proposes a literary practice and a politics founded in the inculcation of a shared experience of language as something somewhat alien, prosthetic, mobile, 'architectonic'.[18] As she suggests in *Meddle English*, it is the work of writing to 'test out, provoke the naturalised edges and bounds of language use and rules', to meddle with identitarian imaginings of language and orient ourselves towards 'a future perfect of English as language practice'.[19]

* * *

The idea of English as a practice runs through this book: specifically, the strategies by which English may be turned from an ideological force which practises on speakers into something which we practise – something we make through doing, individually and collectively, a continuous assemblage. The writers in this book express a range of experiences and positions, of ways of seeing language and the world that come from experiencing English in relation to other kinds of language (and experiencing, often, the concomitant recognition that English is not and never was one language). For some, English emerges as a disaggregated site of experiment: a denaturalised, self-consciously prosthetic medium. For others, it operates as a still self-contained entity in relation to other similarly bounded entities. For all of them, there is no longer any possibility of writing in English as though other languages do not exist. Thought of in these newly relational ways, the versions of English in this book become places to project all kinds of hopes – of new kinds of identity and belonging, new political solidarities, new kinds of signification or exegesis. But they are also the locus of anxiety and fear: fear of being laughed at, fear of not being understood, fear of being marginalised, fear of being excluded, fear of loss in transit. Moving between languages can be alienating as well as exhilarating, exhausting as well as illuminating. It is the signal concern of these writers' work to explore all of this, as an increasingly everyday aspect of lived experience in Britain.

These are often trenchant critiques of a monolingualist national order that shows no signs of disappearing, as I write in the run-up to Britain's exit from the European Union, in intensifying regimes of border security and a fearful logic of linguistic either/or that leads, in the worst scenarios, to fearful eruptions of violence against perceived linguistic alterity. The UK Government's recently published Integrated Communities Strategy Green Paper places a renewed focus on 'integration' that resembles closely other such pronouncements which have been made by different UK Governments since 2002. It is especially important that 'recent migrants should learn to speak and understand our language and values' (the one entailing the other):

> As we leave the European Union and seize the opportunity to create the kind of country we want to be: a global, outward-looking, connected nation, at ease with itself and others, built on the backbone of strong, integrated communities.[20]

In other words, and perhaps paradoxically, it becomes more important than ever that everyone should speak English in a new political landscape in which Britain ceases to be European in order to be global. Though the document nods to the exclusion of white working-class communities, its real focus is revealed by the Home Secretary Sajid Javid, whose Foreword frames the document in relation to his own childhood experience:

> When I was a young child, I sometimes had to miss school so that I could go to the doctor with my mother. But it wasn't because I was ill. It was because more than a decade after arriving from Pakistan she still barely spoke a word of English and needed me – her six year-old-son – to translate for her.[21]

Though Javid's mother later learned English 'fluently'; and though, as Deborah Cameron points out, the suggestion that minority ethnic groups need to learn the majority language is uncontroversial, in the sense of never having been contested by any community; and though the census figure which recurs through the document, of 77,000 people in England aged 16 or over who say they cannot speak English well or at all, represents 0.3 per cent of the population; and though the document acknowledges that existing English language classes are oversubscribed; nevertheless the Green Paper once again associates a supposed lack of English with social ills including school and residential segregation, isolation and unemployment, marginalisation of women, domestic violence, hate crimes, and violent extremism. As Cameron succinctly summarises, this is a variety of discourse in which 'the key opposition is between cohesion, symbolised by English monolingualism, and fragmentation, associated with the maintenance of other languages: fragmentation is figured as a threat, but the nature or source of the threat is only vaguely evoked using generic terms like "extremism" and "radicalization"'.[22] In the context of a proposed Brexit which was largely campaigned for on an anti-immigration agenda (prepared for by Prime Minister Theresa May, during her own time as Home Secretary, with her 'hostile environment for immigration'), though the Paper sets out strategies for putting more resources into language teaching, these and other strands of its supposedly new initiatives are to be resourced through the 'Controlling Migration Fund' – a title which gives a sense of its at-best-conflicted logics. And naturally, one key part of the strategy will be to again 'review' immigration language requirements.[23]

In November 2018, an unknown person painted 'SPEAK ENGLISH' on a wall in Walthamstow, in London. Similar graffiti has gone up elsewhere in Britain, of course, and the same phrase has been shouted at people speaking Spanish or Polish on buses, in streets and Tube carriages. And while these attacks are crude, sometimes violent, they do little more than articulate a sentiment commonplace in news reporting and political discourse. But in an image that went viral on social media and was widely picked up in the press, local artist Chris Walker used Photoshop to doctor the image and posted the result on Twitter.[24] Playfully suggesting the graffiti 'artist' hadn't had time to complete his or her handiwork, Walker claimed to have finished the job, producing an image in which the injunction to 'SPEAK' has become the collective assertion 'WE SPEAK', with 'ENGLISH' joined in scattered arrangement by 'PANJABI' 'LITHUANIAN' 'URDU' 'POLISH' 'ROMANIAN' 'BULGARIAN' 'TURKISH' 'TAMIL' 'BENGALI' 'FRENCH' 'COCKNEY'. Taking the list of languages gleaned from census data published on the Waltham Forest website, Walker turned them into a network of languages in which English features as just one constellated term. It does us all good, he implies, to be part of this 'WE'. It is a vision of the linguistic local that could perhaps be said to fulfil the letter, if not the spirit, of the Integrated Communities Strategy Green Paper's vision of 'a global, outward-looking, connected nation'.

Of course, Walker's Photoshopping could be said to come from a superficially celebratory multiculturalist position (though that would hardly be a fair criticism of his antiracist, activist gesture), but it makes the point that we live, like it or not, in superdiverse times. Like the other linguistic tallies and itineraries we've encountered in this book, it tells a history of class and race, of migration and social change – not least, in its own technological genesis and viral digital spread – and it marks English indelibly by its relationality to other languages. Like the writing examined in this book, it is a fabrication that, as a formal experiment, aims to reflect and comment on the conflicted language politics of our times. In the Twitter thread that followed, several people suggested going to the wall with paint, as a collective, and recreating

2 Image by Chris Walker (@doodlebank)
https://twitter.com/doodlebank/status/1067765392876154882.

3 Image by Chris Walker (@doodlebank)
https://twitter.com/doodlebank/status/1067765392876154882.

Walker's image 'irl' – a nice gesture for the way art might impact materially on the world.

As the chapters in this book have shown, in fact multilingualism
has no fixed politics. It can be a function of elite transnational mobility
or of the radically curtailed mobility of the refugee. It can be grounds
for commonality or solidarity, but also schismatic – along lines of race,
class, gender, sexuality, generation, proficiency, beliefs about language,
and so on. Language is one way we make judgements about each other.
English's historical relationship to empire, meanwhile, and to classed
and regional power, is now also increasingly overlaid by anxieties
about border security, and by political and popular discourses that
articulate the relationship between language and national belonging
in newly intensified ways. At such a moment, it becomes more important than ever to recognise literature's resistant capabilities, to see in
it different ways of thinking about language and the articulation of
different experiences of being at an angle to English – up to and including Bergvall's utopian call to imagine 'a future perfect of English as
language practice'.[25]

Notes

1 Caroline Bergvall, 'Say: "Parsley"'. http://carolinebergvall.com/work/
  say-parsley/.
2 Bergvall, 'Say: "Parsley"'.
3 Caroline Bergvall and Ciarán Maher, 'Say: "Parsley"', Arnolfini, Bristol,
  UK, May–July 2010. www.arnolfini.org.uk/whatson/caroline-bergvall-cir
  an-maher-say-parsley.
4 Caroline Bergvall, 'Say: "Parsley"', Liverpool Biennial, 2004. Quoted in
  'Interview: Caroline Bergvall and Imogen Stidworthy', in Caroline Bergvall,
  Middling English (Southampton: John Hansard Gallery, 2010), p. 60.
5 David Blunkett, 'Integration with diversity: globalization and the renewal
  of democracy and civil society', in Phoebe Griffith and Mark Leonard (eds)
  Reclaiming Britishness (London: Foreign Policy Centre, 2002), p. 77. For
  thorough, careful analysis of Blunkett's connection of language and social
  disorder in this essay, see Adrian Blackledge, *Discourse and Power in a
  Multilingual World* (Amsterdam and Philadelphia: John Benjamins, 2005),
  pp. 193–199 and passim.
6 Bergvall and Maher, 'Say: "Parsley"'.
7 Caroline Bergvall, video for 'Say: "Parsley"', Spacex Gallery/Exeter
  Maritime Museum, Exeter, UK, November 2001. http://carolinebergvall.
  com/work/say-parsley/.
8 Linda A. Kinnahan, 'An interview with Caroline Bergvall', *Contemporary
  Women's Writing* 5:3 (2011), 238.
9 Kinnahan, 'An interview with Caroline Bergvall', 238.
10 Forensic Architecture, 'The Left-To-Die Boat', 11 April 2012. www.foren-
  sic-architecture.org/case/left-die-boat/.
11 Forensic Architecture, 'Project'. www.forensic-architecture.org/project/.
12 Caroline Bergvall, *Drift* (New York: Nightboat, 2014), p. 28.
13 Bergvall, *Drift*, p. 48.
14 Bergvall, *Drift*, p. 134.
15 Forensic Architecture, 'The Left-To-Die Boat'. In the realm of testimony,
  working 'against the grain' also means substituting the shared, collaborative labour of co-investigation for the demand that survivors somehow
  prove the fact of atrocity through narrative that persuasively expresses 'the
  subjective dimension of [their] experience'.
16 Bergvall, *Drift*, p. 180.
17 Bergvall, *Drift*, p. 181.
18 Kinnahan, 'An interview with Caroline Bergvall', 238.
19 Caroline Bergvall, *Meddle English* (New York: Nightboat Books, 2011),
  pp. 16–17, 6.

20 HM Government, 'Integrated communities strategy Green Paper', March 2018, p. 11. https://assets.publishing.service.gov.uk/government/uploads/system/uploads/attachment_data/file/696993/Integrated_Communities_Strategy.pdf.

21 Sajid Javid, 'Foreword by the Secretary of State', in HM Government, 'Integrated communities strategy', p. 9.

22 Deborah Cameron, 'The one, the many and the Other: representing multi- and monolingualism in post-9/11 verbal hygiene', *Critical Multilingualism Studies* 1:2 (2013), 70.

23 HM Government, 'Integrated communities strategy', p. 14.

24 Jasmine Andersson, 'Racist "speak English" graffiti transformed into celebration of diversity by local artist in Walthamstow', *iNews*, 30 November 2018. https://inews.co.uk/news/walthamstow-racist-sign-graffiti-transformed-diversity-local-artist/?fbclid=IwAR17-EFAaktqvZapIXVbj9CtiyCwazNY6_kZknyXzjK3GDomj0jm3gHTYD4. Image by Chris Walker (@doodlebank) https://twitter.com/doodlebank/status/1067765392876154882.

25 Bergvall, *Meddle English*, pp. 16–17, 6.

Bibliography

Reports, legislation, and official documents

Home Office, 'Asylum policy instruction: asylum interviews', version 6.0, March 2015. www.gov.uk/government/uploads/system/uploads/attachment_data/file/410098/Asylum_Interviews_AI.pdf.

Home Office, 'Secure borders, safe haven: integration with diversity in modern Britain', February 2002. https://assets.publishing.service.gov.uk/government/uploads/system/uploads/attachment_data/file/250926/cm5387.pdf.

Home Office, 'Language analysis', version 20.0, February 2017.

HM Government, 'Integrated communities strategy Green Paper', March 2018. https://assets.publishing.service.gov.uk/government/uploads/system/uploads/attachment_data/file/696993/Integrated_Communities_Strategy.pdf.

Nationality, Immigration and Asylum Act, 2002. www.legislation.gov.uk/ukpga/2002/41/section/1/enacted.

Parekh Report. *The Future of Multi-Ethnic Britain* (Runnymede Trust, 2000).

Scarman Report. *The Brixton Disorders 10–12 April 1981* (London: Penguin, 1982).

Swann Report. *Education for All: The Report of the Committee of Inquiry into the Education of Children from Ethnic Minority Groups* (London: Her Majesty's Stationery Office, 1985).

UK Visas and Immigration, 'Code of conduct for the Home Office registered interpreters', December 2008.

UNHCR, *Handbook on Procedures and Criteria for Determining Refugee Status under the 1951 Convention and the 1967 Protocol relating to the Status of Refugees* (Geneva, 1992).

UNESCO, *Universal Declaration of Language Rights*, 2014. www.unesco.org/cpp/uk/delcarations/linguistic.pdf.

United Kingdom Border Agency, 'SET17 – English language requirement', 2010. www.ukba.homeoffice.gov.uk/policyandlaw/guidance/ecg/set/set 17/.

Books and articles

Aboulela, Leila, *The Translator* (Edinburgh: Polygon, 1999).

Aboulela, Leila, 'Moving away from accuracy', *Alif: Journal of Comparative Poetics* 22 (2002), 198–207.

Aboulela, Leila, 'Barbie in the Mosque', in Tom Devine and Paddy Logue (eds) *Being Scottish: Personal Reflections on Scottish Identity Today* (Edinburgh: Edinburgh University Press, 2002), pp. 1–3.

Aboulela, Leila, *Coloured Lights* (Edinburgh: Polygon, 2005).

Aboulela, Leila, *Minaret* (London: Bloomsbury, 2005).

Aboulela, Leila, *Lyrics Alley* (London: Bloomsbury, 2010).

Adams, Catherine and Tania Branigan, 'Refugee sews up his lips, eyes and ears', *Guardian*, 27 May 2003. www.theguardian.com/uk/2003/may/27/immigration.immigrationpolicy.

Agard, John, *Mangoes and Bullets: Selected and New Poems 1972–1984* (London and Sydney: Pluto Press, 1985).

Ager, Dennis, *Ideology and Image: Britain and Language* (Clevedon: Multilingual Matters, 2003).

Aitken, A. J., 'Bad Scots: some superstitions about Scots speech', *Scottish Language* 1 (1982), 30–44.

Alim, H. Samy, Awad Ibrahim, and Alastair Pennycook, *Global Linguistic Flows: Hip Hop Cultures, Youth Identities, and the Politics of Language* (London and New York: Routledge, 2009).

Alim, H. Samy, John R. Rickford, and Arnetha F. Ball, *Raciolinguistics: How Language Shapes our Ideas about Race* (New York: Oxford University Press, 2016).

Alladina, Safder, 'Black people's languages in Britain: a historical and contemporary perspective', *Journal of Multilingual and Multicultural Development* 7:5 (1986), 349–359.

Alladina, Safder, 'South Asian languages in Britain', in Guus Extra and Ludo Verhoeven (eds) *Immigrant Languages in Europe* (Clevedon: Multilingual Matters, 1993), pp. 55–65.

Andersson, Jasmine, 'Racist "speak English" graffiti transformed into celebration of diversity by local artist in Walthamstow', *iNews*, 30 November 2018. https://inews.co.uk/news/walthamstow-racist-sign-graffiti-transformed-diversity-local-artist/?fbclid=IwAR17-EFAaktqvZapIXVbj9CtiyCwazNY6_kZknyXzjK3GDomj0jm3gHTYD4.

Andersson, Ruben, *Illegality, Inc.: Clandestine Migration and the Business of Bordering Europe* (Berkeley: University of California Press, 2014).

Apter, Emily, *The Translation Zone: A New Comparative Literature* (Princeton and Oxford: Princeton University Press, 2006).

Apter, Emily, *Against World Literature: On the Politics of Untranslatability* (London: Verso, 2013).

Apter, Emily, 'Translation at the checkpoint', *Journal of Postcolonial Writing* 50:1 (2014), 56–74.

Appiah, Kwame Anthony, 'Thick translation', *Callaloo* 16:4 (1993), 808–819.

Arnaut, Karel, Jan Blommaert, Ben Rampton, and Massimiliano Spotti (eds) *Language and Superdiversity* (London: Routledge, 2016).

Ashcroft, Bill, *Caliban's Voice: The Transformation of English in Postcolonial Literatures* (London and New York: Routledge, 2009).

Ashcroft, Bill, Gareth Griffiths, and Helen Tiffin, *The Empire Writes Back: Postcolonial Literatures, Theory and Practice* (London: Routledge, 1989); 2nd edition (London and New York: Routledge, 2002).

Auden, W. H., *Spain [A Poem]* (London: Faber, 1937).

Bachner, Andrea, '"Chinese" intextuations of the world', *Comparative Literature Studies* 47:3 (2010), 318–345.

Bakhtin, Mikhail, *The Dialogic Imagination: Four Essays*, trans. Caryl Emerson and Michael Holquist (Austin: University of Texas Press, 1981).

Bakhtin, Mikhail, *Speech Genres and Other Late Essays*, trans. Vern W. McGee, ed. Caryl Emerson and Michael Holquist (Austin: University of Texas Press, 1986).

Ball, Arnetha, Sinfree Makoni, Arthur K. Spears, and Geneva Smitherman (eds) *Black Linguistics: Language, Society and Politics in Africa and the Americas* (London and New York: Routledge, 2003).

Barkham, Patrick, 'The Bard of Dollis Hill', *Guardian*, 18 January 2007.

Barlas, Asma, *'Believing Women' in Islam: Unreading Patriarchal Interpretations of the Qur'an* (Austin: University of Texas Press, 2002).

Battista, Anna, 'Facts and fictions: interview with writer Suhayl Saadi', *Erasing Clouds*. www.erasingclouds.com/0714saadi.html.

Bauman, Richard and Charles Briggs, *Voices of Modernity: Language Ideologies and the Politics of Inequality* (Cambridge: Cambridge University Press, 2003).

Bell, Eleanor, 'Old country, new dreams: Scottish poetry since the 1970s', in Ian Brown (ed.) *Edinburgh History of Scottish Literature. Vol. 3. Modern Transformations: New Identities* (Edinburgh: Edinburgh University Press, 2007), pp. 185–197.

Bell, Eleanor and Gavin Miller (eds) *Scotland in Theory: Reflections on Culture and Literature* (Amsterdam and New York: Rodopi, 2004).

Bell, Henry and Sarah Irving (eds) *A Bird Is Not a Stone: An Anthology of Contemporary Palestinian Poetry* (Glasgow: Freight Books, 2014).

Bergvall, Caroline, 'A cat in the throat: on bilingual occupants', *Jacket* 37 (2009). http://jacketmagazine.com/37/bergvall-cat-throat.shtml.

Bergvall, Caroline, *Middling English* (Southampton: John Hansard Gallery, 2010).

Bergvall, Caroline, *Meddle English* (New York: Nightboat, 2011).

Bergvall, Caroline, *Drift* (New York: Nightboat, 2014).

Bergvall, Caroline, www.carolinebergvall.com.

Bergvall, Caroline and Ric Allsopp, 'Editorial: translations', *Performance Research* 7:2 (2002), pp. 1–3.

Bernstein, Basil, *Class, Codes and Control: Theoretical Studies Towards a Sociology of Language* (London: Routledge, 1971).

Bernstein, Charles, 'Hearing voices', in Marjorie Perloff and Craig Dworkin (eds) *The Sound of Poetry/The Poetry of Sound* (Chicago and London: University of Chicago Press, 2009), pp. 142–148.

Bex, Tony and Richard Watts, *Standard English: The Widening Debate* (London and New York: Routledge, 1999).

Bhabha, Homi, *The Location of Culture* (London and New York: Routledge, 1994).

Bissett, Alan, 'The "New Weegies": the Glasgow novel in the twenty-first century', in Berthold Schoene (ed.) *The Edinburgh Companion to Contemporary Scottish Literature* (Edinburgh: Edinburgh University Press, 2007), pp. 59–67.

Blackledge, Adrian, '"What sort of people can look at a chicken and think Dofednod?": language, ideology and nationalism in public discourse', *Multilingua* 20:3 (2002), 197–226.

Blackledge, Adrian, 'The discursive construction of national identity in multilingual Britain', *Journal of Language, Identity and Education* 1:1 (2002), 67–87.

Blackledge, Adrian, 'Imagining a monocultural community: the racialization of cultural practice in educational discourse', *Journal of Language, Identity and Education* 2:4 (2003), 331–348.

Blackledge, Adrian, *Discourse and Power in a Multilingual World* (Amsterdam and Philadelphia: John Benjamins, 2005).

Blackledge, Adrian and Aneta Pavlenko, 'Negotiation of identities in multilingual contexts', *International Journal of Bilingualism* 5:3 (2001), 2432–2459.

Blommaert, Jan, 'The debate is open', in Jan Blommaert (ed.) *Language Ideological Debates* (Berlin and New York: Mouton, 1999), pp. 1–38.

Blommaert, Jan, 'Investigating narrative inequality: African asylum seekers' stories in Belgium', *Discourse and Society* 12:4 (2001), 413–449.

Blommaert, Jan, 'Commentary: a sociolinguistics of globalization', *Journal of Sociolinguistics* 7:4 (2003), 607–623.

Blommaert, Jan, 'Language, asylum, and the national order', *Current Anthropology* 50:4 (2009), 415–441.

Blommaert, Jan, *The Sociolinguistics of Globalization* (Cambridge: Cambridge University Press, 2010).

Blommaert, Jan, 'Commentary: superdiversity old and new', *Language and Communication* 44 (2015), 82–88.

Blommaert, Jan, Sirpa Leppänen, and Massimiliano Spotti, 'Endangering multilingualism', in Jan Blommaert, Sirpa Leppänen, Päivi Pahta, and Tiina Räisänen (eds) *Dangerous Multilingualism: Northern Perspectives on Order, Purity and Normality* (Basingstoke: Palgrave, 2012), pp. 1–21.

Blunkett, David, 'Integration with diversity: globalization and the renewal of democracy and civil society', in Phoebe Griffith and Mark Leonard (eds) *Reclaiming Britishness* (London: Foreign Policy Centre, 2002), pp. 65–77.

Bonfiglio, Thomas Paul, *Mother Tongues and Nations: The Invention of the Native Speaker* (Berlin and New York: Mouton De Gruyter, 2010).

Bose, Mihir, *Bollywood: A History* (Stroud: Tempus, 2006).

Bourdieu, Pierre, *Outline of a Theory of Practice*, trans. Richard Nice (Cambridge: Cambridge University Press, 1977).

Bourdieu, Pierre, *Language and Symbolic Power*, trans. Gino Raymond and Matthew Adamson (Cambridge, MA: Harvard University Press, 1991).

Bourne, Jill, ' "The grown-ups know best": language policy-making in Britain in the 1990s', in William Eggington and Helen Wren (eds) *Language Policy: Dominant English, Pluralist Challenges* (Amsterdam: John Benjamins, 1997).

Branigan, Tania, 'Kurdish poet finds a voice', *Guardian*, 31 May 2003. www.theguardian.com/uk/2003/may/31/immigrationandpublicservices.immigration.

Brouillette, Sarah, *Postcolonial Writers in the Global Literary Marketplace* (Basingstoke: Palgrave, 2007).

Brouillette, Sarah, *Literature and the Creative Economy* (Stanford, CA: Stanford University Press, 2014).

Bryan, Tim, 'My secret life as coral', *South China Morning Post*, 4 April 2004, n.pag. www.guoxiaolu.com/REV_WR_VS__secret_life_coral.htm.

Butler, Judith, *Excitable Speech: A Politics of the Performative* (London and New York: Routledge, 1997).

Butt, Nadia, 'Negotiating untranslatability in Leila Aboulela's *The Translator*', *Matatu: Journal for African Culture and Society* 36 (2009), 167–179.

Cadwalladr, Carole, 'Heathlow airport? Oh how we laughed', *Observer*, 11 February 2007. www.guardian.co.uk/books/2007/feb/11/fiction.features2.

Cameron, Deborah, *Verbal Hygiene*, 2nd edition (London and New York: Routledge, 2012).

Cameron, Deborah, 'The one, the many and the Other: representing multi- and monolingualism in post-9/11 verbal hygiene', *Critical Multilingualism Studies* 1:2 (2013), 59–77.

Capildeo, Vahni, *Measures of Expatriation* (Manchester: Carcanet, 2016).

Capildeo, Vahni, '*A Brighter Sun*: "I still want to see how the story unfolds" – Conversations with a novel', in Malachi McIntosh (ed.) *Beyond Calypso: Rereading Sam Selvon* (Kingston, Jamaica: Randle, 2016) [ebook], n.pag.

Capildeo, Vahni, *Venus as a Bear* (Manchester: Carcanet, 2018).

Capildeo, Vahni, 'Mother tongues: multilingual identities' panel discussion, *Multilingualisms in World Literature*, School of Oriental and African Studies, 18 January 2018.

Cariello, Marta, 'Searching for room to move: producing and negotiating space in Leila Aboulela's *Minaret*', in Layla Al Maleh (ed.) *Arab Voices in Diaspora: Critical Perspectives on Anglophone Arab Literature* (Amsterdam: Rodopi, 2009), pp. 339–350.

Cassin, Barbara (ed.) *Dictionary of Untranslatables: A Philosophical Lexicon* (Princeton: Princeton University Press, 2014).

Cassin, Barbara and Michael Wood, 'Introduction', in Barbara Cassin (ed.) *Dictionary of Untranslatables: A Philosophical Lexicon* (Princeton: Princeton University Press, 2014), n.pag.

Chambers, Claire, 'An interview with Leila Aboulela', *Contemporary Women's Writing* 3:1 (2009), 86–102.

Chambers, Claire, ' "Meddl[ing] with my type": an interview with Daljit Nagra', *Crossings: Journal of Migration and Culture* 1 (2010), 87–96.

Chambers, Claire, *British Muslim Fictions: Interviews with Contemporary Writers* (Basingstoke: Palgrave, 2011), pp. 1–32.

Chambers, Claire, 'Recent literary representations of British Muslims', in Michael Bailey and Guy Redden (eds) *Mediating Faiths: Religion and Socio-Cultural Change in the 21st Century* (Farnham: Ashgate, 2011), pp. 175–188.

Ch'ien, Evelyn Nien-Ming, *Weird English* (Cambridge, MA: Harvard University Press, 2004).

Chikwava, Brian, *Harare North* (London: Vintage, 2010).

Chomsky, Noam, *Language and Problems of Knowledge* (Cambridge, MA: MIT Press, 1988).

Chow, Rey, *Not Like a Native Speaker: On Languaging as a Postcolonial Experience* (New York: Columbia University Press, 2014).

Clark, Alan, 'A prize insult to the courage of Scotland's finest', *Mail on Sunday*, 23 October 1994.

Coard, Bernard, *How the West Indian Child Is Made Educationally Subnormal in the British School System* (London: New Beacon, 1971).

Cohen, P. and C. Gardner, *It Ain't Half Racist Mum: Fighting Racism in the Media* (London: Comedia, 1982).

Connell, Liam, 'Modes of marginality: Scottish literature and the uses of postcolonial theory', *Comparative Studies of South Asia, Africa and the Middle East* 23:1–2 (2003), 41–53.

Connell, Liam and Victoria Sheppard, 'Race, nation, class and language use in Tom Leonard's *Intimate Voices* and Linton Kwesi Johnson's *Mi Revalueshanary Fren*', in Michael Gardiner, Graeme Macdonald, and Niall O'Gallagher (eds) *Scottish Literature and Postcolonial Literature: Comparative Texts and Critical Perspectives* (Edinburgh: Edinburgh University Press, 2011), pp. 173–184.

Cooke, Miriam, *Women Claim Islam: Creating Islamic Feminism Through Literature* (New York: Routledge, 2001).

Corbett, John, *Written in the Language of the Scottish Nation: A History of Literary Translation into Scots* (Clevedon: Multilingual Matters, 1998).

Corbett, John, 'World Scots and global culture', *Translation and Literature* 9:2 (2000), 171–3.

Corbett, John, 'A double realm: Scottish literary translation in the twenty-first century', in Berthold Schoene (ed.) *The Edinburgh Companion to Contemporary Scottish Literature* (Edinburgh: Edinburgh University Press, 2007), pp. 336–344.

Côté, Nicole, 'Leila Aboulela's *The Translator*: a translated text?', in Suzanne Jill Levine and Katie Lateef-Jan (eds) *Untranslatability Goes Global* (London and New York: Routledge, 2018), pp. 113–127.

Craig, Cairns (ed.) *The History of Scottish Literature, Vol. 4: The Twentieth Century* (Aberdeen: Aberdeen University Press, 1987).

Craig, Cairns, *The Modern Scottish Novel: Narrative and National Imagination* (Edinburgh: Edinburgh University Press, 1999).

Craig, Cairns, 'Scotland and hybridity', in Gerard Carruthers, David Goldie, and Alastair Renfrew (eds) *Beyond Scotland: New Contexts for Twentieth-Century Scottish Literature* (Amsterdam and New York: Rodopi, 2004), pp. 229–253.

Craig, Cairns, 'Beyond reason: Hume, Seth, Macmurray and Scotland's postmodernity', in Eleanor Bell and Gavin Miller (eds) *Scotland in Theory: Reflections on Culture and Literature* (Amsterdam and New York: Rodopi, 2004), pp. 249–283.

Craith, Mairead Nic, *Europe and the Politics of Language: Citizens, Migrants and Outsiders* (Basingstoke: Palgrave, 2006).

Crawford, Robert, *A Scottish Assembly* (London: Chatto & Windus, 1990).

Crawford, Robert, *Devolving English Literature* (Oxford: Clarendon, 1992).

Crawford, Robert, 'Scottish literature and English studies', in Robert Crawford (ed.) *The Scottish Invention of English Literature* (Cambridge: Cambridge University Press, 1998), pp. 225–246.

Crawford, Robert, 'Wund', in Tom Devine and Paddy Logue (eds) *Being Scottish: Personal Reflections on Scottish Identity Today* (Edinburgh: Edinburgh University Press, 2002), pp. 55–56.

Crawford, Robert and W. N. Herbert, *Sterts and Stobies: Poems in Scots* (Oxford: Obog Books, 1985).

Crawford, Robert and W. N. Herbert, *Sharawaggi: Poems in Scots* (Edinburgh: Polygon, 1990).

Crawford, Robert, W. N. Herbert, David Kinloch, Peter McCarey, Richard Price, and Alan Riach, *Contraflow on the Super Highway* (London: Southfields Press and Gairfish, 1994).

Crowley, Tony, *Language in History: Theories and Texts* (London: Routledge, 1996).

Crowley, Tony, *Standard English and the Politics of Language,* 2nd edn (Basingstoke: Palgrave, 2003).

Crown, Sarah, 'A flighty mix-up country', *Guardian*, 24 February 2007. www.guardian.co.uk/books/2007/feb/24/featuresreviews.guardianreview25.

Cutter, Martha J., *Lost and Found in Translation: Contemporary Ethnic American Writing and the Politics of Language Diversity* (Chapel Hill: University of North Carolina Press, 2005).

Dawson, Ashley, *Mongrel Nation: Diasporic Culture and the Making of Postcolonial Britain* (Ann Arbor: University of Michigan Press, 2007).

Deleuze, Gilles, and Félix Guattari, *Kafka: Towards a Minor Literature,* trans. Dana Polan (Minneapolis: University of Minnesota Press, 1986).

Derrida, Jacques, *Monolingualism of the Other; or, The Prosthesis of Origin*, trans. Patrick Mensah (Stanford: Stanford University Press, 1998).

Devine, T. M. *Scotland's Empire 1600–1815* (London: Allen Lane, 2003).

Dhondy, Farrukh, *East End at Your Feet* (London: Topliners, 1976).

Dhondy, Farrukh, *Come to Mecca and Other Stories* (London: Collins, 1978).

Dhondy, Farrukh, *Bombay Duck* (London: Jonathan Cape, 1990).

Dolar, Mladen, *A Voice and Nothing More* (Cambridge, MA and London: MIT Press, 2006).

Doloughan, Fiona, *Contemporary Narrative: Textual Production, Multimodality and Multiliteracies* (London and New York: Continuum, 2011).

Doloughan, Fiona, *English as a Literature in Translation* (London and New York: Bloomsbury, 2016).

Doloughan, Fiona, 'Translation as a motor of critique and invention in contemporary literature: the case of Xiaolu Guo', in Rachael Gilmour and

Tamar Steinitz (eds) *Multilingual Currents in Literature, Translation and Culture* (London and New York: Routledge, 2018), pp. 150–167.

Dósa, Attila, *Beyond Identity: New Horizons in Modern Scottish Poetry* (Amsterdam: Rodopi: 2009).

Edwards, Viv, *West Indian Language: Attitudes and the School* (Derby: National Association for Multi-Racial Education, 1976).

Edwards, Viv, *The West Indian Language Issue in British Schools: Challenges and Responses* (London: Routledge and Kegan Paul, 1979).

Edwards, Viv, *Language in a Black Community* (Clevedon: Multilingual Matters, 1986).

Eliot, T. S., 'London letter', *The Dial* 71:4 (1921), 452–455.

Eliot, T. S., 'The music of poetry' (1942) in *Selected Prose of T. S. Eliot*, ed. Frank Kermode (New York: Harcourt Brace & Co., 1988), p. 113.

Eliot, T. S., *The Waste Land and Other Poems* (London: Faber, 1949).

Evans, Max, 'School becomes first in Britain to teach English as a FOREIGN language', *Daily Express*, 24 March 2014. www.express.co.uk/news/uk/466 589/British-school-to-teach-English-as-a-FOREIGN-language.

Fanon, Frantz, *Black Skin, White Masks*, trans. Charles Lam Markmann (London: Pluto Press, 1986).

Farrier, David, *Postcolonial Asylum: Seeking Sanctuary Before the Law* (Liverpool: Liverpool University Press, 2011).

Flett, Alison, *Whit Lassyz Ur Inty* (Edinburgh: Thirsty Books, 2004).

Forensic Architecture, 'The Left-To-Die Boat', 11 April 2012. www.forensic-arc hitecture.org/case/left-die-boat/.

Foster, Leonard, *The Poet's Tongues: Multilingualism in Literature* (Cambridge: Cambridge University Press, 1970).

Gabrielatos, Costas and Paul Baker, 'Fleeing, sneaking, flooding: a corpus analysis of

discursive constructions of refugees and asylum seekers in the UK press, 1996–2005', *Journal of English Linguistics* 36 (2008), 5–38.

Galbraith, Iain, 'To hear ourselves as others hear us: towards an anthology of twentieth-century Scottish poetry in German', *Translation and Literature* 9:2 (2000), 153–170.

Galloway, Janice, *The Trick is to Keep Breathing* (Edinburgh: Polygon, 1989).

Gardiner, Michael, 'Democracy and Scottish postcoloniality', *Scotlands* 3:2 (1996), 24–41.

Gibb, Robert and Anthony Good, 'Interpretation, translation and intercultural communication in asylum status determination procedures in the UK and France', *Language and Intercultural Communication* 14:3 (2014), 385–399.

Gikandi, Simon, *Maps of Englishness: Writing Identity in the Culture of Colonialism* (New York: Columbia University Press, 1996).

Gikandi, Simon, 'Between roots and routes: cosmopolitanism and the claims of locality', in Janet Wilson, Cristina Sandru, and Sarah Lawson Welsh (eds) *Rerouting the Postcolonial: New Directions for the New Millennium* (London and New York: Routledge, 2009), pp. 22–35.

Gilmour, Rachael, 'Doing voices: reading language as craft in black British poetry', *Journal of Commonwealth Literature* 49:3 (2014), 343–357.

Gilmour, Rachael, '"Sight, sound and meaning": voice/print transitions in black British poetry', in Kate McLoughlin (ed.) *Flower/Power: British Literature in Transition Volume 2, 1960–1980* (Cambridge: Cambridge University Press, 2019), pp. 86–101.

Gilmour, Rachael and Tamar Steinitz (eds) *Multilingual Currents in Literature, Translation and Culture* (London and New York: Routledge, 2018).

Gilroy, Paul, *There Ain't No Black in the Union Jack*, revised edition (London: Routledge, 2002).

Gilroy, Paul, *After Empire: Melancholia or Convivial Culture?* (London and New York: Routledge, 2004).

Glissant, Édouard, *Poetics of Relation*, trans. Betsy Wing (Ann Arbor: University of Michigan Press, 1997).

Gourevitch, Philip, *We Wish to Inform You that Tomorrow We Will Be Killed with Our Families* (London: Picador, 1999).

Graham, William, *The Scots Word Book* (Edinburgh: Ramsay Head Press, 1978).

Gramling, David, *The Invention of Monolingualism* (London and New York: Bloomsbury, 2016).

Grant, William, 'Introduction', in William Grant (ed.) *The Scottish National Dictionary, Vol. 1* (Edinburgh: Scottish National Dictionary Association, 1931), p. xxvii.

Grew, Tony, 'Eric Pickles: keep the faith', *The House*, 9 March 2012. www.politicshome.com/uk/article/48272/?edition_id=998.

Groes, Sebastian, *The Making of London: London in Contemporary Literature* (Basingstoke: Palgrave, 2011).

Gunning, Dave, 'Daljit Nagra, Faber poet: burdens of representation and anxieties of influence', *Journal of Commonwealth Literature* 43:3 (2008), 95–108.

Guo, Xiaolu, *A Concise Chinese-English Dictionary for Lovers* (London: Vintage, 2007).

Guo, Xiaolu, 'Visions in a whirling head', 5 April 2008. www.guoxiaolu.com/WR_visions_whirling_head.htm.

Guo, Xiaolu, *Twenty Fragments of a Ravenous Youth* (London: Anchor Books, 2009).

Guo, Xiaolu, *UFO in her Eyes* (London: Chatto & Windus, 2009).

Guo, Xiaolu, *Lovers in the Age of Indifference* (London: Chatto & Windus, 2010).

Guo, Xiaolu, *I Am China* (London: Chatto & Windus, 2014).

Guo, Xiaolu, 'Words from a brick in the wall (or, what the dialectical poet tries to say but fails to say, and what he might whistle or sing)', *ARIEL: A Review of International English Literature* 47:1–2 (2016), 391–395.

Guth, Stephan, 'Appropriating, or secretly undermining, the secular literary heritage? Distant echoes of *Mawsim al-Hijra* in a Muslim writer's novel: Leila Aboulela, *The Translator*', in Luc Deheuvels, Barbara Michalak-Pikulska, and Paul Starkey (eds) *Intertextuality in Modern Arabic Literature since 1967* (Durham: Durham Modern Language Series, 2006), pp. 65–82.

Hall, Stuart, Chas Critcher, Tony Jefferson, John Clarke, and Brian Roberts, *Policing the Crisis: Mugging, the State, and Law and Order* (London: Macmillan, 1978).

Halliday, Josh and Libby Brooks, 'Johnson pledges to make all immigrants learn English', *Guardian*, 5 July 2019. www.theguardian.com/politics/2019/jul/05/johnson-pledges-to-make-all-immigrants-learn-english.

Harris, Roxy, *New Ethnicities and Language Use* (Basingstoke: Palgrave, 2006).

Hart, Matthew, *Nations of Nothing but Poetry: Modernism, Transnationalism, and Synthetic Vernacular Writing* (Oxford: Oxford University Press, 2010).

Harrison, Tony, *Collected Poems* (London: Viking, 2007).

Hassan, Waïl, 'Agency and translational literature: Ahdaf Soueif's *The Map of Love*', *PMLA* 121:3 (2006), pp. 753–768.

Hassan, Waïl, 'Leila Aboulela and the ideology of Muslim immigrant fiction', *Novel: A Forum on Fiction* 41:2/3 (2008), pp. 298–319.

Heller, Monica, 'Code-switching and the politics of language', in Lesley Milroy and Pieter Mysken (eds) *One Speaker, Two Languages: Cross-Disciplinary Perspectives on Code-Switching* (Cambridge: Cambridge University Press, 1995), pp. 158–173.

Heller, Monica, *Linguistic Minorities and Modernity: A Sociolinguistic Ethnography* (London: Longman, 1999).

Heller, Monica and Bonnie McElhinny, *Language, Capitalism, Colonialism: Toward a Critical History* (Toronto: University of Toronto Press, 2017).

Herbert, W. N., 'A sense of porpoise', *Gairfish* 1 (1990), i–v.

Herbert, W. N., 'Carrying MacDiarmid on', *Chapman* 69–70 (1992), 18–24.

Herbert, W. N., *Forked Tongue* (Newcastle: Bloodaxe, 1994).

Herd, David and Anna Pincus (eds) *Refugee Tales* ([Manchester]: Comma Press, 2016).

Herd, David and Anna Pincus (eds) *Refugee Tales II* ([Manchester]: Comma Press, 2017).

Hills, Susannah, 'Children who speak English as their main language at home are now in the MINORITY in 1,600 schools across Britain', *Daily Mail*,

22 March 2012. www.dailymail.co.uk/news/article-2118846/Children-English-home-language-MINORITY-1-600-school-Britain.html.

Hodson, Jane, *Dialect in Film and Literature* (Basingstoke and New York: Palgrave, 2014).

Honey, John, 'The Language Trap: Race, Class and the "Standard English" Issue in British Schools' (Middlesex: National Council for Educational Standards, 1983).

Honey, John, *Does Accent Matter?* (London: Faber, 1989).

Honey, John, *Language is Power: The Story of Standard English and its Enemies* (London: Faber, 1997).

Hubbard, Tom, 'Contemporary poetry in Scots', in Matt McGuire and Colin Nicholson (eds) *The Edinburgh Companion to Contemporary Scottish Poetry* (Edinburgh: Edinburgh University Press, 2009), pp. 36–48.

Huggan, Graham, *The Postcolonial Exotic: Marketing the Margins* (London and New York: Routledge, 2001).

Husband, Charles, 'Racist humour and racist ideology in British television, or I laughed til you cried', in Chris Powell (ed.) *Humour in Society: Resistance and Control* (London: Macmillan, 1988), pp. 149–178.

Innes, Kirstin, 'Mark Renton's bairns: identity and language in the post-*Trainspotting* novel', in Berthold Schoene (ed.) *The Edinburgh Companion to Contemporary Scottish Literature* (Edinburgh: Edinburgh University Press, 2007), pp. 301–309.

Irvine, Judith T. and Susan Gal, 'Language ideology and linguistic differentiation', in Paul Kroskrity (ed.) *Regimes of Language: Ideologies, Polities, and Identities* (Santa Fe: School of American Research Press, 2000), pp. 35–83.

Jacquemet, Marco, 'Transcribing refugees: the entextualisation of asylum seekers' hearings in a transidiomatic environment', *Text and Talk* 29:5 (2009), 525–546.

Jenkins, Simon, 'An expletive of a winner', *The Times*, 15 October 1994, 20.

Johnson, Linton Kwesi, *Mi Revalueshanary Fren: Selected Poems* (London: Penguin, 2002).

Jones, Lewis, '*Pigeon English* by Stephen Kelman', *Daily Telegraph*, 7 March 2011. www.telegraph.co.uk/culture/books/bookreviews/8362385/Pigeon-English-by-Stephen-Kelman-review.html.

Jørgensen, Jens Normann, M. S. Karrebæk, L. M. Madsen, and J. S. Møller, 'Polylanguaging in superdiversity', *Diversities* 13:2 (2011). www.mmg.mpg.de/fileadmin/user_upload/Subsites/Diversities/Journals_2011/2011_13-02_art2.pdf.

Joseph, Anthony, *Teragaton* (London: Poison Engine Press, 1997).

Kay, Jackie, James Procter, and Gemma Robinson, *Out of Bounds: British Black and Asian Poets* (Tarset: Bloodaxe, 2012).

Kellman, Steven G., *The Translingual Imagination* (Lincoln and London: University of Nebraska Press, 2000).

Kelman, James, *Some Recent Attacks: Essays Cultural and Political* (Stirling: A K Press, 1992).

Kelman, James, *The Busconductor Hines* (London: Orion, 1992).

Kelman, James, 'Elitist slurs are racism by another name', *Scotland on Sunday*, 16 October 1994, Spectrum supplement, p. 2.

Kelman, James, *How Late It Was, How Late* (London: Vintage, 1998).

Kelman, James, *Translated Accounts: A Novel* (Edinburgh: Polygon, 2009; first published Secker and Warburg, 2001).

Kelman, James, *'And the Judges Said …': Essays* (Edinburgh: Polygon, 2008; first published Secker and Warburg, 2002).

Kelman, James, *You Have to be Careful in the Land of the Free* (London: Penguin, 2004).

Kelman, Stephen, *Pigeon English* (London: Bloomsbury, 2011).

Khair, Tabish, 'The Nortoning of Nagra', *Massachusetts Review* 60:2 (2019), 325–335.

Kinloch, David, 'The apology of a dictionary trawler', in Robert Crawford, W. N. Herbert, David Kinloch, Peter McCarey, Richard Price, and Alan Riach, *Contraflow on the Super Highway* (London: Southfields Press and Gairfish, 1994), pp. 3–7.

Kinloch, David, *Paris-Forfar* (Edinburgh: Polygon, 1994).

Kinloch, David, *Un Tour d'Écosse* (Manchester: Carcanet, 2001).

Kinloch, David, 'A queer Glaswegian voice', in Dimitris Asimakoulas and Margaret Rogers (eds) *Translation and Opposition* (Bristol: Multilingual Matters, 2011), pp. 129–160.

Kinnahan, Linda A., 'An interview with Caroline Bergvall', *Contemporary Women's Writing* 5:3 (2011), 232–251.

Knepper, Wendy and Sharae Deckard, 'Towards a radical world literature', *ARIEL: A Review of International English Literature* 47:1–2 (2016), 1–25.

Kövesi, Simon, *James Kelman* (Manchester: Manchester University Press, 2007).

Kress, Gunther, *Multimodality: A Social Semiotic Approach to Contemporary Communication* (London and New York: Routledge, 2010).

Kroskrity, Paul, 'Language ideologies', in Alessandro Duranti (ed.) *A Companion to Linguistic Anthropology* (London: Blackwell, 2004), pp. 496–517.

Lambert, Iain, 'This is not sarcasm believe me yours sincerely: James Kelman, Ken Saro-Wiwa and Amos Tutuola', in Michael Gardiner and Graeme Macdonald (eds) *Scottish Literature and Postcolonial Literature* (Edinburgh: Edinburgh University Press, 2011), pp. 198–209.

Lauret, Maria, *Wanderwords: Language Migration in American Literature* (New York: Bloomsbury, 2014).

Lennon, Brian, *In Babel's Shadow: Multilingual Literatures, Monolingual States* (Minneapolis: University of Minnesota Press, 2010).

Leonard, Tom (ed.) *Radical Renfrew: Poetry from the French Revolution to the First World War by Poets Born, or Sometime Resident in, the County of Renfrewshire* (Edinburgh: Polygon, 1990).

Leonard, Tom, *Reports from the Present: Selected Work 1982-1994* (London: Jonathan Cape, 1995).

Leonard, Tom, *Intimate Voices: Selected Work 1965-1983* (Buckfastleigh: etruscan books, 2003).

Leonard, Tom, *Definite Articles: Selected Prose 1973-2012* (Okehampton: etruscan books / Edinburgh: WP Books, 2013).

Macaulay, Thomas Babington, 'Minute on Indian education' [2 February 1835], in *Selected Writings*, ed. J. Clive and T. Pinney (Chicago: Chicago University Press, 1972), pp. 237-251.

McBride, Eimear, *A Girl is a Half-Formed Thing* (Norwich: Galley Beggar Press, 2013).

Macdonald, Graeme, 'Postcolonialism and Scottish studies', *New Formations* 59 (2006), 115-131.

Macdonald, Graeme, 'Scottish extractions: "race" and racism in devolutionary Scotland', *Orbis Litterarum* 65:2 (2010), 79-107.

McGlynn, Mary, *Narratives of Class in New Irish and Scottish Literature* (Basingstoke: Palgrave, 2008).

McIntosh, Malachi (ed.) *Beyond Calypso: Rereading Sam Selvon* (Kingston, Jamaica: Randle, 2016).

McKay, John, '"All livin language is sacred": Tom Leonard's use of dialect', in J. Derrick McClure, Karoline Szatek-Tudor, and Rosa E. Penna (eds) *'What Countrey's This? And Whither are we Gone?': Papers presented at the Twelfth Conference on the Literature of Region and Nation* (Newcastle: Cambridge Scholars Publishing, 2010), pp. 250-266.

MacKenzie, John M. and T. M. Devine (eds) *Scotland and the British Empire* (Oxford: Oxford University Press, 2011).

McLean, Duncan, 'James Kelman interviewed', *Edinburgh Review* 71 (1985), 64-80.

McLeod, John, *Postcolonial London: Rewriting the Metropolis* (London and New York: Routledge, 2004).

McLeod, John, 'European tribes: transcultural diasporic encounters', in Michelle Keown, David Murphy, and James Procter (eds) *Comparing Postcolonial Diasporas* (Basingstoke: Palgrave, 2009), pp. 19-36.

McLeod, Wilson and Jeremy Smith, 'Resistance to monolinguality: the languages of Scotland since 1918', in Ian Brown (ed.) *Edinburgh History of Scottish Literature, Vol. 3. Modern Transformations: New Identities* (Edinburgh: Edinburgh University Press, 2007), pp. 21–30.

McClure, J. Derrick, 'Lowland Scots: an ambivalent national tongue', in J. Derrick McClure (ed.) *Scots and its Literature* (Amsterdam: Benjamins, 1995), pp. 5–19.

MacMeacail, Aonghas, 'Being Gaelic, and otherwise', *Chapman* 89–90 (1998), 152–157.

McMillan, Neil. 'Wilting, or the "poor wee boy" syndrome: Kelman and masculinity', *Edinburgh Review* 108 (2001), 41–55.

McMurtry, Áine, 'Giving a syntax to the cry: Caroline Bergvall's *Drift* (2014)', *Paragraph* 41:2 (2018), 132–148.

McPhilemy, Kathleen, 'Poetry in Scots: a view from the outside', *Gairfish: The McAvantgarde* (1992), 121–130.

Makoni, Sinfree and Alastair Pennycook (eds) *Disinventing and Reconstituting Languages* (Clevedon: Multilingual Matters, 2007).

Malak, Amin, *Muslim Narratives and the Discourse of English* (New York: State University of New York Press, 2005).

Malkani, Gautam, *Londonstani* (London: Harper Collins, 2006).

Mandair, Arvind, 'Interdictions: language, religion and the (dis)orders of Indian identity', *Social Identities* 13:3 (2007), 337–361.

Mandair, Arvind, *Religion and the Specter of the West: Sikhism, India, Postcoloniality, and the Politics of Translation* (New York: Columbia University Press, 2009).

Mandair, Navdeep, 'Re-enchanting Englishness: multiculturalism and the matter of Britain', *Social Identities* 13:3 (2007), 283–306.

Marx, John, *The Modernist Novel and the Decline of Empire* (Cambridge: Cambridge University Press, 2005).

Maryns, Katrijn, 'Displacement in asylum seekers' narratives', in Mike Baynham and Anna de Fina (eds) *Dislocations/Relocations: Narratives of Displacement* (Manchester: St Jerome, 2005), pp. 174–193.

Maryns, Katrijn, *The Asylum Speaker: Language in the Belgian Asylum Procedure* (Manchester: St Jerome, 2006).

Maryns, Katrijn, 'Multilingualism in legal settings', in Marilyn Martin-Jones, Adrian Blackledge, and Angela Creese (eds) *Routledge Handbook of Multilingualism* (London: Routledge, 2012), pp. 297–313.

Matthews, Kirsten, 'A democracy of voices', in Matt McGuire and Colin Nicholson (eds) *The Edinburgh Companion to Contemporary Scottish Poetry* (Edinburgh: Edinburgh University Press, 2009), pp. 65–79.

Mignolo, Walter, *Local Histories/Global Designs: Coloniality, Subaltern Knowledges, and Border Thinking* (Princeton: Princeton University Press, 2000).

Miller, Gavin, "Persuade without convincing … represent without reasoning': the inferiorist mythology of the Scots language', in Eleanor Bell and Gavin Miller (eds) *Scotland in Theory: Reflections on Culture and Literature* (Edinburgh: Edinburgh University Press, 2004), pp. 197–209.

Miller, Joshua L., *Accented America: The Cultural Politics of Multilingual Modernism* (Oxford and New York: Oxford University Press, 2011).

Miller, Mitch and Johnny Rodger, *The Red Cockatoo: James Kelman and the Politics of Commitment* (Dingwall: Sandstone, 2011).

Miller, Mitch and Johnny Rodger, "The writer as tactician: James Kelman's everyday practice', *Scottish Literary Review* 4:1 (2012), 151–168.

Milne, Drew, 'Broken English: James Kelman's *Translated Accounts*', *Edinburgh Review* 108 (2001), 106–115.

Mirsky, Jonathan, 'Cute pidgin pie', *Spectator*, 15 February 2007. http://archive.spectator.co.uk/article/17th-february-2007/25/cute-pidgin-pie.

Mitchell, Nick, 'Interview – Suhayl Saadi: *Psychoraag*', *Spike Magazine*, 1 April 2006. www.spikemagazine.com/0406-suhayl-saadi-psychoraag-interview.php.

Mohdin, Aamna and Niamh McIntyre, '"Discredited" test used on two in five Syrian asylum seekers in UK', *Guardian*, 17 July 2019. www.theguardian.com/uk-news/2019/jun/17/discredited-test-used-on-two-in-five-syrian-asylum-seekers-in-uk.

Morey, Peter, '"Halal fiction" and the limits of postsecularism: criticism, critique, and the Muslim in Leila Aboulela's *Minaret*', *Journal of Commonwealth Literature* 53:2 (2018), 301–315.

Morris, Adelaide (ed.) *Sound States: Innovative Poetics and Acoustical Technologies* (Chapel Hill and London: University of North Carolina Press, 1997).

Morris, Mervyn, *Is English We Speaking and Other Essays* (Kingston: Randle, 1999).

Mufti, Aamir R., *Forget English! Orientalisms and World Literatures* (Cambridge, MA: Harvard University Press, 2016).

Mugglestone, Linda, *Talking Proper: The Rise and Fall of the English Accent as a Social Symbol* (Oxford: Oxford University Press, 2003).

Mühleisen, Susanne, 'What makes an accent funny, and why? Black British Englishes and humour televised', in Susanne Reichl and Mark Stein (eds) *Cheeky Fictions: Laughter and the Postcolonial* (Amsterdam: Rodopi, 2005), pp. 225–243.

Mundair, Raman, 'Introduction', in Poloumi Deson and Parminder Sekhon,

Red Threads: The South Asian Queer Connection in Photographs (London: Diva Books, 2003), pp. 5–8.

Mundair, Raman, *Lovers, Liars, Conjurers and Thieves* (Leeds: Peepal Tree Press, 2003).

Mundair, Raman, *A Choreographer's Cartography* (Leeds: Peepal Tree Press, 2007).

Mundair, Raman (ed.) *Incoming: Some Shetland Voices* (Lerwick: Shetland Museum and Archives, 2014). www.shetlandamenity.org/the-incoming-project.

Mundair, Raman, 'The Rose of the Rock', in Linda Andersson Burnett (ed.) *Archipelagos: Poems from Writing the North* (n.p.: AHRC/University of Edinburgh, 2014). www.writingthenorth.com/wp-content/uploads/2014/04/archipelagos-for-download.pdf.

Mundair, Raman, 'Your land is my land: perspectives from an immigrant', *Bella Caledonia*, 5 January 2018. https://bellacaledonia.org.uk/2018/01/05/your-land-is-my-land-perspectives-from-an-immigrant/.

Mundair, Raman, 'Sow, Reap and Slowly Savour', Centre for Contemporary Art Glasgow, June 2019. www.cca-glasgow.com/programme/raman-mundair-sow-reap-and-slowly-savour-workshop.

Mundair, Raman, 'Mu Vich, Ajeeb Jeeb – In My Mouth, Strange and Curious Tongue' [2019]. https://soundcloud.com/user-724492265/mu-vich-ajeeb-jeeb?fbclid=IwAR2eicrgvp_kpz_Kgbnpq3paURkDb1qF-OP15zywkK3SFt55K11ZElHK6Fg.

Murphy, Terence Patrick, '"Getting rid of that standard third party narrative voice": the development of James Kelman's early authorial style', *Language and Literature* 15:2 (2006), 183–199.

Nagra, Daljit, *Look We Have Coming to Dover!* (London: Faber, 2007).

Nagra, Daljit, *Tippoo Sultan's Incredible White-Man-Eating Tiger-Toy Machine!!!* (London: Faber, 2011).

Nagra, Daljit, '*Hobson-Jobson*: a very English enterprise', BBC Radio 4, 13 July 2012. www.bbc.co.uk/programmes/b01kksr0.

Nagra, Daljit, *Ramayana: A Retelling* (London: Faber, 2013).

Nagra, Daljit, *British Museum* (London: Faber, 2017).

Nairn, Tom, '*Break-Up*: twenty-five years on', in Eleanor Bell and Gavin Miller (eds) *Scotland in Theory* (Amsterdam and Philadelphia: Rodopi, 2004), pp. 17–34.

Nayar, Pramod K., *Colonial Voices: The Discourses of Empire* (Oxford: Wiley-Blackwell, 2012).

Neubauer, Jürgen, *Literature as Intervention: Struggles over Cultural Identity in Contemporary Scottish Fiction* (Marburg: Tectum Verlag, 1999).

Nichols, Grace, *The Fat Black Woman's Poems* (London: Virago, 1984).

Noorani, Yaseen, 'Hard and soft multilingualism', *Critical Multilingualism Studies* 1:2 (2013), 7–28.

North, Michael, *The Dialect of Modernism: Race, Language, and Twentieth-Century Literature* (Oxford and New York: Oxford University Press, 1994).

Nowell Smith, David, 'Langwij a thi guhtr', in Abigail Lang and David Nowell Smith (eds) *Modernist Legacies: Trends and Faultlines in British Poetry Today* (Basingstoke: Palgrave, 2015), pp. 177–191.

Noxolo, Patricia, 'Towards an embodied securityscape: Brian Chikwava's *Harare North* and the asylum seeking body as site of articulation', *Social and Cultural Geography* 15:3 (2014), 291–312.

O'Grady, Sarah, 'Migrants shun the English language', *Daily Express*, 31 January 2013. www.express.co.uk/news/uk/374550/Migrants-shun-the-English-language.

Oliphant, Vickiie, 'More than one MILLION schoolchildren do not speak English as first language', *Daily Express*, 2 September 2017. www.express. co.uk/news/uk/849283/immigration-news-children-speak-english-first-second-language-school.

O'Rourke, Daniel (ed.) *Dream State: The New Scottish Poets* (Edinburgh: Polygon, 1994).

Orwell, George, *Inside the Whale and Other Essays* (London: Gollancz, 1940).

Page, Norman, *Speech in the English Novel*, 2nd edition (New Jersey: Humanities Press International, 1988).

Parmar, Sandeep, 'Not a British subject: race and poetry in the UK', *Los Angeles Review of Books*, 6 (December 2015), n.pag. https://lareviewofbooks.org/article/not-a-british-subject-race-and-poetry-in-the-uk/.

Paulin, Tom, *A New Look at The Language Question* (Derry: Field Day, 1983).

Pavlenko, Aneta, *Emotions and Multilingualism* (Cambridge: Cambridge University Press, 2005).

Pearce, Lynne, Corinne Fowler, and Robert Crawshaw, *Postcolonial Manchester: Diaspora Space and the Evolution of Literary Culture* (Manchester: Manchester University Press, 2015).

Pennycook, Alastair, 'The right to language: towards a situated ethics of language possibilities', *Language Sciences* 20:1 (1998), 73–87.

Pennycook, Alastair, 'English as a language always in translation', *European Journal of English Studies* 12:1 (2008), 33–47.

Pennycook, Alastair and Emi Otsuji, *Metrolingualism: Language in the City* (London and New York: Routledge, 2015).

Phillipson, Robert, *Linguistic Imperialism* (Oxford: Oxford University Press, 1992).

Pittin-Hedon, Marie-Odile, *The Space of Fiction: Voices from Scotland in a Post-Devolution Age* (Glasgow: Scottish Literature International, 2015).

Potter, Russell, *Spectacular Vernaculars: Hip-Hop and the Politics of Postmodernism* (New York: State University of New York Press, 1995).

Pratt, Mary Louise, 'Linguistic utopias', in Nigel Fabb, Derek Attridge, Alan Durant, and Colin McCabe (eds) *The Linguistics of Writing* (Manchester: Manchester University Press, 1987).

Pratt, Mary Louise, 'Harm's way: language and the contemporary arts of war', *PMLA* 124:5 (2009), 1515–1531.

Price, Richard, 'Approaching the Informationists', in Robert Crawford, W. N. Herbert, David Kinloch, Peter McCarey, Richard Price, and Alan Riach, *Contraflow on the Super Highway* (London: Southfields Press and Gairfish, 1994), pp. i–xii.

Price, Richard, 'Atlantis', *Verse* 15:1–2 (1998), 25.

Primorac, Ranka, 'Making new connections: interview with Brian Chikwava' in JoAnn McGregor and Ranka Primorac (eds) *Zimbabwe's New Diaspora: Displacement and the Cultural Politics of Survival* (Oxford and New York: Berghahn Books, 2010), pp. 255–260.

Procter, James, *Dwelling Places: Postwar Black British Writing* (Manchester: Manchester University Press, 2003).

Procter, James, 'The postcolonial everyday', *New Formations* 58 (2006), 62–80.

Procter, James, 'Imtiaz Dharker', *British Council* (2010). https://literature.brit ishcouncil.org/writer/imtiaz-dharker.

Quinn, Ben, 'David Starkey claims "the whites have become black"', *Guardian*, 13 August 2011. www.theguardian.com/uk/2011/aug/13/david-starkey-claims-whites-black.

Ramazani, Jahan, *The Hybrid Muse: Postcolonial Poetry in English* (Chicago: University of Chicago Press, 2001).

Ramazani, Jahan, 'Black British poetry and the translocal', in Neil Corcoran (ed.) *The Cambridge Companion to Twentieth-Century English Poetry* (Cambridge: Cambridge University Press, 2007).

Ramazani, Jahan (ed.) *Norton Anthology of English Literature: The Twentieth and Twenty-First Centuries* (London and New York: Norton, 2018).

Rampton, Ben, 'Stylization and the dynamics of migration, ethnicity and class', in Natalie Braber and Sandra Jansen (eds) *Sociolinguistics in England* (Basingstoke: Palgrave, 2018), pp. 97–125.

Rampton, Ben, Roxy Harris, and Constance Leung, 'Multilingualism in England', *Annual Review of Applied Linguistics* 17 (1997), 224–241.

Rampton, Ben, Jan Blommaert, Karel Arnaut, and Massimiliano Spotti, 'Introduction: superdiversity and sociolinguistics', *Tilburg Papers in Culture Studies* (2015), 1–17.

Randhawa, Ravinder, *A Wicked Old Woman* (London: The Women's Press, 1987).

Reichl, Susanne and Mark Stein (eds) *Cheeky Fictions: Laughter and the Postcolonial* (Amsterdam: Rodopi, 2005).

Riach, Alan, 'Tradition and the new alliance: Scotland and the Caribbean', *Gairfish: The McAvantgarde* (1992), 135–144.

Riach, Alan, 'Wilson Harris interviewed by Alan Riach', in Alan Riach and Mark Williams (eds) *The Radical Imagination: Lectures and Talks by Wilson Harris* (Liège: Université de Liège, 1992), pp. 33–65.

Rodríguez González, Carla, 'The rhythms of the city: the performance of time and space in Suhayl Saadi's *Psychoraag'*, *Journal of Commonwealth Literature* 51:1 (2016), 92–109.

Rosa, Jonathan, 'Standardization, racialization, languagelessness: sociolinguistic ideologies across communicative contexts', *Journal of Linguistic Anthropology* 26:2 (2016), 162–183.

Rosa, Jonathan, *Looking Like a Language, Sounding Like a Race: Raciolinguistic Ideologies and the Learning of Latinidad* (New York: Oxford University Press, 2017).

Rosello, Mireille and László Marácz, *Multilingual Europe, Multilingual Europeans* (Amsterdam: Rodopi, 2015).

Ross, Michael, *Race Riots: Comedy and Ethnicity in Modern British Fiction* (Montreal and Kingston, London, Ithaca: McGill-Queen's University Press, 2006).

Rushdie, Salman, *The Satanic Verses* (London: Viking, 1988).

Saadi, Suhayl, *The Burning Mirror* (Edinburgh: Polygon, 2001).

Saadi, Suhayl, *Psychoraag* (Edinburgh: Chroma, 2004).

Saadi, Suhayl, '*Psychoraag*: the gods of the door', *Spike Magazine*, 1 February 2006, n.pag. www.spikemagazine.com/0206-suhayl-saadi-censorship-in-the-uk.php.

Saadi, Suhayl, 'In Tom Paine's kitchen: days of rage and fire', in Berthold Schoene (ed.) *The Edinburgh Companion to Contemporary Scottish Literature* (Edinburgh: Edinburgh University Press, 2007), pp. 28–33.

Saadi, Suhayl, 'Infinite diversity in new Scottish writing', *The Association for Scottish Literary Studies* (2000). http://asls.arts.gla.ac.uk/SSaadi.html.

Saadi, Suhayl, 'Being Scottish', in Tom Devine and Paddy Logue (eds) *Being Scottish: Personal Reflections on Scottish Identity Today* (Edinburgh: Edinburgh University Press, 2002), pp. 239–241.

Saadi, Suhayl, '*Londonstani*, by Gautam Malkani: a tale of gangsta Sikh', *Independent*, 21 April 2006. www.independent.co.uk/arts-entertainment/books/reviews/londonstani-by-gautam-malkani-6103175.html.

Saadi, Suhayl, 'Extra Time in Paradise' (English Version)/ 'Extra Time in Paradise' (Glaswegian-ish Version), *Devolving Diasporas* (n.d.). www.devolvingdiasporas.com/writing.htm.

Sakai, Naoki, *Translation and Subjectivity* (Minneapolis: University of Minnesota Press, 1997).

Sapir, Edward, 'The status of linguistics as a science', *Language* 5 (1929), 207–214.

Saro-Wiwa, Ken, *Sozaboy: A Novel in Rotten English* (New York: Longman, 1994).

Sassi, Carla, 'Acts of (un)willed amnesia: dis-appearing figurations of the Caribbean in post-Union Scottish literature', in Giovanna Covi, Joan Annim-Addo, Velma Pollard, and Carla Sassi (eds) *Caribbean-Scottish Relations: Colonial and Contemporary Inscriptions in History, Language and Literature* (London: Mango Publishing, 2007), pp. 131–198.

Sassi, Carla, 'Issues of memory, issues of identity: interrogating Scotland's mnemonic fictions of the Caribbean', in J. Derrick McClure, Karoline Szatek-Tudor, and Rosa E. Penna (eds) *'What Country's This? And Whither are we Gone?': Papers Presented at the Twelfth Conference on the Literature of Region and Nation* (Newcastle: Cambridge Scholars Publishing, 2010), pp. 97–117.

Sauerberg, Lars Ole, *Intercultural Voices in Contemporary British Literature: The Implosion of Empire* (Basingstoke: Palgrave Macmillan, 2001).

Schneider, Britta, *Linguistic Human Rights and Migrant Languages* (Frankfurt: Peter Lang, 2005).

Schoene, Berthold, 'A passage to Scotland: Scottish literature and the British postcolonial condition', *Scotlands* 2:1 (1995), 107–122.

Schoene, Berthold, 'Going cosmopolitan: reconstituting "Scottishness" in post-devolution criticism', in Berthold Schoene (ed.) *The Edinburgh Companion to Contemporary Scottish Literature* (Edinburgh: Edinburgh University Press, 2007), pp. 7–16.

Schwarz, Bill, 'Creolization, West One. Sam Selvon in London', *Anthurium: A Caribbean Studies Journal* 11:2 (2014), 1–22.

Scott, Jeremy, *The Demotic Voice in Contemporary British Fiction* (Basingstoke: Palgrave Macmillan, 2009).

Sebba, Mark, '"English a foreign tongue": the 2011 census in England and the misunderstanding of multilingualism', *Journal of Language and Politics* 16:2 (2017), 264–284.

Selvon, Samuel, *The Lonely Londoners* (Harlow: Longman, 1986; London: Penguin, 2006).

Selvon, Samuel, *Ways of Sunlight* (London: Longman, 1979).

Seyhan, Azade, *Writing Outside the Nation* (Princeton and New York: Princeton University Press, 2001).

Shaogong, Han, *A Dictionary of Maqiao*, trans. Julia Lovell (New York: Dial Press, 2005).

Singh, Rajendra (ed.) *The Native Speaker: Multilingual Perspectives* (New Delhi: Sage, 1998).

Skoblow, Jeffrey, *Dooble Tongue: Scots, Burns, Contradiction* (Newark: University of Delaware Press, 2001).

Skutnabb-Kangas, Tove and Robert Phillipson (eds) *Linguistic Human Rights – Overcoming Linguistic Discrimination* (Berlin: De Gruyter, 1995).

Slaughter, Joseph R., *Human Rights Inc.: The World Novel, Literary Form, and International Law* (New York: Fordham University Press, 2007).

Smith, Ali, 'Life beyond the M25', *Guardian*, 18 December 2004.

Smith, Zadie, *White Teeth* (London: Penguin, 2001).

Smyth, Brendan, 'To love the Orientalist: masculinity in Leila Aboulela's *The Translator*', *Journal of Men, Masculinities and Spirituality* 1:2 (2007), 170–182.

Sollors, Werner (ed.) *Multilingual America: Transnationalism, Ethnicity, and the Languages of American Literature* (New York: New York University Press, 1998).

Sommer, Doris, *Bilingual Aesthetics: A New Sentimental Education* (Durham, NC and London: Duke University Press, 2004).

Spahr, Julianna, *Everybody's Autonomy: Connective Reading and Collective Identity* (Tuscaloosa: University of Alabama Press, 2001).

Spahr, Julianna and David Buuck, 'Poetry and other Englishes: a forum', *Boundary 2* 33:2 (2006), 3–47.

Steinitz, Tamar, 'Back home: translation, conversion and domestication in Leila Aboulela's *The Translator*', *Interventions: International Journal of Postcolonial Studies* 15:3 (2013), 365–382.

Sternberg, Meir, 'Polylingualism as reality and translation as mimesis', *Poetics Today* 2:4 (1981), 221–239.

Stewart, Garrett, *Reading Voices: Literature and the Phonotext* (Berkeley, Los Angeles, and Oxford: University of California Press, 1990).

Sutcliffe, David, *British Black English* (London: Blackwell, 1983).

Sutcliffe, David and Ansel Wong (eds), *The Language of the Black Experience: Cultural Expression Through Word and Sound in the Caribbean and Black Britain* (London: Blackwell, 1986).

Taylor-Batty, Juliet, *Multilingualism in Modernist Fiction* (Basingstoke: Palgrave, 2013).

Tonkin, Boyd, 'Xiaolu Guo: Far East to East End', *Independent*, 26 January 2007. www.independent.co.uk/arts-entertainment/books/features/xiaolu-guo-far-east-to-east-end-433621.html.

Toury, Gideon, 'Enhancing cultural changes by means of fictitious transla-tions', in Eva Hung (ed.) *Translation and Cultural Change: Studies in*

History, Norms and Image-Projection (Amsterdam: John Benjamins, 2005), pp. 3–17.

Trudgill, Peter, *Language, Dialect and the School* (London: Edward Arnold, 1975).

Tyler, Imogen, ' "Welcome to Britain": the cultural politics of asylum', *European Journal of Cultural Studies* 9:2 (2006), 185–202.

Tymoczko, Maria, 'Postcolonial writing and literary translation', in Susan Bassnett and Harish Trivedi (eds) *Postcolonial Translation: Theory and Practice* (London and New York: Routledge, 1998), pp. 19–40.

Tymockzo, Maria, 'Translations of themselves: the contours of postcolonial fiction', in Sherry Simon and Paul St-Pierre (eds) *Changing the Terms: Translation in the Postcolonial Era* (Ottawa: University of Ottawa Press, 2000), pp. 147–163.

Unger, Johann Wolfgang, *The Discursive Construction of the Scots Language: Language, Education, Politics and Everyday Life* (Amsterdam and Philadelphia: John Benjamins, 2013).

Upstone, Sarah, *British Asian Fiction: Twenty-First-Century Voices* (Manchester: Manchester University Press, 2010).

Venuti, Lawrence, *The Scandals of Translation: Towards an Ethics of Difference* (London and New York: Routledge, 1998).

Vericat, Fabio, 'Letting the writing do the talking: denationalising English and James Kelman's *Translated Accounts*', *Scottish Literary Review* 3:1 (2011), 129–151.

Vertovec, Steven, 'Super-diversity and its implications', *Ethnic and Racial Studies* 30:6 (2007), 1024–1054.

Viswanathan, Gauri, *Masks of Conquest: Literary Study and British Rule in India*, revised edition (New York: Columbia University Press, 2014).

Walcott, Derek, *Collected Poems 1948–1984* (New York: Noonday, 1986).

Walkowitz, Rebecca, *Born Translated: The Contemporary Novel in an Age of World Literature* (New York: Columbia University Press, 2015).

Warwick Research Collective, *Combined and Uneven Development: Towards a New Theory of World-Literature* (Liverpool: Liverpool University Press, 2015).

Watson, Roderick, 'Postcolonial subjects? Language, narrative authority and class in contemporary Scottish culture', *Hungarian Journal of English and American Studies* 4:1–2 (1998), 21–38.

Watson, Roderick, 'The double tongue', *Translation and Literature* 9:2 (2000), 175–178.

Watson, Roderick, 'Living with the double tongue: modern poetry in Scots', in Ian Brown (ed.) *Edinburgh History of Scottish Literature. Vol. 3. Modern*

Transformations: New Identities (from 1918) (Edinburgh: Edinburgh University Press, 2007), pp. 163–175.

Watt, Nichola, 'Eric Pickles warns of non-English-speaking "sub-class" in UK', *Guardian*, 8 March 2012. www.guardian.co.uk/politics/2012/mar/08/eric-pickles-english-sub-class.

Wesling, Donald, 'Bakhtin and the social poetics of dialect', in *Bakhtin and the Social Moorings of Poetry* (Cranbury, NJ, London, and Mississauga, Canada: Associated University Presses, 2003), pp. 61–76.

Wessendorf, Susanne, *Commonplace Diversity: Social Relations in a Super-Diverse Context* (Basingstoke: Palgrave, 2014).

White, Tony, *Foxy-T* (London: Faber, 2004).

Whitlock, Gillian, *Postcolonial Life Narratives: Testimonial Transactions* (Oxford: Oxford University Press, 2015).

Whorf, Benjamin Lee, *Language, Thought and Reality* (Cambridge, MA: MIT Press, 1972).

Whyte, Christopher, 'Nationalism and its discontents: critiquing Scottish criticism', in J. Derrick McClure, Karoline Szatek-Tudor, and Rosa E. Penna (eds) *'What Countrey's This? And Whither are we Gone?': Papers Presented at the Twelfth Conference on the Literature of Region and Nation* (Newcastle: Cambridge Scholars Publishing, 2010), pp. 23–39.

Williams, James, *Multilingualism and the Twentieth Century Novel: Polyglot Passages* (Basingstoke: Palgrave, 2019).

Williams, Raymond, *Keywords: A Vocabulary of Culture and Society* (London: Fontana, 1976).

Wilson, Graeme, 'English is a second language for 40% in parts of Britain', *Sun*, 5 March 2013.

Wirth-Nesher, Hana, *Call it English: The Languages of Jewish American Literature* (Princeton: Princeton University Press, 2006).

Woolley, Agnes, *Contemporary Asylum Narratives: Representing Refugees in the Twenty-First Century* (Basingstoke: Palgrave Macmillan, 2014).

Woolley, Agnes, 'Narrating the "asylum story": between literary and legal storytelling', *Interventions: International Journal of Postcolonial Studies* 19:3 (2017), 376–394.

Wright, David and Gavin Brookes, '"This is England, speak English!": a corpus-assisted critical study of language ideologies in the right-leaning British press', *Critical Discourse Studies* 16:1 (2019), 56–83.

Wroe, Nicholas, 'Glasgow kith', *Guardian*, 2 June 2001. www.theguardian.com/books/2001/jun/02/fiction.artsandhumanities.

Yao, Steven G., *Translation and the Languages of Modernism: Gender, Politics, Language* (Basingstoke: Palgrave, 2002).

Yeh, Diana, 'Contested belongings: the politics and poetics of making a home in Britain', in A. Robert Lee (ed.) *China Fictions/English Language: Literary Essays in Diaspora, Memory, Story* (Amsterdam and New York: Rodopi, 2008), pp. 299–325.

Yildiz, Yasemin, *Beyond the Mother Tongue: The Postmonolingual Condition* (New York: Fordham University Press, 2012).

Yule, Henry and A. C. Burnell, *Hobson-Jobson: A Glossary of Colloquial Anglo-Indian Words and Phrases* (London: John Murray, 1886).

Zetter, Roger, 'More labels, fewer refugees: remaking the refugee label in an era of globalization', *Journal of Refugee Studies* 20:2 (2007), 172–192.

Zhen, Zhang, '"I'm a modern peasant": encountering Xiaolu Guo', *World Literature Today* 82:6 (2008), 45–48.

Index

Note: Literary works can be found under authors' names. 'n' after a page reference indicates the number of a note on that page.

Aboulela, Leila
multilingualism 24–25, 170–171
translation 25, 27, 168–181, 198–199
works
Minaret 170, 175–181, 184
The Translator 169–170, 173–175
Agard, John 12, 53, 148
anticolonialism 15, 20–21, 23, 44, 53
see also internationalism
applied linguistics 17–18, 42–44
Apter, Emily 14, 19, 188, 219, 227
asylum system
legislation 140, 147, 206, 213–215, 237
monolingualist logic 25, 193–195, 205–208
state violence and language 69, 130, 213–217, 230, 236, 240–241
terminology 147, 214–215, 224–229
translation as equivalence 19, 25, 208–212
see also border security; language testing and citizenship; migrants
authenticity 22, 24, 111–113, 142–146, 162–163

Bakhtin, Mikhail 17, 18, 24, 146
Bergvall, Caroline 15–16, 25–27, 236–241, 245
Bernstein, Basil 42–43, 49
bilingualism 172, 177–178
see also moving between languages
Blommaert, Jan 17, 205–206, 210, 213

bodies see embodied idea of language
border security
Britain 18, 58–59, 242
relationship to language 25–26, 33n.51, 236–240, 245
US 67–68
see also asylum system; language testing and citizenship; migrants
borrowings 4, 58, 86, 149–151, 156–158
Brouillette, Sarah 142–143

Cameron, Deborah 4–5, 7, 8, 17, 242–243
Capildeo, Vahni 1–5, 7, 15, 16, 17
Caribbean Artists Movement 15, 38, 44, 69
Caribbean literature
influence of 15, 23, 38–39, 69, 148
language 2–3, 5–6, 42–44
shared history with Scotland 53–55, 69, 80, 94–96
see also Capildeo, Vahni; creole languages; Selvon, Sam; Walcott, Derek
Chikwava, Brian 25, 224–230
Chomsky, Noam 23, 43–44, 49, 68, 215–216
Chow, Rey 3, 17, 23, 101–102, 112, 125, 131, 203n.68
class
exclusion of working class 46, 63–65, 78–79, 155–156, 242

class (*cont.*)
  ideology and monolingualism 4,
    9–10, 28, 41–42, 47, 245
  middle-class Scottish identity 90–91,
    103
  standard English 26, 39–42, 139–140
  transnational solidarity 38–40,
    54–55, 69–70, 109–110
  working-class voices in literature
    19–20, 38–44, 47–70, 144,
    160–162
  see also vernaculars
colonialism
  borrowing between languages
    149–151, 156–158
  cultural 44, 65
  Enlightenment and racial thinking
    108
  histories of language 2–3, 24, 34n.57,
    156–160, 177–178
  imposition of standard English
    41–43, 46–47, 53–54, 58, 141
  Scotland's role in empire 45–47,
    54–55, 108
  see also anticolonialism;
    decolonisation; postcoloniality
Crawford, Robert
  literary criticism 15, 19, 46, 72n.22,
    80
  poetry 23, 81, 84–89, 96
  Sharawaggi 85–89, 98n.27
creole languages
  activism 42, 44, 54
  stigmatisation 10–12, 53, 139–140
  use in literature 5–7, 12, 53, 94–95,
    225, 227
  see also minor(ity) languages;
    vernaculars

decolonisation 5, 19–20, 42
  linguistic 38–39, 65–66
Derrida, Jacques 17, 102, 120
deterritorialised language 178, 188,
  198, 217, 227, 230
dialogue 19–20, 39–40, 57
dictionaries 12, 23, 79, 83–93, 96,
  183–187
  see also etymology; glossaries

Eliot, T. S. 114–115, 135n.55, 152, 153,
  154
embodied idea of language 125–126,
  130–132
empire *see* colonialism

English *see* standard English
etymology 5, 89–90, 93, 147, 151,
  156–159, 162
  see also dictionaries; glossaries

Fanon, Frantz 3, 155
Farrier, David 18, 180, 206, 226
Forensic Architecture 238–240

Gaelic 8, 46–47, 66, 81–85, 126
gendered language 55–56, 110,
  186–187
Gilroy, Paul 147, 152, 161, 214, 229
Glissant, Édouard 16
globalisation
  cultural dominance of West 129,
    187–188
  deterritorialised language 178, 188,
    198, 217, 227, 230
  dominance of English 3, 26, 67–68,
    177, 217
  language of capitalism 83–85, 188,
    227
  multilingualism 2, 7–8, 113,
    119–121
  translation 170–172, 196
glossaries 21, 106–108, 118, 149–151,
  160
  see also dictionaries; etymology
Guo, Xiaolu
  critical reception 28
  limitations of language 169,
    183–185
  self-authorship 25, 186–187, 198
  subversive possibilities of translation
    25, 171, 197–198
  translation as lived experience
    24–25, 169–172, 181–182
  works
    *A Concise Chinese-English
      Dictionary for Lovers* 170, 182,
      183–189
    I Am China 25, 169–170,
      182–183, 189–198
    UFO in Her Eyes 182

Harris, Roxy 44, 53, 69–70
Hassan, Waïl 25, 170, 173, 201n.42
Herbert, W. N. 81, 83, 84, 85, 98n.24,
  98n.27
Hobson-Jobson 16, 149–151, 162
Holmes, Rachel 214
human rights 27, 216–217, 231n.8,
  238–240

immigration *see* asylum system; border security; language testing and citizenship; migrants

Informationist poetry 83–85, 96

internationalism
  anticolonial solidarity 15, 20–21, 23, 44, 53, 66, 68–70
  literary insurgency against standard English 40–41, 44–45, 78
  localism and 39–43, 53–57, 66
  minor(ity) languages 23, 102, 106, 126–127
  Scottish literature 20–23, 38–41, 44–45, 53–57, 78–89, 96, 98n.14, 215–217
  see also translation; transnationalism

Johnson, Linton Kwesi 18, 21, 44, 53, 77n.109, 148

Kay, Jackie 20–21, 55
Kelman, James
  class and language politics 20, 22–23, 66, 70, 104
  critical reception 28, 65
  influences and associations 15, 16, 38–40, 43–44, 69–70, 77n.109, 104
  internationalist language politics 22–23, 25, 38–41, 66–70, 81, 215–217
  works
    '*And the Judges Said...*' 57–58
    The Busconductor Hines 59–60
    How Late It Was, How Late 28, 60–65, 69
    'A reading from the work of Noam Chomsky' 43–44, 68–69, 215–216
    Translated Accounts 25, 27, 69, 216–224, 230
    You Have to Be Careful in the Land of the Free 67–68
Kinloch, David
  influences and associations 81, 90–91
  translation 16, 93
  use of Scots 23, 84, 89–96
  works
    'The apology of a dictionary trawler' 89, 91
    'Dustie-Fute' 90, 92
    'Gurliewhirkie' 92

'The Love That Dare Not' 92–93
'Mamapoules' 94–96
'A queer Glaswegian voice' 90–91

language activism 42–44, 53–54
language testing and citizenship 4–5, 8, 19, 26, 140, 147, 237
  see also asylum system; border security; migrants
La Rose, John 38, 44, 69, 77n.109
Leonard, Tom
  influences and associations 4, 15, 50, 53, 90–91, 93
  internationalism and localism 40–43, 53–57, 70
  language politics 22–23, 40–43, 78–79
  spoken and written language 48, 50–52
  works
    'Ghostie Men' 49–50
    'Honest' 51–52
    'Jist Ti Let Yi Know' 50–51
    'On reclaiming the local' 56–57
    Radical Renfrew 54
    Reports from the Present 56
    'Six Glasgow Poems' 52
    'Unrelated Incidents' 47–49, 51
linguaphobia 13, 28, 243
  see also monolingualism
localism 39–43, 53–57, 66, 109–110, 244

MacDiarmid, Hugh 23, 47, 79, 84, 85, 87, 91, 97n.2
migrants
  deadliness of migrant routes 196, 238–240
  language learning 9–13, 194–195, 242
  literary representations of immigrant experience 5–7, 18, 25, 67–68, 168–199, 210–230
  loss of language 121–122
  as outsiders 36n.90
  racism towards 178, 214–215, 243–244
  see also asylum system; border security; language testing and citizenship; moving between languages
mimicry 24, 95, 141–142, 146–147, 152–156, 164n.18

minor(ity) languages
  internationalism 23, 102, 106,
    126–127
  legislation and policy 8, 163n.5
  linguistic nativism 127–128
  resistance to dominance of English
    67–68, 126–127
  stigmatisation 139–142, 243
  see also creole languages; Gaelic;
    Punjabi; Scots; vernaculars
misogynistic language 110, 154
monolingualism
  asylum system 25, 193–195, 205–208
  education 10–11, 141
  ideology and the state 9, 19, 25,
    56–58, 205–210, 242–243
  linguistic correctness 10–13, 28
  myths 7, 14, 40–41, 101–102
  publishing 21–22, 26–27, 104
'mother tongue' 7, 101, 102, 122–124,
    131, 132n.4, 186
moving between languages 81,
    124–127, 144–145, 185, 237–238,
    242
  see also bilingualism; migrants;
    translation
Mugglestone, Linda 19, 41
Muldoon, Paul 21, 154–155
multimodality 18, 25, 171, 238
Mundair, Raman
  influences and associations 131
  linguistic (un)belonging 21,
    131–132
  migration 121–122, 126–127
  prosthetic language 23–24, 96,
    102–103
  use of Shetland Scots 37n.95, 103,
    126–131
  works
    'Apnea' 126
    'A Choreographer's Cartography'
      126
    'The Folds of my Mother's Sari'
      124
    Incoming: Some Shetland Voices
      127–128
    Lovers, Liars, Conjurers and
      Thieves 122–123
    'The Meeting Point' 125
    'Name Journeys' 122, 124–125
    'Osmosis' 123–124
    'Piercing Flesh' 130
    'Refractions' 125
    '60° North' 127

'Sow, Reap and Slowly Savour'
    121–122
'Stories Fae Da Shoormal'
    128–130
'Terra Infirma' 130
music 107, 110, 113–120, 135n.55

Nagra, Daljit
  authenticity and marketability 22,
    24
  critical reception 143–144, 145–146,
    152, 165n.31
  histories of empire 162–163
  Hobson-Jobson 16, 149–151
  inclusion in anthologies 27, 144,
    164n.25
  influences and associations 148
  Punjabi community and language
    140–141, 144–154, 160–162,
    165n.31
  works
    'A Black History of the English-
      Speaking Peoples' 156–159
    'Bolly Bhaji' 149–151, 160
    'Booking Khan Singh Kumar' 24,
      143
    British Museum 144, 145, 148
    'Cane' 145
    'Darling & Me!' 152–154
    'The Furtherance of Mr Bulram's
      Education' 144
    'The Gob-Smacking Taste of Mine
      Inheritance' 149
    'In a White Town' 145
    'Informant' 146
    'Kabba Considers the Ontology of
      Representation' 145–146, 156
    Look We Have Coming to Dover!
      143–144, 152
    'Look We Have Coming to Dover!'
      144–145
    'The Man Who Would Be English!'
      141, 144, 146
    'The Punjab' 148–149
    'Raju t'Wonder Dog' 151,
      160–162
    'This Be the Pukka Verse' 151
    Tippoo Sultan's Incredible White-
      Man-Eating Tiger-Toy Machine!!!
      149–150
    'Tippoo Sultan's Incredible
      White-Man-Eating Tiger-Toy
      Machine!!!' 159–160
    'Yobbos!' 154–156

national identity
  Britain 4–5, 9–10, 26, 139–140,
    146–150
  language as emanation of place 109,
    129
  Scotland 66, 79–89, 102–103,
    108–113
  threatened by multilingualism 4–5,
    9–10, 106, 139–140
  see also internationalism; language
    testing and citizenship; 'mother
    tongue'; transnationalism
'native speaker' 7, 8–9, 21, 101, 132n.4,
    139–140, 147
nativism, linguistic 103, 120, 127–128
novelistic conventions and standard
    English 19–20, 39–40, 41, 57–60

orientalism see publishing: marketable
    multiculturalism
O'Rourke, Daniel 82–83
orthography see vernaculars: visual-
    textual representation

Paulin, Tom 148
poetry anthologies and journals 27,
    81–84
postcoloniality
  experience of language 19, 101–102,
    110–113, 121–123, 162–163
  London 7, 18, 20, 229
  Scotland 45–46, 54–55, 80
  solidarity between former colonies
    22–23, 38–39, 45, 96, 148
  see also anticolonialism; colonialism;
    decolonisation
Powell, Enoch 10, 13, 156
Price, Richard 83–85
prosthetic language 23–24, 101–132,
    238, 241
publishing
  experimental work 21, 104–105,
    133n.18, 197
  marketable multiculturalism 21–22,
    24, 104, 142–144, 162
  multilingual 14–15, 81
  poetry 81–84
Punjabi 105–112, 121–127, 140–141,
    144–154, 160–162

queer language 89–96

racism
  contemporary immigration

  discourse 29n.11, 147, 214–215,
    229
  Islamophobia 176
  linguistic 24, 33n.51, 141–142,
    243–244
  mimicry 146–147, 152–156, 164n.18
  1970s and 1980s Britain 24, 141–142,
    152
  Scotland 45
refugees see asylum system; border
    security; language testing and
    citizenship; migrants
Refugee Tales 210–215
representation, politics of see
    authenticity
Rushdie, Salman 18, 21, 104, 148, 158,
    172

Saadi, Suhayl
  critical reception 37n.95, 105
  influences and associations 104
  linguistic experimentation 21,
    104–106, 110–115
  music 113–120
  paratexts 106–108, 118, 120
  prosthetic language 23, 96, 120–121,
    131–132
  Psychoraag 37n.95, 104–121,
    131–132
  publication 104–105, 133n.18
  Scots and Scottishness 23, 102–103,
    108–110, 112
  review of Londonstani 22
Saro-Wiwa, Ken 15, 40, 58–59, 60,
    218–219, 224
Sassi, Carla 45, 55
Scarman Report 11–12, 29n.11
Scotland
  deindustrialisation 79–80, 82, 98n.13
  linguistic landscape 21, 78–79,
    81–83, 103, 104, 108–113
  literary internationalism 20–23,
    38–41, 44–45, 53–57, 78–89, 96,
    98n.14
  national identity 66, 79–89, 102–103,
    108–113
  postcoloniality 45–46, 54–55, 80
  role in empire 45–47, 54–55, 108
Scots
  dictionaries 89–93
  literary 22–23, 47–50, 78–96, 97n.2,
    98n.24, 105–106, 109–112
  marginalisation 39, 46–47, 53–54,
    82, 83, 88

Scots (*cont.*)
  Shetland 37n.95, 98n.14, 103,
    126–131
  translation 80–82, 97n.6, 98n.27
  see also Gaelic; standard English:
    literary resistance to; vernaculars
Selvon, Sam
  influence on other writers 38–39
  literary vernacular 5–7, 39–40, 225,
    227
  works
    'Calypso in London' 6
    The Lonely Londoners 5–6, 59,
      225
    'My Girl and the City' 7
    'Working the Transport' 6–7
Sommer, Doris 14, 119–120, 134n.26
spoken and written language 16, 22,
  40–41, 48, 51–54
  see also dialogue; vernaculars
standard English
  class 39–42, 46
  debates 8, 26
  exclusionary 58–64, 240–241
  historical roots in empire 41, 43,
    46–47, 58, 141
  language of authority 60–65, 68–69,
    177, 217, 219–220
  literary resistance to 15, 40, 58, 66,
    80, 85–89, 110, 126–127
  normalisation in the novel 39–40,
    57–58
  proficiency and citizenship 4–5, 8,
    19, 26, 139–140, 147, 237
  threats to 9–13, 236–237
  see also monolingualism
synthetic language *see* vernaculars:
  literary

Tawada, Yoko 15
Tebbit, Norman 9, 146
translation
  capitalist exchange 67–68, 188, 196
  as connection 192–193, 195–196,
    198
  as equivalence 19, 25, 171, 173,
    183–184, 198, 208–212
  facing-page 16, 82, 85–88
  glossaries and dictionaries 21,
    106–108, 118, 149–151, 160

  limitations 169, 183–185, 190–191,
    216–224
  lived experience 24–25, 90–91,
    169–172, 181–182
  religious conception 175, 180–181,
    198
  subversive potential 25, 171,
    197–198
  technology 19, 75n.71
  translated literature 44, 51, 79–82,
    85–88, 97n.6, 98n.27
  translation-ready literature 26–27,
    82
  untranslatability 168–169, 174–176,
    181, 184, 200n.29, 220–224
  see also internationalism;
    moving between languages;
    transnationalism
transnationalism
  class 54–55, 69–70, 109–110
  culture 15–16, 26, 104, 190–191
  religion 24–25, 170, 172, 178–181,
    198, 201n.42
  see also internationalism; translation
Tutuola, Amos 15, 38, 39, 40

vernaculars
  challenge to monolingualism 39–40,
    42–44, 53–54, 70
  comic representations 57, 202n.58
  confinement to dialogue 19–20,
    39–40, 57
  literary 5–7, 54, 79, 85– 91, 97n.2,
    98n.24, 144, 225
  narration 40, 59–60, 183
  stigmatisation 12, 46–47, 87
  visual-textual representation 16,
    19–20, 39–42, 105, 218
  see also class; creole languages;
    minor(ity) languages; spoken and
    written language

Walcott, Derek 158
Walker, Chris 243–245
Walkowitz, Rebecca 19, 27
Watts, Carol 210–212
Williams, Raymond 159
Williams, William Carlos 50

Yildiz, Yasemin 14, 122–123

Ingram Content Group UK Ltd.
Milton Keynes UK
UKHW021304180523
421960UK00034B/376